Papers of the Forty-Seventh Algonquian Conference

Actes du Quarante-Septiéme Congrès des Algonquinistes

PAPERS OF THE ALGONQUIAN CONFERENCES
ACTES DU CONGRÈS DES ALGONQUINISTES

William Cowan
Founding Editor

Monica Macaulay and Margaret Noodin
Editors

Jonathan Jibson and Samantha Litty
Editorial Assistants

Marie-Pierre Bousquet, Wesley Y. Leonard, and Lucy Thomason
Associate Editors

47

Papers of the Forty-Seventh Algonquian Conference

Actes du Quarante-Septiéme Congrès des Algonquinistes

EDITED BY Monica Macaulay and Margaret Noodin

MICHIGAN STATE UNIVERSITY PRESS | EAST LANSING

♾ The paper used in this publication meets the minimum requirements
of ANSI/NISO Z39.48-1992 (R 1997) (Permanence of Paper).

Michigan State University Press
East Lansing, Michigan 48823-5245

Printed and bound in the United States of America.

27 26 25 24 23 22 21 29 19 18   1 2 3 4 5 6 7 8 9 10

ISBN 978-1-61186-269-0 (paperback)
ISBN 978-1-60917-552-8 (PDF)

Book design by Charlie Sharp, Sharp Designs, East Lansing, Michigan
Cover design by Erin Kirk New.
Cover detail of a quill box is used courtesy of Julie L. Loehr.

g green
press
INITIATIVE

Michigan State University Press is a member of the Green Press Initiative and is
committed to developing and encouraging ecologically responsible publishing
practices. For more information about the Green Press Initiative and the use of
recycled paper in book publishing, please visit *www.greenpressinitiative.org*.

Visit Michigan State University Press at *www.msupress.org*

CONTENTS

PREFACE

The Forty-Seventh Algonquian Conference was held in Winnipeg, Manitoba, 22–25 October 2015. It was organized by Will Oxford and Nicole Rosen of the Department of Linguistics at the University of Manitoba, together with their student assistant Vivian Xu. The organizers are grateful to Heather Lee and Terry Janzen in the Department of Linguistics for assistance with conference preparations, and to the staff at the James W. Burns Executive Education Centre and the Fort Garry Hotel. Arden Ogg organized an exhibit of paintings by Dawn Marie Marchand from Cold Lake First Nation and introduced the banquet speaker, Rosanna Deerchild, who gave a powerful reading from her recent book of poetry, *Calling Down the Sky*. Irina Volchók, president of the Linguistics Graduate Students' Association, arranged for the assistance of a large number of students over the conference weekend: Mutasim Al-Deaibes, Chantale Cenerini, Vazna Ghobadi, Steve Kesselman, Lanlan Li, Renée Lint, Hansini Rajatheva, Hai Tran, Akinori Watanabe, and Yaxin Zheng. The conference was sponsored by the Department of Linguistics, the Faculty of Arts Endowment Fund, the Dean of Arts, and the Conference Sponsorship Program (Vice-President Research and International), all at the University of Manitoba.

The editors think Arden Ogg's introduction of Rosanna Deerchild deserves to be included in full:

It was almost thirty years ago that I helped Chris Wolfart and Jennifer Brown organize the 18th Algonquian Conference right here at the Hotel Fort Garry, so I'm delighted to be welcoming so many of you back, and of course to greet new friends as well.

It is my honour this evening to introduce my friend Rosanna Deerchild to all of you, but I'm going to steal a minute first to brag to her a bit about this audience, because I'm kind of proud of them too.

Among this loosely-formed group—getting together here for the 47th time—I have friends who are linguists, ethnohistorians, anthropologists, educators and others, many of whom have made a lifelong commitment to the languages and cultures of Algonquian peoples across North America. Some of them—like Solomon Ratt, and our new co-editor Meg Noodin to name just two—are honouring that commitment from within their own cultures in exactly the way that our founders envisioned with hope.

So while most of North America slumbers on in blissful ignorance of the atrocities that First Nations people continue to live, many of the people in this room have humbly devoted their careers to documentation, recording, support, and even revival of the languages and cultures that have been under constant siege. To use the metaphor of Stephen Augustine, they climbed into canoes that weren't theirs, to try to help paddle. So I want you to know, Rosanna, that our welcome is one that acknowledges First Nations stories and truths, and celebrates with you the powerful spirit of First Nations survival.

Now, for my Algonquianist friends: a word or two about Rosanna.

Rosanna is best known in Winnipeg as an outspoken poet, writer, broadcaster, comedian, and activist. Several times I have heard people wonder whether she'll ever overcome her stage fright—right before they collapse on the floor in laughter.

Her family is Cree from "the Wintering Place"—O-Pipon-Na-Piwin Cree Nation at South Indian Lake, about 850 km north of Winnipeg (ôta!). Her Momsy is a residential school survivor who nevertheless retained her first language of Woods Cree (the *th*-dialect).

Rosanna helped found Winnipeg's Aboriginal Writers' Collective in the late 80s, and she received a literary award for her first published book of poetry, *This Small Northern Town*. Earlier this year, she was an unwilling cover girl for McLean's

Magazine—then turned that experience into a series of healing community-wide conversations about racism. She has recently taken her well-deserved place as host of CBC radio's *UnReserved*, the national radio space for Indigenous community, culture, and conversation.

I have witnessed her verbal super powers in action at the Writers Collective's Cree versus Ojibwe poetry cage match, but maybe best of all, I am thrilled to introduce to you an *okiichitakwe* who knows how to stand in the middle of a crowd of thousands dancing at Portage and Main and shrill out a Xena Princess Warrior whoop that echoes out in all four directions. Please join me in welcoming Rosanna Deerchild.

In addition to the papers published here, the following papers were presented at the conference:

Sara Acton (Eastern Michigan University) and Julie Brittain (Memorial University): Acquiring the Passive in Cree: Evidence from Spontaneous Child-Adult Interactions

Lene Antonsen (Universitetet i Tromsø—Norges arktiske universitet), Antti Arppe (University of Alberta), Atticus G. Harrigan (University of Alberta), Trond Trosterud (Universitetet i Tromsø—Norges arktiske universitet), and Arok Wolvengrey (First Nations University of Canada): Modeling the Plains Cree Verb

Phil Branigan (Memorial University), and Julie Brittain (Memorial University): A Labelling Theoretic Approach to Relative Root Complements in East Cree

Jennifer S. H. Brown (University of Winnipeg): A. I. Hallowell and Adam Bigmouth in Conversation: Medicine Men and Windigos on the Upper Berens River, 1938–1940

Vincent Collette (First Nations University of Canada): Dubitative Suffixes in South East Cree

Dolorès Contré Migwans (Cercle d'apprentissage Dogomig / Université de Montréal): *Naa-Ka-Nah-Gay-Win*—Une Démarche de Pédagogie par Symbols

David Costa (Myaamia Center at Miami University): Diminutive Nouns in Miami-Illinois

Andrea Cudworth (University of Wisconsin–Madison): Comparative Constructions in Menominee

Rose-Marie Déchaine (University of British Columbia): WSIWYG Morphology Applied to Plains Cree Verb Stems

Rick Donovan (University of Winnipeg): Artifact Evidence of Chakapesh and the
  Giants

John Fierst (Central Michigan University): Edwin James in the Introduction to *The
  Captivity and Adventures of John Tanner*

Naatosi Fish (University of Montana/Blackfeet), Bonny Lahey (University of
  Montana), and Mizuki Miyashita (University of Montana): The Application of
  Blackfoot Pitch Studies to Language Education

Brandon Fry (University of Ottawa): Conjunct and Independent VTA Theme-Signs
  in Ojibwe: A Difference in Feature Inheritance

George Fulford (University of Winnipeg): Grammaticalization in Cree: The Concrete
  Verb Final *pani-* 'Move' and Preterit Suffix *–pan*

Erik D. Gooding (Minnesota State University Moorhead): Meshkwaki and Thaaki
  Names and Naming

Patricia Harms (Brandon University): The Store of Peace: The Pauingassi Trading
  Post, 1969–1990

Marie-Odile Junker (Carleton University) et al.: Dictionaries and Linguistic Atlas
  Project: A Progress Report

Daiho Kitaoka (University of Ottawa) and Kathleen Strader (University of Ottawa):
  Discontinuous DPs in Michif: Preverbal Focus Position

Robert Lewis (University of Chicago): Determining Potawatomi Word Order

Anne Lindsay (National Centre for Truth and Reconciliation): Are Archives Animate:
  A Brief Overview of Some of the Collections of the National Centre for Truth
  and Reconciliation at the University of Manitoba

Hunter Lockwood (University of Wisconsin–Madison) and Kira Lin Dallaire
  (Eastern Michigan University): Resilience and Revitalization

Éric Mathieu (University of Ottawa): On the Status of Gender in Algonquian

Éric Mathieu (University of Ottawa) and Kathleen Strader (University of Ottawa):
  On Gender in Michif

Andrew M. Miller (First Nations University of Canada) and Vincent Collette (First
  Nations University of Canada): The Use of Bitumen by the Algonquian Peoples
  of Canada: Archeological, Ethnohistoric, and Linguistic Relationships

Henry Neufeld (independent scholar) and Gerald Neufeld (independent scholar):
  Fifty Years Too Soon: A Struggle Over Language at Pauingassi, Manitoba

Will Oxford (University of Manitoba): Inverse as Elsewhere

Yolanda Pushetonequa (University of Minnesota): Meskwaki Phonology 2015

Kai Pyle (University of Wisconsin–Green Bay): The Role of the Internet in Michif Language Revitalization

Conor McDonough Quinn (University of Maine): Recovering the Penobscot TA Conjunct: Documentary, Analytical, and Revitalization Considerations

Kate Riccomini (University of Ottawa): Structure and Agreement in Ojibwe Transitive Verbs

Nicole Rosen (University of Manitoba) and Carrie Gillon (Arizona State University): Michif "D"

Nicole Rosen (University of Mantiboa), Jesse Stewart (University of Saskatchewan), and Olivia Sammons (University of Alberta): Phonetics of the Synchronic Michif Vowel System

Katherine Schmirler (University of Alberta): Algonquian Quadrupeds: The Origin and Productivity of *-osw and Its Place in Algonquian Prehistory

Graham Still (University of Manitoba): Coda Constraints in Algonquian Sound Change

Alain Takam (University of Lethbridge): Revitalisation des Langues Minoritaires par les Médias: Étude de Quelques Stratégies de Promotion des Langues Autochtones au Canada

Lucy Thomason (Smithsonian Institution): Meskwaki *Kek(i)* Particles

Lynn Whidden (Brandon University): Vocalized Songs as Cultural Archaeology

Arok Wolvengrey (First Nations University of Canada): Preverbs in a Plains Cree Text Corpus: Some Preliminary Findings

Algonquian Verb Paradigms: A Case for Systematicity and Consistency

Antti Arppe, Chris Harvey, Marie-Odile Junker, and J. Randolph Valentine

n this paper we make the case for certain types of systematicity in describing the morphology of Algonquian languages, in particular the inflectional morphology of Algonquian verbs, though these principles would apply to the documentation of any other Indigenous language. By systematicity, we mean well-organized and detailed descriptions of a language's words and their morphological structure, seeking exhaustive descriptions of all word-class paradigm-types, matched with a comprehensive lexicon incorporating paradigm-type specifications. Indeed, this is what most scholars of Algonquian languages in practice seek to produce in their linguistic documentation work. Importantly, we are not advocating for any particular notation or standard, as we know that Algonquian scholars have developed many different systems. But whatever notation is used, it is essential that it be systematic in that it can be deterministically mapped to other notations and representations.

Crucially, in this we are in effect arguing for taking the Model-Controller-View (MCV) architecture developed in computer science for user interfaces, to help us structure and organize our linguistic data (Krasner and Pope 1988; Junker and Stewart 2011). In this approach, the Model consists of the raw information that is stored in the underlying, primary database, in whatever format, as long as that format is systematically followed and explicitly described. The View refers to how users are presented with this information, the design of which can be changed to other Views, depending on application, user need, or user group, without requiring changes in the underlying database/Model. The Controller consists of the software instructions that connect the Model to the View. By separating components in this way, we enable a rapid and robust development environment, and by using this standardized approach we can take advantage of the extensive documentation and large community of other developers following this approach.

We have found that with such an approach one can be surprisingly time-effective in creating computational morphological models that form the basis of several language technology tools to help support the revitalization and continued use of Indigenous languages (Arppe et al. 2015). Importantly, these tools and applications can reach a quality comparable to those available for majority languages. Primary among such tools are intelligent web-based dictionaries (I-DICTs), which are intelligent in that with the computational model they can link almost any inflected form with its appropriate dictionary entry as well as generate word paradigms. Such a computational model can also be adapted into a spell-checker, which, integrated into a word-processing application, can support adherence with one or more existing orthographical conventions, resulting in the production of good-quality texts where the focus can be on content and not orthography. Furthermore, one can create intelligent language training and education applications (ICALLs), which use the computational model for the dynamic generation of large numbers of learning exercises based on combining core vocabulary with finite sets of exercise templates (Antonsen et al. 2013). Finally, one can use the computational model for ongoing linguistic analysis of texts and other research.

In developing linguistic resources for Indigenous languages, we need to recognize that there are multiple audiences, with different levels of linguistic knowledge and proficiency and varying usage needs, who will want to have access to and make use of these resources. Broadly speaking, these audiences can be divided into: (1) the members of the linguistic communities in question, for whom the language is either their mother tongue or a second language important as a vehicle of cultural identity (this also includes people living away from their communities); (2) people external to the language community who are typically interested in it from the perspective of scientific study; (3) students of the language taking courses in K–12 or university contexts; and (4) nonspecialists interested in the language. In the case of endangered languages, the mix of these audiences and their needs is influenced by the state of the endangerment of the language. For instance, different Algonquian languages and dialects exemplify a gradient continuum ranging from robust and broad use, to severely endangered and restricted use, to dormant or extinct.[1] We will exemplify these states with East Cree and Innu (robust), Plains Cree and Southwestern Ojibwe (endangered), and Mahican (dormant).

East Cree, spoken by over 12,000 people in nine communities situated in the James Bay region of Northern Quebec, is still learned by children as their first language and fluently used in schools and in the communities overall, involved in most spheres of life as an oral language. There is basic literacy among the speakers, but written communication tends to be in English or, to a lesser extent, French. Innu, spoken in Quebec and Labrador, illustrates a similar situation. In contrast, Plains Cree, spoken in Alberta and Saskatchewan, is no longer generally learned as a first language by children in the communities, and most children are exposed to their heritage language only in school in the form of weekly language and culture instruction. However, many middle-age and older community members are bilingual, having learned Plains Cree as their first language, but the situations in which Plains Cree is used in these communities is more restricted than in the case of East Cree. Moreover, due to these still-active fluent speakers having grown up in the residential school era, when Indigenous languages were not taught in any way, their proficiency is stronger in the spoken than in the written form of the language. Consequently, the fluent speakers, having less certainty of words' written forms, would benefit from spell-checking when writing their language, while heritage and other learners need information on proper pronunciation (spoken recordings of words individually and in sentential context) as well as assistance with how words are inflected, i.e., the paradigms. Furthermore, teachers and advanced learners could make good use of information on the morphological composition of words.

Southwestern Ojibwe is primarily spoken in Wisconsin and Minnesota. An assessment of speakers in 2009 (Moose et al. 2009) determined that 678 speakers remained in Minnesota and 42 in Wisconsin, the latter distributed over six communities. While access to fluent speakers is obviously very limited in these communities, it is also important to note that nearly half of Wisconsin's American Indian population resides in urban areas. Very few published materials laying out basic inflectional paradigms exist, and dictionaries such as Nichols and Nyholm (1995) follow the standard practice of providing only a couple of key inflectional forms. There is thus a great need to help independent teachers and learners with at least the basic, core inflectional forms, if not fully enumerated paradigms of both nouns and verbs.

Mahican is an Eastern Algonquian language whose last rememberers passed away in the 1930s. The language was fairly well documented by missionaries and native speakers in the eighteenth and nineteenth centuries (mostly religious translations and wordlists survive), with some linguistic elicitation and short stories recorded in the early twentieth century. The modern Mahican community in Wisconsin has access to some of the old written sources, but there has yet to be a thorough interpretation of these sources, especially in a way that makes them accessible to Mahican people interested in the language. Centrally, this involves identifying and modeling paradigms, and presenting these alongside an online dictionary, in ways useful to both researchers and language learners (Harvey 2015), which then function as the means by which individual learning or curriculum development can begin. Accessible paradigms are critically important for dormant languages where there are no speakers to consult.

In light of the context discussed above, we discuss and exemplify the following topics in this paper: (1) the desiderata of a formal model that would best accommodate the Algonquian verb; (2) the desiderata for any standard for labeling and organizing Algonquian verbal paradigms (i.e., should one split or chunk morphemes or both?); (3) how we might best pursue consistency for the underlying primary databases across Algonquian languages, to allow for the maximal efficiency in the adaptation of applications developed for one Algonquian language to the rest, as well as for ease of comparability in language learning and linguistic research; (4) what is lexical vs. paradigmatic (i.e., which morphological processes are productive?); and (5) the desiderata on the different ways in which we can display information from the primary databases so that it is useful for the various audience types—first language speakers, heritage language learners, nonheritage language learners, instructors, linguistic researchers—and takes into account the reality of the language's relative vitality.

Templates

A few key notions are generally agreed on when describing the Algonquian verb.[2] There are four basic morphological classes that subsume certain persons and their particular grouping; and there are varying numbers of inflectional paradigms, distributed in three orders: Independent, Conjunct, and Imperative. General characteristics of the three orders across Algonquian languages are as follows: verbs in the Independent order take personal prefixes (Conjunct and Imperative verbs do not); Conjunct verbs can undergo initial change; and the set of persons used in the Imperative is restricted.

Out of these generalizations, templates can be derived that can be used for both structuring a verb database and displaying verb conjugations for different audiences. Of the four Algonquian morphological verb classes, the Transitive Animate (VTA) verb, so called for its animate object, has the largest number of forms, which are best organized by grouping together LOCAL or I-You interactions (Speech Act Participants [SAPs] only), NON-LOCAL or third person interactions only, and MIXED person interactions involving SAP and third persons. The VTA passive has a person set that patterns like the person set of the Transitive Inanimate (VTI) verb, so called for its inanimate object, and the Animate Intransitive (VAI) verb, which takes animate subjects. Inanimate Intransitive (VII) verbs, which take inanimate subjects, only have third person inanimate subjects. VTI and VAI verbs also have relational inflection, which excludes obviative subjects, and passive or unspecified actor forms, which often have the same person affix sets as Inanimate Intransitive verbs, though not in all languages. All of the above is summarized in (1) and illustrated in Figure 1 for Innu VTA verbs.

(1)   Basic Template for the four classes of Algonquian verbs:

VTA verb
- LOCAL (I-YOU interactions, Speech Act Participants [SAP] only)
- MIXED (SAP and 3rd)
- NON-LOCAL (3rd person interactions)
- Passive set (similar to AI and TI verbs)

VTI and VAI verbs
- Regular
- Relational
- Unspecified actor sets (similar to II verbs)

VII verb

FIGURE 1. Display of an Innu VTA Verb, based on templates, and exhibiting a numbering system of subparadigms in the pop-up window (verbe.innu-aimun.ca)

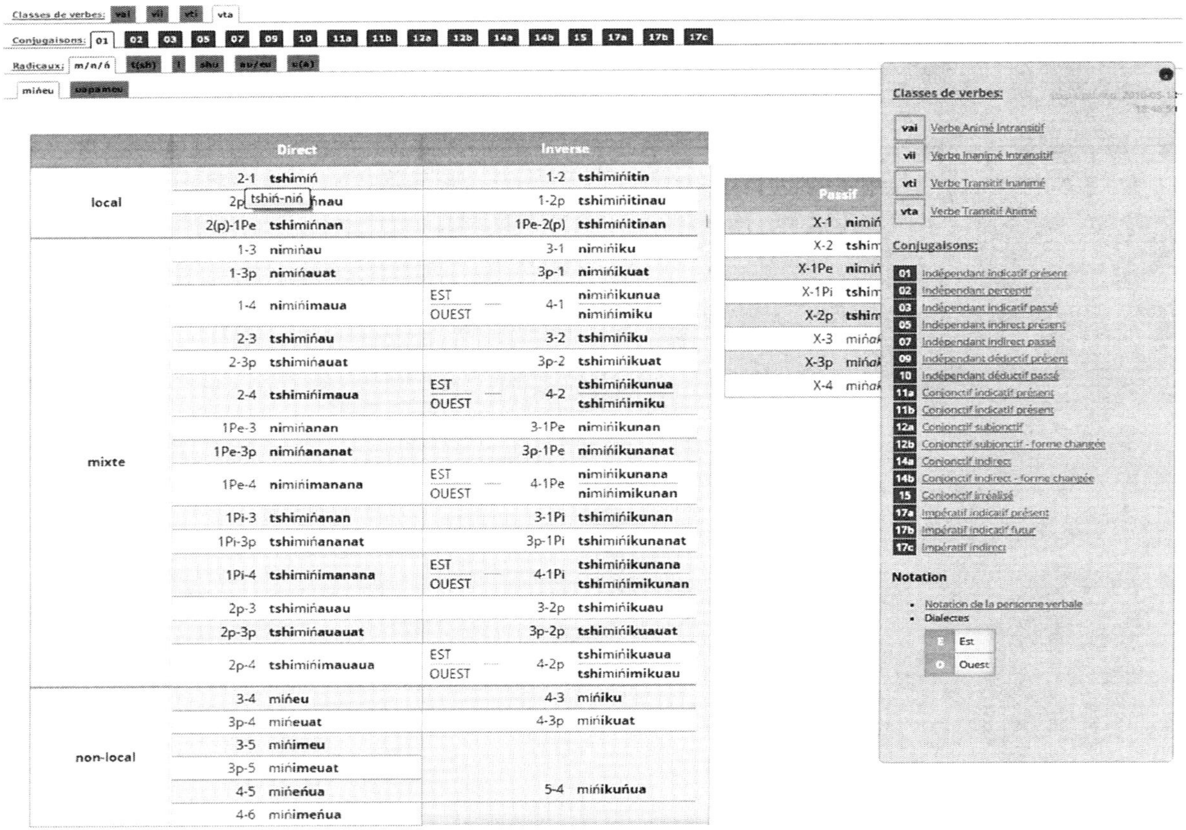

Person Labeling and Notation

As one can see from Figure 1, a numbered notation is used to index person and number. Consistency is crucial. There can be many ways to DISPLAY the person marking, but we recommend that standardization across Algonquian verb databases be seriously pursued. Issues can range from choice of a notation that is ambiguous or uninterpretable to technical difficulties in importing and manipulating the data on a computer, which can result in software malfunctions or even loss of data. For example, from the perspective of cross-Algonquian comparability, if a language neutralizes number for animate obviative forms, it could be preferable to use 4(p) or 3′(p) rather than just 4 or 3′, because there are Algonquian languages where obviative singular and plural are distinguished, such as northwestern Ontario dialects of Ojibwe. Nevertheless, as long as one label (e.g., 4) is used consistently and is clearly described to represent a number-wise underspecified obviative person form, conversion to some other notation can be done with ease. Furthermore, using numbers to refer to grammatical person might well make sense to linguists but makes little sense to lay speakers.[3] Below is a short list of various person notations currently found in Algonquian Verb databases that need clear descriptions and mappings of equivalences, a task that we must leave for the future:

(2) Various Person Notations:

Inanimates: 3 or 0?

Obviative animates: 3, 3′, 3″ or 3, 4, 5, . . . ?

Obviation: ′, ″ or OBV?

Plural (vs. Singular): 22 or 2p? ; 4, 4(p) 4s or 4p ?

Inclusive-Exclusive distinction: 12, 21, 21p, 21(p), 1Pi ? / 1p or 1Pe?

Transitivity and direction—direct: 3-4, 3>4, 3→4, 3+4 ; inverse: 4→3 or 4←3?

VTI verbs: 1-0 or 1?

Passive and unspecified actor forms: X-1 or 1, X, X′, . . .

Glossing and Displaying with Templates

Once a consistent notation is adopted, glossing templates can be developed for pedagogical displays and comparative purposes. Displays can be adapted to various user types and needs. For example, in the Innu and East Cree verb conjugation applet,[4] the solution was to use a mouse-over of the abstract person number to display a gloss, established in consultation with the speakers and users, that contains

TABLE 1. VII glossing template for Innu

PRONOUN	ENGLISH SUBJECT PRONOUN	PRONOM SUJET FRANÇAIS	INNU PRONOUN
0	it	ça, il	tshekuan
0p	they	ça, ils	tshekuana
0′	it [obviative]	ça, il [obviatif]	tshekuanńu
0′p	they [obviative]	ça, ils [obviatif]	tshekuanńua

TABLE 2. VTA glossing template (21p mixed) across Innu and East Cree dialects

PRONOUN	ENGLISH SUBJECT	ENGLISH OBJECT	INNU PRONOUN	SEC PRONOUN	NEC PRONOUN
3→21p	s/he	us (you and me)	uiń→tshińanu	wî→chîyânû	wîyi→chîynaâniu
21p→3	we (you and I)	him/her	tshińanu→uiń	chîyânû→wî	chîyâniu→wîyi
3p→21p	they	us (you and me)	uińuau→tshińanu	wîwâu→chîyânû	wîyiwâu→chîyâniu
21p→3p	we (you and I)	them	tshińanu→uińuau	chîyânû→wîwâu	chîyâniu→wîyiwâu
21p→4	we (you and I)	him/her/them [obviative]	tshińanu→neńua (utauassima)	chîyânû→aniyûh (utawâshimh)	chîyâniu→aniyâyiuh (ukusis-h)
4→21p	s/he or they [obviative]	us (you and me)	neńua (utauassima) →tshińaniu	aniyûh (utawâshimh) →chîyâniu	aniyâyiuh (ukusis-h) →chîyâniu

a corresponding emphatic pronoun in the Indigenous language (see Tables 1 and 2 and Figure 1). The French and English glossing templates were developed not only to generate English and French glosses of verb forms but also to check and suggest consistency with the bilingual dictionary definitions of such verbs.

Tables 1 and 2 illustrate some issues encountered in seeking to help different user types and the solutions that were adopted: How much metalanguage (terms like OBVIATIVE, PLURAL) do we use? Does the list include all possible cases, and do we give examples? For instance, consider how both emphatic and indefinite pronouns are used in the templates, how some examples are added in parentheses, and how grammatical information is indicated in brackets. Since there are no emphatic obviative pronouns, a set of remote demonstratives was used instead (gloss for person 4, *neńua*). For inanimate subjects, the inflected obviative form of *tshekuan* was used, but for unspecified actor VAI forms, the corresponding *auen* was NOT used, as a decision was made not to offer any pronominal gloss for impersonal verbs.

Such templates can also be used to generate code to control the display of forms. The display (or View) of our verb forms can follow different orderings of pronouns, based on users' habits or preferences. The order for VTI or VAI verbs in (3a) follows what bilingual Innu-French speakers are used to from their French grammar schooling experience, while the order (3b) follows the animacy/person hierarchy.

(3)   a. 1, 2, 1p, 21p, 2p, . . .

      b. 2, 2p, 21p, 1, 1p, . . .

Labeling Paradigms

Labeling paradigms should be as consistent as possible, within and across Algonquian languages. One solution first proposed by MacKenzie (1980) is to adopt a numbering system based on cognate suffixes across languages and dialects. Different labels can then be applied in the displays to reflect the semantics of each paradigm in a particular dialect and the different users' preferences: those of a linguist, Indigenous teachers, and so forth. Figure 1 also illustrates such a list and its realizations in Innu. This numbering system can also be used to display paradigms economically in tabs, as in the Innu and East Cree verb applets in Figure 1, which also have a legend that links paradigm labels to web pages covering the corresponding grammar, with examples. Such an equivalence-based labeling system could be extended to include Eastern Algonquian languages and diachronic dimensions.

Generating Forms

All the examples given so far have concerned fairly vigorous languages, for which model verbs could be fully documented with many speakers, with fluent teachers and speakers as users. Generating verb forms for these languages is so far happening behind the scenes and for search engine purposes only (see next section). When the language is no longer spoken except by a few elders, the need to automatically generate and display all possible verb forms increases. While the principles of database organization stay the same, some new display issues arise.

FIGURE 2. Western Ojibwe verb paradigm (generated)

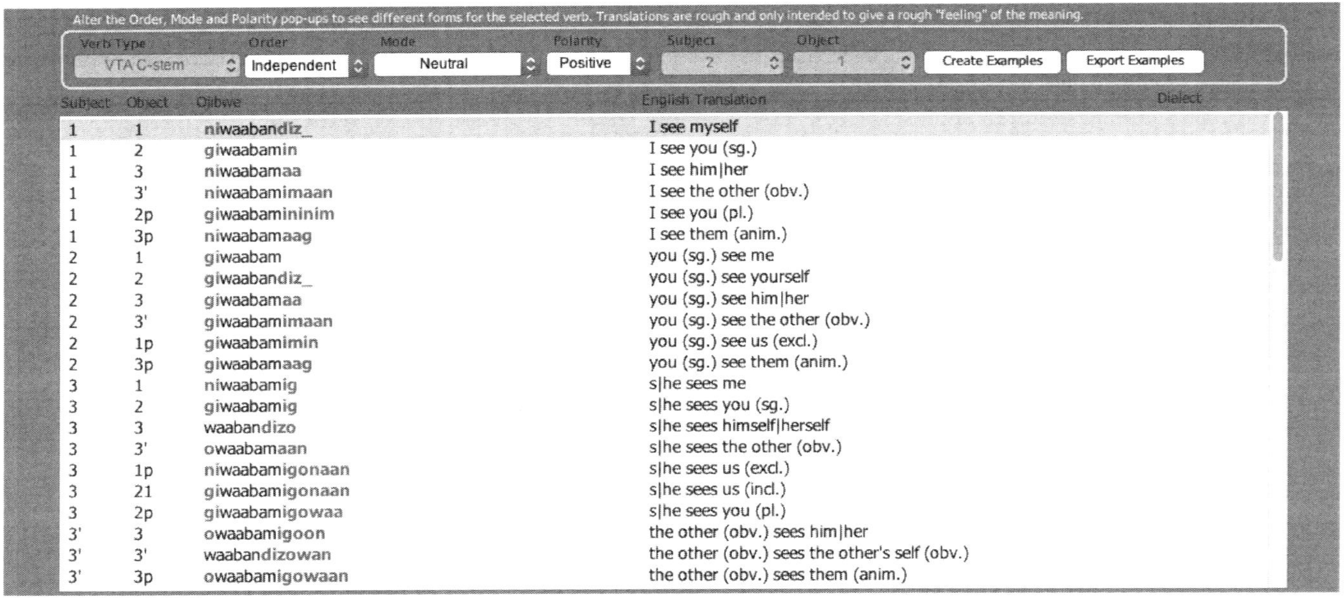

Alter the Order, Mode and Polarity pop-ups to see different forms for the selected verb. Translations are rough and only intended to give a rough "feeling" of the meaning.

Verb Type	Order	Mode	Polarity	Subject	Object	Create Examples	Export Examples
VTA-C-stem	Independent	Neutral	Positive	2	1		

Subject	Object	Ojibwe	English Translation	Dialect
1	1	niwaabandiz_	I see myself	
1	2	giwaabamin	I see you (sg.)	
1	3	niwaabamaa	I see him|her	
1	3'	niwaabamimaan	I see the other (obv.)	
1	2p	giwaabamininim	I see you (pl.)	
1	3p	niwaabamaag	I see them (anim.)	
2	1	giwaabam	you (sg.) see me	
2	2	giwaabandiz_	you (sg.) see yourself	
2	3	giwaabamaa	you (sg.) see him|her	
2	3'	giwaabamimaan	you (sg.) see the other (obv.)	
2	1p	giwaabamimin	you (sg.) see us (excl.)	
2	3p	giwaabamaag	you (sg.) see them (anim.)	
3	1	niwaabamig	s|he sees me	
3	2	giwaabamig	s|he sees you (sg.)	
3	3	waabandizo	s|he sees himself|herself	
3	3'	owaabamaan	s|he sees the other (obv.)	
3	1p	niwaabamigonaan	s|he sees us (excl.)	
3	21	giwaabamigonaan	s|he sees us (incl.)	
3	2p	giwaabamigowaa	s|he sees you (pl.)	
3'	3	owaabamigoon	the other (obv.) sees him|her	
3'	3'	waabandizowan	the other (obv.) sees the other's self (obv.)	
3'	3p	owaabamigowaan	the other (obv.) sees them (anim.)	

The Western Ojibwe Dictionary (Valentine and Ningewance 2009), as shown in Figure 2, offers a basic display for each verb, for which both numeric abbreviations and computer-generated English glosses (based on person templates as discussed above) are provided. Note also that, given the length of some Ojibwe inflected forms, when a form is selected, a computer-generated syllabification is provided as a pronunciation aid. Finally, for pedagogical reasons, not only is the VTA inflection provided but also the derived reflexive (VAI) verb inflection.

We can see here how the predominant user groups one has in mind will determine how to present verb paradigms. In addition to the inflectional subsets discussed above (orders, moods), polarity is added and generated, since there are distinct negative forms in all three orders. The Western Ojibwe Dictionary only displays a grammatically specified subset of inflections in its viewing area. Users can select which subcategories they want to see by using drop-down menus (top of Figure 2) or by using a help system that requires less linguistic knowledge through an interactive window to the right, by which they can specify in simple terms the grammatical context in which a form will be used (its order), its polarity (positive or negative), and its subject and object person/number/obviation features.

In order for verb paradigms to be generated like this, a number of decisions have to be made, which will influence both the documentation work and the form of the data entered in the database. A full discussion of the advantages and disadvantages of database structural types is beyond the scope of this paper (but see Junker et al. 2013), though we recommend relational databases for consistency and economy. Importantly, when lexical and morphological information is documented and stored in a well-structured and systematic way, in standard databases that linguists routinely use, such linguistic information can be converted into platform-independent, portable computational models that can in turn be packaged as software modules, e.g., as spell-checkers, which can be integrated with a word-processing application. One widely used technology for such computational models are Finite-State Machines (e.g., Beesley and Karttunen 2003). They are well-known computational data structures, are extremely fast and efficient, have a calculus allowing for powerful manipulations, allow rule-based definition of paradigms for various verb types, and are easily portable to different operating systems and platforms, and thus can be integrated with other applications. Here, one can consider the finite-state machine as another instantiation of the underlying Model, the output of which can again be adapted by a Controller to produce various Views. We have done this successfully with Plains Cree (Harrigan et al. 2016), where the computational modeling work has been substantially facilitated by a consistently structured lexical database (the one underlying Wolvengrey 2001) which is systematically matched with descriptions of the verb paradigms (Wolvengrey 2011), building upon prior work by Wolfart (1973), Ellis (1971), and others. Combined with a Plains Cree lexical database, this computational model can be used create an intelligent dictionary (I-DICT), allowing for the generation of a variety of Views on the verb paradigms, available for any verb in the dictionary (cf. *itwêwina* n.d.)

With these considerations in mind, how should we analyze the data and represent the morphemes that constitute verb inflection?

Analyzing and Representing Morphemes: To Split or to Chunk?

One linguistic tradition in representing the morphological structure of words is maximal decomposition, so that each morphosyntactic feature is matched with some overtly observable and delineable sequence in the word (the ITEM-AND-AR-RANGEMENT approach); take, for example, the the five morphemes and associated features (4a–b) from Wolvengrey (2011:56) for Plains Cree. Note that the only difference in form here is the theme sign, *-â-* vs. *-iko-* (Direct vs. Inverse), which switches which of the two referents expressed by the verb is the Actor and the Goal.

(4)   a. niwîcihânânak   b. niwîcihikonânak
          ni-wîcih–â–nân–ak (split)   ni-wîcih–iko–nân–ak (split)
          ni-wîcih-ânânak (chunked)   ni-wîcih-ikonânak (chunked)
          1-help.VTA-DIR-1p-3p   1-help.VTA-INV-1p-3p
          'We (excl.) help them.'   'They help us (excl.).'

For many Algonquian languages, such splitting can be undertaken in a relatively straightforward manner for the most part, but there are word forms where this is not easy at all. For example, Nichols (1980) analyzes Southwestern Ojibwe as having 14 suffix position classes. Certain negative forms appear to show the reinsertion of morphological elements, such as *niwaabam<u>aa</u>siw<u>aa</u>naan* 'we (excl.) do not see him', which shows the TA direct theme sign /-aa/ both before and after the negative suffixes $_4$/-si/ and $_5$/-w/. An alternative item-and-arrangement approach is to treat the entire suffix complex as a unit, in the spirit of the word and paradigm approach to morphology as exemplified in Blevins (2006; cf. also Harrigan et al. 2016). Entire suffix-complex strings were used to generate inflections in the Ojibwe dictionary illustrated in Figure 2. For learners, too, learning entire suffix complexes would seem much easier than attending to individual, sequentialized morphemes in 14 positions.

From the perspective of computational modeling, being able to describe complex word structure as minimally as possible with possibly extensive sets of rules for morpheme concatenation and for morphophonological processes was desirable early on, due to limits on computer memory. Devising such rules so that they are both complete and accurate is a time-consuming task, and in some cases simply enumerating chunks of less-regularly decomposable morpheme sequences and their associated features would be a more efficient option, and likely a psychologically more valid one as well. Moreover, the exponential increase of computer memory and processing speed has turned the chunking strategy into a viable one. Thus, we can instead present the Plains Cree forms in (3a–b) as consisting of two chunks, a circumfix-like element (made up of a prefix and suffix sequence) and the intervening stem, both associated with one or more morphosyntactic features. Because there are much fewer morpheme junctures (two in this case), one needs fewer rules to deal with potential morphophonological variation. Lexical databases often already contain such a chunked decomposition as a part of documentation work, so in order to create a computational model a linguist does not need to spend more time on devising and testing myriad rules to split these chunks further. For the VTA examples (3a–b), we can thus instead specify the Actor and Goal as first person plural (exclusive) and third person plural, or with the roles inverted, based on the entire *ni . . . ânânak* (1 . . . 1p→3p) or *ni . . . ikonânak* (1- . . . -3p→1p) chunks enveloping the stem *wîcih-*, without any need for further splitting.

Sometimes, chunking can even include stem or stem-final material to allow for more consistent string matching to determine stem classes. For the East Cree search engine (Junker and Stewart 2008), the verbal 'suffix' included the final stem vowel or consonant. The database (the Model) can thus include several layers of analysis, with different representations stored up (including sound files), which can be queried by different rules (the Controller) to offer different displays (the View). In Table 3 (from the database of East Cree model verbs), the third person relational dubitative form of the n-stem verb *takushin* contains multiple representations.[5] Furthermore, even if one opts for maximal chunking, such chunks can be marked with preidentified morphological splits (e.g., line [e] in Table 3), when known

TABLE 3. Southern East Cree VAI n-stem takushin relational third person independent indicative dubitative neutral

a. ᑕᑯᔑ ᓄᐍᐨ	Word form in standard SEC syllabic spelling
b. takushinuweche	Word form in standard SEC roman spelling
c. takushinuuhche	Older spelling, converted from legacy syllabics
d. takushi-nuweche	Search Engine chunks
e. takushin-u-weche	Morpheme cuts for display: italics, bold
f. takushinw-we-ʔche	Morpheme break with underlying forms

or applicable, thus not requiring any dynamically implemented morphological decomposition.

Relationships with Dictionaries

Representations of verb paradigms are intimately linked to dictionary databases. Two basic pieces of information are essential for modeling: verb class indicated as part of speech and stem type. A number of restrictions to prevent overgenerating forms must also be stored in the lexicon. Here, we give a few examples of common problems and solutions for Algonquian languages we have worked with, and we show how modeling with dictionary databases can lead to better documentation of verb paradigms.

Number Restrictions

Some verbs only appear in the plural, which must be indicated in the dictionary database (Model), in a dedicated field, and read by the Controller to block singular forms from being generated, e.g., for numeral verbs (5a). Conversely, forms only used in the singular, like impersonal verbs (5b), also need to be marked in the dictionary. These examples are from the East Cree Dictionary (Junker et al. 2012):

(5)   a. nîshuwich (VAI) stem: *i* , **pl.** 'they (anim.) are two'.

       b. chimûn (vai) stem: *n*, **impersonal** 'it is raining'.

Derivational Information

We saw that the Western Ojibwe Dictionary generates all the reflexive forms of a VTA verb, but how should one treat reciprocal forms? Should these be stored in the lexicon or in the paradigms? Where do we encode 'productivity'? Dictionaries tend to have representative samples of relative root addition (6), reduplication, reciprocal and reflexive verbs, and secondary derivation processes like causatives or applicatives, but for modeling we need to be able to restrict generation rules on the level of each individual lexical entry. While some restrictions can be deduced based on pragmatic reasoning, in many cases we can discover the actual restrictions on inflectional generality/productivity only with corpus work.

(6) apû   >   itapû
     'she sits'   >   'she sits a certain way'

Lexicalized Forms

Lexicalized forms can be a challenge. Which grammatical category do we give to lexicalized forms such as passive (unspecified actor) forms of VAI verbs like (7b) or inflected verb forms in the Cree conjunct subjunctive like (8b)? Some guiding principles can be derived from modeling constraints, in terms of what information is minimally necessary and sufficient for a user to be able to conjugate such verbs. One solution is to create a special subtype for parts-of-speech, e.g., 'VII, impersonal' in (7b) or 'VII, subj. (VII conjunct subjunctive)' in (8b).

(7) a. makusheu (VAI) stem: *e* 's/he feasts'

     b. makushânû (VII, impersonal) stem: û 'there is a feast' (East Cree Dictionary)

(8) a. uapan (VII) VII stem: *n*; CONJ. uapak; SUBJ. uapaki 'it is dawn, daylight'

     b. uapaki (VII, subj) 'tomorrow', conjunct form of *uapan* (Innu Dictionary)

Other lexicalization patterns commonly found in Algonquian include VTA inverse forms that only take an inanimate agent, often labeled VAI in Cree dictionaries and VTAI in Ojibwe. But what is the conjugation class of these new derived

FIGURE 3. Modeling initial change for East Cree verbs

ecn	12b-N (0)	14-N (0)
chihtin	chihtinichh	chihtinikwaa
aah uhchi uhpiniikuniwich	No example for stem: unknown	No example for stem: unknown
aahchinaakun	iyaahchinaakuhchh	iyaahchinaakunikwaa
aahchinihkaataau	iyaahchinihkaataachh	iyaahchinihkaataakwaa
aahchipihtaamikin	iyaahchipihtaamikihchh	iyaahchipihtaamikinikwaa
aahchipiyiu	iyaahchipiyichh	iyaahchipiyikwaa
aahchishtaau	iyaahchishtaachh	iyaahchishtaakwaa
aahchiyiwaapiyiu	iyaahchiyiwaapiyichh	iyaahchiyiwaapiyikwaa
aahchiyiwaau	iyaahchiyiwaachh	iyaahchiyiwaakwaa
aahkuhiiwaau	iyaahkuhiiwaachh	iyaahkuhiiwaakwaa
aahkuhtiwaapischihtin	iyaahkuhtiwaapischihtihchh	iyaahkuihtuiwaapischihtinikwaa
aahkuhtiwishtaau	iyaahkuhtiwishtaachh	iyaahkuihtuiwishtaakwaa
aahkuhtuwipiihchihtin	iyaahkuhtuwipiihchihtihchh	iyaahkuihtuwipiihchihtinikwaa
aahkun	iyaahkuhchh	iyaahkunikwaa
aahkuvihtuwipiihchistin	iyaahkuvihtuwipiihchistihchh	iyaahkavyihtuwipiihchistinikwaa
aahkwaachipiyiu	iyaahkwaachipiyichh	iyaahkwaachipiyikwaa
aahkwaahkiititaau	iyaahkwaahkiititaachh	iyaahkwaahkiititaakwaa
aahkwaakimitaau	iyaahkwaakimitaachh	iyaahkwaakimitaakwaa
aahkwaakunaautin	iyaahkwaakunaautihchh	iyaahkwaakunaautinikwaa
aahkwaapisistaau	iyaahkwaapisistaachh	iyaahkwaapisistaakwaa
aahkwaasinaakun	iyaahkwaasinaakuhchh	iyaahkwaasinaakunikwaa
aahkwaaskitin	iyaahkwaaskitihchh	iyaahkwaaskitinikwaa
aahkwaataaskitiin	iyaahkwaataaskitiitichh	iyaahkwaataaskitinikwaa
aahkwaataayihtaakun	iyaahkwaataayihtaakuhchh	iyaahkwaataayihtaakunikwaa
aahkwaatin	iyaahkwaatiihchh	iyaahkwaatiinikwaa
aahtaakimipiyiu	iyaahtaakimipiyichh	iyaahtaakimipiyikwaa
aahtaaputaau	iyaahtaaputaachh	iyaahtaaputaakwaa
aahtaaskupiyiu	iyaahtaaskupiyichh	iyaahtaaskupiyikwaa
aahtikutaau	iyaahtikutaachh	iyaahtikutaakwaa

forms? Sometimes, new paradigms have to be created to accommodate these. For example, for VAI forms lexicalized from the VTI passive in Innu, we created a new model conjugation, ending in -*kanu*, treating this form as a VAI stem.

Modeling for Accurate Documentation

Modeling not only allows us to generate forms and build search engines, it also has the advantage of allowing us to check large amounts of real data against the model. For example, in 2007 Junker investigated the rules of initial change in East Cree. With Terry Stewart, they modeled two changed forms for each verb in the Cree dictionary, and during a workshop with elders, Junker and her Cree collaborators went through a list of over 20,000 Cree verbs, doing spot checks to verify and improve the descriptive rules for initial change (Figure 3).[6]

Linking Things Together

Many potential audiences must be able to access the paradigm/dictionary database, including language learners, educators, first language speakers, and linguists. Each of these audiences can have a DISPLAY or VIEW specific to their needs, which is generated from the same underlying database. There are a variety of ways to display the paradigms. One way familiar to many users is a wiki-driven web-based site, accessible anywhere even by means of mobile devices. A wiki, out of the box, excels at searching, linking, and tagging information from the underlying database. There are built-in tools for handling multimedia (sound, images, and video), and it is relatively easy to set up with instant online access.

A good case study is a Mahican language database developed by Harvey (2015) which combines the written corpus (interlinearized) with a dictionary database and dynamic paradigm generator—an example web page from the wiki display is in Figure 4. Any instance of a lemma or affix can be linked to its proper lexical entry page. Such a lexical entry wiki page shows several selected fields directly from the database (derivation, definition, part of speech, notes, etc.). The list of instances from the corpus is built dynamically via wiki tools. Each wiki page also has a list of tags or categories that flag potential points of interest. Here, clicking, e.g., "redupl" would extract and present a list of all reduplicative verbs in the corpus. This is particularly useful when the researcher discovers an unusual or unknown form or

FIGURE 4. Example lexical entry page in Mahican lexical database

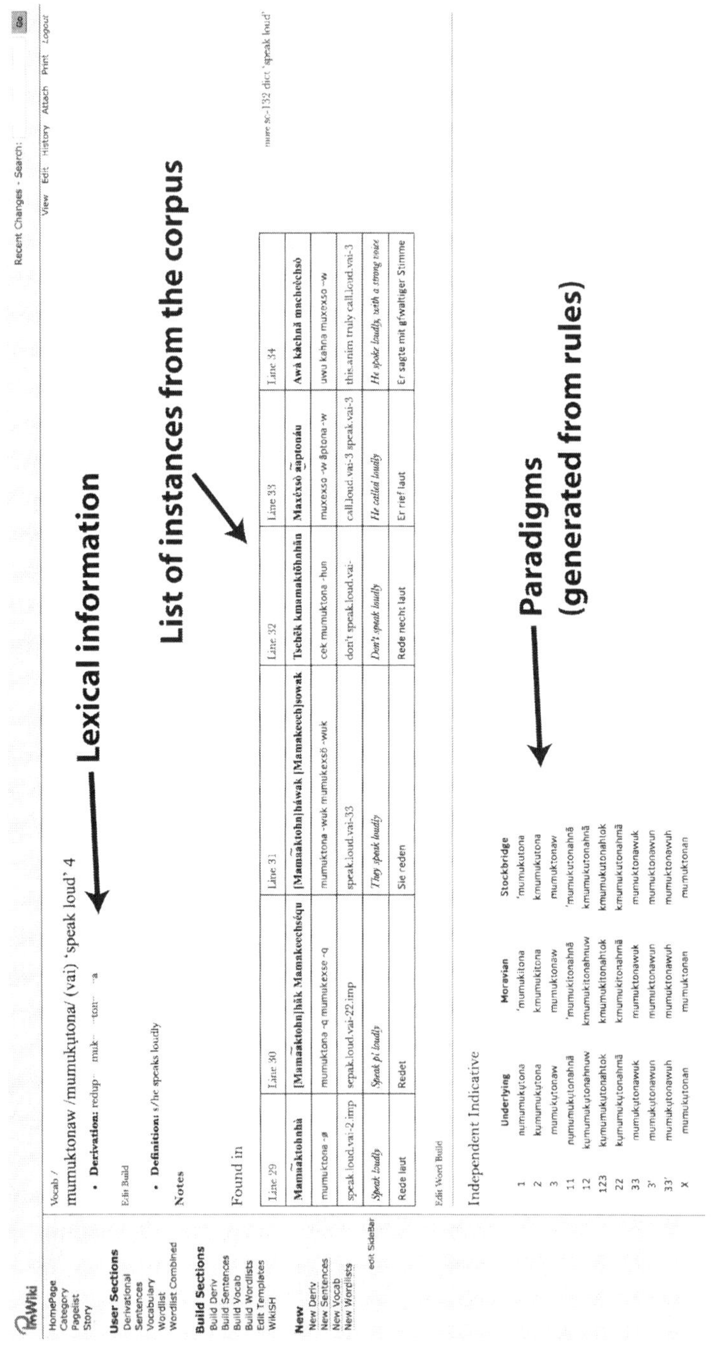

mw-tw-1312 dict 'speak loud'

Recent Changes - Search:

View   Edit   History   Attach   Print   Logout

KWiki

HomePage
Category
Pagelist
Story

User Sections
Derivational
Sentences
Vocabulary
Wordlist
Wordlist Combined

Build Sections
Build Deriv
Build Sentences
Build Vocab
Build Wordlists
Edit Templates
WikiSH

New
New Deriv
New Sentences
New Vocab
New Wordlists

edit Sidebar

Lexical information

Vocab /
mumuktonaw /mumuk̈utona/ (vai) 'speak loud' 4

- **Derivation:** redup muk- -ton -a

Edit Build

- **Definition:** s/he speaks loudly

Notes

List of instances from the corpus

Found in

	Line 30	Line 31			
Mamaktohnhū	**[Mamaktohnu]hūk Mamakeecheēqu**	**[Mamaktohu]hūwak [Mamakeeeh]sowak**			
mumuktona-∅	mumuktona-q mumukesse-q	mumuktona -wok mumukess0 -wok			
speak.loud.vai-2.imp	speak.loud.vai-22.imp	speak.loud.vai-33			
Speak p loudly	*Speak pl loudly*	*They speak loudly*			
Rede laut	Redet	Sie reden			

Line 32	Line 33	Line 54	
Tschīk kmumakiōhnhiu	**Maxīxso āiptoniu**	**Awā kāchnā mschēēchsō**	
cek mumuktona -hun	muxexag -w āptona -w	uwu kahta muxexso -w	
don't speak.loud.vai-	call.loud.vai-3 speak.vai-3	this.anim truly call.loud.vai-3	
Don't speak loudly	*He called loudly*	*He spoke loudly, with a strong voice*	
Rede nicht laut	Er rief laut	Er sagte mit gewaltiger Stimme	

Edit Word Build

Paradigms (generated from rules)

Independent Indicative

	Underlying	Moravian	Stockbridge
1	numumukụtona	'mumukitona	'mumukutona
2	kumumukụtona	kmumukitona	kmumukutona
3	mumukụtonaw	mumukitonaw	mumuktonaw
11	numumukụtonahnā	'mumukitonahnā	'mumukitonahnā
12	kumumukụtonahnuw	kmumukitonahtuow	kmumukutonahilok
123	kumumukụtonahtiok	kmumukitonahtiok	kmumukutonahilok
22	kumumukụtonahnā	kmumukitonahnā	kmumukutonahnā
33	mumukụtonawok	mumuktonawok	mumuktonawok
3'	mumukụtonawun	mumuktonawun	mumuktonawun
33'	mumukụtonawuh	mumuktonawuh	mumuktonawuh
x	mumukụtonan	mumuktonan	mumuktonan

structure in the data; this can be tagged and analyzed with other examples of the same form at a later date. Finally, the verb paradigm is generated by combining principal parts from the lexical database to appropriate affix chunks, where morphophonological rules are applied just before actual display.

As seen in Figure 4, the audience here is the linguist comparing instances in the corpus to a model of the verb paradigm. Where the generated paradigms on the wiki page disagree with the attested forms, the lexeme or the model (affix chunks and morphophonology) can be immediately corrected.[7] However, if the target audience is second language learners, different display forms can be selected when the wiki page is output: the person numbers (1, 2, 3, . . .) could be replaced by Mahican pronouns (*nia*, *kia*, *naakmã*, . . .), the user could select a specific dialect, the interlinear form could instead be shown as an example sentence, and any notes could be omitted.

Conclusions

The most important consideration at the beginning of any project is the design and construction of the database in a consistent and systematic way, guaranteeing future compatibility and portability, and the ability to compare information with other linguistic databases as seamlessly as possible. Employing the database model outlined in this paper, systematic and consistent work can be easily and instantaneously tailored to a broad range of potential users. There are clear benefits to such a system for verb paradigms: researchers can test their model paradigms against a corpus; native speakers can have quick access to a source for standardized spelling; educators can plan curriculum derived from this resource; and learners can have a place to look up those verbs when they need them, in real-life situations where conversation requires an unfamiliar form.

NOTES

1. "Dormant" refers to a language with no speakers or semispeakers but for which ample documentation exists and there is a community that recognizes the language as part of their cultural heritage.

2. For influential twentieth-century models, see Ellis 1971, updated in Ellis 2016, and Wolfart 1973.

3. Also, using certain characters that have a special function in most computer code, such as an apostrophe for indicating obviation, e.g., 3', instead of the proper unicode character for 'prime' (02B9), or symbols for indicating Actor-Goal direction that are also angle brackets, e.g., 2>3, instead of the unicode arrow 2→3, can lead to severe difficulties in importing data into a computer database, and the use of such characters should be avoided.

4. See Baraby and Junker 2011–2014 and Junker and MacKenzie 2010–2015, 2011–2015. The glossing templates owe much to discussions with Bill Jancewicz and Rand Valentine.

5. There is a clear pedagogical advantage for language learners to associate conjugations with verb classes, based on their Algonquian verb finals. For example, in the above example, a subclass with the final -*shin* 'on the horizontal' could be coded to further predict the conjugation pattern of semantically related verbs. In Ojibwe, identifying the VAI final -*ose* 'walk' can successfully predict the conjugation of a whole series of 'walking' verbs such as: *animose, aagimose, babaamose, babimose, bedose, bimose, bimwewedaawangose, bimweweyaagonewose*, etc. (see Ojibwe People's Dictionary for translations, http://ojibwe.lib.umn.edu/). We suggest that those tasks are best handled by and within dictionaries.

6. Similarly, the imperative forms of all 1,645 *u* stem AI verbs of the Innu dictionary were generated with two possible imperatives in 2014, to allow Innu editor Yvette Mollen to select the correct form, which is the test for long and short *u* stems. As a result, three categories of *u* stems were created for the database: *long u, short u*, and just *u* for verbs that are always in the plural where underlying length is not determinable.

7. One example is the verb suffix -*sa* (cognate with the Delaware present aspect suffix). At first, the paradigm generator did not produce this form—there were so few instances that one could not determine precisely what -*sa* means in a given sentence. During interlinearization, the suffix -*sa* was tagged wherever it appeared, and a link was automatically created. Throughout this process, the tag-link could be clicked, and all instances of -*sa* were listed in their context. Its extant functions now apparent, and with a sufficient number of instances on the corpus to be sure of the form of the suffix, it could then be added to paradigm generator. This method has been very useful in finding unpredicted forms and variation.

REFERENCES

Antonsen, Lene, Ryan Johnson, Trond Trosterud, and Heli Uibo. 2013. Generating modular grammar exercises with finite-state transducers. *Proceedings of the second workshop on NLP for computer-assisted language learning at NODALIDA 2013*, pp. 27–38. NEALT Proceedings Series, vol. 17 / Linköping Electronic Conference Proceedings, vol. 86. Linköping: Linköping University Electronic Press.

Arppe, Antti, Lene Antonsen, Trond Trosterud, Sjur Moshagen, Dorothy Thunder, Conor Snoek, Timothy Mills, Juhani Järvikivi, and Jordan Lachler. 2015. Turning language documentation into reader's and writer's software tools. Fourth International Conference on Language Documentation and Conservation (ICDLC 4), 26 February–1 March 2015, Honolulu.

Baraby, Anne-Marie, and Marie-Odile Junker. 2011–2014. 3e éd. *Conjugaisons des verbes innus*. http://verbe.innu-aimun.ca.

Beesley, Kenneth R., and Lauri Karttunen. 2003. *Finite state morphology*. Stanford, CA: CSLI Publications.

Blevins, James. 2006. Word-based morphology. *Journal of Linguistics* 42:531–573.

Ellis, C. Douglas. 1971. Cree verb paradigms. *International Journal of American Linguistics* 37(2):76–95.

———. 2016. Verb Paradigms. In *Spoken Cree glossary*. Ottawa: Carleton University. spokencree.org.

Harrigan, Atticus, Lene Antonsen, Antti Arppe, Dustin Bowers, Trond Trosterud, and Arok Wolvengrey. 2016. Learning from the computational modeling of Plains Cree verbs. Workshop on computational methods for descriptive and theoretical morphology, Seventeenth International Morphology Meeting, Vienna, 18–21 February 2016.

Harvey, Christopher. 2015. *Wiki-generated paradigm tools*. Fourth International Conference on Language Documentation and Conservation (ICDLC 4), 26 February–1 March 2015, Honolulu.

itwêwina. N.d. *itwêwina*—Intelligent on-line dictionary for Plains Cree. Alberta: University of Alberta. http://altlab.ualberta.ca/itwewina/.

Junker, Marie-Odile, and Marguerite MacKenzie. 2010–2015. *East Cree (Northern Dialect) verb conjugation*. 4th ed. http://verbn.eastcree.org.

———. 2011–2015. *East Cree (Southern dialect) verb conjugation*. 4th ed. http://verbs.eastcree.org.

Junker, Marie-Odile, Marguerite MacKenzie, Luci Bobbish-Salt, Alice Duff, Ruth Salt, Anna Blacksmith, Patricia Diamond, and Pearl Weistche (eds). 2012. *The Eastern James Bay Cree dictionary on the web: English-Cree and Cree-English, French-Cree and Cree-French (Northern and Southern dialects)*. http://dictionary.eastcree.org/.

Junker, Marie-Odile, and Terry Stewart. 2008. Building search engines for Algonquian languages. *Papers of the Thirty-Ninth Algonquian Conference*, ed. by Karl S. Hele and

Regna Darnell, pp. 378–411. London: University of Western Ontario Press.

———. 2011. A linguistic atlas for endangered languages: www.atlas-ling.ca. *Proceedings of the Eleventh International Conference on Education and New Learning Technologies (EDULEARN 11)*. Barcelona.

Junker, Marie-Odile, Delasie Torkornoo, and J. Randolph Valentine. 2013. Relational databases for Cree, Innu, and Ojibwe dictionaries. Forty-Fifth Algonquian Conference, University of Ottawa, October 2013.

Krasner, Glenn E., and Stephen T. Pope. 1988. A cookbook for using the model–view controller user interface paradigm in Smalltalk-80. *Journal of Object-Oriented Programming* 1(3):26–49.

MacKenzie, Marguerite. 1980. Towards a dialectology of Cree-Montagnais-Naskapi. PhD thesis, University of Toronto.

Mailhot, José, Marguerite MacKenzie, and Marie-Odile Junker. 2013. *Online Innu dictionary*. http://www.innu-aimun.ca/dictionary.

Moose, Lawrence Leonard, Mary Moose, Gordon Jourdain, Marlene Stately, Leona Wakonabo, Eugene Stillday, Anna Gibbs, Rosemarie DeBungie, and Nancy Jones. 2009. *Aaniin Ekidong: Ojibwe vocabulary project*, ed. by Anton Treuer and Keller Papp. St. Paul: Minnesota Humanities Center.

Nichols, John D. 1980. Ojibwe morphology. PhD thesis, Harvard University.

Nichols, John, and Earl Nyholm. 1995. *Concise dictionary of Minnesota Ojibwe*. Minneapolis: University of Minnesota Press.

Valentine, J. Randolph, and Patricia N. Ningewance. 2009. Western Ojibwe dictionary. Computer application, University of Wisconsin–Madison.

Wolfart, H. Christoph. 1973. *Plains Cree: A grammatical study*. Transactions of the American Philosophical Society, n.s., 63(5). Philadelphia: American Philosophical Society.

Wolvengrey, Arok (ed.). 2001. ᓀᐦᐃᔭᐍᐏᐣ: ᐃᑗᐏᓇ / *nēhiýawēwin: itwēwina / Cree: Words*. Regina: Canadian Plains Research Center.

———. 2011. *Semantic and pragmatic functions in Plains Cree syntax*. Ultrecht, The Netherlands: LOT.

Historical Concepts and Perceptions of Snakes in Western Algonquian Bows

Roland Bohr

"Snakes bear symbolic connotations in many cultures, be they beneficent or ominous . . . for they combine in disturbing ways the comforting and familiar with the terrifying and repellent. Linking desire with fear, and attraction with repulsion, such images, often highly erotic, exercise a strong hold on the imagination" (Lapatin 2002:76, 77, 79).

Research at various museums in Canada, the United States, and Europe on Indigenous hunting weapons, primarily the bow and arrow, revealed several bows from the northern Plains and the Plateau region that had their backs covered with snakeskin. Most of the snakeskin-covered bows examined were covered with rattlesnake skins; but three were covered with garter snake skins instead. All three of these likely came from Blackfoot-speaking peoples,[1] with collection dates ranging from before 1846 to the early 1900s.[2]

Most of these snakeskin-covered bows were sinew-backed bows, meaning that each bow had one or more layers of sinew fibers glued to its back, i.e., the side that faces the target when the bow is drawn. Sinew backing was a common way for Indigenous bow makers in western North America to utilize short or flawed pieces of wood to make powerful bows, as the sinew, rather than the wood, took up the

FIGURE 1. Sinew-backed wooden bow, covered with garter snake skin, decorated with ermine skin fringe, held in place by porcupine quillwork; collected by George Dorsey on the Blood Reserve in Alberta in 1897. Field Museum Chicago, Cat. No. 51662. Drawing by Steve Allely, in Allely and Hamm (2002:138). Reprint courtesy of Steve Allely and Jim Hamm.

tension strain when the bow was drawn, relieving the wood of tension and avoiding stress to knotholes or other flawed areas on the back of the bow.

Because sinew fibers were usually applied to the wood with a variety of water-soluble glues made from animal parts, the conventional technological explanation for gluing snakeskin to the back of a bow is that the snakeskin served to protect the underlying matrix of sinew and glue from moisture. Thus, the snakeskin covering could be explained as important for the proper physical functioning of the bow. However, a few of the bows I examined have the snakeskin cover directly on top of plain wood with no sinew underneath. On these bows, the snakeskin cover would not serve an actual functional purpose, but instead must have been applied for reasons other than the mere functionality of the weapon.

Blackfoot and Lakota Elders, who examined bows in several collections in Canada and the United States with me, insisted that bows with snakeskins on their backs could not possibly have come from their communities, because snakes carried very negative connotations in their cultures. I initially assumed that these comments stemmed from the effects of more than a century of enforced Christianization. Especially so, since non-Aboriginal sojourners on the northern Plains, such as the fur trader Alexander Henry the Younger, while traveling through the Intermountain West in the early nineteenth century, noted that local Aboriginal people used rattlesnake skins to cover the sinew backings of their bows and that they sold such weapons to the Blackfoot and other Plains peoples, who would pay a horse or a gun in exchange for a sinew-backed bow (Gough 1988–1992:524).[3] Traveling the western Plains in 1833/34, the German naturalist Prince Maximilian of Wied noted that some bows among the Piegan-Blackfeet were covered with snakeskins, while Crow people in western Montana also made sinew-backed sheep-horn or elk antler bows, covered with rattlesnake skins (Witte and Gallagher 2010:204, 250). Thus, by the early 1800s, while by no means common, snakeskin-covered bows were in demand as trade items and were in use among Blackfoot-speaking peoples at that time, possible negative connotations in regard to snakes notwithstanding. In the first half of the 1800s, the German naturalist Paul von Wuerttemberg collected a snakeskin-covered bow from Assiniboine peoples, where he had observed such weapons in action.[4]

Another traditional cultural practice contravening present-day negative notions about snakes in some Plains Aboriginal cultures has to do with amulets made to contain the navel cords of newborns. Such navel amulets were often covered in quillwork or beadwork. Among Blackfoot-speaking peoples, navel amulets for girls were made in the shapes of turtles or toads, while those for boys were shaped like a snake (Wissler and Duval 1975 [1909]:127, footnote 3).[5] The beadwork designs on several such snake-shaped navel amulets coming from Kainai and Pikani people resemble the longitudinal dark-and-light stripe patterns found on garter snakes. While this may indicate a connection between garter snakes and masculinity in Blackfoot culture, some of these navel amulets also display transverse alternating bands of light and dark beadwork, representative of the light and dark banded tail

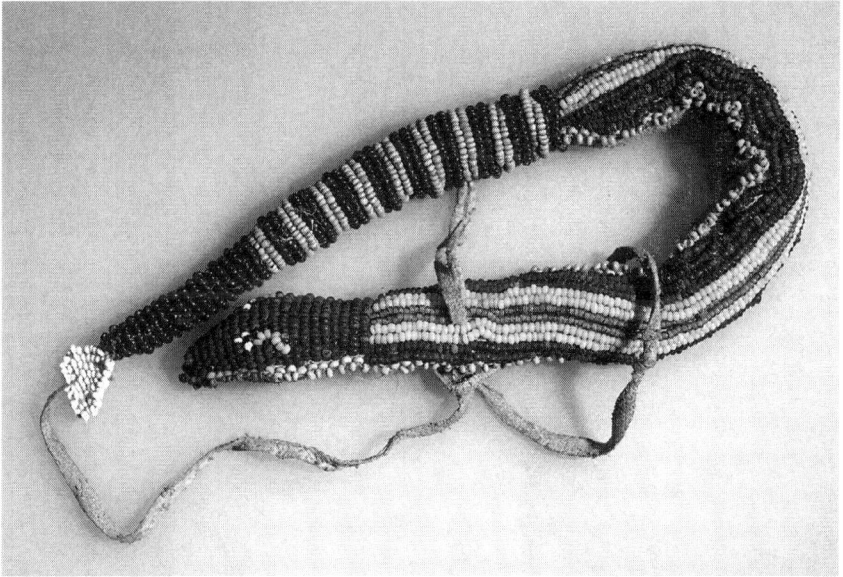

FIGURE 2. Piegan (Pikani) navel amulet, American Museum of Natural History, Cat. No. 50.2/2854A, collected by Clark Wissler on the Blackfeet Reservation in Montana, in 1903. Note the stripes parallel to the "body" of the snake, reminiscent of the color pattern of a garter snake, as well as the transverse bands of alternating light and dark colors near the "tail," similar to the banding on a rattlesnake tail.

FIGURE 3. Plains garter snake, *Thamnophis radix*. Copyright and photo by Steve Byland, 123RF.com.

FIGURE 4. Western Diamondback Rattlesnake, *Crotalus atrox*. Note the similarity of the alternating bands of black and white on the animal's tail near the rattle to the alternating dark and light bands of quillwork on the left tip of the horn bow in Figure 6. Copyright and photo by Steve Byland, 123RF.com.

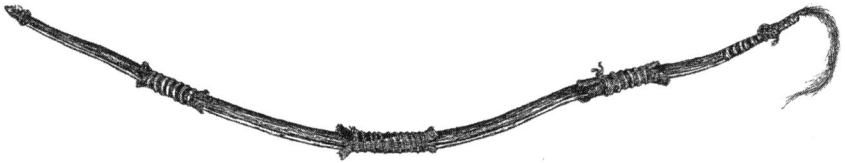

FIGURE 5. Note the upper tip of this bow in the right section of this image for an example of the alternating light and dark quillwork decorations on an elk antler bow. This bow was collected by Dr. Washington Matthews, US Army, on the Fort Berthold Reservation in North Dakota among the Mandan, Hidatsa, and Arikara in the 1870s; now at the Smithsonian Institution. Drawing by Steve Allely, in Allely and Hamm (2002:147). Reprint courtesy of Steve Allely and Jim Hamm.

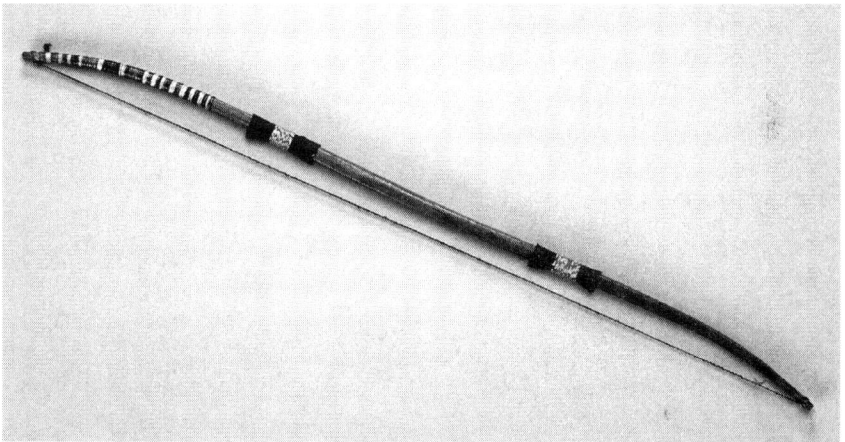

FIGURE 6. This Blackfoot bow at the Canadian Museum of History shows another example of the "rattlesnake tail" decoration. Cat. Number: Bow: V-X-297. Museum records date an accompanying quiver and bow case (V-X-296 a-r) for this bow to 1841, or earlier. Photo courtesy of Canadian Museum of History.

of a rattlesnake. Such bands of alternating light- and dark-colored quill work also appear on the tips of several nineteenth-century Plains bows, likely indicating a connection between archery and rattlesnakes.

The late nineteenth-century ethnographer George Bird Grinnell recorded a Blackfoot story titled "The Woman Who Married a Snake." In this story, a male snake transforms into a young man, wearing a bison robe with the hair side out, as well as a yellow plume in his hair (Wissler and Duval 1975 [1909]:150). These colors are reminiscent of the color scheme of a garter snake. As garter snakes mainly live near streams and ponds, they may represent a connection to water and to the underwater world, an integral part of Blackfoot cosmology.

Similar motifs appear in a traditional Plains Cree story that has a Cree woman killing a metallic-looking coppery scaled horned serpent by the shore of a river (Bloomfield 1934:159). Snakes also figure prominently in Plains Cree versions of the "Rolling Head" story, where they become the lovers of an adulterous woman and are being killed by her enraged husband (Bloomfield 1934:271–274). Christianized Algonquian persons may have seen a similarity between this seduction scene and the biblical motif of the seduction of Eve by a snake in the Garden of Eden.

In eastern and central Algonquian cultures, very different perceptions of snakes exist. For example, Penobscot and Montagnais people used snakeskins as a cure for rheumatism. They were said not to have feared snakes and, on occasion, to have put them inside their shirts to carry them about (Speck 1923:275). Maliseet people stated that a snakeskin, worn around the hat, or as a hat band, could ward off enemies (Speck 1923:278).

Anishinaabe (Ojibwa) people in the White Shell region of Ontario and Manitoba, using rocks and stones, created petro forms in the shape of snakes. These may have been created in conjunction with the Midéwiwin, or Grand Medicine Society, in an effort to address the cultural breakdown, disease, and population loss that came with waves of various European epidemic diseases (Pettipas 2015:1). The Midéwiwin is a secret society devoted to the preservation and transmission of knowledge, which continues to be active in contemporary Anishinaabe communities. In Great Lakes Anishinaabe cultures, the Missisauga rattlesnake symbolized the highest level of the Midéwiwin society. Because of their rattles, these snakes were associated with shamans and the rattles they use (Hamell and Fox 2005:127, 130, 134). The regalia used by the highest-ranking Midéwiwin practitioners include items made from rattlesnakes. For example, rattlesnake skins were used in the construction of Midéwiwin medicine bags. Ojibwa people in what is now Minnesota adorned the tail sections of these snakeskin bags with small brass bells or thimbles, imitating the snake's rattle (Hamell and Fox 2005:138). These contexts all present snakes in a more positive than negative context, associating them with healing and protection.

Le Sonnant, or "the Rattle," an early nineteenth-century leader of a mixed Plains Cree/Saulteaux band, may represent a western extension of this concept. The American fur trader Robert Campbell, who met with Le Sonnant in 1833, indicated in a letter to his brother Hugh that Le Sonnant was approximately sixty years of age at the time of the meeting (MacCulloch 2009:151). On occasion, his name was rendered into English as "the Rattlesnake" (MacCulloch 2009:149–150;

FIGURE 7. Water color portrait of Le Sonnant aka Mahsette-Kuiuab, Cree Chief, 1833, pencil and wash on paper by Karl Bodmer (Swiss, 1809–1893), Joslyn Art Museum, Omaha, Nebraska, Gift of the Enron Art Foundation, 1986.49.230.

Thwaites 1966:200–201).[6] Le Sonnant was also a signatory to the 1816/17 Selkirk Treaty, signed at the Red River Settlement, in what is now southeastern Manitoba (see Carter 1994). Non-Aboriginal travelers and sojourners who came into contact with Le Sonnant described him as a highly accomplished "conjurer," respected but also feared by friend and foe alike (Thwaites 1966:201).

The contemporary Plains Cree artist Louise Bernice Halfe Skydancer expressed similar sentiments in regard to the ambiguous perception of spiritually powerful persons within their own communities. She stated that "the gifts of the snake are powerful. My Grandmother was a healer. She used snake skins to heal those in need, yet she received more fear than respect in spite of the healing that occurred" (Skydancer 2006).

The late nineteenth/early twentieth-century Plains Cree leader Fine Day was said to have derived some of his personal medicine powers from a rattlesnake as well. He owned a large rattlesnake effigy belt, beaded in dark blue and white pony

FIGURE 8. The Kainai (Blood) leader Onista 'sakaxsin, or Calf Shirt (1844–1901), handling a rattlesnake. Image courtesy of Glenbow Archives, Calgary, NA-716-4.

beads. The alternating blue and white stripes at the tail section of this rattlesnake effigy are similar to the alternating dark and light bands of quillwork found on some Plains and Plateau bows and on some Blackfoot navel amulets. Fine Day's grandmother was said to have made this belt upon his request, because a vision of a rattlesnake was said to have revealed to him an escape route out of an encirclement of his war party by Blackfoot opponents (Miller and Corey 2007:19; Mandelbaum 2001 [1940]:4).[7]

Another individual who drew power from rattlesnakes was the Kainai (Blood) leader Onista 'sakaxsin, or Calf Shirt (1844–1901). Calf Shirt claimed to have received power over rattlesnakes in a vision in the late 1870s, or early 1880s. In this vision, a person was said to have appeared to Calf Shirt, stating: "I'm from the Big Snake tribe; our people are rattlesnakes. When you die, you'll become one of us" (Dempsey 1994:140). This seems reminiscent of the mythical community of big snakes, defeated by a Blackfoot culture hero in the Kutuyis/Blood Clot story mentioned below.

After this event, Calf Shirt kept one or more large rattlesnakes in a pit in the earthen floor of his home and was known to carry at least one large rattlesnake coiled around his body under his shirt. He often performed with several of his snakes at public events. Nonetheless, his Kainai compatriots were said to have feared him and his snake powers (Dempsey 1994:140–149).

The late nineteenth/early twentieth-century Oblate missionary Leon Doucet, who had extensive contacts with Blackfoot-speaking communities, noted Calf Shirt and another man, Kakko-Stamik, a relative of the Blood (Kainai) leader Red Crow, as specialists in handling rattlesnakes.[8] These men were clearly seen as exceptional, which may indicate that at least by the late 1800s, rattlesnakes held largely negative connotations among Blackfoot-speaking people (Dempsey 1994:138–149).

Joe Healy (aka Potaina, aka Flying Chief) and Eagle Rib (Petoqpekis), both men who lived on the Blood Reserve around the turn of the twentieth century, may have had connections to snakes as well, as they carved bowls from a soft greenish stone found near Lethbridge, Alberta, featuring the image of a dog and a snake for tourists, as well as for domestic use (Brownstone 2008:55).

In his 1903 report on Blackfoot material culture, anthropologist Clark Wissler described a Pikani (Piegan) archery set collected by George Bird Grinnell on the Blackfeet Reservation in the 1870s. The set includes a sinew-backed wooden bow. Its sinew-backing has been painted green, another reference to the Underworld/ Underwater Beings in Blackfoot culture. Dark green paint and duck or mallard feathers also appear on a garter snake skin–covered bow at the Manitoba Museum. Furthermore, the quiver/bow case combination of this archery set was made from river otter skins, yet another reference to water and the Underwater Beings. Lastly, Wissler described a peculiar small object attached to the quiver:

> At the top of the quiver is a peculiar upright object about 15 cm high made by wrap-
> ping a strip of rawhide around a piece of brass wire. According to our information,
> this was always placed in quivers, but knowledge of its significance has been lost.
> The size is that of an ordinary lead pencil. The surface is beaded and to the top
> are tied two small strips of otter skin. This is probably a charm. (Wissler 1910:158)[9]

This object may have been a section of a stiffening stick, attached to quivers to keep them from folding when arrows were withdrawn and to serve as a point of attachment to tie the quiver, bow case, and carrying strap together. The brass wire may have been a further reference to water and the Underwater Beings.

The Royal Ontario Museum holds an otter skin quiver collected from the Bloods in around 1875, with a similar ornamented detail. It is decorated with three beaded white and blue stripes and a finial composed of two strips of furred weasel hide and a hank of deer hair. This decorative element terminates in a long stick about the thickness of a pencil that serves the function of stiffening the juncture of the two parts to the quiver set.[10] Brass and otter fur could in this context be seen as references to the Underwater Beings, connected to projectile weapons in a culture where archery sets could also function as society bundles (Crowshoe and Manneschmidt 2002:27).

Among Blackfoot-speaking peoples, as well as among other Plains cultures, the bow and arrow were imbued with deep spiritual meaning. In Algonquian languages, including Blackfoot, inanimate objects, such as weapons and tools, could be treated as animate objects, based on the concept that both humans and objects had souls. As Blackfoot people explained to the missionary John MacLean on the Blood Reserve in the late 1800s: "As men on earth when they are living must live on material things, so spirits who are not flesh and blood must live on spiritual food. The spirits take the spirit of bows and arrows and shoot with them, they eat the spirit of the buffalo meat, and they smoke the spirit of tobacco" (Brownstone 2008:57).

Snakes also appeared in personal names among Blackfoot-speaking peoples. For example, between 1833 and 1842, Alexander Culbertson, a trader with the American Fur Company, lived at Fort McKenzie in present-day Montana, where he married a Kainai woman named Medicine Snake Woman (Natamista Iksana) (Crowshoe and Manneschmidt 2002:56).

Nineteenth-century Plains Cree people had a warrior society, known as the "rattlesnakes" (Bloomfield 1934:17–19). Bow lances were among the insignia of several Plains warrior societies, especially among Siouan-speaking peoples, such as the Assiniboine, Lakota, and Dakota. These ceremonial weapons consisted of a lance shaft shaped like a double-curved Plains bow, with a stone or a metal lance point on one end. One of the earliest recorded descriptions of a bow lance comes from the journals and drawings of George Back, a midshipman on the Franklin expeditions to the Arctic, who observed a group of Assiniboine people near Fort Carlton carrying this type of weapon (Houston 1994:40, figure 28). Some bow lances, while not only resembling the shape of a snake in their wavy profile, included portions of rattlesnake skin. For example, among the Oglala Lakota, in the second half of the nineteenth century, there existed a Sacred Bow Society whose leading officers wielded a bow-lance in battle to which, among other items, rattlesnake skins were attached (Blish 1934:183).

In contrast to the more or less positive interpretations of snakes in Eastern and Central Algonquian communities, ancient Cree traditions often contain rather unfavorable views on snakes. For example, local Cree people created snake-shaped petro forms in the Flin-Flon/Denare Beach area, near the central Manitoba-Saskatchewan border, to commemorate the death of a small girl who was said to have been eaten by snakes. This story may be connected to old Cree stories relating to an ancient time, when the great snake Misekenapik was said to have eaten people until the culture hero Wesakedjak defeated it (Pettipas 2015:3).

Several Blackfoot and Plains Cree stories speak of women encountering mythical snake beings near bodies of water. According to Michel-Gerald Boutet, Algonquian but also some Siouan cultures perceived snakes as representing water, partly because their bodies resemble meandering river courses and partly because snakes can survive in very dry conditions for fairly long. However, they have also come to be associated with concepts of evil, as in these cultures snakes can also be representative of devastating floods (Boutet n.d.:1).[11] Boutet stated in this regard that "the Sioux also entertain such terrible stories with the Unktehila water dragon. These accounts conclude with its destruction by the fiery Thunderbird" (Boutet n.d.:3). Boutet went on to explain the etymology of terms for "snake" from several Algonquian languages:

> One of the Proto-Algonquian terms, *kenwepyikwa for 'snake', was constructed using the Ojibwe kine:pik, Menominee kenu:pik, Miami-Illinois kineepikwa and Cree kene:pik forms (Hewson 1993, Costa 1992). Etymologically, the term literally means "long tailed water animal" (*kenw- 'long', with the link vowel *-e:-, *-epy 'water' and *-ikw 'animal with prominent tail'). Although most snakes are land animals, they are occasionally seen in water and are mythologically linked to the Water Spirit. (Boutet n.d.:2)

Variations of this term seem to refer to snakes in general. However, several Plains languages, such as Ojibwa, Cree, and Lakota, while including general terms for "snake," also maintained distinct terms to denote rattlesnakes.[12]

The Lakota spiritual leader Black Elk, who lived around the turn of the twentieth century, described details of his vision to the ethnographer John Neihardt.

> I remembered that the grandfather of the west had given me a wooden cup of water and a bow and arrow and with this bow and arrow I was going to destroy the enemy with the power of the fearful road. With the wooden cup of water I

was to save mankind. This water was clear and with it I was to raise a nation (like medicine). (DeMallie 1985:119)

Black Elk expressed this dualism of healing and destruction for water and the bow and arrow again in several other passages: "The Thunder-Beings [lightning] have the power to kill and the water the power to heal. We could depend on the water to live on and the lightning to kill with" (DeMallie 1985:123). A similar dualism appeared in another part of Black Elk's vision: "This man's name was One Side. One Side had [a] bow and arrow in one hand and a cup of water in the other" (DeMallie 1985:130). In conjunction with the Lakota horse dance ceremony, the same dualism appeared: "The flowering stick was carried by one of the virgins; one of them had the pipe with the spotted eagle on it; another one had a bow and arrow and a cup of water; the other girl had the herb from the north" (DeMallie 1985:215). And also, "We put a cup full of water on the west side and we made a bow and arrow and laid it across the cup of water" (DeMallie 1985:217).

The Pikani, Kainah, and Siksika have several painted lodges, often associated with medicine bundles. One of the oldest of these painted tipi designs is the snake-painted lodge. Snakes painted on tipis are often horned, which marks them out as sacred in Blackfoot culture. The ancient Blackfoot story of Kutuyis, or Blood Clot, includes an explanation for the origin of the "snake painted lodge" (Hungry Wolf 1982:160–161). In this story, the mythological hero Kutuyis freed mankind from the tyranny of giant bears and snakes, who kept all the rich food for themselves, while allowing humans to eat only scraps. Through Kutuyis's intervention balance was restored and humans regained access to more nutritious foods. Several variants of snake-painted lodges and their associated ceremonial complexes exist. In the context of a bundle opening ceremony at the Museum of the Plains Indian, in Browning, Montana, in 1941, Mrs. Green Grass Bull, a Pikani Elder, explained that "the greatest power of this bundle was the getting of food" (Hungry Wolf 2006:368–371). The fact that snake-painted lodges often included medicine bundles may suggest that snake-skin covered bows could have been part of a bundle associated with such a lodge. In any case, considering that the principal power of the snake-painted lodge and its associated medicine bundles was the procurement of food, adding a snakeskin to a hunting weapon, such as a bow, may have been seen as a way to transfer some of this power to the hunter using such a bow.

It is interesting to note that some of the zoomorphic images on snake-painted Blackfoot lodges resemble eels, rather than snakes. Cree people referred to eels as *kinebikoinkosew* 'snake fish' (Chamberlain 1901:672).

FIGURE 9. Thunder Chief, Kainai (Blood), photographed by Frederick Steele & Co., Glenbow Archives, NA-118-14.

The garter snake skin–covered, sinew-backed bow now at the Field Museum in Chicago was collected on the Blood Reserve in 1897 by the anthropologist George Dorsey. Very similar bows appear in two photographs of Kainai people taken at one of the photo studios of Frederick W. Steele, either in Winnipeg or in Alberta, in the late 1800s. It is possible that the bows in these images are actually the same bow, one of the many artifacts that Steele and other photographers of the period used as props to "adorn" their Indigenous photo subjects. However, the quality of the photographs is insufficient to determine whether the bows in the picture are one and the same and whether they are backed with garter snake skin.

The man in Figure 9 is Thunder Chief; the man in Figure 10 is Flying Chief, aka Joe Healy. Both of these men carry bows adorned with porcupine quillwork and ermine skin fringes. The jacket worn by Joe Healy also appears in Steele photographs of three other Kainai men; Black Plume, Charcoal (Bad Young Man) and Red Crow

FIGURE 10. This photo of Joe Healy, aka Flying Chief, was originally titled "Blood Indian Warrior." Photo by Frederick Steele & Co., United Church of Canada Archives, Toronto, 93.049P/955.

as well as in a photograph of Crow Eagle (North Peigan). Thus, the bow(s?) may have been Steele's prop(s) as well. It is possible that the photos of Flying Chief and Red Crow wearing the same jacket were already taken in 1886, when Red Crow and other Plains Aboriginal leaders traveled through Winnipeg on their way to Ottawa to meet with Prime Minister John A. MacDonald (Marsh 2103). However, it is more likely that these photos were taken closer to the reserves of Blackfoot-speaking peoples in Alberta, as Frederick Steele maintained subsidiary photo studios there (Silversides 1994:3). Steele worked in Winnipeg as a photographer from June 1886 until at least 1910.[13]

Several similar bows, attributed to Blackfoot-speaking peoples, show the same double-curved profile and very similar quillwork decorations on each midlimb section, holding ermine skin fringes in place. However, these bows seem to be covered with rattlesnake skin, not with garter snake skin. One such bow is now at the National Museum of Denmark in Copenhagen. Unfortunately, no other provenance information than the Blackfoot attribution could be obtained. Another bow, now at the British Museum in London, England, was collected on the Blood Reserve from the Kainai leader Strangle Wolf by Frederick Deane-Freeman, an employee of the Department of Indian Affairs (Brownstone 2002:38–49, 73–77).[14] Another similar bow, now at the Royal Ontario Museum in Toronto, came from the estate of the Mohawk/English poet and author Pauline Johnson, who had received it as a gift from a Northwest Mounted Police officer.[15]

The presence of ermine skin on most of these bows suggests that they held considerable spiritual significance among Blackfoot-speaking peoples. Since shirts and leggings adorned with ermine skin fringe, known as "weasel suits," could be perceived as independent medicine bundles, it is possible that these ermine skin–adorned bows were also medicine bundles, or part of a medicine bundle, perhaps in the context of one of the men's societies. In 1834, Prince Maximilian observed an Indigenous man at Fort McKenzie, named White Buffalo ("Tomek-sih-soksinam"), carrying a bow beautifully decorated with ermine fringe on each bow limb. Wied stated that White Buffalo had taken this bow from a Salish opponent in battle (Witte and Gallagher 2010:355, 389).[16] However, other types of bows that served as regalia in men's societies among Blackfoot-speaking peoples, such as the Pigeon Society or the Bear Braves, usually seem to have had very little adornment of quillwork and ermine skin fringe.

If Algonquian people held similar associations of archery and the Thunder Beings with destructive powers and water with the Underworld Beings, but also with healing, this dualism may have been expressed by combining the thunder being origin of a bow with a snakeskin, representing water and the Underwater Beings. In that case, the snakeskin would not be representative of the actual animal, but of the concept. Thus, the species of snake that the skin came from may not have been considered to be of crucial importance; any snakeskin may have sufficed. Combining references to the Thunder Beings and the Underwater Being in one item may have been a way to spiritually draw on opposite but equally powerful forces.

While negative perceptions of snakes may well have existed before Christianization, these historic examples present rather ambiguous views on snakes in western Algonquian cultures, dating back to a time before the establishment of reserves and reservations in Canada and the United States at the end of the nineteenth century.

Plains peoples' views on snakes combined aspects of healing and hunting prowess with the embodiment of destructive powers to be wielded in battle. While these examples do not fully explain the presence of snakeskins on some bows used by Algonquian peoples and other cultures on the Plains and in the Plateau region, they indicate a rich and complex system of beliefs and practices around snakes that gradually changed over time and could also differ between individuals of the same culture, based on individual connections or aversions to these reptiles and the concepts they represented.

NOTES

1. There are three main groups of Blackfoot-speaking Peoples; the Kainai, or Blood; and the Siksika, or Blackfoot, and the Pikani. The Pikani's homelands were intersected by the enforcement of the Canada-US border in the mid-1800s. Those living in Alberta are referred to as "Peigan," those in Montana as "Piegan," or "Blackfeet," while the term "Pikani" can be used in contexts before this division took place.

2. Garter snake skin–covered bows: Field Museum Chicago, Cat. No. 51662, sinew-backed wooden bow, collected by George Dorsey on the Blood Reserve in Alberta, in 1897; see also Van Stone 1992. Manitoba Museum, Winnipeg, Hudson's Bay Company Collection, No. 156 A, selfbow, collected on the Blood Reserve by Indian Agent T. J. Fleetham in the early twentieth century; Ethnologisches Museum Berlin, Germany, Cat. No. IV B 143, sinew-backed wooden bow, obtained from Friedrich Koehler, a member of the German diplomatic corps to the United States, ca. 1846, possibly Blackfoot.

3. Wednesday, 13 February 1811.

4. Lindenmuseum Stuttgart, Cat. No. 94636, sinew-backed wooden bow, collected by Duke Paul of Wuerttemberg, ca. 1824–1850, ascribed to the Assiniboine.

5. This practice was connected to the story of the mythological character Whirlwind Boy, who was said to have picked the shapes of these animals because of their robust health and longevity.

6. Manitoba Archives–Hudson's Bay Company Archives, Brandon House Journal for 1811–1812, B.22/a/18b, December 1811.

7. Fine Day's snake effigy belt is now at the Royal Alberta Museum in Edmonton.

8. "An old man named Calf Shirt, snake charmer, showed off a tame rattlesnake that he always carried on his person. Another, a relative of Red Crow named Kakko-Stamik, specializes in handling without fear these kinds of deadly snakes. He either has a medicine or a gift to instantly heal the bite of these terrible reptiles … that is what these Indians claim, at last [sic]." (Doucet, n.d., 14) Crowshoe/Manneschmidt 2002:86.

9. See also American Museum of Natural History Cat. No. 50.2/2854A.

10. Royal Ontario Museum, Cat. No. ROM2005_5123_1, collected by Reverend John W. McLean.

11. For ancient Algonquian and Iroquoian stories of giant snake/man beings devouring humans, see also Hamell and Fox 2005:128, figure 2.

12. For example, in Cree, the word *sesikwew* denotes a rattlesnake, while other snakes are referred to as *kinebik*. In Ojibwa, the terms *shishikwe* and *sinawe* ('rattler') denote rattlesnakes, while *kinepik* is used for other snakes. Chamberlain 1901:679, 680. In Lakota, a Siouan language, *sinte hla* is used for rattlesnakes, while other snakes are referred to as *zuzeca*.

13. Manitoba Historical Society, Manitoba Photographers: Frederick W. Steele.

14. See also British Museum, Cat. No. Am-1903-88.

15. Royal Ontario Museum, Cat. No. HK1811.

16. The tribal affiliation of White Buffalo is not clear. He may have been Blackfoot or Gros Ventre des Prairies.

REFERENCES

American Museum of Natural History. Photo of Cat. No. 50.2/28.54A https://anthro.amnh.org/anthropology/databases/common/image_dup.cfm?catno=50%20%20%2F%204526.

Blish, Helen H. 1934. The ceremony of the sacred bow of the Oglala Dakota. *American Anthropologist* 36(2):180–187.

Bloomfield, Leonard. 1934. *Plains Cree texts*. G. E. Stechert.

Boutet, Michel-Gerald. n.d. *The Great Long Tailed Serpent: An iconographical study of the serpent in Middle Woodland Algonquian culture*. Laval, Quebec. http://www.midwesternepigraphic.org.

British Museum. Photo of Am-1903–8 8. http://www.britishmuseum.org/research/collection_online/collection_object_details.aspx?objectId=531720&partId=1&searchText=Am1903,-.88&page=1.

Brownstone, Arni. 2002. Ancestors: The Deane-Freeman Collection from the Bloods. *American Indian Art Magazine* (Summer):38–49, 73–77.

———. 2008. Reverend John MacLean and the Bloods. *American Indian Art Magazine* (Summer):44–57, 106–107.

Carter, Sarah A. 1994. KĀ-KĪWISTĀHĀW. *Dictionary of Canadian biography*. Vol. 13. http://www.biographi.ca/en/bio/ka_kiwistahaw_13E.html.

Chamberlain, Alexander F. 1901. Significations of certain Algonquian animal names. *American Anthropologist,* n.s., 3(4):669–683.

Costa, David J. 1992. Miami-Illinois animal names. *Algonquian and Iroquoian Linguistics* 17:19–44.

Crowshoe, Reg, and Sybille Manneschmidt. 2002. *Akak'stiman: A Blackfoot framework for decision-making and mediation processes*. Calgary: University of Calgary Press.

DeMallie, Raymond J. 1985. *The Sixth Grandfather: Black Elk's teachings given to John G. Neihardt*. Lincoln: University of Nebraska Press.

Dempsey, Hugh A. 1994. *The amazing death of Calf Shirt and other Blackfoot stories*. Markham, ON: Fifth House Publishers.

Gough, Barry M. (ed.). 1988–1992. *The journal of Alexander Henry the Younger, 1799–1814*. Champlain Society.

Hamell, George, and William A. Fox. 2005. Rattlesnake tales. *Ontario Archaeology* 79/80:127–149.

Healy, Joe. Photo of Joe Healy aka Flying Chief. United Church of Canada Archives, Toronto. 93.049P/955. http://uccdigitalcollections.ca/items/show/368.

Hewson, John. 1993. *A computer-generated dictionary of proto-Algonquian*. Canadian Ethnology Service Papers, vol. 125. Canadian Museum of Civilization.

Houston, Stuart (ed.). 1994. *Arctic artist: The journal and paintings of George Back, Midshipman with Franklin, 1819–1822*. McGill-Queen's University Press.

Hungry Wolf, Adolf. 2006. *Pikunni ceremonial life*. Blackfoot Papers, vol. 2. Skookumchuck, BC: The Good Medicine Cultural Foundation.

Hungry Wolf, Beverly. 1982. *The ways of my grandmothers*. Fort Mill, SC: Quill.

Lapatin, Kenneth. 2002. *Mysteries of the Snake Goddess*. Cambridge, MA: Da Capo Press.

MacCulloch, Patrick C. 2009. *The Campbell quest: A saga of family and fortune*. St. Louis: Missouri History Museum.

Mandelbaum, David. 2001 (1940). *The Plains Cree: An ethnographic, historical and comparative study*. Regina: Canadian Plains Research Center–University of Regina.

Manitoba Archives–Hudson's Bay Company Archives, Brandon House Journal for 1811–1812, B.22/a/18b, December 1811.

Manitoba Historical Society. Manitoba Photographers: Frederick W. Steele. http://www.mhs. mb.ca/docs/photographers/steele_fw.shtml.

Marsh, James H. 2013. Red Crow. *The Canadian encyclopedia*. http://www. thecanadianencyclopedia.ca/en/article/red-crow-feature.

Miller, Preston E., and Carolyn Corey. 2007. *The new Four Winds Guide to Indian weaponry, trade goods and replicas*. Atglen, PA: Schiffer Publishing.

Pettipas, Leo. 2015. Snake petroforms in the north. *Manitoba Archaeological Society* (April 2014):1–4.

Royal Ontario Museum, Photo of Cat. No. HK1811. http://images.rom.on.ca/public/index. php?function=image&action=detail&sid=&ccid=.

Silversides, Brock. 1994. *The face pullers: Photographing Native Canadians, 1871–1939.* Markham, ON: Fifth House Publishers.

Skydancer, Louise Bernice Halfe. 2006. Keynote address: The rolling head's "grave" yard. *Studies in Canadian Literature /* Études *en littérature canadienne* 31(1):65–74.

Speck, Frank, 1923. Reptile lore of the Northern Indians. *Journal of American Folklore* 36(141):273–280.

Thunder Chief. Photo of Thunder Chief. Glenbow Archives. http://ww2.glenbow.org/search/archivesPhotos.

Thwaites, Reuben Gold (ed.). 1966. *Early Western Travels, 1748–1846.* Vol. 23, *Part II of Maximilian, Prince of Wied's, Travels in the Interior of North America, 1832–1834.* AMS Press.

Van Stone, James W. 1992. *Material culture of the Blackfoot (Blood) Indians of Southern Alberta.* Chicago: Field Museum of Natural History.

Wissler, Clark. 1910. *Material culture of the Blackfoot Indians.* New York: American Museum of Natural History.

Wissler, Clark, and D. C. Duval. 1975 [1909]. *Mythology of the Blackfoot Indians.* New York: AMS Press.

Witte, Stephen S., and Marsha V. Gallagher (eds.). 2010. *The North American Journals of Prince Maximilian of Wied.* Vol. 2. Norman, OK: University of Oklahoma Press.

She Beads like a Cocom but Designs like a Young Person: An Exploration of Beading as Anishnaabe Epistemology

Chuck Bourgeois

ndigenous knowledge occupies a rather vague and tenuous space in present-day academia. Situating Indigenous epistemologies alongside or within mainstream Euro-Western knowledge systems has been an ongoing struggle for many scholars. This study seeks to present beading, not as an anthropological oddity, or a peripheral element of Indigenous culture, but rather as a valid and rigorous epistemology that is intimately connected to each practitioner's sense of identity and understanding of reality. In addition, this study situates beading as an inseparable part of a larger framework of epistemologies that inform an Indigenous worldview.

Self-in-Relation

"An Indigenous worldview seeks that you identify yourself to the Spirit, the people and the Spirit of the work you intend on doing to establish the beginning of re-spectful practise" (Absolon 2010:75). In observance of this edict, I begin by situating myself in relation to this research. I am of French/Métis/Saulteaux ancestry from the historic Métis community of *Wazhushk Ziibins*, which is also known by the colonial settler name of St-Pierre Jolys, in the unceded Indigenous territory of southern Manitoba. Beading occupies a central and revered place in Métis culture, as we are often referred to as The Flower Beadwork People. As a child, I spent many hours admiring my grandfather's small but dazzling collection of beaded moccasins and gauntlets, which he proudly displayed in his home. Over the past fifteen years, while exploring my Métis heritage, it has been my distinct pleasure to learn from and live with my ancestral relatives, the *Anishnaabe* (Ojibwe), throughout our traditional territory. In some ways, the present work represents a continuance of this ancestral partnership and seeks to build upon the early historic relationships between Métis people and the *Anishinaabe* (Fiola 2015).

Indigenous Epistemology

The study of Indigenous epistemology has only recently gained popularity within academic circles. Indigenous scholars throughout the globe are exploring their ancestral heritages and are beginning to articulate the unique, comprehensive nature of these epistemologies. While it is beyond the scope of this study to examine the ongoing effects of colonization (Smith 1999), the supremacy of Western thinking (Reddekop 2014), and the often contested space of Indigenous knowledge in academia (Wane 2013), it is nonetheless essential to at least acknowledge this tension. It is also imperative to recognize Indigenous epistemologies, in all their vastness, diversity, and complexity as standalone systems of knowledge and not merely the by-products of colonial interactions (Battiste 2013). In light of this, I draw heavily on Ermine's (2007:195) concept of "ethical space," which he defines as "a way of ethically examining the diversity and positioning of indigenous peoples and Western society" in order to avoid a Euro-Western evaluation of Indigenous knowledges.

There is an increasing body of literature emerging from the study of Indigenous epistemology. Gegeo and Watson-Gegeo (2001:58) defines it as "a cultural group's ways of thinking and of creating, reformulating, and theorizing about knowledge via traditional discourses and media of communication, anchoring the truth of the discourse in culture." Ermine (1995:102), in a more philosophical approach, opines that "Aboriginal epistemology" is an effort to understand the reality of existence and harmony with the environment by utilizing an incorporeal knowledge paradigm. Meyer (2001:126) asserts that Hawaiian epistemology "is a long-term idea that is both ancient and modern, . . . and a distinct feature of our culture that cannot easily be distinguished from the fabric it is sewn into."

Wane (2013:95) posits simply that Indigenous epistemology connects a person to "ancestral philosophical and pedagogical traditions." Based on these definitions it is possible to situate all aspects of Indigenous life, from hunting, to ceremonial practices, to child rearing, to medicinal plant knowledge, to traditional artistic expressions within the umbrella of Indigenous epistemology. Throughout this discussion, I present beading as a distinct area of knowledge within the larger body of Indigenous epistemologies.

Beading as Epistemology

Beadworking was integrated into existing Indigenous epistemologies when beads were first imported as fur trade commodities by Europeans during the colonization of North America. Far from a homogenous tradition, the patterns, styles, designs, and specific uses of beaded artwork depended largely on the maker, community, and region. Individual families developed their own unique style of beading that functioned, among other uses, as "a means of communicating status and social space" (Farrell-Racette 2004:1).

It is perhaps helpful here to conceptualize beading, not as an isolated skill, but rather as an inseparable part of an infinite and intricate tapestry of knowledge that has evolved and adapted along with ndigenous peoples for millennia. The interrelatedness of Indigenous knowledges is described by Absolon (2010:75) as "an intermixing of the past, present, future; the ecology of creation such as earth, sun, water and air and all their occupants; and the values that retain the balance and harmony of all of the above."

Beading continues to be an intimate and essential part of life, and learning, for many Indigenous families throughout Turtle Island, as evidenced by this reflection from Farrell (2008:40):

Growing up, I would visit my Cocom (my grandmother), who was a gifted crafter, and watch as she made moccasins, and mukluks—only a couple of the many traditional arts and crafts that she knew how to make. I particularly remember watching as she sewed with deft hands, each bead into a perfect, taut line. I would watch as she transformed each bead upon bead into a beautifully shaped and colorful flower or leaf. I would watch her and my mother as well, making these things. It was only when I was older I realized that by watching her, I was learning.

While the practice of beadwork—its patterns, forms, and applications—varies greatly between Indigenous nations, communities, and families, a common element is the level of emotional investment practitioners devote to their craft. The act of beading is holistic in nature, and stimulates emotional, spiritual, physical, and mental processes. How could it be otherwise? The level of focus required to create even the most basic piece connects practitioners to their work in deep and intimate ways. Beading is also a popular social activity and is often practiced in groups, or alongside other traditions such as storytelling, and food preparation. Many practitioners build collections of their favorite patterns and reproduce them frequently. As Tracy (2003:180) noted while working with a Métis elder for her master's thesis, "[t]he emotional and spiritual value Mrs. Umpherville placed on her patterns helped me to understand the depth of meaning they held for her."

These insights depict beading as far more than a secular pastime, and reveal some of the evocative and intimate connotations it represents for Indigenous beadworkers. By emphasizing the subtler aspects of beading, an understanding of its function as an epistemology becomes possible.

Statement of Purpose

The purpose of this work, in many ways, is as complex as the beading patterns contained within its pages. From a broad perspective, I am inspired by Wane (2013:102) to explore Indigenous knowledges as a means of "asserting the place of Indigeneity in the academy [and] recognizte and validate the legitimacy of Indigenous knowledges as a pedagogic, institutionally communicative tool." I am also deeply interested in understanding more about how Indigenous epistemologies have survived colonialism, and continue to resist, and persist, from within the pervasiveness of Western society. Herein, I approach beading not as a static, historical, or unchanged practice, but rather I consciously endeavor not to isolate or confine it in a way that denies its living and dynamic nature (Simpson 1999).

While several studies look at Indigenous epistemologies in general terms (Absolon 2010; Gegeo and Watson-Gegeo 2001; Simpson 1999; Weber-Pillwax 1999), the primary purpose of this work is to present a more personal description of the poignant and influential nature of Indigenous knowledges and to examine how they are valued, and understood by my research collaborator, Missy (a pseudonym).

My secondary purpose is to position beading and all its accompanying knowledge as a fluid, living entity that grows and expands through the process of incorporating the central tenants of traditional culture into a modern context.

Methodology and Method

This research was undertaken as a phenomenological case study. It draws from case study, as it is "bound by time and activity" (Creswell 2014:14), as well as from phenomenology, as it examines "the dialogue between a person and her world" (Groenewald 2004:4). Case study methodology lent itself well to the present work as it provides an "in depth description of a process, a program, an event or an activity" (Creswell and Maietta 2002:162). It is through this in-depth lens that some of the more subtle and nuanced elements of beading became evident.

Phenomenology, in addition to being useful as a research methodology, also contributed an intriguing philosophical context from within which to interpret the data collected. Contrary to a more positivist approach that would observe participants, the act of beading, the social context of beading, and the beads themselves each as independent research subjects, phenomenology allowed for an examination of how observable and unobservable phenomena are assembled and embedded with deep meaning through the "intentional consciousness" (Giorgi 1997:239) of the research collaborator. Also from phenomenology, the concept of bracketing was used to focus the study and "bracket" the knowledge of beading from other related Indigenous knowledges (Groenewald 2004:12). Expert and purposive sampling were used to identify the research collaborator who is extremely knowledgeable and whose particular expertise formed the basis for the research.

Method

I asked Missy to bring in photographs and exemplars of her beadwork that were of particular significance to her and representative of her journey of learning and understanding in beading. She was very generous and shared one exemplar as well as several photographs of her work. I developed three semistructured interview questions that I would ask her about three select pieces and shared them with her in advance. During the interview, I made an audio recording, used speech-to-text software, and took anecdotal notes.

Missy answered the questions by sharing personal narratives, which corresponds with the relational nature of Indigenous knowledge (Reddekop 2014) in addition to helping me "understand the depth of meaning" beading held for her (Tracy 2003:180). This is also in accordance with Bruner's (1996:xiv) assertion that it is through "narrative that cultures have created and expressed their world views and have provided models of identity and agency to their members." Finally, member checking was used to provide "respondents the opportunity to assess adequacy of data" (Angen 2000:381).

Limitations

Time constraints limited the study in some ways. While I am confident that the interview with Missy yielded trustworthy, insightful data, I must acknowledge Creswell's (2014:14) assertion that phenomenology should include the perceptions of "SEVERAL individuals who have all experienced the phenomenon" (emphasis added). After data collection, I almost immediately began to formulate new lines of inquiry. How would Missy's perceptions compare with those of other beadworkers? Would their experiences be comparable or radically dissimilar? Would the experience vary significantly for different age groups or between male and female participants? How might beading contribute to decolonization? As is often the case, my research has produced more questions than concrete answers.

In addition, it became apparent while reviewing the data that beading is a far more complex area of study than I had first believed. Beading is a social activity, it connects practitioners to family and history, it can provide financial income, it is intimately connected to Pow Wow culture, it encompasses larger themes of traditional gift-giving and intergenerational knowledge transmission, it is used to depict sacred stories and teachings, and it can be used signify tribal affiliation. While Missy casually alluded to each of these themes (among others), our singular, brief interview did not allow for a more profound examination of them. Time constraints also prevented me from acquiring a variety of data sources in order to "build a coherent justification for the themes" (Creswell 2014:201). Missy gladly agreed to share her beadwork with me and graciously provided pictures to include in this study. I became deeply interested, however, in observing the entire process firsthand, from the color and pattern selection, to the variety of tools and accessories utilized, to the specific techniques, to the social aspects of beading. Participant observations of this nature would have buttressed the interview data and allowed for a more thorough analysis. Acknowledging these limitations not only helps to define the parameters of this study but will also inform future research.

Data Collection

Lavallée (2009:28) asserts that "the use of the tobacco as a gift to participants demonstrates respect for the knowledge that the participant will be providing and ensures that the research is done in a good way." In observation of this teaching, far in advance of our interview, I presented Missy with a gift, and a tobacco offering as a sign of respect, and to initiate our exchange through a traditional protocol. In addition to my prepared interview questions some additional clarifying questions arose during the interview, which were retrieved from the audio recording and included in the data transcription. These supplementary questions allowed me to spontaneously explore areas I felt were pertinent to the research and also gave Missy a chance to expand on some of her thoughts.

It quickly became apparent how intimate and personal beading is for Missy. Her narratives elevated beading beyond a mere craft and revealed vibrant networks of interdependent knowledge deeply connected to her family history and cultural identity. She knowledgeably discussed both traditional and contemporary aspects of beading, and it was difficult at times to distinguish the line between the narrative and the knowledge; the two are obviously inseparable elements of this epistemology. As I began working with the data, I distinctly felt that I was examining only a minute portion of a far more expansive body of knowledge. With Absolon's (2010) concept of respectful practice in mind, I identified "broad patterns" (Creswell 2014:66) and recurring themes with which to frame Missy's insights.

Thematic Analysis

Interrelation with Other Epistemologies

Missy frequently referenced other related skills and knowledge she learned in conjunction with beading. She expressed this in more general terms: "I learned so much during those times," but she also gave more specific examples. At a certain point in her beading apprenticeship, Missy began drawing her own designs as opposed to using set patterns, demonstrating her growing expertise. "I used to doodle these designs in class and later on these drawings started to get bigger and bigger and kind of flowery and I was like 'I can bead this!'"

Pow Wows have a complex set of protocols, teachings and ceremonies associated with them. Each piece of regalia holds particular significance for a dancer and is crafted in accordance with traditional edicts (McConney 2006). Missy's regalia is no exception, and the jingle dress she made with her grandmother is accentuated by her own beadwork. A featured piece of her regalia is a belt, which she brought for our interview. Here, the epistemic interrelatedness of Missy's beading and Pow Wow dancing is particularly evident: "My granny helped me make my dress and I did all the beadwork for my belt, so whenever I dance, I dance with this pattern around my waist. It fills me with a sense of pride when people see me dancing and compliment it."

During the latter part of our interview, Missy discussed how she decided to investigate the significance of beading for other practitioners as part of her Honours Thesis in Indigenous Learning. It was in fact while she was beading the belt for her regalia that the notion to do so struck her. Thus, Missy too was engaged in "carving out safe space" (Wane 2013:102) for Indigenous knowledge within the academy and was successful in expressing this epistemology in a scholarly context. By sharing simply that the "unique thing about beadwork [is that] everyone has their own specific way and they do it for their own reasons," Missy acknowledged the vast complexity of beading.

Connection to Family and Family History

As Farrell (2008:26) asserts, "the manner in which [traditional skills] are shown or taught is also interconnected with the purpose and reasons for doing such an activity." For Missy, the tenets of beading were not taught to her in a classroom, with a book or a video tutorial; she was expertly mentored in the same way that

FIGURE 1. Missy's jingle dress belt

skills have been passed down in her family for millennia. This relational ontology, where knowledge transmission and even the perception of reality itself is mediated through intimate relationships, is a central feature of Indigenous epistemology, and common to indigenous peoples throughout the globe (Reddekop 2014).

Missy speaks with great fondness of her granny, and during our interview, it is clear how highly she values their time together. "Sitting there with my granny, she's doing her own beadwork too; it was a time we all got to spend together." Missy also shared how she chose the pattern for the belt in her jingle dress regalia.

Growing up, my family always had these *tikinagans* [infant cradle boards] laying around and they were decorated with a certain kind of pattern. As I grew up and started to care more about it, I asked my granny who beaded them and how come that pattern seems to be repeated so often? She said that that was actually made by my great-grandmother's mother and she made this *tikinagan* for one of my great uncles when he was born way back in the 1930s. I wouldn't be doing beading today if it weren't for patterns like that. For them [the patterns] to survive for so long, that's amazing.

Much like the Métis elder featured in Tracy's research (2003:242), the intimate nature of Missy's family traditions gives her a profound understanding of "not only who she is, but also who her family was."

Beading as a Communicative Medium

In addition to deepening her relationship with her granny and other family members, beading acts as a communicative medium for Missy and allows her to develop relationships and meet people from various walks of life. Indeed, her beadwork becomes much more than simple trinkets or decorative accessories. Farrell-Racette (2004:191) describes how, for the indigenous people of Canada both in the past and today, "beadwork is only an object until it becomes animated through use or infused with memory and story. Who made it? Who wore it? How is it placed on the body? When is it worn? How does it move? In order to understand the social meaning of material culture, it is important to understand the context in which it is used."

Missy described how one of her favorite pieces, which combined traditional and modern elements, became infused with memory and story. "I did a Storm Trooper, but it has traditional floral designs around it. I gave it to my best friend for her wedding." Considering Missy's intimate family connection with beading and the value she places on her practice, it is difficult to imagine a more appropriate or meaningful way to commemorate their friendship.

Missy's beadwork adorns her regalia and is given as gifts, but in addition, her skill is such that her work is regularly purchased by admirers at craft shows and other venues. She recalls this compliment from an elderly gentleman: "'I'm not a very rich man, but when I see this type of artwork, I scoop it up whenever I can. This is gonna hang in my rec room and I'll be able to say that a nice Ojibwe woman from up north made it.' I thought that was so sweet that he valued it as much as he did. It's nice to meet people who know the value of the work that goes into beading."

Missy admits, however, that her greatest compliment came from another gentleman well-versed in the various styles and forms of beadwork at the same art show. She recalls his insightful observation: "You know what my first thought was when I saw this work? I thought, 'Whoever made this beads like an old Cocom [grandmother], but designs like a young person!'" This comment not only affirmed Missy's mastery but also captures her beadwork's seemingly effortless blend of traditional and contemporary imagery.

FIGURE 2. Missy's storm trooper

Another one of Missy's creations featuring a beautiful floral pattern she drew herself was advertised on a local art gallery's website. It quickly sold and now sits, bearing her name and community, in the Sequoyah National Research Centre in Little Rock, Arkansas. In this instance, Missy's beadwork transcended interpersonal communication and positioned her, her craft, and her family's hereditary knowledge on an international platform among the work of other proud indigenous peoples.

Conclusion

I quickly became aware that it would not be possible to exclusively isolate Missy's experience with and knowledge of beading during our discussion. Each of her narratives, accompanied by pictures of her intricate and skillful beadwork, deftly interwove family history, Pow Wow teachings, Ojibwe pride and childhood memories. Perhaps ANISHNAABE EPISTEMOLOGY is too impersonal and insufficient a term to describe this complex body of knowledge. The characterization of Indigenous

FIGURE 3. Missy's museum piece

knowledges as holistic, all-encompassing, and relational (Absolon 2010; Farrell 2008; Reddekop 2014) is astute, and, as I had initially suspected, a project of far greater scope would be necessary in order to truly appreciate its enormity.

While in some ways Missy's experience with beading coincided with the insights of other practitioners reviewed in the literature, it is evident that the significance of beading is unique and singular to each individual. As Missy herself opined: "to some people it's a means of making a living; for other people, it brings them a sense of cultural pride and other people just think 'it's pretty so I do it.'"

Aware of the delicate relationship between Indigenous knowledges and the academy, I am satisfied that the narratives included herein were presented in a respectful way and did not transgress any ethical boundaries, either scholarly or cultural. Oriented by a phenomenological framework, I have made every effort to be as unobtrusive as possible in my exploration of this very nuanced and expansive Indigenous epistemology. The personal and holistic nature of Indigenous epistemologies requires us to experience them directly, and to create meaning from this knowledge for ourselves. Examining beadwork as an epistemology, rather than simply as art, provides insight into each practitioner's worldview, and also allows us to see how this worldview connects them to wider spheres of Indigenous knowledge and experience. In closing, I would like to leave the reader with a final quote, one that situates Missy alongside a growing critical mass of indigenous people who, in an age of rampant globalization, are returning to their ancestral heritage for inspiration and interpreting these vibrant ways of knowing in new and powerful ways. "Indigenous people are in a state of resurgence and revitalization and at this time in our long history we are recovering, re-emerging, and reclaiming our knowledge base. The context of our past has vastly changed, yet we remain: We are Indigenous and we carry our ancestor' stories, teachings and knowledge" (Absolon 2010:78).

REFERENCES

Absolon, Kathy. 2010. Indigenous wholistic theory: A knowledge set for practice. *First Peoples Child & Family Review* 5(2):74–87.

Angen, Michael. 2000. Evaluating interpretive inquiry: Reviewing the validity debate and opening the dialogue. *Qualitative Health Research* 10:378–395.

Battiste, Marie. 2013. *Decolonizing education: Nourishing the learning spirit.* Saskatoon: Purich Publishing.

Bruner, Jerome. 1996. *The culture of education.* Cambridge, MA: Harvard University Press.

Creswell, John. 2014. *Research design: Qualitative, quantitative, and mixed methods approaches.* Thousand Oaks, CA: Sage Publications.

Creswell, John, and R. Maietta. 2002. *Handbook of research design and social measurement.* Thousand Oaks, CA: Sage Publications.

Ermine, Willie. 1995. Aboriginal epistemology. *First Nations education in Canada: The circle unfolds,* ed. by Marie Battiste and Jean Barman, pp. 101–112. Seattle: University of Washington Press.

———. 2007. Ethical space of engagement. *Indigenous Law Journal* 6:193–201.

Farrell, Amy. 2008. Kakanjegawin, to know. Anishnawbe epistemology and education: A philosophical and holistic exploration of Anishnawbe approaches to knowledge and implications in education. MA thesis, Lakehead University.

Farrell-Racette, Sherry. 2004. Sewing ourselves together: Clothing, decorative arts and the expression of Métis and Half Breed identity. PhD thesis, University of Manitoba.

Fiola, Chantal. 2015. *Re-kindling the sacred fire: Métis ancestry, Anishnaabe spirituality and identity.* Winnipeg: University of Manitoba Press.

Gegeo, David, and Karen Watson-Gegeo. 2001. How we know: Kwara'ae rural villagers doing Indigenous epistemology. *The Contemporary Pacific* 13:55–88.

Giorgi, Amedeo. 1997. The theory, practice, and evaluation of the phenomenological method as a qualitative research procedure. *Journal of Phenomenological Psychology* 28:235–260.

Groenewald, Thomas. 2004. A phenomenological research design illustrated. *International Journal of Qualitative Methods* 3:1–26.

Lavallée, Lynne. 2009. Practical application of an Indigenous research framework and two qualitative Indigenous research methods: Sharing circles and Anishnaabe symbol-based reflection. *International Journal of Qualitative Methods* 8:21–40.

McConney, Denise. 2006. Dance your style: Towards understanding some of the cultural significances of Pow Wow references in First Nations' literatures. PhD thesis, University of Saskatchewan.

Meyer, Manulani. 2001. Our own liberation: Reflections on Hawaiian epistemology. *The Contemporary Pacific* 13:123–198.

Reddekop, Jarred. 2014. Thinking across worlds: Indigenous thought, relational ontology, and the politics of nature; or, if only Nietzsche could meet a yachaj. PhD thesis, University of Western Ontario.

Simpson, Leanne. 1999. The construction of traditional ecological knowledge: Issues, implications and insights. PhD thesis, University of Manitoba.

Smith, Linda. 1999. *Decolonizing methodologies: Research and indigenous peoples.* Zed Books.

Tracy, Michelle. 2003. A bead box of my own: The beadwork of Métis artist Philomene Umpherville. MA thesis, University of Alberta.

Wane, Njoki. 2013. [Re]claiming my Indigenous knowledge: Challenges, resistance, and opportunities. *Decolonization: Indigeneity, Education & Society* 2:93–107.

Weber-Pillwax, Cora. 1999. Indigenous research methodology: Exploratory discussion of an elusive subject. *Journal of Educational Thought* 33:31–45.

Root Syntax: Evidence from Algonquian

Rose-Marie Déchaine and Natalie Weber

oots do not have a uniform morphology within and across Algonquian languages.[1] They vary with respect to: (i) how many morphemes a stem containing a root has; (ii) whether they are restricted to particular categories; and (iii) whether they code valency, event type, and DP features. We propose that root morphology reflects where and how roots merge with the syntactic spine: roots adjoin to XP or X, with the latter precompiled "offline" (and stored) or computed "online" in the syntax. Inasmuch as morphology mirrors syntax, this predicts that roots pattern differently depending on where and how they merge with the verb spine. Developing the analysis with Blackfoot and Plains Cree data, we deploy diagnostics that detect: (i) if the merge site of √ROOT is XP or X; and (ii) if an X-adjoined √ROOT is precompiled or computed online.

Background Assumptions

In Algonquian languages, the morphological root corresponds to the INITIAL component of a stem, which may be simplex (√ROOT only) or complex (√ROOT plus other components). Algonquian roots divide into two groups (Bloomfield

1927): NOMINAL roots are restricted to nominal contexts; GENERAL roots are found in nominal, verbal, and particle contexts. For example, the Plains Cree nominal root √ISKWÊW 'woman' occurs as a bare root in N contexts (1a), and inflects for plural (1b) or obviative (1c). The general root √OHP 'high' does not occur as a bare root, and must be categorized by a FINAL suffix, which derives verbal (2a), nominal (2b), or particle (2c) stems.[2]

(1) *Plains Cree nominal root*

    a. **iskwêw**

        √WOMAN.*n*

        'woman'

    b. **iskwêw**-ak

        √WOMAN.*n*-PL

        'women'

    c. **iskwêw**-a

        √WOMAN.*n*-OBV

        'woman/women, obviative'

(2) *Plains Cree general root*

    a. **ohp**-î-w

        √HIGH-V-3

        's/he/it jumps up, goes up'

    b. **ohp**-iwin

        √HIGH-NMLZ

        'leaping'

    c. **ohp**-im

        √HIGH-PRT

        'off to the side, away'

In what follows, we lay out our assumptions about clause structure and √ROOT merger, and show how this predicts the occurrence of three classes of general roots, illustrating and discussing each root class in turn. As it is key to our proposal, we note that we follow the widely accepted morphological segmentation of Algonquian languages (in particular, Frantz 2009 for Blackfoot and Wolfart 1973 for Plains Cree). Below, we show there is essentially a one-to-one relationship between the morphemes that realize verbal heads and the DPs they introduce. This motivates the structures in (3). Intransitive verbs contain a V-head that selects one DP, (3a). Transitive verbs contain two heads (big V and little *v*), with V selecting DP_{THEME}, and *v* selecting DP_{AGENT}, (3b). (See Hale and Keyser 1993; Kratzer 1996; and Marantz 1997 on the decomposition of transitive verbs into two heads.)

(3) a. *Intransitive VP*   b. *Transitive vP*

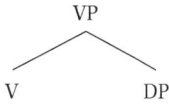

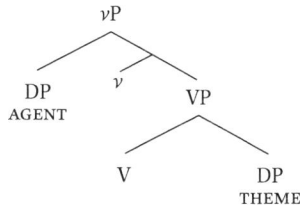

```
        VP                                      vP
       /  \                                    /  \
      /    \                                  /    \
     V      DP                              DP      v
                                           AGENT   /  \
                                                  /    \
                                                 V      VP
                                                       /  \
                                                      /    \
                                                     V      DP
                                                           THEME
```

V and *v* restrict the features of their local DP; we model this with AGREE, where
a head probes for a matching feature (Chomsky 2000, 2001). Regarding event type
(e.g., state, change-of-state, event, process) we adopt a version of first phase syntax
(Ramchand 2008), with VP/*v*P the locus of event type. Intransitive VPs can denote
individual-level states (*tall*), stage-level states (*tired*), changes-of-state (*become dry*),
or processes (*boil*). Transitive *v*Ps can denote individual-level states (*like*) or events
(*cut*). The locus of event type is V for intransitive verbs, and is distributed across *v*
and V for transitive verbs.

We claim that √ROOT can merge in two ways (Déchaine 2002; Déchaine and
Weber 2015): (i) by adjoining to a phrase (XP); or (ii) by adjoining to a head (X).
Adjunction to XP yields two outputs: adjunction to VP or *v*P. Likewise adjunction to
X yields two outputs—adjunction to V or *v*—and is further distinguished according
to whether the tree—is precompiled offline or computed online. This predicts a
total of six outputs.[3]

Adjunction to XP via Online Computation

Roots can adjoin to intransitive VP (4a) or transitive *v*P (4b). As adjuncts, they
impose no selectional restrictions on the constituent they merge with. Therefore,
this √ROOT class is category-neutral, and not restricted to verb contexts. It is a-valent,
and freely combines with VP/*v*P shells, with the latter determining valency. It is
also neutral with respect to event type, and compatible with state, change-of-state,
event, or process denotations. The √ROOT adjoins to the left or right of the stem,
with left-adjunction being the norm in Algonquian languages.

(4) *Adjunct-merge to XP (via online computation)*

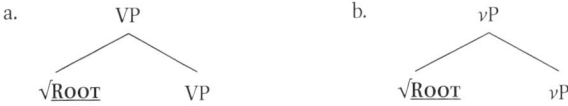

a.
```
        VP
       /  \
   √ROOT   VP
```

b.
```
        vP
       /  \
   √ROOT   vP
```

Adjunction to X via Online Computation

If the √ROOT adjoins to a head, as in (5), it mirrors the category and valency of that head. Such a √ROOT is restricted to a particular category (verb), valency (intransitive, transitive), event type (state, event, process), and DP type (animate, inanimate). The heads V/v condition category, valency, event type, and DP type; the √ROOT is not specified for any of these.

(5) *Adjunct-merge to X (via online computation)*

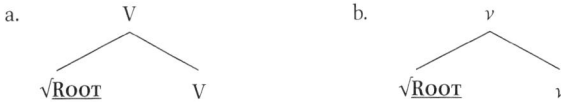

a.
```
         V
       /  \
   √ROOT   V
```

b.
```
         v
       /  \
   √ROOT   v
```

Adjunction to X via Offline Precompilation

Some roots are precategorized in that they come prebundled with a covert v/V head. Our claim that categorizing features are prebundled with some lexical items but project as independent heads elsewhere has a long pedigree in inflectional morphology; we apply this idea to derivational morphology to account for the behavior of precategorized roots. We label precategorized V roots as √ROOT$_V$, and precategorized v roots as √ROOT$_v$. Prebundling is a special case of adjunction to X, which is precompiled offline and stored as a precategorized unit, (6).[4] Precompiled verb roots are restricted to a particular category (verb, noun), valency (intransitive, transitive), event type (state, event, process), and DP type (animate, inanimate). Roots adjoining to V derive monomorphemic [√ROOT$_V$] stems; roots adjoining to v derive bimorphemic [√ROOT$_v$+V] stems.

(6) *Adjunct-merge to X (via offline precompilation)*

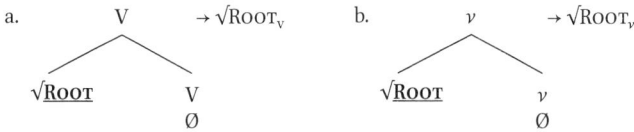

a.   V   → √ROOT$_v$ b. v → √ROOT$_v$

```
        V                              v
      /   \                          /   \
  √ROOT    V                     √ROOT    v
           ∅                              ∅
```

In (6), a √ROOT adjoins to a phonologically null head, deriving a bare root with an abstract bimorphemic structure. This roughly corresponds to the DM analysis of English roots, where a null verbalizer (v) merges with *fall*, *laugh*, or *eat*. A crucial difference is that, in our data, morphological exponence almost always maps transparently to syntax, and bare roots arise only with precompiled adjunction to V. We take this to indicate that a transparent morphology-syntax mapping is optimal as it is more learnable. Accordingly, we posit zero heads only if they are paradigmatically conditioned.

The two merge strategies (adjunction to XP or X), together with the possibility of offline precompilation versus online computation, correlate with the diagnostics in Table 1.

Diagnostic 1, which counts morphemes, assumes that roots do not generally adjoin to phonologically null heads in syntactic derivation. Accordingly, roots merged in the syntax derive bimorphemic intransitive [√ROOT+V] stems and

TABLE 1. Detecting where and how roots merge

		XP-ADJOINED	X-ADJOINED	
		COMPUTED	COMPUTED	PRECOMPILED
	DIAGNOSTIC	(ADVERBIAL)	(VERB-LIKE)	(VERB)
1.	*Morpheme count* (i.e., minimal stem) (a) bimorphemic intransitive stem	✓	✓	✗
	(b) trimorphemic transitive stem	✓	✓	✗
2.	*Category restriction* root restricted to particular category	✗	✓	✓
3.	*Selectional restriction* (a) root restricted to particular valency	✗	✓	✓
	(b) root restricted to particular event type	✗	✓	✓
	(c) root restricted to particular DP type	✗	✓	✓

trimorphemic transitive [√ROOT+v+V] stems. In contrast, precompiled roots derive monomorphemic intransitive [√ROOT$_V$] stems and bimorphemic transitive [√ROOT$_v$+V] stems. Diagnostic 2 tracks categorical restrictions: XP-adjoined roots are not categorically restricted, but X-adjoined roots are. Diagnostic 3 tracks restrictions on valency, event type, and DP features: XP-adjoined roots are not restricted, but X-adjoined ones are. Overall, XP-adjoined roots are akin to adverbs, X-adjoined roots are verblike, and precompiled roots are precategorized as verbs. Diagnostic 1 distinguishes verblike roots from precategorized roots, and Diagnostics 2 and 3 distinguish adverbial roots from verb(like) roots. In the next sections, we show that these tests confirm that Bloomfieldian general roots divide into three classes. We begin with XP-adjoined roots, and then consider X-adjoined roots.

XP-Adjoined Roots Are Adverbs

After exemplifying Plains Cree and Blackfoot verbal stems where each verbal head (V/v) from the structures in (3) maps to a phonologically overt suffix, we discuss the morphology-syntax mapping. We show that while suffixes behave like verbal heads, roots do not, and this motivates our analysis of roots as XP adjuncts. Finally, we use the diagnostics from Table 1 to confirm that these roots are XP-adjoined.

There is agreement that light VP/vP determines event type in Algonquian (Hirose 2003; Brittain 2003; Quinn 2006). In intransitive VPs, V (realized by AI/ II finals) specifies event type and probes for DP features: probing for ANIMATE derives an AI stem, probing for INANIMATE derives an II stem. Consider (7), where the √ROOT is a VP adjunct: Plains Cree -(i)si probes for ANIMATE; -$â$ probes for INANIMATE. Blackfoot AI -ssi and II -ii behave similarly. (DP is a *pro* that agrees in animacy with V.)

(7) *VP-adjoined root*

　　a. *Plains Cree*

　　　　[$_{VP}$ √MIYO   [$_{VP}$[$_V$ -isi_{AN}]   pro$_{AN}$]]   ***miyo-si-w***   y is good   AI
　　　　[$_{VP}$ √MIYO   [$_{VP}$[$_V$ -$â_{IN}$]   pro$_{IN}$]]   ***miyw-â-w***   y is good   II

　　b. *Blackfoot*

　　　　[$_{VP}$ √ISSP   [$_{VP}$[$_V$ -ssi_{AN}]   pro$_{AN}$]]   *iik-**ssp**-ssi-wa*   y is tall/important   AI
　　　　[$_{VP}$ √ISSP   [$_{VP}$[$_V$ -ii_{IN}]   pro$_{IN}$]]   *iik-**ssp**-ii-wa*   y is tall/high   II

Now consider the transitive stems in (8), where the √ROOT adjoins to vP, and two verbal heads are present: v is realized by TA/TI finals, accounting for why they occur only in transitive contexts. The theme suffix realizes V, accounting for why it codes animacy (and definiteness in Blackfoot) of DP$_{THEME}$. (We do not treat complex v/V here.) Plains Cree AI(T) finals derive syntactically transitive stems that are morphologically intransitive, and show agreement only with the DP$_{AGENT}$. Blackfoot AI+O finals derive stems whose indefinite object resembles an incorporated noun.

(8) vP-adjoined root

    a.   *Plains Cree*[5]

$[_{vP} √\text{WIYAT}[_{vP} \text{pro}[_{v'} [_v \text{êyim}_{AN}]$ $[_{VP}[_V \text{-}ê_{AN}]$ $\text{pro}_{AN}]]$
wiyat-êyim-ê-w   x find y funny   TA

$[_{vP} √\text{WIYAT}[_{vP} \text{pro}[_{v'} [\text{-}\text{êyiht}_{IN}]$ $[_{VP}[_V \text{-}am_{IN}]$ $\text{pro}_{IN}]]$
wiyat-êyiht-am-(w)   x find y funny   TI

$[_{vP} √\text{WIYAT}[_{vP} \text{pro}[_{v'} [\text{-}iht_{IN}]$ $[_{VP}[_V \text{-}â_D]$
wiyat-iht-â-w   x make y funny   AI(T)

    b.   *Blackfoot*[6]

$[_{vP} √\text{IKKAHS}[_{vP} \text{pro}[_{v'} [_v imm_{AN}]$ $[_{VP}[_V \text{-}Ø_{AN}]$ $\text{pro}_{AN}]]$
ikkahs-imm-Ø-ii-wa   x find y funny   TA

$[_{vP} √\text{IKKAHS}[_{vP} \text{pro}[_{v'} [_v i't]$ $[_{VP}[_V \text{-}i_{IN}]$ $\text{pro}_{IN}]]$
ikkahs-i't-i-m-wa   x find y funny   TI

$[_{vP} √\text{IKKAHS}[_{vP} \text{pro}[_{v'} [_v \text{-}i't]$ $[_{VP}[_V \text{-}aki_{IND}]$ $\text{pro}_{IND}]]$
ikkahs-i't-aki-wa   x find (y) funny   AI+O

The trees in (9) show the AGREE relations for vP. Little v probes for an ANIMATE DP$_{AGENT}$ and selects for a concordant VP complement (Déchaine 1999; Hirose 2003); this holds of Plains Cree and Blackfoot. In Plains Cree, animacy agreement is active with TA/TI/AI(T) finals, located in V: in (9a), V probes for D.ANIMATE with TA finals, for D.INANIMATE with TI finals, and for D with AI(T) finals. In Blackfoot, V probes for animacy AND definiteness (Weber and Matthewson 2014, 2017), probing for DEFINITE.ANIMATE with TA finals, for DEFINITE.INANIMATE with TI finals, and for INDEFINITE with AI+O finals.

(9) a. *Plains Cree TA/TI/AI(T)*

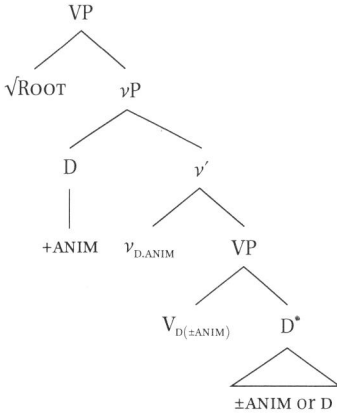

```
                VP
              /    \
        √ROOT       vP
                  /    \
                 D      v′
                 |     /  \
              +ANIM  v_D.ANIM   VP
                            /    \
                      V_D(±ANIM)   D*
                                  /  \
                              ±ANIM or D
```

b. *Blackfoot TA/TI/AI+O*

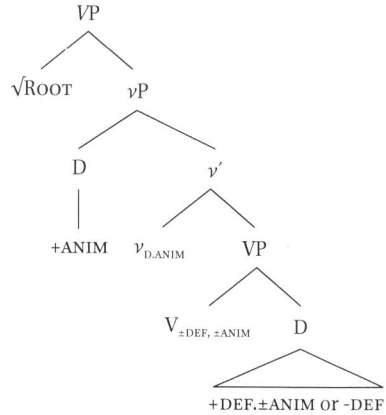

```
                VP
              /    \
        √ROOT       vP
                  /    \
                 D      v′
                 |     /  \
              +ANIM  v_D.ANIM   VP
                            /    \
                    V_±DEF, ±ANIM   D
                                  /    \
                          +DEF.±ANIM or -DEF
```

We now examine how the diagnostics in Table 1 apply to XP-adjoined roots. Diagnostic 1 counts morphemes: with XP-adjoined roots, intransitive stems are bimorphemic, transitive stems trimorphemic. Consider the intransitive stems in (10–11), which are minimally bimorphemic: Plains Cree √MIYO 'good' and Blackfoot √SSP 'high' do not directly inflect with agreement; rather, they combine with a verbalizing suffix, followed by agreement. Transitive stems are trimorphemic (12–13), with √ROOT combining with *v* (a transitive final) and V (a theme sign). The ill-formed (12a) and (13a) examples show that it is insufficient to add only a theme suffix selecting the DP_THEME.

(10) *Plains Cree intrans. stem*
   a. *[**miyô**]   -w

   b. [**miyo**-si]   -w
       √GOOD-V.AI-3
       's/he is good'

(11) *Blackfoot intrans. stem*
   a. *[**ssp**]   -wa

   b. [**ssp**-ssi]   -wa
       √HIGH-V.AI-3
       's/he is tall/high'

(12) *Plains Cree trans. stem*
   a. *[**miyw**   -am]-wak

   b. [**miyo**   -n-am]-wak
       √GOOD-by.hand-V.TI-3PL
       'they improve it'

(13) *Blackfoot trans. stem*
   a. *[**issp**   -i]-m-wa

   b. [**issp**   -inn -i]-m-wa
       √HIGH-by.hand-V.TI-DIR-3
       's/he lifts it'

Diagnostic 2 tracks whether roots are restricted to categorical contexts. XP-adjoined roots are unrestricted, and occur in verbal or nominal contexts. For Plains Cree, √KIMOT 'steal' in (14) can generate root-derived verbs (14a) or nouns, with the latter entity-denoting (14b) or event-denoting (14c). Blackfoot √ISTTSIK 'slick' in (15) can generate root-derived stative (15a) and entity-denoting nouns (15b). Event nominalizations like (16) (from √PASSKAA 'dance') use stem-level nominalizations in Blackfoot (Bliss et al. 2016). Crucially, categorization in Plains Cree and Blackfoot is expressed via suffixes, not by the root.

(14) *Plains Cree root categorization*

    a. [kimot-i]-w
       √STEAL-V-3
       's/he steals' (AI)

    b. o-[kimot-iw]
       AGT-√STEAL-NMLZ
       'thief' (NA)

    c. [kimot-iwin]
       √STEAL-NMLZ
       'theft' (NI)

(15) *Blackfoot root categorization*

    a. [isttsik-ii]-wa
       √SLICK-V-3
       'it is slippery' (II)

    b. [isttsik-anoko]-yi
       √SLICK-cloth.*n*-IN
       'linoleum, leather, oil cloth' (NI)

(16) *Blackfoot stem categorization*

    [[passkaa]-n]-yi
    √DANCE.V]-NMLZ]-NI
    'dance' (NI)

One question that arises for Plains Cree is whether root-derived event nominals such as (14c) are instances of serial categorization, where the root is first verbalized, and then nominalized. Serial categorization in Plains Cree only arises in the context of stem-derived event-denoting nominals, where both categorizers are phonologically overt; in the Algonquian literature, these are treated as SECONDARY DERIVATION. The contrast between root-derived versus stem-derived event nominals in Plains Cree challenges Borer's (2012) claim that event nominals always contain a layer of verbal structure. For related discussion and analysis based on data from Nata (eastern Bantu), see Déchaine et al. 2017.

Diagnostic 3 tracks valency, event type, and DP type to detect whether a root shows selectional restrictions. XP-adjoined roots impose no selectional restrictions; as such, they derive intransitive or transitive stems, and are compatible with various event types and DP types. Derivational paradigms (Bauer 1997) of intransitive and transitive stems confirm this. Consider the intransitive stems in (17–20) for Plains Cree √MIYO 'good' and Blackfoot √SSP 'high'. In Plains Cree, a verbalizing suffix—analyzed as V—determines whether the stem denotes a state (17) or change-of-state (18). V also determines valency (intransitive) and DP features (animacy). In Blackfoot, V likewise determines valency (intransitive), event type (individual-level/stage-level), and animacy. In addition, Blackfoot aspectual prefixes narrow the event type: -iik in (19) selects an individual-level construal, iit- in (20) selects a stage-level one. (We have no examples of a stage-level construal with an inanimate DP, but expect such examples to be well formed; see Weber 2016.) Crucially, XP-adjoined √ROOTs do not determine category, valency, event type, or DP type.

(17) *Plains Cree intrans. state*
   a. [**miyo**-si]-w
      √GOOD-V.AI-3
      's/he is good/nice/beautiful'

   b. [**miyw**-âsin]
      √GOOD-V.II
      'it is good/nice/beautiful/valuable'

(18) *Plains Cree change-of-state*
   a. [**miyo**-payi]-w
      √GOOD-move.AI-3
      's/he got lucky'

   b. [**miyo**-payin]
      √GOOD-move.II
      'it runs/works well'

(19) *Blackfoot intrans. state*
   a. iik-[**ssp**-itaa]-wa
      DEG-√HIGH-V.AI-3
      's/he is/was tall'

   b. iik-[**ssp**-ii]-wa
      DEG-√HIGH-V.II-3
      'it is/was tall/high'

(20) *Blackfoot change-of-state*
   a. iit-[**ssp**-itaa]-wa
      LOC-√HIGH-V.AI-3
      '(at that time) s/he got tall'

Roots derive transitive stems—(21–22) for Plains Cree, (23–24) for Blackfoot—that can be stative or eventive, and whose DP_{THEME} is [±anim]. The stem can be morphologically intransitive, but syntactically transitive: this derives Plains Cree AI(T) stems, (21c, 22c) and Blackfoot AI+O stems, (23c, 24c).

(21) *Plains Cree trans. state*

    a. [**kask**-êyim-ê]-w
        √PREVAIL-by.mind-V.TA-3
        's/he is sad over him/her (TA)'

    b. [**kask**-êyiht-am]
        √PREVAIL-by.mind-V.TI
        's/he is sad over it it'

    c. [**kask**-iht-â]-w
        √PREVAIL-CAUS-V.AI(T)-3
        's/he is able to do it'

(22) *Plains Cree trans. event*

    a. [**miyo**-n-ê]-w
        √GOOD-by.hand-V.TA-3
        's/he improves him/her'

    b. [**miyo**-n-am]
        √GOOD-by.hand-V.TI
        's/he improves it'

    c. [**miyo**-ht-â]-w
        √GOOD-CAUS-V.AI(T)-3
        's/he made it fit well'

(23) *Blackfoot trans. state*

    a. [**issak**-imm-Ø]-ii-wa
        √RECOVER-by.mind-V.TA-DIR-3
        's/he recovered from losing him/her'

    b. [**issak**-i't-i]-m-wa
        √RECOVER-by.mind-V.TI-DIR-3
        's/he recovered from losing it'

    c. [**issak**-i't-aki]-wa
        √RECOVER-by.mind-V.AI+O-3
        's/he recovered from losing s.o./s.t.'

(24) *Blackfoot trans. event*

    a. [**issp**-inn-Ø]-ii-wa
        √HIGH-by.hand-V.TA-DIR-3
        's/he lifts him/her'

    b. [**issp**-inn-i]-m-wa
        √HIGH-by.hand-V.TI-DIR-3
        's/he lifts it'

    c. [**issp**-inn-aki]-wa
        √HIGH-by.hand-V.AI+O-3
        's/he lifts s.o./s.t.'

Examples (17–24) indicate that *v*P/VP-adjoined roots are modifiers unspecified for category, valency, event type, or DP features. Rather, these properties are conditioned by suffixes of the root. As modifiers, roots stack (25a, 26a) and modify NPs (25b, 26b).

(25) *Plains Cree roots as modifiers*

    a. [**miyw**-[**asin**-[ah-am]]]-(w)

        [√GOOD-[√DRAW-[by.tool-v.TI]]]-3

        's/he writes something well'

    b. [**miyo**-[kikway]]

        [√GOOD-[√THING.*n*]]

        'good thing'

(26) *Blackfoot roots as modifiers*

    a. [**inikks**-[**iistap**-[oo]]]-wa

        [√ANGRY-[√AWAY-[v.AI]]]-3

        's/he went away angry'

    b. [**inikk**-[itapi]]-iksi

        [√ANGRY-[√PERSON]]-PL

        'angry people'

Treating √ROOT as XP-adjoined captures the fact that it is insensitive to category, valency, event type, and DP features. Adjuncts are usually optional, so it is surprising that the roots we analyze as *v*P/VP are obligatory. Syntactic analyses of Algonquian verb stems agree that the elements that realize *v*/V are light verbs. It seems that Algonquian verbs have a morphosyntactic requirement to contain a root (perhaps for morphophonological reasons), so if none is present, one must be adjoined. That this is a syntactic requirement is confirmed by the fact that verb stems can be formed with a dummy adjunct, which adds no specific meaning and reveals the semantic contribution of *v*. This is shown in (27), where *v*P is restricted by the manner modifier 'thus' (Plains Cree *is-/it-*, Blackfoot *anist-*). Adjunction of a dummy morpheme is predicted if adverbial modification is a syntactic restriction.

(27) *Default adverbial adjunction*

    a. *Plains Cree*

ADV	[-*v*	-V]	-AGR	GLOSS
is	[-*îh*	-*ê*]	-*w*	x make y thus
it	[-*in*	-*ê*]	-*w*	x hold y thus
is	[-*inaw*	-*ê*]	-*w*	x see y thus

    b. *Blackfoot*

ADV	[-*v*	-V]-AGR-AGR	GLOSS
anist	[-*o't*	-*o*] -*yii-wa*	x take y thus
anist	[-*inn*	-*o*] -*yii-wa*	x hold y thus
anist	[-*in*	-*o*] -*yii-wa*	x see y thus

Not all roots are modifiers; a class of roots are verblike, and we discuss these next.

Precompilied X-Adjoined Roots Are Like Verbs

A precompiled X-adjoined root yields a $[\sqrt{\text{ROOT}_X}]$ formative that behaves like a syntactic atom; such roots pattern like verbs. Consider (28), where Plains Cree $\sqrt{\text{NIPI}}$ and Blackfoot $\sqrt{\text{I'NI}}$ 'die' are precompiled with V and so have a fixed value for valency (intransitive), event type (eventive), and DP feature (animate). A root precompiled with v, (29), derives transitive stems, where v is followed by a suffix that instantiates V.[7] In Plains Cree, V is the theme suffix that controls the animacy of DP$_{\text{THEME}}$. In Blackfoot, V is an abstract final (Frantz 2009) controlling the animacy and definiteness of DP$_{\text{THEME}}$ (Weber and Matthewson 2014).

(28)   *Precompiled V-adjoined root*

    a.   *Plains Cree* $[_{\text{VP}}[_{\text{V}}\sqrt{\text{NIPI}}]$ pro]]   ***nipi-w***   y died   AI

    b.   *Blackfoot* $[_{\text{VP}}[_{\text{V}}\sqrt{\text{I'NI}}]$ pro]]   ***i'ni-wa***   y died   AI

(29)   *Precompiled v-adjoined root*

    a.   *Plains Cree* $[_{v\text{P}}\text{pro}\,[_{v'}[_{v}\sqrt{\text{MOW}}]\,[_{\text{VP}}[_{\text{V}}\text{-}\hat{e}]$ pro]]   ***mow-ê-w***   x ate y   TA

    b.   *Blackfoot* $[_{v\text{P}}\text{pro}\,[_{v'}[_{v}\sqrt{\text{OOW}}]\,[_{\text{VP}}[_{\text{V}}\text{-}at]$ pro]]   *oow-at-ii-wa*   x ate y   TA

Precompiled roots are a corner case in Plains Cree, but are common in Blackfoot. To see this, compare Plains Cree XP-adjoined roots with Blackfoot precompiled cognates: (30–31) contrasts Plains Cree $\sqrt{\text{SÊK}}$ 'afraid/frighten' with Blackfoot $\sqrt{\text{IKO'PO}}$ 'afraid' and $\sqrt{\text{SSKI'TSI}}$ 'frighten'. While Plains Cree XP-adjoined root derives intransitive or transitive stems, Blackfoot precompiled roots are suppletive, with different roots selected according to whether they precompile with V ($\sqrt{\text{IKO'PO}_V}$ 'afraid') or v ($\sqrt{\text{SSK'TSI}_v}$ 'frighten'). Also compare XP-adjoined Plains Cree $\sqrt{\text{MASIN}}$ 'mark, write' with Blackfoot $\sqrt{\text{SINA}_v}$ 'draw', which is precompiled with v. While the former adjoins to vP or VP (32), the latter is restricted to vP contexts (33).

(30) *Plains Cree VP-merged root*

  a. [**sêk**-isi]-w

  √AFRAID-V.AI-3

  's/he is afraid' (AI)

  b. [**sêk**-ih-ê]-w

  √AFRAID-*v*-V.TA-3

  's/he frightens him/her' (TA)

(31) *Blackfoot precompiled root*

  a. [**iko'po**]-mm-wa

  √AFRAID$_V$-AN-3

  's/he is afraid' (AI)

  b. [**sski'tsi**-Ø]-yii-wa

  √FRIGHTEN$_v$-V-DIR-3

  's/he frightens him/her' (TA)

(32) *Plains Cree XP-merged root*

  a. [**masin**-ahw-ê]-w

  √DRAW-by.tool-V.TA-3

  's/he marks/pictures him/her'

  b. [**masin**-âso]-w

  √DRAW-V.AI-3

  's/he is marked/striped/branded'

(33) *Blackfoot precompiled root*

  a. [**sina**-Ø]-yii-wa

  √DRAW$_v$-V-DIR-3

  's/he drew/photographed him/her'

  b. [**sina**-Ø]-aa-wa

  √DRAW$_v$-V-INV-3

  's.o. drew/photographed him/her'

We now run through our battery of diagostics. With diagnostic 1—morpheme count—precompilation with V derives monomorphemic stems, but with *v* it derives bimorphemic stems. This is confirmed by (34) for Plains Cree and (35) for Blackfoot.

(34) *Plains Cree precompiled roots*

  a. [**nipi**]-w

  √DIE$_V$-3

  's/he died' (AI)

  b. [**mow**-ê]-w

  √EAT$_v$-V.TA-3

  's/he ate him/her, e.g., bread' (TA)

(35) *Blackfoot precompiled roots*

  a. [**i'ni**]-wa

  √DIE$_V$-3

  's/he died' (AI)

  b. [**oow**-at]-ii-wa

  √EAT$_v$-V.TA-DIR-3

  's/he ate him/her, e.g., bread' (TA)

With diagnostic 2—which tracks category restrictions—precompiled roots are like precategorized verbs. As illustrated in (36) and (37) for 'die', such roots directly inflect for agreement, and participate in stem (rather than root) nominalization.

(36) *Plains Cree*

    a. [**nipi**]-w

       √DIE$_V$-3

       's/he died'

    b. [**nipi**]-win

       √DIE$_V$-NMLZ

       'death'

    c. *[**nip**]-a

       √DIE-PL

       Intended: 'deaths'

(37) *Blackfoot*

    a. [**i'ni**]-wa

       √DIE$_V$-3

       's/he died'

    b. [**i'ni**]-hsin-wa

       √DIE$_V$-NMLZ-3

       'death'

    c. *[**i'ni**]-iksi

       √DIE-AN.PL

       Intended: '(the) dead (pl.)'

With diagnostic 3—which tracks valency, event type, and DP type—precompiled roots restrict valency (intransitive or transitive), code event type (stative or eventive), and select for DP type (animate, inanimate). See (31) and (33) above for Blackfoot. In sum, precompiled roots are precategorized verbs and contrast with adverbial XP-adjoined roots, which are a-categorical.

X-Adjoined Roots Are Verblike

The final class of roots we consider, X-adjoined roots, adjoin to V or *v*, (38–39).

(38) *V-adjoined root*

    a. *Plains Cree*

       [$_{VP}$√PIM   [$_{VP}$[$_V$√OHT-*ê*] pro]]   ***pim-oht-ê-w***   x walks along   AI

    b. *Blackfoot*

       [$_{VP}$√ITAP   [$_{VP}$[$_V$√SSKAP-*i*]pro]]   ***itap-sskap-i-wa*** x crawls toward AI

(39) *v-adjoined root*

    a. *Plains Cree*

       [$_{vP}$pro [$_{v'}$[$_v$√POST-*iskaw*] [$_{VP}$[$_V$-*ê*]   pro]] ***post-iskaw-ê-w*** x put y on   TA

       [$_{vP}$pro [$_{v'}$[$_v$√POST-*isk*]   [$_{VP}$[$_V$-*am*] pro]] ***post-iska-m-(w)*** x put y on   TI

b. *Blackfoot*

$[_{vP}\text{pro} [_{v'}[_v \sqrt{\text{SIN}}\text{-}ip]$ $[_{VP}[_V\text{-}\emptyset]$ pro$]]$ *sin-ip-Ø-wa*   x licked y   TA

$[_{vP}\text{pro} [_{v'}[_v \sqrt{\text{SIN}}\text{-}iht]$ $[_{VP}[_V\text{-}i]$ pro$]]$ *sin-iht-i-wa*   x licked y   TI

$[_{vP}\text{pro} [_{v'}[_v \sqrt{\text{SIN}}\text{-}iht]$ $[_{VP}[_V\text{-}aki]$ pro$]]$ *sin-iht-aki-wa*   x licked s.o/s.t.   AI+O

For Diagnostic 1, which counts morphemes, V- and *v*-adjoined roots create trimorphemic stems. Consider first intransitive stems: as shown in (38), V-adjoined roots differ from VP-adjoined roots (which are bimorphemic) and roots precompiled with V (which are monomorphemic) in that they derive trimorphemic stems. Notably, V-adjoined roots require a preceding root, indicating they are complex verbalizing suffixes. This converges with traditional accounts, which treat them as complex finals. Consider now transitive stems derived from *v*-adjoined roots: as shown in (39), *v*-adjoined roots like Plains Cree √POST 'put on' and Blackfoot √SIN 'lick' are followed by *v* and V heads, deriving trimorphemic stems. The *v*-adjoined roots do not require a preceding root, indicating that they are still roots (rather than complex finals). Thus, V-adjoined versus *v*-adjoined roots are resolved differently.

Diagnostic 2 tracks categorical restrictions and identifies a class of roots that are restricted to verb contexts. In the present analysis, these correspond to X-adjoined roots. Such roots can bear verbal inflection or be nominalized via deverbal stem nominalization, but they cannot directly bear nominal inflection. This is illustrated for transitive roots in (40) for Plains Cree √POST 'put on' and in (41) for Blackfoot √SIN 'lick'.

(40)   *Plains Cree*

     a.   [**post**-iskaw-ê]-w

        √PUT.ON-by.body-V.TA-3

        's/he put s.o. (clothing) on'

     b.   [**post**-ayiwinis]-iwin

        √PUT.ON-clothes-NMLZ

        'putting clothes on' (NI)

     c.   *[**post**]-iwin

        √PUT.ON-NMLZ

        Intended: 'putting on' (NI)

(41)   *Blackfoot*

     a.   [**iisin**-ip-Ø]-ii-wa

        √LICK-by.mouth-V.TA-DIR-3

        's/he licked s.o.'

     b.   ot-[**iisin**-ip-Ø]-aa-wa

        3-√LICK-by.mouth-V.TA-INV-3

        'the ones s/he licked

     c.   *[**sin**]-hsin-iksi

        √LICK-NMLZ-AN.PL

        Intended: '(the) licks'

Relative to Diagnostic 3—which tracks valency, event type, and DP type—roots do not encode these properties, but reflect the properties of the V/*v* they adjoin to. As (42–43) show, V-adjoined roots derive intransitive stems, occurring in transitive stems only via secondary derivation. Likewise, as (44–45) show, *v*-adjoined roots derive transitive stems and are incompatible with AI/II finals. (It is significant that these complex forms are verbs of motion, which are morphologically complex in numerous languages. We leave this to future research.)

(42) *Plains Cree*

    a. [pim-**oht**-ê]-w
        √ALONG-√WALK-V.AI-3
        's/he walks along'

    b. wîci-[pim-**oht**-ê]-m-ê-w
        with-√ALONG-√WALK-V-AI-AP
        PL-TH-3
        's/he walks (with) s.o.'

    c. *wîci-[pim-**oht**]-im-ê-w
        with-√ALONG-√WALK-APPL-TH-3
        Intended: 's/he walks (with) s.o.'

(43) *Blackfoot*

    a. [itap-**sskap**-i]-wa
        √TO-√DRAG-V.AI-3
        's/he crawls towards'

    b. [itap-**sskap**-at-Ø]-ii-wa
        √TO-√DRAG-APPL- V.TA-DIR-3
        's/he drags s.o.'

    c. *[itap-**sskap**-hk-o]-yii-wa
        √TO-√DRAG-by.body-v. TA-DIR-3
        Intended: 's/he drags s.o. by body'

(44) *Plains Cree*

    a. *[**post**-isi]-w
        √PUT.ON-V.AI-3
        Intended: 's.o. is put on'

    b. *[**post**-â]-w
        √PUT.ON-V.II-3
        Intended: 's.t. is put on'

(45) *Blackfoot*

    a. *[**iisin**-ssi]-wa
        √LICK-V.AI-3
        Intended: 's.o. is licked'

    b. *[**iisin**-ii]-wa
        √LICK-V.II-3
        Intended: 's.t. is licked'

Comparison with Previous Analyses

In Blackfoot and Plains Cree, differences relating to morpheme count, as well as categorical and selectional restrictions, reflect two types of merge (adjunction of √ROOT to XP or X) as well as the contrast between offline precompilation and online computation. There remains the question of how our approach compares to previous analyses. We consider, in turn, approaches that treat roots as part of a morphological template, as a-categorical, or as defective.

Templatic Analysis of Roots

Bloomfieldian accounts posit a tripartite [INITIAL-MEDIAL-FINAL] template, with roots being INITIAL (Bloomfield 1946; Goddard 1990). We illustrate in (46) how Goddard (1990) would treat a Plains Cree stem, with √OHP 'high' an INITIAL followed by a FINAL that determines transitivity and event type (Denny 1984; Wolfart 1973:49ff).[8] The optional MEDIAL can be filled with a nominal, as in (45d) *as-* 'wind'. INITIALS mostly co-occur with a FINAL, but a few Plains Cree stems consist of only an initial, (47).

		[INITIAL + (MEDIAL) + (FINAL)]			THEME	AGR		
(46)	a.	*ohp*		*-in*	*-ê*	*-w*	's/he lifts s.o.'	TA
	b.	*ohp*		*-in*	*-am*	(*-w*)	's/he lifts s.t.'	TI
	c.	*ohp*		*-î*		*-w*	's.o./s.t. jumps/goes up'	AI/II
	d.	*ohp*	*-âs*	*-i*		*-w*	's.o. is raised by the wind'	AI
(47)	a.	*nipi*				*-w*	's/he is dead'	AI
		mîci				*-w*	's/he eats s.t.'	AI(T)
	b.	*kost*			*-ê*	*-w*	's/he fears s.o.'	TA
		kost			*-am*	(*-w*)	's/he fears s.t.'	TI
		it			*-ê*	*-w*	's/he says thus to/about s.o.'	TA
		it			*-am*	(*-w*)	's/he says thus to/about s.t.'	TI
	c.	*miy*			*-ê*	*-w*	's/he gives (it/him) to s.o.'	TA

The [INITIAL-MEDIAL-FINAL] template captures the fact that the root qua INITIAL is obligatory, while MEDIALS and FINALS are optional. However, it fails to explain why Plains Cree roots are integrated into the stem in a non-uniform manner: most roots MUST occur with a final (46), but a small number of roots MUST occur alone, (47). Of course, in a templatic account, the distinction between the multimorphemic stems of (46) and the monomorphemic stems of (47) may simply be a matter of morphological arbitrariness. However, this fails to capture the systematicity of the two strategies; monomorphemic stems are restricted with respect to category, valency, and event type in a way that multimorphemic stems are not. In our account, the contrast between (46) and (47) reflects two merge strategies: VP/vP-adjoined roots predictably require a final (46); precompiled roots, precategorized as V/v, predictably prohibit a final (47).

A-Categorial Analysis of Roots

In our proposal, roots merge with the verb spine at different points of the derivation, contra DM analyses that argue for a uniform insertion algorithm. In DM, roots are a-categorial formatives introduced as sister to a categorizing head (Marantz 1997). Many treatments of Algonquian verbs (Hirose 2003; Brittain 2003; Quinn 2006) adopt this approach, treating FINALS as categorizing heads that merge with a √ROOT, (48). On this view, the stems in (46–47) derive from the combination of an a-categorial root (the INITIAL) plus an overt or covert v head (the FINAL). Such DM-style approaches leave (at least) two issues unresolved. First, INITIALS like those in (47) are not a-categorial; as we have shown, they exhibit all the properties of precategorized verbs. Second, some DM-style analyses treat roots as complements (Siddiqi 2009) to a categorizing head. But if roots are syntactic atoms, they should be able to be introduced as heads, complements, or adjuncts. Recall that Algonquian roots stack (see (25–26)) confirming they are introduced as adjuncts. This is compatible with more recent developments in DM (Marantz 2013), which acknowledges the modificational nature of roots.

(48) a. Verbalizing context $[\, [\, \sqrt{\text{ROOT}} \,] \, v_{\text{FINAL}}]$

 b. Nominalizing context $[\, [\, \sqrt{\text{ROOT}} \,] \, n_{\text{FINAL}}]$

In DM, properties of a lexical item (category, phonological form, semantic denotation) are distributed across the grammar in three different lists, as in (49). Members of List 1 are "units of structural computation" (Harley 2014) and participate in MERGE, MOVE, and AGREE. Clearly, the notion of √ROOT we are working with belongs to List 1. List 2 specifies phonological exponence (VOCABULARY ITEMS in DM) of terminal nodes at PF. List 3 specifies semantic denotations that map onto the terminal nodes (ENCYCLOPEDIA in DM).

(49)   *Distributed morphology model* (adapted from Harley 2014, (1))

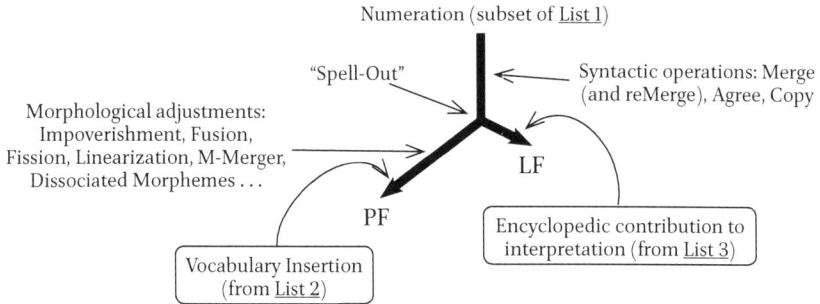

Numeration (subset of List 1)

"Spell-Out"   Syntactic operations: Merge (and reMerge), Agree, Copy

Morphological adjustments: Impoverishment, Fusion, Fission, Linearization, M-Merger, Dissociated Morphemes . . .

LF

PF

Encyclopedic contribution to interpretation (from List 3)

Vocabulary Insertion (from List 2)

Of interest here is the relation of suppletion to vocabulary items. Some treatments (Marantz 1995) adopt late insertion, where roots (from List 1) are not individuated until PF-insertion applies (Harley 2014); e.g., √[+COUNT] is resolved as [kæt] or [dág] at PF. In Harley (2014), root INSERTION is late, but subject to competition, so root INDIVIDUATION exists in List 1, and is relevant throughout the syntax and semantics. On this view, Plains Cree and Blackfoot roots would be individuated in List 1, but be inserted late. In Harley (2014), one diagnostic for insertion timing is vocabulary competition, with suppletion being the hallmark feature. In this context, it is significant that roots that adjoin to XP show no suppletion, (7–9), but roots that adjoin to X do, (31). Though this contrast does not follow from the DM insertion algorithm, it does follow from the structural hypothesis outlined here, in combination with Bobaljik's (2012) proposal that suppletion cannot be conditioned across an XP boundary. While X-adjoined roots are local to a conditioning head, XP-adjoined roots are separated from potential conditioning contexts by an XP boundary, and so are (correctly) predicted to be immune from suppletion.

Another point of divergence between our analysis and DM-style treatments lies in how precategorized roots are treated. As far as we can determine, a DM account can appeal to (at least) one of three mechanisms. First, precategorized roots could arise via FUSION, a DM operation that turns two syntactic nodes into one (Harley and Noyer 1999, 2000). Second, DM can constrain vocabulary insertion of the relevant root-realizing items to only verbal contexts (Ramchand 2008). Both mechanisms—fusion and constrained vocabulary insertion—are morphological adjustments triggered by specific lexical items. But we are considering the behavior of a large class of roots that behave like precategorized verbs, so both solutions are overly stipulative. A third solution would be to have precategorized verb roots undergo LABEL without merging with a categorical head. But the need for labeling independent of merge is contentious: for example, Chomsky (2013) models labeling as internal merge of one member of a symmetric set with the set itself. Moreover, applying LABEL without merge requires that roots be marked as special in some way (Marantz 2002; Embick 2010; Levinson 2010). The data we consider here indicates that this root class is not special; rather, it reduces to (precompiled) adjunction to X.

Structural Deficiency of Roots

Some approaches argue that roots are structurally deficient because they participate in FIRST merge (Borer 2003; de Belder 2011), the initial step of the derivation. The roots-as-adjuncts analysis challenges this view. Adjunct-merge to VP/vP is not first merge, yet XP-adjoined roots are deficient: they are unspecified for category, valency, event type, and DP features. In the present analysis, roots are deficient because they are adjuncts; this converges with de Belder (2011) who considers that only categorized items project. This predicts that a-categorical roots can only be introduced via adjunction, exactly what the present analysis shows is the case.

Conclusion

Variation in root morphology reflects the locus of merge, and follows without stipulation: a √ROOT can adjoin to XP or X, with the latter predictably falling into two subclasses according to whether it is derived via offline precompilation or online syntactic computation. Data from Plains Cree and Blackfoot confirm the proposal, but also raise the question of which strategy is canonical in a given system. While Plains Cree usually deploys adjunction to XP, Blackfoot prefers lexical precompilation, and in both languages syntactic adjunction to X is found more often with intransitive stems than transitive ones. Future research should shed light on the source of these differences.

NOTES

1. Thanks to two anonymous reviewers as well as to H. Borer, B. Bullshields, T. Cardinal, R. Cloud, R. Compton, J. Crippen, D. Frantz, I. Genee, I. Goddard, T. Hirose, J. Legate, E. Mathieu, M. Mizumoto, C. Mudzwinga, R. Rhodes, L. Russell, R. Scout, D. Si, P. Svenonius, M. Wiltschko, H.C. Wolfart, and F. Zúñiga.

2. Conventions (in addition to Leipzig glosses): [. . .] = verb stem, AGT = agent nominal, AI+O = AI plus indefinite object, AI(T) = AI transitive, AI = animate intransitive, AN = animate, D = definite, DEG = degree, DIR = direct, IC = initial change, II = inanimate intransitive, INCH = inchoative, INV = inverse, IN = inanimate, ND = indefinite, PRT = particle, √ROOT = root, s.o. = someone (animate), s.t. = something (inanimate), TA = transitive animate, TI = transitive inanimate.

3. For discussion of the connection of *v* to Voice, see Harley (2013), Folli et al. (2005), and Crippen and Déchaine (2015).

4. Déchaine and Weber (2015) analyze precategorized roots as insertion of a root into *v*/V. A precedent for this is found in Rizzi and Roberts (1989:107), who argue that, in French, Infl can be inserted into C in main clauses. Here we present "insertion of a root into v/V" in terms of precompiled *v*/V roots.

5. The translations in (8a) reflect the contribution of *v*: Plains Cree *-êyim* and *-êyiht* are the TA and TI forms of 'act on s.o./s.t. by mind', *-iht* is a general purpose causativizer 'act on s.o/s.t'. In all cases, the root √WIYAT 'funny' is construed as a result state.

6. Blackfoot null V, found in TA stems like (8b), is paradigmatically conditioned and contrasts with overt V found in TI and AI+O stems.

7. Our analysis extends to ditransitive 'give' (Plains Cree √MIY, Blackfoot √OHKOT), which arises if a root precompiles with an applicative *v*P, (i).

(i) *Precompiled Applicative-Adjoined Root*

   a. *Plains Cree*

   $[_{AP}$pro $[_{AP'}[_{AP}$ √MIY$]$ $[_{vP}$pro $[_{v}[_{v}$ Ø$]$ $[_{VP}[_{V}$ -ê$]$ pro$]]$ **miy-ê-w**   x gave (it/him) to y   TA

   b. *Blackfoot*

   $[_{AP}$pro $[_{AP'}[_{AP}$ √OHKOT$]$ $[_{vP}$pro $[_{v}[_{v}$ Ø$]$ $[_{VP}[_{V}$ Ø$]$ pro$]]$ **ohkot-Ø-ii-wa**   x gave (it/him) to y   TA

8. An INITIAL may combine with a final that is derived from a stem. In this way, Goddard's template allows for iterated roots, which we analyze as stacked modifiers.

REFERENCES

Bauer, Laurie. 1997. Derivational paradigms. *Yearbook of Morphology 1996*, ed. by Geert Booij and Jaap van Marle, pp. 243–256. Dordrecht: Kluwer Academic Publishers.

Bliss, Heather, Elizabeth Ritter, and Martina Wiltschko. 2016. Blackfoot nominalization patterns. *Papers of the Forty-Fourth Algonquian Conference*, ed. by Monica Macaulay, Margaret Noodin, and J. Randolph Valentine, pp. 1–21.

Bloomfield, Leonard. 1927. The word-stems of Central Algonquian. *Festschrift Meinhof*, ed. by Franz Boas, pp. 393–402. Hamburg: L. Friederichsen.

———. 1946. Algonquian. *Linguistic Structures of Native America* 6:85–129.

Bobaljik, Jonathan D. 2012. *Universals in comparative morphology: Suppletion, superlatives, and the structure of words*. Cambridge, MA: MIT Press.

Borer, Hagit. 2003. Exo-skeletal versus endo-skeletal explanations: Syntactic projections and the lexicon. *The nature of explanation in linguistic theory*, ed. by John More and Maria Polinsky, pp. 31–67. Stanford, CA: CSLI Publications.

———. 2012. In the event of a nominal. *The theta system: Argument structure at the interface*, ed. by Martin Everaert, Marijana MArelj, and Tal Siloni, pp. 103–149. Oxford: Oxford University Press.

Brittain, Julie. 2003. A distributed morphology account of the syntax of the Algonquian verb. *2003 CLA Proceedings*, pp. 25–39.

Chomsky, Noam. 2000. Minimalist inquiries: The framework. *Step by step: Essays on minimalist syntax in honor of Howard Lasnik,* ed. by Roger Martin, David Michaels, Juan Uriagereka, and Samuel Jay Keyser, pp. 89–155. Cambridge, MA: MIT Press.

———. 2001. Derivation by phase. *Ken Hale: A life in language*, ed. by Michael J. Kenstovicz, pp.1–54. Cambridge, MA: MIT Press.

———. 2013. Problems of projection. *Lingua* 130:33–49.

Crippen, James, and Rose-Marie Déchaine. 2015. Syntax and semantics of the Tlingit classifier. *Proceedings of WSCLA 20*.

de Belder, Marijke. 2011. Roots and affixes: Eliminating lexical categories from syntax. PhD thesis, Utrecht University.

Déchaine, Rose-Marie. 1999. What Algonquian morphology is really like. *MITOPL* 17:25–72.

———. 2002. On the significance of (non-)augmented roots. Paper presented at CLA 2002, University of Toronto.

Déchaine, Rose-Marie, Dayanqi Si, and Joash Gambarage. 2017. Nata deverbal nominalizations. *Africa's endangered languages: Documentary and theoretical approaches*, ed. by Jason Kandybowicz and Harold Torrence. Oxford: Oxford University Press.

Déchaine, Rose-Marie, and Natalie Weber. 2015. Head-Merge, Adjunct-Merge, and the syntax of root categorisation. [WCCFL 33]. *SFUWPL* 5:38–47.

Denny, Peter. 1984. Semantic verb classes and abstract finals. *Papers of the Fifteenth Algonquian Conference,* ed. by William Cowen, pp. 241–271.

Embick, David. 2010. *Localism versus globalism in morphology and phonology.* Cambridge, MA: MIT Press.

Folli, Raffaella, Heidi Harley, and Simin Karimi. 2005. Determinants of event type in Persian complex predicates. *Lingua* 115:1365–1401.

Frantz, Donald G. 2009. *Blackfoot grammar.* 2nd ed. Toronto: University of Toronto Press.

Goddard, Ives. 1990. Primary and secondary stem derivation in Algonquian. *IJAL* 56(4):449–483.

Hale, Ken, and Samuel Jay Keyser. 1993. On argument structure and the lexical expression of syntactic relations. *The view from building 20: Essays in Linguistics in honor of Sylvain Bromberger*, ed. by Kenneth L. Hale and Samuel Jay Keyser, pp. 53–110. Current Studies in Linguistics, vol. 24. MIT Press.

Harley, Heidi. 2013. External arguments and the Mirror Principle: On the distinctness of Voice and *v*. *Lingua* 125:34–57.

———. 2014. On the identity of roots. Unpublished manuscript, University of Arizona.

Harley, Heidi, and Rolf Noyer. 1999. Distributed morphology. *Glot International* 4(4):1–9.

———. 2000. Licensing in the non-lexicalist lexicon. *The lexicon/encyclopaedia interface*, ed. by Bert Peeters, pp. 349–374. Amsterdam: Elsevier Press.

Hirose, Tomio. 2003. *Origins of predicates.* Abingdon: Routledge.

Kratzer, Angelika. 1996. Severing the external argument from its verb. *Phrase structure and the lexicon*, ed. by Johan Rooryck and Laurie Ann Zaring, pp. 109–137. Springer.

Levinson, Lisa. 2010. Arguments for pseudo-resultative predicates. *NLLT* 28(1):135–182.

Marantz, Alec. 1995. A late note on late insertion. *Explorations in generative grammar*, ed. by Young-Sun Kim, Byung-Choon Lee, Kyoung-Jae Lee, Kyun-Kwon Yang, and Jong-Kuri Yoon, 396–413. Seoul: Hankuk Publishing Co.

———. 1997. No escape from syntax. *PWPL* 4:201–225.

———. 2002. Phases and Words. Unpublished manuscript, New York University. http://babel.ucsc.edu/~hank/mrg.readings/Phases_and_Words_Final.pdf.

———. 2013. Verbal argument structure: Events and participants. *Lingua* 130:152–168.

Quinn, Conor. 2006. Referential access dependency in Penobscot. PhD thesis, Harvard University.

Ramchand, Gillian. 2008. *Verb meaning and the lexicon: A first phase syntax.* Cambridge: Cambridge University Press.

Rizzi, Luigi, and Ian Roberts. 1989. Complex inversion in French. *Probus* 1(1):1–30. [Reprinted in Belletti and Rizzi (eds.). 1996. *Parameters and functional heads: Essays in comparative syntax*, pp. 91–116. Oxford: Oxford University Press.]

Siddiqi, Daniel. 2009. *Syntax within the word*. Amsterdam: John Benjamins.

Weber, Natalie. 2016. Predicate features and imperfectivity in Blackfoot. *Proceedings of the Qualifying Papers Mini-conferences 2013–2014*, pp. 249–273. University of British Columbia Working Papers in Linguistics, vol. 44.

Weber, Natalie, and Lisa Matthewson. 2014. Reflections of complement type. *MITWPL* 71(2):275–298.

———. 2017. The semantics of Blackfoot arguments. *Papers of the Forty-Fifth Algonquian Conference*, pp. 213–232, ed. by Monica Macaulay, Margaret Noodin, and J. Randolph Valentine. East Lansing: Michigan State University Press.

Wolfart, H. Christoph. 1973. *Plains Cree: A grammatical study*. Transactions of the American Philosophical Society, n.s., vol. 63, part 5. Philadelphia.

Blackfoot and Core Algonquian Inflectional Morphology: Archaisms and Innovations

Ives Goddard

lackfoot is clearly the most divergent language in the Algonquian family.[1] Many cognates shared with other languages have been identified or claimed (Michelson 1935; Taylor 1960; Thomson 1978: Proulx 1989; Berman 2006, 2007), but Blackfoot has not contributed to the reconstruction of Proto-Algonquian (PA) phonology or morphology. The other languages smear west to east, losing phonetic contrasts in stages (Goddard 1994), but all appear to continue the same reconstructible inflectional morphology (Bloomfield 1946; Goddard 1967, 1979, 2000, 2007, 2015b; Costa 2003).[2]

The many features of Blackfoot morphology that differ from the other languages raise obvious questions: (1) Can any of these differing features be shown to be archaisms that point to the existence of a Proto–Algonquian-Blackfoot (PAB) that was older than Proto-Algonquian (the proto-language of Core Algonquian)? (2) Are there features in Core Algonquian that can be shown to be shared innovations that originated as something more like Blackfoot? One challenge to investigating these questions is the imperfect state of current knowledge of Blackfoot and Proto-Algonquian comparative phonology. Many correspondences have been observed, but many unresolved details remain, and the approach taken here is in some cases necessarily superficial and ad hoc.[3]

Noun Inflection

Blackfoot noun inflection has most of its morphology from Proto-Algonquian. The peripheral (outer) suffixes on nouns and demonstrative pronouns (1) are generally inherited. The semivowels in |-wa| anim. sg. and |-yi| inan. sg., obv. do not appear after a consonant; they are set up by Frantz (1991:8, 12) to account for their appearance after vowels, but historically they reflect a PA *w that is part of the stem and lost in some forms by contraction (with Bl /-yi/ < PA *-wi).

(1)   Peripheral suffixes on nouns (Blackfoot and Proto-Algonquian)

	BLACKFOOT	PROTO-ALGONQUIAN
anim. sg.	-a (Frantz |-wa|)	*-a
inan. sg.	-i (|-yi|)	*-i
anim. pl.	-iksi	*-aki (Bl /i/ < PA *a; Bl /ksi/ < PA *ki)
inan. pl.	-istsi	*-ari
obv. sg.	-i (|-yi|)	*-ari OBsg, *-ahi OBpl
indef.	-i (|-i|)	(none)

Bl *-istsi* inan. pl. is not from PA *-ari* but from PA *-iri*, the form taken by this suffix in demonstrative pronouns and some other forms; note Bl *-istsi* inan. pl. in *annistsi* 'those (inan.)' (apparently < PA *ini* 'that (inan.)' + *iniri* 'those (inan.)'; cf. Goddard 2003:80). Bl *-i* obv. sg. regularly continues PA *-ahi* obv. pl. (Bl /-i/ < *-ii* < *-ihi* < PA *-ahi*): Bl *otáni* 'his daughter' < PA *ota'nahi* 'his daughters'. The proximate (i.e., non-obviative) animate plural suffix is used instead of a distinct obviative plural: Bl *otániksi* 'his daughters'. The use of the original obviative plural also for the singular is found in three languages or contiguous areas: Cheyenne, Western Mahican, and Southern New England Algonquian and Western Abenaki. The use of the proximate plural also where an obviative would be expected is attested from some speakers of Unami (for indefinite object nouns) and Munsee (Goddard 2015a:218–219). The indefinite suffix is unique to Blackfoot, at least in this function; it is unmarked for number.[4]

Possessed nouns in Blackfoot have the possessed-theme marker Bl -(i)m (< PA *-em) on lexically specified stems: *nitómitaama* 'my dog' (cf. *imitááwa* 'dog'). Possessors are marked with prefixes and central (or inner) suffixes that generally correspond to Proto-Algonquian (2).

(2)   Inflection for possessor

	BLACKFOOT		PROTO-ALGONQUIAN	
1s	ni(t)-	-Ø	*ne(t)-	-Ø
2s	ki(t)-	-Ø	*ke(t)-	-Ø
3s	o(t)-	-Ø	*o(t)-	-Ø
1p	ni(t)-	-innaan-	*ne(t)-	*-ena'n-
12	ki(t)-	-innoon-	*ke(t)-	*-enaw-
2p	ki(t)-	-oaawa-	*ke(t)-	*-wa'w-
3p	o(t)-	-oaawa-	*o(t)-	*-wa'w-
3'	o(t)-	-(w)a- (sg. only)	*o(t)-	*-iriw-

The prefixes insert /t/ before a vowel in nondependent stems. The plural-possessor suffixes have shapes influenced by the suffixes marking the same categories in certain TA inflections (see below). The inclusive suffix, which is not used on verbs, appears to have partially assimilated to the exclusive; an older shape -innawan- was recorded by Mary R. Haas in 1967 (Taylor 1969:154).

The peripheral suffixes (1) appear after the plural-possessor suffixes (2): nitómi-taaminnaan<u>a</u> 'our (exc.) dog' (cf. PA *neta'nena'n<u>a</u> 'our (exc.) daughter'); nitánin-naan<u>iksi</u> 'our (exc.) daughters'; nookóówannaan<u>i</u> 'our (exc.) home'; kookóówannoon<u>i</u> 'our (inc.) home'; kookóówannoon<u>istsi</u> 'our (inc.) homes'. The suffix set up synchron-ically as -oaawa- 2p,3p combines with peripheral suffixes as -oaawawa 2p+ANsg (haplological variant -oaawa), -oaawaiksi 2p+ANpl, and -oaawayi 3p+OB. Histor-ically these endings incorporate a suffix -oaa(w)- 2p,3p that spread from the TA inverse, where it is phonetically regular (see below), and the syllables following this are the portion that reflects the Proto-Algonquian ending, which would have been undercharacterized after regular sound changes: kitán<u>oaaw</u>awa 'your (pl.) daughter' ← -oaaw- 2p + pre-Bl *ki-tán-aw-a < PA *ke-ta'n-wa'w-a 'your (pl.) daughter'. The ending for obviative possessor continues that for third plural possessor: otánayi 'his (obv.) daughter (obv.)' < PA *ota'nwa'wahi 'their daughters (obv.)'. This form was presumably repurposed by a sort of proportional analogy after otánoaawayi 'their daughter (obv.)' was created to replace it with plural reference: in other paradigms with -oaaw- 3p (which has no obviative counterpart) the corresponding singular lacks this.

Animate and Inanimate Intransitive

In the Blackfoot animate intransitive (AI) paradigm, the first and second person forms can be straightforwardly understood by comparing those of the Proto-Algonquian independent indicative, but the third person forms and those of the inanimate intransitive (II) show significant differences.

(3) Animate intransitive inflection

	BLACKFOOT		PROTO-ALGONQUIAN	
1s	nit-		*ne(t)-	-Ø
2s	kit-		*ke(t)-	-Ø
1p	nit-	-hpinnaana	*ne(t)-	-hmena˙
12		-ʔpa	*ke(t)-	-hmena
2p	kit-	-hpoaawa	*ke(t)-	-hmwa˙
X		-ʔpa		*-hmi
3s,0s	-wa		AI *-wa 3s, II *-wi 0s	
3p,0p	-yi		AI *-waki 3p, II *-wari 0p	
3′	-yini (sg. only)		AI *-riwari 3′s, II *-riwi 0′s	

Only the variants of the prefixes with intercalated /t/ are found with Blackfoot verbs, because all verb stems begin with a vowel (or an underlying |i|; see below). The suffixes that pluralize the first (exclusive) and second persons were shortened in Proto-Algonquian by the regular loss of word-final consonants, but the full forms have been restored in Blackfoot (matching possessed-noun inflection and transitive verbs); the same innovation occurred independently in Menominee. These suffixes begin with the formative element /hp/ < PA *hm, while that for indefinite person (abbreviated X; "unspecified subject" [Frantz 1991:22]), which is now more commonly used for first person inclusive (12), has the unexplained variant /ʔp/ (/oʔp/) after elided stem-final /i/). All these suffixes are followed by an empty morpheme -a (a "predictable addition" [Frantz 1991:22]), a default suffix that prevents a disallowed word-final consonant. Frantz (1991:22) takes the second plural ending as having -oaawa (cf. 2), but historically this has -oaaw- 2p,3p, the short form of the suffix appearing also in the TA inverse and the TI (see below). When -oaaw- 2p,3p was introduced into pre-Blackfoot *-hpa (the expected reflex of PA *-hmwa˙ 2p), the result was Bl -hpoaawa 2p, with a final -a (the remnant of

PA *-wa·) that was semantically superfluous and was evidently extended to all the endings of this set as what now appears as the empty -a.

The third person peripheral suffixes on verbs differ from those marking the same categories on nouns. The AI ending -wa 3s matches PA *-wa 3s but is also the ending on II stems: siksinááttsiwa 'it is black' (contrast PA *-wi). It will be argued below that Bl -a on verbs as inanimate singular, Bl -i (Frantz: -yi) as the corresponding plural for both genders, and -yini OBsg can be understood as resulting from linked innovations that replaced the original peripheral suffixes that were identical to those in noun inflection.

Transitive Inanimate

The Blackfoot transitive inanimate (TI) has what appears to be an absolute paradigm (one not marking the object) with the singular and plural peripheral suffixes of the third person AI (3) added in the first (and indefinite) and second persons (4).

(4) Transitive inanimate

	BLACKFOOT		PROTO-ALGONQUIAN (TI CLASS 1, ABSOLUTE)	
1s–Os	nit-	-iihpa	*ne(t)-	-e·
1s–Op	nit-	-iihpi		
2s–Os	kit-	-iihpa	*ke(t)-	-e·
2s–Op	kit-	-iihpi		
1p–Os	nit-	-iihpinnaana	*ne(t)-	-e·hmena·
1p–Op	nit-	-iihpinnaani		
12–Os		-ii?pa	*ke(t)-	-e·hmena
12–Op		-ii?pi		
2p–Os	kit-	-iihpoaawa	*ke(t)-	-e·hmwa·
2p–Op	kit-	-iihpoaayi		
X–Os		-ii?pa		*-e·hmi
X–Op		-ii?pi		
3s–0		-ima		*-amwa
3p–0		-imi		*-amo·ki
3's–0		-imini		*-amiriwari (or *-ameriwari)

The first and second person endings differ from those of the AI in having a theme sign |-ii| and, instead of the empty -a, a suffix for a singular or plural object (-a sg. or -i pl., the peripheral suffixes in the third person forms in the AI [3]). (Also, /ʔp/ in place of /hp/ is here "perfectly acceptable" [Frantz 1991:43]). The third person endings, in contrast, have the theme sign |-im|, with the peripheral suffixes of the corresponding AI endings marking the subject and no suffix for the object. The sufixes -ii and -im continue PA *-eˑ and *-am, the suppletive theme signs of the Class 1 TI absolute paradigm (Goddard 2007:266). Some verbs have instead -oo and -oom; these have generalized -oo as the theme sign of the Class 2 TI (PA *-aw with contraction to *-oˑ and *-aˑ), and added -m from the Class 1 TI in the third person.[5] The formative element -hp was retained in the first and second singular before the (uniquely Blackfoot) peripheral suffixes, but it is absent in the corresponding AI forms because PA *-hm was regularly lost word-finally (3). If, as seems likely, the Blackfoot peripheral suffixes are an innovation, it is still possible for -hp (< PA *-hm) to have survived in the singular before modal suffixes (though these have disappeared); e.g., PA *nemeθkoeˑhmesaha 'I have found (it, them [indef.])' (with present mode *-esaha; cf. Men nepoˑnɛˑmesah 'so I'm putting it in the pot').

Transitive Animate

The transitive animate (TA) direct paradigm continues the Proto-Algonquian objective inflections in the first, second, and indefinite person forms and the absolute inflections in the forms for third person subject.

(5) Transitive animate direct

	BLACKFOOT		PROTO-ALGONQUIAN	
			(objective)	
1s–3s	nit-	-awa	*ne(t)-	-aˑwa
1s–3p	nit-	-ayi	*ne(t)-	-aˑwaki
2s–3s	kit-	-awa	*ke(t)-	-aˑwa
2s–3p	kit-	-ayi	*ke(t)-	-aˑwaki
1p–3s	nit-	-annaana	*ne(t)-	-aˑwenaˑna
1p–3p	nit-	-annaani	*ne(t)-	-aˑwenaˑnaki
12–3s		-awa	*ke(t)-	-aˑwenawa
12–3p		-ayi	*ke(t)-	-aˑwenawaki

2p–3s	kit-	-awaawa	*ke(t)-	-aˑwaˑwa
2p–3p	kit-	-awaayi	*ke(t)-	-aˑwaˑwaki
X–3s		-awa		*-aˑwa
X–3p		-ayi		*-aˑwaki
				(absolute)
3s–3′		-iiwa[6]		*-eˑwa (3s–3′)
3p–3′		-iiyi		*-eˑwaki (3p–3′)

The TA direct inflections in Blackfoot reflect those given in (5) for Proto-Algonquian (Goddard 2007:265–266), except that the plural suffix Bl -yi (-i) does not match PA *-aki. As in the AI and TI, the inherited indefinite subject inflection is used for first plural inclusive. Some Blackfoot verbs have the direct theme sign (PA *-aˑ-) as Bl -a- (5; e.g., nitsikákomimm**a**wa 'I love him'), but others have Bl -aa- (e.g., nitsúpohkis-stoyaawa 'I shaved him'), perhaps conditioned by the preceding semivowel (Frantz 1971:5). In the first plural exclusive suffix Bl -nnaan- the -nn- is the reflex of PA *-wen-, arising by vowel syncope and the usual Blackfoot consonant assimilation in secondary clusters.[7] The -nn- in this ending (of the TA direct) was generalized to the exclusive central suffix in all paradigms (2, 3, 4, 6).

The TA inverse paradigm also continues the Proto-Algonquian objective inflections in the first and second person forms, but it has a mixture of absolute and objective inflections for third person object. The inverse theme sign -ok < PA *-ekw has the vowel colored by the lost *w.[8]

(6) Transitive animate inverse

	BLACKFOOT		PROTO-ALGONQUIAN	
			(objective)	
3s–1s	nit-	-oka	*ne(t)-	-ekwa
3p–1s	nit-	-oki	*ne(t)-	-ekoˑki
3s–2s	kit-	-oka	*ke(t)-	-ekwa
3p–2s	kit-	-oki	*ke(t)-	-ekoˑki
3s–1p	|nit-	-Okinnaana|	*ne(t)-	-ekonaˑna
3p–1p	nit-	-okinnaani	*ne(t)-	-ekonaˑnaki
3s–12		|-Okiwa|	*ke(t)-	-ekonawa
3p–12		|-Okiyi|	*ke(t)-	-ekonawaki
3s–2p	|kit-	-Okoaawa|	*ke(t)-	-ekowaˑwa
3p–2p	kit-	-okoaayi	*ke(t)-	-ekowaˑwaki

3'–3s	ot-	-oka	*o(t)-	*-ekoˑhi (3'p–3s)
				(*-ekwa ((3')–3s [absolute]))
3'–3p	ot-	-okoaayi	*o(t)-	*-ekowaˑwahi (3'p–3p)

The inflections for first and second person objects reflect those of Proto-Algonquian, with the subjects marked by Bl -a sg. and -i pl. (The forms for inclusive object may continue derived passives formed on the inverse theme sign.) The inflection for obviative on third singular has the third person prefix from the objective inflection and the ending from the absolute paradigm. The inflection for obviative on third plural directly reflects that for obviative plural on proximate plural. In these forms for obviative subjects, obviative singular and plural are treated as the same, in contrast to other paradigms, in which the obviative is only singular and obviative plural is the same as proximate plural. In ot–okoaayi 3'–3p the suffix -i, which marks obviative singular on nouns, refers to an obviative subject that is either singular or plural. This would have been the earlier meaning of the suffix, after PA *-ahi OBpl was generalized to the obviative singular.

The Peripheral Suffixes on Verbs

In fact, the key factor that led to the restructuring of the peripheral suffixes on verbs in Blackfoot was the development of Bl -i out of PA *-ahi OBpl by regular sound changes (see above). This would have resulted in a set of suffixes that had Bl -i as inanimate singular and obviative plural, beside the inherited homophony of the inanimate plural and the obviative singular (< PA *-ari). Iconic consistency was introduced at the expense of largely redundant distinctness when the obviative plural suffix Bl -i spread to mark to plural of all categories on verbs, while in the singular Bl -a was adopted to mark inanimate as well as animate (replacing *-i INsg). These changes did not introduce any ambiguity of gender but merely reduced the multiple exponence of gender marking, given the distinctness of AI and II stems and of TA and TI stems and theme signs. But the suffix Bl -i was also extended in another direction to become the obviative suffix for both singular and plural. This stage, with Bl -i for both numbers of the obviative, is reflected by the inflection ot–okoaayi 3'–3p (i.e., for obviative singular or plural on third plural proximate) (6). The same change must have taken place in the inflection of nouns (and demonstrative pronouns), before Bl -iksi ANpl was extended to the obviative plural (1).

The generalization of Bl -*i* to mark all plurals and obviatives would have resulted in a verbal suffix -*i* that had multiple meanings as the marker of the subject of an AI or a TI. This suffix was retained for proximate plural and obviative plural (the same dual function as -*iksi* on nouns and demonstratives)[9] and for inanimate plural, but added -*ni* (giving -(*y*)*ini*) to specify obviative singular (3, 4). The added -*ni* in -*yini* OBsg can be explained as the reduced form of a demonstrative. The demonstrative *anni* 'that (inan.)' is presumably derived by compounding PA *ini 'that (inan.)' with itself and the other forms of this set: PA *ini + *ini > Bl *anni*.[10] The uncompounded demonstrative is preserved in Bl *nitánistawa* 'I told him' (Donald Frantz, personal communication 2016), which continues PA *neteθaʼwa with the addition of a default oblique complement *ani 'that (inan.)' (< PA *ini) as a preverb and elision of the final vowel of this before PA **iθ-* 'say {so} to'. The suffix -*ni* added to mark an obviative singular can directly reflect PA *inihi 'those (obv.)' from the same paradigm (with the usual extension to obviative singular); cf. *anni* 'that (obv. [sg.])' (homophonous with *anni* 'that (inan.)').

Although the restructuring of the peripheral suffixes on Blackfoot verbs that has to be reconstructed was extensive, there are at least two reasons why taking these Blackfoot suffixes as an archaic subset dating back to Proto–Algonquian-Blackfoot would not be a viable alternative. For one thing, there is really no place in Proto-Algonquian for an additional set of peripheral suffixes, since the specific morphology that marks subjects and objects in the independent indicative is derived from the formation and inflection of possessed nouns and must therefore have originally had the same peripheral suffixes (Goddard 2007). And for another thing, forms that match the Proto-Algonquian independent indicative are inherited in Blackfoot as participles ("nominals"), with heads marked by peripheral suffixes that do match those on nouns (Frantz 1991:65, 115–130). The forms with animate singular heads are identical with the corresponding verbs, sharing a suffix -*a* ANsg (7a, 7d), but those with plural, obviative, or inanimate heads differ.

(7)   Blackfoot participles

     a. *áyoʔkaawa* 'the sleeping one' (-wa < PA *-wa 3s; also 'he is sleeping')

     b. *áyoʔkaiksi* 'the sleeping ones' (-iksi < PA *-waki 3p)
        (not 'they are sleeping'; cf. *ííksspitaayi* '(they [anim.]) are tall')

c. iʔnitsíí<u>ksi</u> 'the ones that killed him' (-*ííksi* < *-*í*'-w-iksi < PA *-e'waki 3p–(3'))
    (cf. iʔnitsíí<u>yi</u> 'they killed him', with -(y)i ANpl)

d. nitsíínoannaan<u>a</u> 'the one we (exc.) saw' (also 'we (exc.) saw him')
    (nit–annaana < PA *net–a'wena'na 1p–3p)

e. nitsíínoannaan<u>iksi</u> 'the ones we (exc.) saw'
    (nit–annaaniksi < PA *net–a'wena'naki 1p–3p)
    (not 'we saw them'; cf. nitsikákomimmannaan<u>i</u> 'we (exc.) love them (anim.)')

f. <u>ots*íín*o</u>ayi 'the one (obv.) he saw' (ot–ayi < *ot–a'wi < PA *ot–a'wahi 3s–3'p)
    (cf. iʔnits*íí<u>wa</u>* 'he killed him, them (obv.)'

g. siksinááttsi<u>yi</u> 'black thing', siksinááttsii<u>stsi</u> 'black things'[11]
    (cf. siksinááttsi<u>wa</u> 'it is black')

The use of forms like those in (7) as participles is a Blackfoot innovation, but their inflections continue the Proto-Algonquian verbal paradigms that had peripheral suffixes like those on nouns. Participles like (7f) continue an objective form that has disappeared from Blackfoot as a finite verb. The functionally equivalent participles in Core Algonquian languages are a mode of the conjunct order, which must have been more archaic than the independent order and which has disappeared from Blackfoot. The Blackfoot participles can be understood as arising out of a use of forms of the independent indicative, which replaced the older participles and were partly differentiated from the corresponding finite verbs when these innovated the new set of peripheral suffixes.

Indefinite Objects

The feature of Blackfoot noun inflection that is most divergent from Core Algonquian is a form used specifically for an indefinite singular or plural primary object of either gender. A noun marked as indefinite always follows an intransitive active verb that is either derived from a synonymous transitive verb or the basis for deriving the corresponding transitives.

(8) *áóoyiyaawa* owáí

a-	ooyi-	-yi	-aawa	owaa-	-i
dur	eat.AI	3p	pl	egg	indef

'They are eating egg(s).' (Frantz 1991:40)

The verb in (8) is intransitive (*ooyi-* AI 'eat' presumably < **oowi-*); the (homophonous) transitive stems are derived from it: *oowat-* TA, TI(2) 'eat (anim., inan.)'. The form *owáí* (underlying |owaa-i|) 'egg(s) (indef.)' contrasts with *owááyi* 'egg' (|owaa-yi|) and *owáístsi* (|owaa-istsi|) 'eggs'. The distinctness of *owáí* 'egg(s) (indef.)' and *owááyi* 'egg' is accounted for synchronically by the contrast between |-i| and |-yi| and the regular shortening of a vowel before another vowel. But historically there could have been no old phonemic vowel sequences. Bl *owááyi* 'egg' reflects a post-PA **o-wa·w-i* (reshaped exactly like Sh *howa·wi* from PA **wa·wari* [cf. Goddard 2010:30]); the stem-final PA **w* is retained as *y* before word-final *-i* but lost before the *i* of a longer suffix or *-i* indef. (Compare the loss of the /y/ from the longer forms of the distinct-third-person pronouns [see below].) The absence of *y* before the plural and indefinite suffixes is paralleled by the deletion of stem-final *n*, *m*, and *s* before the same morphemes in certain nouns (which are set up with underlying |N|, |M|, and |S|): *isttoána* 'knife' (pl. *isttoáíksi* pl., *isttoáí* indef.); *atsikíni* 'shoe' (*atsikíístsi* pl., *atsikíí* indef.). A full set of examples is not available, but apparently a form identical with the indefinite form was used as a prenoun in some cases: *kóópis-i* 'broth, soup' (pl. *kóópiistsi*), prenoun *kóópii* in *kóópii*[-]*sopoistsi* 'chinooks' (lit. 'broth winds'); *pomís-i* 'fat' (pl. *pomíístsi* 'fat drippings'), prenoun *pomíí* in *pomíí*[-]*sistsiiksi* 'goldfinches' (lit. 'grease birds'); cf. *moʔtsís-i* 'arm, hand' (pl. *noʔtsíístsi* 'my arms'), *moʔtsíí* indef.; *pookááwa* 'child; catbird' (pl. *pookáíksi*), *pookááyi* obv., *pookáí* indef.; *áápotskinawa* 'cow' (pl. *áápotskinaiksi*), prenoun *áápotskinai* in *áápotskinai*[-] *sahkomaapiwa* 'cowboy' (a literal calque).[12]

Prenouns were made from noun stems of either gender in Proto-Algonquian (and still in, for example, Meskwaki) with a suffix **-i* (Bloomfield 1946:103–104):

(9) Prenoun in Meskwaki

Mes okima·wa 'chief' → okima·wi PN 'of chief':

okima·wi-oškinawe·ha 'young man of chief's family' (lit., 'chief('s)-youth')

okima·wi-wi·kiya·pi 'chief's lodge'

Prenouns thus have exactly the form and properties of the Blackfoot indefinite forms. Preverbs made from nouns (in the same way) are less common, but examples can be found of such preverbs with the semantic role of object:

(10)   Preverbs as semantic objects of syntactically intransitive verbs
        Mes   okima·wi-nehta·we·mikatwi 'it [disease] killed a chief'
                (nehta·we·- AI 'kill' + -mikat II [makes an II from an AI])
        Unami name (1799):   ⟨Tulpe Najundam⟩ "he that carries a turtle" (Gipson 1938:29)
                (Un †tó·lpe 'turtle sp.'; nayúntam TI-O 'he carries something on his back')

In Meskwaki (at least) some preverbs often appear as homophonous free particles that immediately follow the verb for emphasis. If this optional postposing (and recategorization) of preverbs was inherited from Proto-Algonquian (as is likely), no additional assumptions are necessary to derive the Blackfoot indefinite nouns from postposed preverbs that referred to syntactic objects. The origin of -i (indef.) in preverbs also explains why nouns with this have the shapes otherwise found only in longer forms.

It appears, then, that although the Blackfoot way of indicating indefinite objects is unique in the family, it, too, derives historically from morphology that must be reconstructed for Core Algonquian.

You-and-Me (Local) Forms

The Blackfoot TA inflections for action by a second person on a first person or the reverse have the structure of the reconstructed Proto-Algonquian paradigms made on theme 3 (PA *-i 1.obj) and theme 4 (PA *-eθ 2.obj) and use the AI person markers in the same pattern, but they have different theme signs. The forms for second person on first use the inverse theme sign in the shape -oki (Frantz 1991:59), and in fact kitsikákimimmoki can mean 'you (sg.) love me' as well as 'they love you (sg.)'. This ambiguity probably reflects the fact that the use of the inverse theme sign for second person on first (replacing PA *-i) is a recent innovation. The replacement of PA *-eθ by Bl -o for first person on second (Frantz 1991:58) is unexplained.

Fused Enclitics

In addition to the verbal inflections in (3–6) Blackfoot also has fused pronominal enclitics (Frantz: "attached pronouns") that refer to third person arguments (Fox and Frantz 1979; Frantz 1991:20–21, 33, 46–49, 103, 2009:21–22). A form inflected ambiguously as either proximate or obviative plural, like *ííksspitaayi* 'they are tall', is used only if the subject follows: *ííksspitaayi nohkóíksi* 'my sons are tall'; *ííksspitaayi ohkóíksi* 'his sons are tall'. If the subject is not named or precedes the verb, *=aawa* is added to a proximate or inanimate plural and *=aiksi* is added to an obviative plural (with some vowel elision): *ííksspitaayaawa* 'they (prox.) are tall'; *ííksspitaayaiksi* 'they (obv.) are tall'. The set that contains *=aiksi* also includes *=áyi* OBsg and INsg and *=aistsi* INpl; this set is used "when there is another third person in the immediate context" and is referred to as the "distinct third person pronoun" (Frantz 1991:47). Two non-identical enclitic pronouns may be used together, but there is no enclitic for proximate singular: *áakohpommatoomáyi* 'he will buy it' (*-ooma* 3s–0; *=áyi* INsg); *áakohpommatoomiaawaistsi* 'they (prox.) will buy them (inan.)' (*-oomi* 3p–0; *=aawa* 3p; *=aistsi* INpl).

The enclitic *=aawa* 3p (anim. and inan.) is cognate with PA **-wa·w* pl (word-finally **-wa·*), a bound suffix. This is used with the pronominal prefixes PA **ke-* 2 and **o-* 3 in the inflection of possessed nouns and objective independent order verbs (2–6), but it is also used without an associated prefix to pluralize second persons and animate third persons elsewhere. For example, in the conjunct order PA **-t* 3 was pluralized as **-t-wa·w* 3p (as reflected in Cree and Menominee); in the Unami delayed imperative *-me* 2s is pluralized as *-mɔ́·e* 2p (< **-mwa·we*) (Goddard 1979:145); the third person emphatic pronoun PEA **ne·kəma* has a plural **ne·kəma·wa*, with a plural suffix PEA **-wa* (pointing to PA **-wa·* < pre-PA **-wa·w*). Only the last of these could come directly from an incorporated enclitic (and this has no non-Eastern cognate), but PA **-wa·w* is evidently cognate with Wiyot *wow* ([waw]), a postposed word that pluralizes Wiyot *khíl* 'you (sg.)' as *khíl wow* 'you (pl.)', a comparison supported by the cognacy of the Wiyot word *hinòd* 'we' and the pluralizing suffix PA **-ena·n* 1p (Karl V. Teeter in Haas 1958:167–168). For the phonology, compare Bl *áápi* 'white, light-colored' and PA **wa·pi*; underlying word-initial semivowels are dropped by a general phonological rule (Frantz 1991:151). The final *-a* is presumably the Blackfoot empty *-a*, added by rule after a consonant (see above, after 3).

The distinct-third-person enclitics can be compared directly to the forms of PA **aya*, the place-holder pronoun or "noun substitute" (Proulx 1988:317; LeSourd

2003). Blackfoot has =*áyi* INsg (< PA **ayi*), =*aiksi* ANpl (< PA **ayaki*), =*aistsi* INpl (reshaped as if **ay-iri* ← PA **ayari*), and =*áyi* OBsg (< PA **ayahi* OBpl). The Algonquian word is used as a hesitation form and the like (Cr *aya*, Menominee *aya·h* anim., *i·h* inan.; Mal *ĭyá* anim. sg. [pl. *íyək*], *ĭyé* inan. sg. [pl. *íyəl*]), and also as an empty noun or noun final ('one') combined with adjectival prenouns or initials: Cr *osk-a·ya* 'a young one' (< |oski-aya|); Men *oske·h-aya·h* 'a new one'; EAb *kčáy* 'old person'; Mun *kíhkay* 'chief' (< 'old chief' < 'elder'). Although there is no synchronic or diachronic account of Blackfoot accent, it seems reasonable to take the accent on =*áyi* OBsg and INsg (in some occurrences) as reflecting an earlier status as an independent word.

In contrast to the basic verbal inflections, the Blackfoot attached pronouns appear to go back to an earlier stage of the proto-language than the one the Core Algonquian languages descend from. Bl =*aawa* 3p (anim. and inan.) still betrays its origin as an enclitic that is not part of the basic ending complex, while PA **-wa·(w)* is in all cases a word-internal suffix. The Blackfoot distinct-third-person enclitics are purely abstract bearers of inflectional categories, while the Core Algonquian noun substitute has developed a specialized function.

Post-Inflectional Suffixes

A feature of Blackfoot noun phrases not found in Core Algonquian is the series of "post-inflectional suffixes," which can be added to demonstratives (of five sets) and, optionally, their accompanying nouns after the inflectional suffixes of gender and number (Frantz 1991:64–65); they have also been called "deictic suffixes" for "spatial/temporal proximity" (Taylor 1969:201) and "referent/region configuration suffixes" (Schupbach 2013:60–73).

(11) Post-inflectional suffixes

    a. -ma   stationary

    b. -ya   Frantz: moving, but not toward speaker (possibly at another time); Schupbach: motion away from anchor, around (to and fro); presentative

    c. -ka   proximity information relates to a time other than present; Schupbach: motion toward anchor, back (along path);

d. -hka   not visible to the speaker; Greg Thomson (cited by Frantz): less salient;
            Schupbach: indiscernible, invisible

Examples:

a. amo<u>ma</u> miistsísa '(he will sit) on this tree' (amo 'this (anim.)')

b. amo<u>ya</u> áyoʔkaawa 'this sleeping one (was going about all night)'

c. amí<u>ka</u> nookóówayi<u>ka</u> '(when I get home I'll fix up) my house' (ami 'that (inan.)')
    ámoksí<u>ka</u> isttsííksinaiʔkokaiksi<u>ka</u> 'ones who (used) snake-painted lodges here'

d. anná anná<u>hka</u> *kínna<u>hka</u>*? 'Where is your father?' (anna 'that (anim.)')
    anná<u>hka</u> áwáaistóówa<u>hka</u> '(I know) who is coming.'

Although the peripheral suffixes of Core Algonquian are word-final (1), the absentative suffixes (12) appear to show a trace of a following suffix. The absentative is used variously for entities that are absent, dead, departed or departing, or further removed.

(12) Absentative endings in Proto-Algonquian

	normal	absentative	
anim. sg.	*-a	*-aˑ	< *-a + X
inan. sg.	*-i	*-eˑ	< *-i + X
anim. pl.	*-aki	*-akeˑ	< *-aki + X
	(etc.)	(etc.)	

The lost suffix (here represented abstractly as "X") lengthened the preceding vowel, shifting *i to *eˑ; it would have been in the same slot as the Blackfoot post-inflectional suffixes but does not appear to have been cognate with any of them, and none of them adds the specific core meaning 'deceased'. In demonstrative pronouns the animate singular added *-kaˑ: PA *$ina\cdot ka\cdot$ 'that (anim. abs.)' (cf. PA *ina 'that (anim. sg.)'). In Eastern Algonquian the *k of this suffix was extended throughout the paradigm, and the endings on nouns begin with PEA *-ənk (13). In these languages the absentative is used variously for what is absent, dead, asleep, destroyed, or no longer possessed.

(13)   Absentative endings in Proto–Eastern-Algonquian

	nouns & verbs	demonstratives
anim. sg.	*-a	*-ka
inan. sg.	*-ē	*-kē
anim. pl.	*-ənkakē	*-kakē
	(etc.)	(etc.)

Typical examples in Unami are: *náka lə́nəwa* 'that deceased man'; *nikáhke lənúnkahke* 'those deceased men'; there is also a more common shortened form for plural nouns: *lənúnka*.

The closest parallel between the absentative and the Blackfoot post-inflectional suffixes appears to be in the use of the Meskwaki absentative demonstratives that have animate singulars in *-ka* for another that is visible but further away (*iˑyaˑka*) or is in another place (*iˑnaˑka*).

(14)   Meskwaki demonstratives in *-ka*

a.   mana   =čaˑh   nekoti,   iˑyaˑka   naˑhka.
     this.ANSG   so   one   this.removed.ANSG   also
     "Here is one, and there is another." (Jones 1907:51)

b.   iˑnaˑka   =keˑh=   pašitoˑha ...   eˑh=anemehkaˑči.
     that.removed.ANSG   moreover   old.man   he.walks.on
     'Meanwhile that old man forged on ...'

Now, what is odd about PA *inaˑkaˑ* 'that (anim. abs.)' (> Mes *iˑnaˑka*, EAb *nə̀ka*, Un *náka*; the Eastern forms guarantee the original final long vowel) is that it appears to be *|in-aˑ-k-aˑ|*, with a repetition of the absentative singular suffix *-aˑ*. This anomaly is explained if the medial *-aˑ-* was the original absentative suffix and followed by a post-inflectional suffix *-ka* (cf. 8c) that originally referred in some way to another time or place and was analogically reshaped to be like a word-final absentative suffix. This analysis would postulate a sequence of two post-inflectional suffixes, but as the first of these (the "X" of (12)) has no Blackfoot cognate this sequence would not be inconsistent with anything that Blackfoot actually attests.

In fact, additional support in Core Algonquian for an original post-inflectional suffix *-ka* is provided by PA *awiyaka* 'someone' (> Cr *awiyak*, Old Innu /awiyak/ ⟨a8iak⟩ [Silvy 1974:15], Men *weyak*; Mes *owiyeˑha* 'someone, anyone, someone else', reshaped as a formal diminutive). This has a morphologically unmotivated syllable *-ak- that is absent from the stem *awiy- that appears in other forms of the paradigm: PA *awiyaki 'some people', obv. *awiyari > Cr awiyak, awiya; Old Innu /awiyač/ ⟨A8ïats⟩ 'someone, other people' ("qlqn, autruy"; Fabvre 1970:27); Men weyak, weyan.[13] If PA *awiy-_ak_-a was originally *awiy-a-_ka_ it would have the shape of a regularly inflected singular *awiya with a post-inflectional suffix *-ka that would match Bl -ka (8c), presumably adding the notion 'other'. It seems also reasonable to compare PEA *-ank (13), the suffix appearing before the peripheral suffixes in the absentative endings of nouns and verbs, with Bl -hka 'invisible, not-salient' (8d), despite the difference in the order of the suffixes. The Illinois vocative plural suffix /-enka/ may also belong in this set.

It seems clear that the absentative inflections are best understood as an innovation of the Core Algonquian languages that incorporated remnants of a set of post-inflectional suffixes like those of Blackfoot.

Initial *i*- in Blackfoot Verbs

A prominent phonological difference between Blackfoot and Core Algonquian is the abundance of verb stems that begin with Bl /iC-/, in contrast to the complete absence of PA *i- before most single consonants. PA *i- was found only in a restricted class of environments: before consonant clusters (some but not all); before PA *r (only reconstructible in PA *iren- 'ordinary'); in demonstratives (e.g., *iyo· 'this [inan.]', *ini 'that [inan.]'); and in relative roots (*iθ- ~ *iš- '{so}; to {somewhere}'; *iha'- AI 'go to {somewhere}' [3s *ihe·wa]; *iθ- ~ *iš- TA 'say {so} to' [and note *ikwa·(obv.) says {so} to him']; *i- ~ *iyo- AI 'say {so}' [3s *iwa], and stems derived from these). No initial begins with PA *ip-, *ič-, *it-, *ik-, *is-, *iš-, *im-, or *in-. In contrast, Blackfoot has verbs listed under ip-, ik-, etc., but none under p-, k-, or any other single obstruent, except for some given with s- (Frantz and Russell 1989). In fact, all Blackfoot verb stems basically begin with a vowel; stems appearing in some forms with an initial consonant have deleted an initial |i-| that must be set up in the underlying form and is sometimes present on the surface. Consequently, the pronominal prefixes appear on verbs only with the intercalated /t/ that is required before a vowel (3–6). For example, the verb cited as siksip- TA 'bite' (Frantz and Russell 1989:242) has an /i-/ in isiksipáwa 'he was bitten' (Frantz 1971:12) and an underlying |i-| in nítssiksipawa 'I bit him' (< *nitsisiksipawa < |nit-isikIp-a:wa|; cf. PA *sakipw- TA).[14]

Stem-initial syllables in Proto-Algonquian have other limitations, including the absence of initial clusters of true consonants and the lack of a contrast between *i and *e. These constraints suggest that such syllables had undergone phonetic reduction. An evident example of such word-initial erosion is provided by the relative roots beginning with PA *t- (~ *-ent-; with initial change *e·nt-). For example, PA *taθ- '{somewhere}' with the prefix *ne(t)-1 is *netentaθ- and with initial change is *e·ntaθ-: e.g., Un té·kəne talá·wsu 'he lives in the woods'; ntəntala·wsí·ne·n 'for us to live there'; yú entala·wsíenk 'here where we live'. The allomorphy in these initials indicates that they must originally have begun with pre-PA *ent- and that this was reduced to PA *t-; this sound change acounts for why there are no reconstructible stems beginning with PA *int-.

The fact that the cognates of PA verb stems beginning with a consonant commonly have Bl |iC-| (/iC-/ ~ /C-/) can be accounted for by assuming that Proto–Algonquian-Blackfoot had stems that began with *iC- and that this sequence was reduced by sound law to PA *C-. Independently, under synchronic conditions that have not been described, word-initial Bl |iC-| is sometimes realized as C-, and this appears to be the regular outcome in nouns.

(15) Stems with Blackfoot iC- and PA *C-

　　a. Bl ipon- 'terminate, end, be rid of' : PA *po·n- 'cease':
　　　　nitsipónihta 'I paid'; ponihtáát 'pay!' (cf. Mes po·nike·wa 'he pays his debt')

　　b. Bl iksistohs- TI 'warm over heat' : PA *ki·šow- 'warm' + *-es TI(1) 'by heat':
　　　　iksístohsima 'he warmed it, them (inan.)', iksístohsit 'warm it!'

　　c. Bl ikimm- TA 'show kindness to, bestow power on' : PA *ketem- (initial)
　　　　(cf. Mes keteminaw- 'take pity on, bless with supernatural power'):
　　　　ikímmiiwa 'he bestowed power on him', nitsíkimmoka 'he — me'

　　d. Bl issksino- TA, issksin- TI 'know'[15] : PA *keskinaw- TA, *keskin- TI(1):
　　　　issksínoyiiwáyi 'he knows him', issksinímayi 'he knows it',
　　　　nítssksinoawa 'I know him' < *nítsissksinoawa; nítáíssksinoawa 'I think of him'

It is likely that there were also stems that began with PAB *C- and that word-initial Bl |i-| was extended to them analogically on the model of the stems with Bl |iC-| (i.e., /iC-/ ~ /C-/) that went back to PAB *iC-. Direct evidence for this is provided by stems that begin synchronically with |iC-| but have initial change on the vowel that follows this (without the |i-|): e.g., *siiksipáwa* 'he was bitten', synonymous with *isiksipáwa*, mentioned above (Frantz 1971:12). Initial change in Blackfoot marks past tense by modifying the first vowel of a stem (Taylor 1967; Frantz 1971:12, 1991:36); in Proto-Algonquian it marked participles. A form like *siiksipáwa* can also be used as a participle meaning 'the one who was bitten'.[16] In Proto-Algonquian this would have been expressed by a conjunct participle, but (as discussed above) forms identical with the independent indicative have taken over this function in Blackfoot, with the suffixes that were inherited on nouns (7). Blackfoot initial change may thus be a relic of an earlier use of initial change on participles: Bl *siik-* < PA **se·k-*, the initial PA **sak-* (> Bl |sik-|) with initial change.[17] In any case, its presence on the syllable |sik-| of |sikIp-| TA 'bite' (< PA **sakipw-* TA) indicates that this was an initial syllable at the relevant earlier time period.

The analogical creation of allomorphs with initial Bl |i-| for all originally consonant-initial verb stems would account for the fact that the pronominal prefixes on verbs always occur with an incorporated |t|, which indicates that they only occurred before a vowel.

Conclusion

Some of the morphological features of Blackfoot that are very different from anything in Core Algonquian (notably the peripheral suffixes on verbs and the indefinite suffix on nouns) can be derived historically from a Proto-Algonquian reconstructed on the basis of the other languages, but others (notably the post-inflectional suffixes) must derive from an historical stage earlier than Proto-Algonquian. The generalization of vowel-initial verb stems points to the same conclusion. Blackfoot must therefore descend from a branch of the family that separated from the branch from which all the other languages descend, after which the ancestor of Core Algonquian (classical Proto-Algonquian) independently underwent shared innovations reflected in the descendant languages.

Many other features of Blackfoot morphology and lexicon remain to be explained in historical terms.

NOTES

1. Versions or sections of this paper were also presented at the Fifteenth and Sixteenth Spring Workshops on Theory and Method in Linguistic Reconstruction, Ann Arbor, Michigan, March 2014 and April 2016. I am grateful to Donald G. Frantz and Inge Genee for assistance with data and sources.

2. Some of the sound changes that will be encountered in this paper are these: PA *a > Bl i or a; PA *a˙ > Bl a or aa (underlying |a:| is set up for $a \sim aa$ [Frantz 1991:79–80]); PA *e > Bl i; PA *e˙ > Bl ii; medial PA *t, *$č$, *$š$, *$θ$, and *r > Bl t (i.e., -(s)t(s)-); intervocalic *h > Ø. PA *w and *y are lost after any consonant. Post-vocalic PA *w (> Bl |w|) > Bl y before word-final Bl -i and (at least in some cases) > Ø before word-medial Bl i (with shortening of a preceding long vowel). Bl t > ts before Bl i of any origin. Bl k > ks before Bl i if from PA *i (underlying Bl |I| [Frantz 1991:150]). Bl t > st after Bl i from PA *i (Bl |I|).

   Proto-Algonquian is reconstructed with *r for Bloomfield's *l and *sk for *xk (Goddard 1994:205). Also, *i- is written for underlying |e-| (instead of *e-), and initial and medial PA *o is written instead of *we, reverting to Bloomfield's (1925:133) reconstruction of *i- and *u (Goddard 2002:45, n. 2; cf. for *i- Proulx 1989:58, 68). There may, however, have been a contrastive PA *we across morpheme boundaries involving a few non-initial elements, as this is the situation in Meskwaki (Goddard 2001:174–175) and Shawnee (examples in Voegelin 1938–1940:81, 333), which have generally archaic vowel systems.

3. Abbreviations: abs. = absentative; AI = animate intransitive; AN, anim. = animate; Bl = Blackfoot; Cr = Plains Cree; DUR durative; EAb = Eastern Abenaki; ex. = example; exc. = exclusive; II = inanimate intransitive; IN, inan. = inanimate; inc. = inclusive; indef., INDEF = indefinite; Mal = Maliseet; Men = Menominee; Mes = Meskwaki (Fox); Mun = Munsee (Canadian Delaware); OB, obv, obv. = obviative; OBJ = object; p, pl, pl. = plural; PA = Proto-Algonquian; PAB = Proto–Algonquian-Blackfoot; PEA = Proto–Eastern Algonquian; PN = prenoun; prox. = proximate (non-obviative); s, sg, sg. = singular; Sh = Shawnee; TA = transitive animate; TI = transitive inanimate; TI-O = objectless transitive inanimate; Un = Unami.

   1 = first person; 1p = exclusive; 12 = inclusive; 2 = second person; 3 = third person animate; 3′ = third person animate obviative; 0 = third person inanimate; 0′ = third person inanimate obviative; 3′p–3s and 3′p–3p = third plural animate obviative acting on third singular and plural (objective); (3′)–3s third animate obviative acting on third singular (absolute).

   Arrows (← and →) indicate derivation or change by a morphological process, development, or reshaping; the signs > and < indicate phonological change. Bars (pipes: |...|) enclose abstract underlying forms (following the analysis of Frantz 1991,

2009); slashes (/. . ./) enclose phonemicizations; pointed brackets (⟨. . .⟩) enclose exact transcriptions of the source; * marks a reconstruction (assumed to have existed); † marks a phonemicization based on a non-phonemic transcription.

4. The indefinite inflection is no longer used by some speakers (Frantz 2009:viii). The term "indefinite" is used here in the standard sense it has in linguistics and logic, in preference to "non-referring" (Frantz 1991:10, 2009:11), "non-particular" (Frantz 1991:40, 2009:41), or "non-specific" (Taylor 1969:192). Nouns with this inflection are not non-referring expressions as this term is used in logic (since they can refer to real things), and they can be used for particular things, as in sentences like (8), in which specific eggs that might be seen and described are referred to.

5. The description of TI inflections as sorting into classes with different theme signs follows Bloomfield (1962:158–160); Frantz (1991:44) analyzes the vowels of the theme signs as part of the stem, taking -i as a morphologically conditioned shortening of -ii.

6. The third person endings are set up synchronically as |-yiiwa| and |-yiiyi|, but the |y| they begin with goes back to a stem-final PA *w, for example in forms that have Bl oy reflecting a stem-final PA *aw (as in (15d) below) or Bl iy reflecting PA *ahw.

7. The secondary origin of Blackfoot geminate consonants was demonstrated by Thomson (1978), who noted the apparent anomaly of the nn in the first plural suffix.

8. Underlying forms are listed where no whole-word examples were found (Frantz 1991:54–56); underlying |O| is realized as /o/, /Ø/ /, or /oo/, depending on the shape of the stem.

9. In sentences fused enclitic pronouns differentiate these forms when a subject noun does not follow the verb (Frantz 1991:20–22, 2009:21–22).

10. For compounding, initial-vowel reduction, and other processes that derive demonstratives in Algonquian languages, see Goddard (2003:80–86).

11. Forms from Donald Frantz (personal communication, 2016). Inanimate heads may also be objects (Frantz 1991:128).

12. Berman (2006:283, n. 34) has examples of noun stems dropping a final |S| or |N| before the noun final -ikin (or -iikin) 'bone'.

13. Ojibwe awiya 'somebody, anybody' is more likely an analogical refashioning of the expected inherited *awiyak (< PA *awiyaka) than a unique case of the retention of a final vowel in a three-syllable word. The paradigm has assimilated to that of monosyllabic nouns like nikka 'Canada goose', pl. nikkak.

14. In Frantz (2009:154) the ts in the prefix in such cases is accounted for by a rule geminating post consonantal s across a morpheme boundary; the generality of this rule is unclear, but apparently the preceding consonant can only be t or k, the two consonants

subject to assibilation before *i*. Another rule inserts *i* before stem-initial *s* under certain conditions. Berman (2006:265, 268, 271) discusses environments in which the "*i*-prefix" is inserted. On the available evidence it would seem preferable to take this variably present *i* as an underlying segment, with moderately complex conditions on its deletion, rather than to take it as an *i* inserted by phonologically unnatural rules.

15. Lemmata "ssksino" and "ssksini" but with a cross-reference to "issksini" (Frantz and Russell 1989:262, 1995:225); by the criterion for determining the stem given by Frantz and Russell (1995:xix) the stems begin with *i*-, since this is what follows the durative prefix *a*-. The *i* included at the end of the TI stem is part of the theme sign in third person endings (4); cf. n. 5.

16. Frantz (1991:126) has such a passive participle used for an inclusive subject.

17. Cf. Berman (2006:271), but initial change could not have been on a second syllable.

REFERENCES

Berman, Howard. 2006. Studies in Blackfoot prehistory. *International Journal of American Linguistics* 72:264–284.

———. 2007. A Blackfoot syncope rule. *International Journal of American Linguistics* 73:239–240.

Bloomfield, Leonard. 1925. On the sound-system of Central Algonquian. *Language* 1:130–156.

———. 1946. Algonquian. *Linguistic structures of Native America*, ed. by Harry Hoijer et al., pp. 85–129. Viking Fund Publications in Anthropology, vol. 6. New York: Wenner-Gren Foundation.

———. 1962. *The Menomini language*, ed. by Charles F. Hockett. New Haven, CT: Yale University Press.

Costa, David J. 2003. *The Miami-Illinois language.* Lincoln: University of Nebraska Press.

Fabvre, Bonaventure. 1970. Racines montagnaises. Transcribed by L. Angers and G. E. McNulty. Quebec: Université Laval.

Fox, Jacinta, and Donald G. Franz. 1979. Blackfoot clitic pronouns. *Papers of the Tenth Algonquian Conference*, ed. by William Cowan, pp. 152–166. Ottawa: Carleton University.

Frantz, Donald G. 1971. *Toward a generative grammar of Blackfoot (with particular attention to selected stem formation processes).* Norman: Summer Institute of Linguistics of the University of Oklahoma.

———. 1991. *Blackfoot grammar.* Toronto: University of Toronto Press.

———. 2009. *Blackfoot grammar.* 2nd ed. Toronto: University of Toronto Press.

Frantz, Donald G., and Norma Jean Russell. 1989. *Blackfoot dictionary of stems, roots, and affixes.* Toronto: University of Toronto Press.

———. 1995. *Blackfoot dictionary of stems, roots, and affixes.* 2nd ed. Toronto: University of Toronto Press.

Gipson, Lawrence Henry (ed.). 1938. *The Moravian Indian mission on White River.* Indianapolis: Indiana Historical Bureau.

Goddard, Ives. 1967. The Algonquian independent indicative. *Contributions to anthropology, Linguistics I (Algonquian),* ed. by A. D. DeBlois, pp. 66–106. National Museum of Canada Bulletin 214. Ottawa.

———. 1979. *Delaware verbal morphology: A descriptive and comparative study.* New York: Garland.

———. 1994. The west-to-east cline in Algonquian dialectology. *Actes du 25ᵉ Congrès des Algonquinistes,* ed. by William Cowan, pp. 187–211. Ottawa: Carleton University.

———. 2000. The historical origins of Cheyenne inflections. *Papers of the Thirty-First Algonquian Conference,* ed. by John D. Nichols, pp. 77–129. Winnipeg: University of Manitoba.

———. 2001. Contraction in Fox (Meskwaki). *Actes du Trente-Deuxième Congrès de Algonquinistes,* ed. by John D. Nichols, pp. 164–230. Winnipeg: University of Manitoba.

———. 2002. Explaining the double reflexes of word-initial high short vowels in Fox. *Diachronica* 19:43–80.

———. 2003. Reconstructing the history of the demonstrative pronouns of Algonquian. *Essays in Algonquian, Catawban, and Siouan linguistics in memory of Frank T. Siebert, Jr.,* ed. by Blair A. Rudes and David L. Costa, pp. 41–113. Winnipeg: University of Manitoba.

———. 2007. Reconstruction and history of the independent indicative. *Papers of the Thirty-Eighth Algonquian Conference,* ed. by H. C. Wolfart, pp. 207–271. Winnipeg: University of Manitoba.

———. 2010. Linguistic variation in a small speech community: The personal dialects of Moraviantown Delaware. *Anthropological Linguistics* 52(1):1–48.

———. 2015a. Three nineteenth-century Munsee texts: Archaisms, dialect variation, and problems of textual criticism. *New voices for old words,* ed. by David J. Costa, pp. 198–314. Lincoln: University of Nebraska Press.

———. 2015b. Arapaho historical morphology. *Anthropological Linguistics* 57(4):345–411.

Haas, Mary R. 1958. Algonkian-Ritwan: The end of a controversy. *International Journal of American Linguistics* 24:159–173.

Jones, William. 1907. *Fox texts.* American Ethnological Society Publications, vol. 1. Leiden: E. J. Brill for the American Ethnological Society.

LeSourd, Philip. 2003. The noun substitute in Maliseet-Passamaquoddy. *Essays in Algonquian,*

Catawban, and Siouan linguistics in memory of Frank T. Siebert, Jr., ed. by Blair A. Rudes and David L. Costa, pp. 141–163. Winnipeg: University of Manitoba.

Michelson, Truman. 1935. Phonetic shifts in Algonquian languages. *International Journal of American Linguistics* 8:131–171.

Proulx, Paul. 1988. The demonstrative pronouns of Proto-Algonquian. *International Journal of American Linguistics* 54:309–330.

———. 1989. A sketch of Blackfoot historical phonology. *International Journal of American Linguistics* 55:43–82.

Schupbach, Shannon Scott. 2013. The Blackfoot demonstrative system: Function, form, and meaning. MA thesis, University of Montana.

Silvy, Antoine. 1974. *Dictionnaire montagnais-français (ca 1678–1684)*. Transcribed by L. Angers, D. E. Cooter, and G. E. McNulty. Montreal: Les Presses de l'Université du Québec.

Taylor, Allan R. 1960. Blackfoot historical phonology: A preliminary survey. Ms. in the Survey of California and other Indian languages, University of California at Berkeley.

———. 1967. Initial change in Blackfoot. *Contributions to Anthropology: Linguistics I (Algonquian)*, pp. 147–156. National Museum of Canada Bulletin 214, Anthropological Series, vol. 78. Ottawa.

———. 1969. A grammar of Blackfoot. PhD thesis, University of California, Berkeley.

Thomson, Gregory E. 1978. The origin of Blackfoot geminate stops and nasals. *Linguistic studies of Native Canada*, ed. by E.-D. Cook and J. Kaye, pp. 89–109. Lisse: Peter de Ridder Press, and Vancouver: University of British Columbia Press.

Voegelin, Carl F. 1938–1940. Shawnee stems and the Jacob P. Dunn Miami dictionary, Parts I–V. *Indiana Historical Society Prehistory Research Series* 1:63–108, 135–167, 289–323, 345–406, 409–478.

On Ordering and Reordering Arguments

Michael David Hamilton

A cross Algonquian languages, it is common for the inner suffix (or Slot 6; Bloomfield 1946) to index either the subject or object, depending on the content of their person-features (φ-features).[1] There are two recent syntactic accounts that derive the distribution of the inner suffix in specific languages by reordering (Coon and Bale 2014) or equalizing (Oxford 2014) the relative structural asymmetry of subjects and objects in transitive forms. However, reordering or equalizing of subjects and objects in the syntax should be detectable via diagnostics for structural height. In this paper I outline the distribution of the inner suffix in the Listuguj dialect of Mi'gmaq and explore the applicability of versions of these syntactic movement accounts. Following Hamilton (2015), I employ Long-Distance Agreement (LDA) as a diagnostic for the structurally highest argument in embedded clauses in Mi'gmaq. This allows me to test the predictions that syntactic movement accounts make for the relative height of subjects and objects. Ultimately, I conclude that an account that does not involve reordering or equalizing the asymmetry between arguments is the most appropriate for inner suffixes and LDA in Mi'gmaq. The main descriptive point is that there is no clear link between inner suffix indexing and the patterning of LDA in Mi'gmaq. This leads to the main theoretical point that there need not be a link between agreement and argument movement, and assuming such leads to a much simpler account of syntactic derivation in Mi'gmaq.

The paper is organized as follows: in the next two sections, I introduce the distribution of inner suffixes and the patterning of LDA, respectively, in Mi'gmaq. Following this, I outline two accounts of inner suffixes, and test their applicability to Mi'gmaq based on their prediction of the relative height of subjects and objects with LDA data. Before concluding, I present an alternative proposal that derives inner suffix indexing and the LDA data in a simpler manner.

Inner Suffix

The inner suffix is a verbal affix that typically indexes the φ-features of a single argument, regardless of how many arguments are present in the structure. Table 1 shows the inventory of inner suffixes in Mi'gmaq.

TABLE 1. Mi'gmaq inner suffixes

PERSON	SINGULAR	PLURAL
1	-∅	-eg (EX), -gw (IN)
2	-n	-oq
3	-t/-g	-'tit

Across Algonquian languages, the inner suffix displays a preference for plural Speech Act Participant (SAP) arguments over all other arguments regardless of grammatical role. This is also common in Mi'gmaq. I present transitive forms in three groupings: local (only SAP arguments), mixed (one SAP and one third person argument), and third person (only third person arguments). In local forms, SAP plural forms are indexed when present, regardless of grammatical role. If both arguments are plural, then first person plural is preferentially indexed, rather than second person.[2] This is shown in (1), as first person plural is indexed if it is the subject (1b) or object (1a).[3] If one argument is plural, it is always indexed. If both are singular, only the subject is indexed. Local forms are summarized in Table 2.

TABLE 2. Local forms

2PL> 1PL(EX)	*-eg*	1PL(EX) > 2PL	*-eg*
2PL >1	*-oq*	1> 2PL	*-oq*
2> 1PL(EX)	*-eg*	1PL(EX) >2	*-eg*
2 >1	*-n*	1 >2	*-∅*

(1) a. 2/2PL> 1PL

    ges-al-i-**eg**

    love-AN-1OBJ-1PL

    'You(-all) love **us(EX)**'

  b. 1PL > 2/2PL

    ges-al-uln-**eg**

    love-AN-2OBJ-1PL

    '**We(EX)** love you(-all)'

In mixed forms, in which there is one SAP and one third person argument, SAP plural forms are similarly indexed preferentially. This is shown in the first three rows in Table 3. When SAP plural forms are absent, third person is indexed preferentially. This is shown in the last two rows in Table 3 and in (2). Here, third person is indexed regardless of whether it is the subject (2b) or object (2a). (2b) is somewhat special in that it appears to be a portmanteau of third person subject and second person object (*-'sg*).[4]

(2) a. 2> 3

    ges-al-**t**

    love-AN-**3**

    'You love **her/him**'

  b. 3 > 2

    ges-al-**'sg**

    love-AN-**3>2**

    '**S/he** loves you'

TABLE 3. Mixed forms

1PL(EX) >3	-eg	3> 1PL(EX)	-eg
1PL(IN) >3	-gw	3> 1PL(IN)	-gw
2PL >3	-oq	3> 2PL	-oq
1> 3	-t/g	3 >1	-t/g
2> 3	-t/g	3 > 2	-'sg

TABLE 4. 3rd person forms

3 >4(PL)	-t/g	4 >3(PL)	-t/g
3PL >4(PL)	-tit	4PL >3(PL)	-tit

Third person forms pattern with SAP singular local forms in that the subject is always indexed. When we change the grammatical role of third person singular in (3), it is indexed by the inner suffix when it is the subject (3a) but not when it is the object (3b).[5] Table 4 summarizes third person forms. Note that only the plurality of the subject is important in these forms.[6]

(3) a. 3 >4PL

   Mali ges-al-a-j-i

   Mary love-AN-3OBJ-3-3PL

   '**Mary** loves them'

   b. 4PL >3

   ges-al-gwi'-**tit**-l

   love-**AN-INV-3PL**-OBV

   'S/he loves **them**'

In sum, any potential account needs to address both: (i) preferences that are independent of grammatical role in the majority of forms (e.g., 1PL in local and mixed forms, otherwise third person in mixed forms), as well as (ii) the importance of grammatical role in others (e.g., subjects with SAP singular local forms and third person forms). In the next section, I outline the patterning of LDA in Mi'gmaq. I use this as a diagnostic for the structural height of embedded arguments. This becomes important in assessing accounts that derive inner suffix indexing via argument movement.

Long-Distance Agreement

Long-Distance Agreement involves forms in which multiple clauses share the same
argument (e.g., Polinsky and Potsdam 2001; Branigan and MacKenzie 2002). In a
slight revision of Dahlstrom (1991), Hamilton (2015) uses the restricted LDA pattern
in Mi'gmaq as a means to determine the relative structural height of embedded
arguments.[7] In Mi'gmaq, LDA is restricted only to the embedded subject, except in
third person inverse forms, in which it is restricted to the object. In this section I
show the LDA pattern by embedding the local, mixed, and third person examples
from the previous section.

Beginning with local forms, if we embed the examples from (1), we see that
LDA is only possible with the embedded subject, as shown in the (a) examples, but
not the object, as shown in the (b) examples.[8] The argument in bold is the one that
the matrix verb targets for LDA, and the underlined argument is the one that the
inner suffix on the embedded verb indexes.

(4) EMBEDDED 2PL>1PL FORM

    a. LDA WITH EMBEDDED SUBJECT

        gej-ugsi-**oq**   [ges-al-i-<u>eg</u>]

        know.AN-3>SAPPL-**2PL**   [love-AN-1OBJ-<u>1PL</u>]

        'S/he knows that **you(-all)** love <u>us (EXC)</u>'

    b. No LDA WITH EMBEDDED OBJECT

        *gej-ugsi-**eg**   [ges-al-i-<u>eg</u>]

        know.AN-3>SAPPL-**1PL**   [love-AN-1OBJ-<u>1PL</u>]

        intended: 'S/he knows that you(-all) love **us (EXC)**'

(5) EMBEDDED 1PL>2PL FORM

    a. LDA WITH EMBEDDED SUBJECT

        gej-ugsi-**eg**   [ges-al-uln-<u>eg</u>]

        know.AN-3>SAPPL-**1PL**   [love-AN-1OBJ-<u>1PL</u>]

        'S/he knows that <u>**we (EXC)**</u> love you(-all)'

    b. No LDA WITH EMBEDDED OBJECT

        *gej-ugsi-**oq**   [ges-al-uln-<u>eg</u>]

        know.AN-3>SAPPL-**2PL**   [love-AN-1OBJ-<u>1PL</u>]

        intended: 'S/he knows that <u>we (EXC)</u> love **you(-all)**'

In (4), the matrix verb can only LDA with the second person plural embedded subject, as evidenced by the fact that the matrix verb can appear with a second person plural inner suffix (-*oq*) in (4a) but not a first person plural inner suffix (-*eg*) in (4b). Similarly, when the grammatical roles of the embedded arguments are switched in (5), the matrix verb can only LDA with the first person plural embedded subject. This is shown by the fact that the matrix verb can now appear with a first person plural inner suffix (-*eg*) in (5a) but not with a second person plural inner suffix (-*oq*) in (5b).

Also note that the argument that is indexed as the inner suffix on the embedded verb can also be the argument that the matrix verb targets for LDA, e.g., first person plural in (5a). However, this need not be the case, as first person plural is indexed by the embedded verb in (4), but it cannot be the target of LDA, as shown by the unacceptability of (4b). This will also hold for the mixed and third person forms below.

Continuing with mixed forms, if we embed the examples from (2), LDA continues to only be possible with the embedded subject, as in the (a) examples, but not the object, as in the (b) examples.

(6) Embedded 2>3 form

　　a. LDA with embedded subject

　　　　gej(i)-**u'l**　　　　[ges-al-ṭ]

　　　　know.AN-**2OBJ**　　[love-AN-3̱]

　　　　'I know that **you** love <u>her/him</u>'

　　b. No LDA with embedded object

　　　　*geji'-**g**　　　　[ges-al-ṭ]

　　　　know.AN-**3**　　　[love-AN-3̱]

　　　　intended: 'I know that you love **<u>her/him</u>**'

(7) Embedded 3>2 form

　　a. LDA with embedded subject

　　　　geji'-**g**　　　　[ges-al-'ṣg]

　　　　know.AN-**3**　　　[love-AN-3̱>2]

　　　　'I know that <u>s/he</u> loves <u>you</u>'

b. No LDA WITH EMBEDDED OBJECT

    *gej(i)-**u'l**   [ges-al-'sg]

    know.AN-**2OBJ**   [love-AN-3>2]

    intended: 'I know that s/he loves **you**'

In (6), the matrix verb can only LDA with the second person singular embedded subject, as evidenced by the fact that the matrix verb can appear with a second person plural theme sign (*-u'l*), as in (6a), but not a third person inner suffix (*-g*), as in (6b). Similarly, when the grammatical roles of the embedded arguments are switched in (7), the matrix verb can now only LDA with the third person embedded subject. This is shown by the fact that the matrix verb can appear with a third person inner suffix (*-g*), as in (7a), but not with the second person plural theme sign (*-u'l*), as in (7b).

However, turning to third person forms, while the LDA is still limited to the subject in the direct, as in (8a), in the inverse it is limited to the object, as in (9b).

(8)   EMBEDDED 3>4P FORM

    a. LDA WITH EMBEDDED SUBJECT

        geji'-**g**   [ges-al-a-j-i]

        know.AN-**3**   [love-AN-3OBJ-3-3PL]

        'I know that s/he loves them'

    b. No LDA WITH EMBEDDED OUBJECT

        *geji'-g-**ig**   [ges-al-a-j-i]

        know.AN-3-**3PL** [love-AN-3OBJ-3-3PL]

        intended: 'I know that s/he loves **them**'

(9)   EMBEDDED 4P>3 FORM

    a. No LDA WITH EMBEDDED SUBJECT

        *geji'-g-**ig**   [ges-al-gwi'-tit -l]

        know.AN-3-**3PL** [love-AN-INV-3PL-OBV]

        'I know that **they** love her/ him'

b. LDA WITH EMBEDDED OBJECT

geji'-**g**   [ges-al-<u>gwi'</u>-tit-l]

know.AN-**3**   [love-AN-INV-<u>3PL</u>-OBV]

intended: 'I know that <u>they</u> love **her/him**'

In the embedded direct form in (8), the matrix verb can only LDA with the third
person singular embedded subject, as evidenced by the fact that the matrix verb can
appear with a third person inner suffix (-*g*), as in (8a), but not additionally a third
person plural outer suffix (-*ig*), as in (8b). Unlike the other forms we have seen so
far, when the grammatical roles of the embedded arguments are switched, as in the
embedded inverse form in (9), the matrix verb can only LDA with the third person
singular embedded object. This is shown by the fact that the matrix verb can still
only appear with a third person inner suffix (-*g*), as in (9b), but not additionally
with the third person plural outer suffix (-*ig*), as in (9a).

   In sum, LDA is limited to the subject in all local, mixed, and direct third person
forms. Third person inverse forms are exceptional in that LDA is limited to the object. At first glance, the commonality for either the subject or object being indexed
by the inner suffix appears to contrast with the typical rigidity of LDA to be limited
to the subject in Mi'gmaq. This would appear to make accounts of the inner suffix
that reorder or equalize subject-object asymmetries unlikely to be able to account
for LDA patterns. In the next section I outline two recent accounts, apply them to
Mi'gmaq, and show that they cannot capture both sets of inner suffix and LDA data
without numerous assumptions. I then present a simpler nonmovement account.

Potential Accounts

In this section I present two different accounts, both of which assume: (i) a probe-
goal account of AGREE (Chomsky 2000), in which a functional head with a probe
bearing features (e.g., person features) can search its local domain for an argument
with matching features; (ii) the inner suffix is indexed on a functional head above
the verbal domain, e.g., T^0 or $Infl^0$; and (iii) subjects are base-generated in the
verbal domain structurally higher than objects (i.e., grammatical role is crucially
linked to structural position). I will not take issue with any of these assumptions.
The accounts I present either reorder or equalize the assumed base-generated
subject-object asymmetry in order to account for the distribution of the inner

suffix. I will assess the applicability of these accounts for Mi'gmaq in terms of both the inner suffix data and the consequences for subject-object asymmetries via the LDA data.

Coon and Bale (2014)

The first account proposes that the argument indexed as the inner suffix is also the structural highest argument, which results in the reordering of arguments when the object is indexed. This account is driven by a proposed intermediate functional projection (FP) between TP and VoiceP. This is headed by F^0, which has a fused number (#) and person (π) probe that has the ability to search both the subject and object, as shown in (10).

(10)

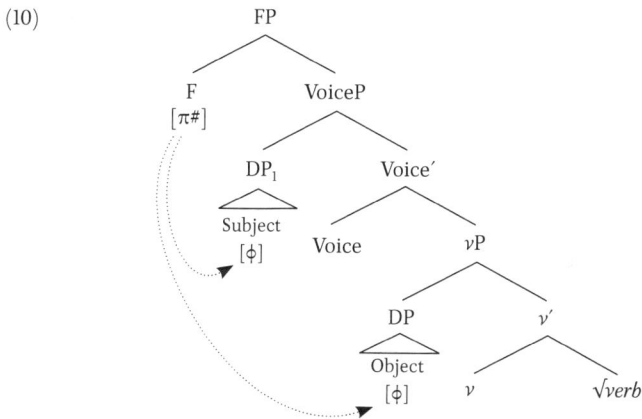

In the fused probe, the #-probe has a built-in preference for plural, and the π-probe has built-in preferences for SAP, e.g., via a [PARTICIPANT] feature. Only if an argument is both plural and SAP is the probe fully satisfied. This derives the preference for SAP plural arguments. The preference for first person over second person is derived via an additional feature on the π-probe, e.g., [SPEAKER].[9] In order to derive the full inner suffix pattern, in addition to Coon and Bale's fused # and π-probe, the φ-probe needs to have a feature that searches for third person arguments, e.g., [D]. This would derive the preference for third person when an SAP plural argument is not present. An example of this probe is shown in (11).

(11)

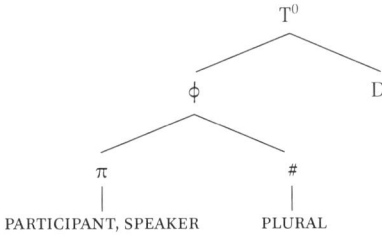

Additionally, one way to derive the higher-ranking preference for subjects is to assume that the probe searches the subject first and the object second, e.g., via Cyclic Agree (Béjar and Rezac 2009). The probe would only index the object if it more fully satisfies the probe, such as if the object is: (i) first person plural, (ii) second person plural when the subject is not first person plural, or (iii) third person when the subject is not SAP plural. The set of assumptions regarding probe preferences would derive the inner suffix pattern.

Once F^0 agrees with the argument that most fully satisfies the probe, Coon and Bale (2014) posit that it attracts this argument to Spec-FP via an EPP feature, as shown in (12). This can either be the subject, as in (12a), or the object, as in (12b), which moves over the subject in a manner similar to a Bruening-style (2001, 2009) inverse movement. Once F^0 has attracted the relevant argument, T^0 agrees with it via a φ-feature probe, and raises it to Spec-TP via an EPP feature. Thus, it is always the case that the same DP that is attracted to Spec-FP is also attracted to Spec-TP. In fact, the sole purpose of FP appears to be to ensure that T^0 agrees with the most satisfying argument, therefore providing a potential position for the object to move over the subject.

(12)   a.

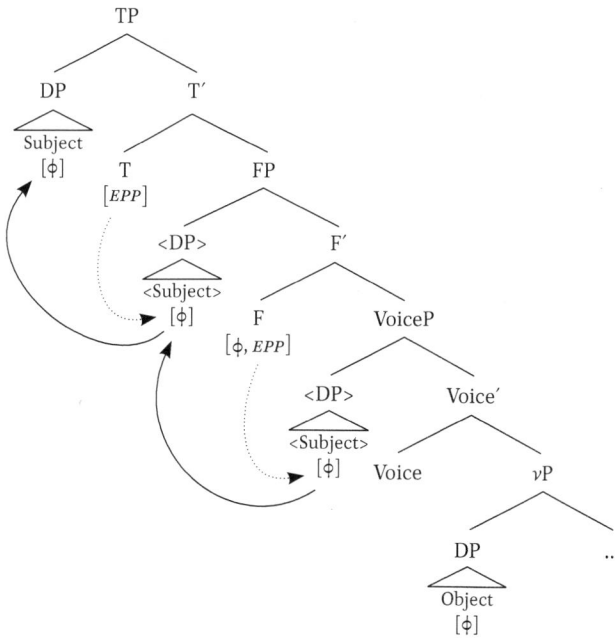

b.

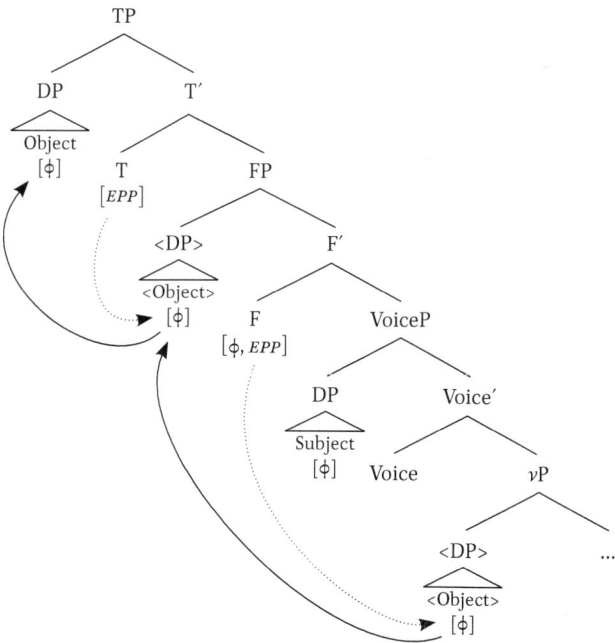

TABLE 5. Coon & Bale (2014): LDA predictions

	PREDICTIONS		ATTESTED	
Local	2PL>[1PL]	[1PL]>2PL	[2PL]>1PL	[1PL]>2PL
	[2PL]>1	1>[2PL]	[2PL]>1	[1]>2PL
	2>[1PL]	[1PL]>2	[2]>1PL	[1PL]>2
	[2]>1	[1]>2	[2]>1	[1]>2
Mixed	[2PL]>3	3>[2PL]	[2PL]>3	[3]>2PL
	[1PL(EX)]>3	3>[1PL(EX)]	[1PL(EX)]>3	[3]>1PL(EX)
	[1PL(IN)]>3	3>[1PL(IN)]	[1PL(IN)]>3	[3]>1PL(IN)
	2>[3]	[3]>[2]	[2]>3	[3]>2
	2>[3]	[3]>1	[1]>3	[3]>1
3rd person	[3]>4	[4]>3	[3]>4	4>[3]

This account crucially links inner suffix indexing to structural height. This is because the argument that the inner suffix indexes is attracted to a derived position in Spec-TP, which is always structurally higher than the non-indexed argument in its base-generated position. This makes the prediction that LDA should only be possible with the embedded argument that is indexed as the inner suffix on T^0. This is shown in the predictions column in Table 5. However, several of these are incorrect, as we can see when compared to the actual pattern in the attested column of Table 5. Incorrect predictions are highlighted.

Whenever the subject is indexed, it will remain the structurally highest, and this account correctly predicts it to be the only one available for LDA, e.g., local 2(PL)>1, mixed 2PL>3, and third person (direct) 3>4. Whenever the object is indexed, it is hypothesized to move over the subject, and this account would incorrectly predict it to be the only one available for LDA, e.g., local 2PL>1PL and mixed 3>2PL. The only exceptions to these two patterns are when: (i) both the subject and object are indexed, e.g., 3>2, as both should be available for LDA assuming that they are both attracted to F^0 and T^0 (although only third person is present in these forms); and (ii) third person inverse 4>3 forms, in which the fourth person subject is predicted to undergo LDA (but only the third person object can).

In order to revise this account, we would need to assume that a higher functional head, e.g., C^0, always attracts the subject (except in the third person inverse cases), thus retaining its position as the structurally highest, even when the object has moved over it. However, we would additionally need to assume that subjects and objects have a corresponding feature in the syntax apart from their base-generated position, in order to distinguish them when their relative order is reversed, e.g., when the object is attracted over the subject to F^0 and T^0. These would be two additional stipulations to this account, in addition to the multiple existing assumptions regarding the extra FP, probe specification, probe searching, and the EPP features on both F^0 and T^0.

Oxford (2014)

The second account proposes that the ability for either the subject or object to be indexed as the inner suffix is indicative of both being equidistant from the φ-probe on $Infl^0$, which drives inner suffix indexing. Under this account, $Voice^0$ has a φ-feature and an EPP feature such that it agrees with the object DP and attracts it to Spec-VoiceP, as shown in (13).[10] Following Chomsky (2000), among others, Oxford (2014) assumes that multiple DPs in the specifier position of the same functional projection are equidistant from higher probes.

(13)

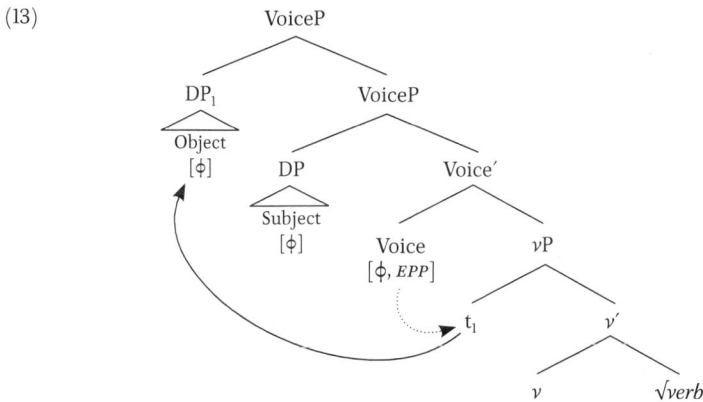

Under this account there is an InflP above VoiceP and below NegP (similar to Coon and Bale's [2014] FP) and $Infl^0$ has a complex φ-probe. Since the subject and object DPs are equidistant from $Infl^0$, both can be searched and agreed with by $Infl^0$, as shown in (14).

(14)

```
                          InflP
                    _____/_____
                   /              \
                Infl             VoiceP
                [φ]          ___/\___
                            /        \
                          DP         Voice′
                        __/\__    ___/\___
                       Object    /        \
                        [φ]      DP       Voice′
                               __/\__   ___/\___
                              Subject  /        \
                               [φ]   Voice     ...
```

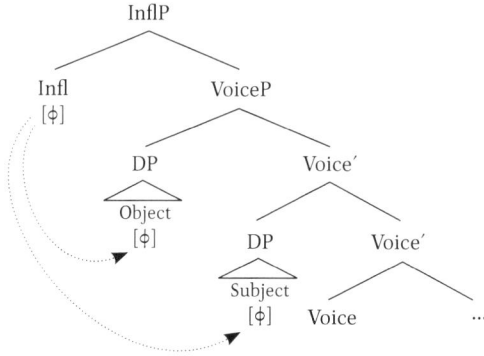

The process by which the probe selects an argument could occur in the syntax itself, similar to the probe specification and probe search assumptions discussed for Coon and Bale (2014). However, since both are equidistant structurally, an additional mechanism or feature is necessary in order to distinguish the subject from the object.[11] Another option is that selection could occur postsyntactically, so the probe would simply collect the φ-features of both arguments and the distribution of the inner suffix would then be determined by post-syntactic Vocabulary Insertion rules (e.g., Halle 1997).[12] Regardless of which method is chosen, the end result of this process is that the inner suffix appears postsyntactically as agreement on T^0 (Bobaljik 2008).

As this account stands, if both arguments are equidistant from higher probes, then either the subject or object should be able to undergo LDA. However, LDA is only ever possible with a single argument, thus additional assumptions are necessary. Oxford (2014) proposes the possibility of the highest-ranking argument being attracted by an EPP feature on T^0. In order to limit attraction to one argument, and therefore to make the analysis more plausible for our LDA data, I depart from Oxford (2014) and propose a strict Person Hierarchy, such as 1>2>3>4. The resulting predictions for LDA are shown in the predictions column in Table 6. Compared with the actual data in the attested column, the incorrect predictions are highlighted.

TABLE 6. Oxford (2014) revised: LDA predictions

	PREDICTIONS		ATTESTED	
Local	[2PL]>1PL	1PL>[2PL]	[2PL]>1PL	[1PL]>2PL
	[2PL]>1	[1]>[2PL]	[2PL]>1	[1]>2PL
	[2]>1	1>[2]	[2]>1	[1]>2
	[2]>1	1>[2]	[2]>1	[1]>2
Mixed	[2PL]>3	3>[2PL]	[2PL]>3	[3]>2PL
	[1PL(EX)]>3	3>[1PL(EX)]	[1PL(EX)]>3	[3]>1PL(EX)
	[1PL(IN)]>3	3>[1PL(IN)]	[1PL(IN)]>3	[3]>1PL(IN)
	[2]>3	3>[2]	[2]>3	[3]>2
	[1]>3	3>[1]	[1]>3	[3]>1
3rd person	[3]>4	4>[3]	[3]>4	4>[3]

This revised account correctly predicts the distribution of LDA in third person forms, since LDA is limited to third person arguments, which are assumed to be higher on the Person Hierarchy than fourth persons. However, in local and mixed forms, only correct predictions are made when the subject is ranked higher than the object, e.g., first person subjects in local forms and SAP subjects in mixed forms. When the object outranks the subject, e.g., first person objects in local forms and SAP objects in mixed forms, it would be predicted to move over the subject, thus incorrectly predicted to be structurally higher and the only argument available to undergo LDA. It is important to note that even if we use a 2>1>3>4 Person Hierarchy, the same incorrect predictions would occur in mixed forms and an equal number—but different set—of local forms would be incorrect. Thus, linking structural height to the Person Hierarchy does not approximate the LDA pattern in Mi'gmaq.

An alternate revision, suggested by a reviewer, is to assume that T^0 has an EPP feature that always attracts the subject, which is similar to the revision necessary for Coon and Bale's (2014) account as well. The predictions column in Table 7 shows this revised account, assuming that there is a nonstructural mechanism available to distinguish the subject from the object.

TABLE 7. Oxford (2014) + Subject EPP: LDA predictions

	PREDICTIONS		ATTESTED	
Local	[2PL]>1PL	[1PL]>2PL	[2PL]>1PL	[1PL]>2PL
	[2PL]>1	[1]>2PL	[2PL]>1	[1]>2PL
	[2]>1PL	[1PL]>2	[2]>1PL	[1PL]>2
	[2]>1	[1]>2	[2]>1	[1]>2
Mixed	[2PL]>3	[3]>2PL	[2PL]>3	[3]>2PL
	[1PL(EX)]>3	[3]>1PL(EX)	[1PL(EX)]>3	[3]>1PL(EX)
	[1PL(IN)]>3	[3]>1PL(IN)	[1PL(IN)]>3	[3]>1PL(IN)
	[2]>3	[3]>2	[2]>3	[3]>2
	[1]>3	[3]>1	[1]>3	[3]>1
3rd person	[3]>4	[4]>3	[3]>4	4>[3]

This revised account covers all forms, except for third person ones, since the subject in the inverse 4>3 form is predicted to undergo LDA, but only the object can participate. This fares much better than the Person Hierarchy revision of this theory or Coon and Bale (2014). However, there are many assumptions involved, including object shift, equidistance, either a syntactic or post-syntactic process for indexing the inner suffix, a nonstructural mechanism for distinguishing arguments, and an EPP feature on T^0. Taking a step back, essentially this revised account equalizes the assumed base-generated subject-object asymmetry for the purposes of probing, only to then reintroduce the very same asymmetry again in order to derive the LDA data. This can be avoided if the probe has the ability to search multiple non-equidistant arguments, such as the probe proposed on F^0 by Coon and Bale (2014). In the next section I propose an account that employs such a probe in order to derive the distribution of the inner suffix while avoiding unnecessary DP movement altogether.

Proposal

Previously, I showed that the inner suffix typically indexes either the subject or object, while LDA is typically restricted to embedded subjects. Then I showed that accounts that link inner suffix indexing to argument movement had a difficult time accounting for the Mi'gmaq LDA data without additional stipulations. In this section, I outline a simpler account that does not involve argument movement, but relies on the ability of the probe on T^0 to search multiple arguments.

To begin, I make the same basic assumptions as the three previous accounts: (i) a probe-goal account of AGREE, (ii) the inner suffix is indexed by a probe on T^0, and (iii) subjects are base-generated structurally higher than objects. Based on the third assumption alone, we can account for the same range of LDA data as the revised Oxford (2014) account in Table 7: local, mixed, and third person direct forms. All we need to assume additionally is a means to derive the distribution of the inner suffix without argument movement, thus, simply based on the properties of the probe alone. We can do this by following the assumptions about the probe on F^0 in Coon and Bale (2014), although I depart from their account by assuming that this probe (i) is on T^0, and (ii) does not have an EPP feature, so it does not attract an argument to its specifier. This is shown in (15).

(15)

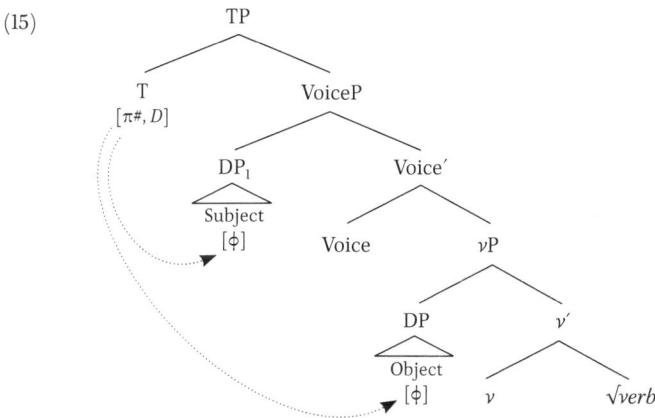

The proposal that a probe can search two arguments is similar to the assumption made by Coon and Bale (2014), and departs from Oxford (2014) in not assuming that equidistance is a necessary precondition for the probe to search multiple arguments. But it is important to take a closer look at the possibilities for how probe searching could occur. For our purposes, there are three different possibilities, as the probe can: (i) search arguments one-by-one, (ii) search arguments all at once, or (iii) search only the two structurally highest arguments. The first would be to assume that the probe searches arguments one-by-one (e.g., Cyclic Agree; Béjar and Rezac 2009). This was outlined for the Coon and Bale (2014) account and had the additional possibility to give primacy to the subject in indexing. One potential complication of such an account is that forms with an SAP plural subject would be predicted to not have portmanteau forms, since the probe would never search the object as it is satisfied with the subject. Although this is not a problem for the Mi'gmaq inner suffix data presented here, it may become an issue if applied to other inner suffix data sets, such as the conjunct forms in Oxford (2014).

The second option is for the probe to search and gather all of the person features of all the arguments in the syntax, and for selection to be determined post-syntactically (e.g., Multiple Agree; Nevins 2011). This was outlined as a possibility for the Oxford (2014) account. One advantage of such an account is that since the argument indexed by the inner suffix is not determined in the syntax, we would not expect there to be any syntactic reflex, such as DP movement. This fits well with the LDA data in Mi'gmaq. One possible complication of this account is that since my proposal does not include object shift or equidistance, the person features of all arguments would be gathered, which in ditransitive forms would include all three arguments. However, inner suffix indexing is limited to the two structurally highest arguments (the subject and indirect object). Thus in ditransitive 1>2>3 forms, we might predict the third person to be indexed by the inner suffix, given the preference for third person in 1>3 and 2>3 forms. However, this is not the case, as the lowest argument (the direct object) is never indexed by the inner suffix, thus, a 1>2>3 form is indexed the same as a 1>2 form.

The third option, which avoids the Multiple Agree problem, would be to specify that the probe can only search the two structurally highest arguments relative to the probe, regardless of whether there is a third argument present in the syntax (e.g., Despić et al. 2016). The distribution of the inner suffix could then be derived in the syntax, as in the first option, or post-syntactically, as in the second option.

Independent of which option we chose, my proposal only relies on assumptions necessary to all potential accounts: (i) probe searching, (ii) location of probe preferences (syntactic or post-syntactic), and (iii) an additional mechanism for deriving the inverse, e.g., an EPP feature higher head, such as C^0 (following Hamilton's [2015] account of LDA), or on T^0 itself (if we follow Lochbihler and Mathieu's [2016] account of LDA). This proposal improves the empirical coverage of Coon and Bale (2014) without relying on many of their assumptions, such as an additional FP, EPP features on F^0 and T^0, and a (potentially) higher probe to raise the subject. This proposal also equals the empirical coverage of the second revised version of Oxford (2014) without relying on as many assumptions, e.g., object shift, equidistance, and an EPP feature on T^0. Thus, an account of inner suffix indexing and LDA, which does not necessarily link agreement to argument movement (e.g., EPP features), is relatively simpler and provides equal or greater empirical coverage.

Conclusion

In this paper I presented data from Mi'gmaq on the distribution of the inner suffix and LDA side-by-side in order to show that they are largely independent of each other. Grammatical role is largely irrelevant for inner suffix indexing, apart from a limited number of forms, while it is very important in the patterning of LDA. I showed that theories that employ argument movement as a means to derive the distribution of the inner suffix need a host of additional assumptions in order to approximate the restricted LDA pattern in Mi'gmaq. I proposed a simpler account that does not rely on argument movement, but simply on probe preferences and inverse movement, which any account needs to assume, in order to derive both inner suffix and LDA patterning.

While this paper focused specifically on Mi'gmaq, future research is necessary to investigate whether this proposal can also account for other Algonquian languages. Restricted LDA patterns have also been reported for Plains Cree (Dahlstrom 1991) and two dialects of Ottawa (Rhodes 1994); thus, these would be the best places to continue research. Since it is much more difficult to discern subject-object asymmetries in languages with less-restricted LDA patterns, such as Passamaquoddy (Bruening 2001) and Innu-aimûn (Branigan and MacKenzie 2002), it would be necessary to employ different subject-object diagnostics in order to see what, if any, relationship structural height has with inner suffix indexing in these languages.

NOTES

1. I would like to thank Janine Metallic, Mary Ann Metallic, Janice Vicaire, and Joe Wilmot for sharing their knowledge of Mi'gmaq; and Jessica Coon, Alan Bale, Miloje Despić, Sarah E. Murray, and the Cornell Syntax Circle for their helpful feedback. All errors are entirely my own responsibility.

2. In forms in which there are both second and first person plural arguments, Algonquian languages vary in whether they preferentially index one or the other. First person plural is preferentially indexed over second person plural in Mi'gmaq, Menominee, Blackfoot,

Plains Cree, Atikamekw, East Cree, Betsiamites, and Moisie (MacKenzie 1980; Macaulay 2009); second person plural is preferentially indexed instead of first person plural in Moose Cree, Swampy Cree and Davis Inlet Cree (MacKenzie 1980; Macaulay 2009)

3. Abbreviations: 1 = first person, 2 = second person, 3 = animate third person singular proximate (discourse salient), AN = animate, DIR = direct, EX = exclusive, IN = inclusive, INV = inverse, LOC = local, OBJ = object, PL = plural, SAP = speech act participant (first and/or second person), X>Y = X agent, Y patient.

4. Note that this portmanteau does not appear in the negative form, as shown in (i). The negation suffix (-u) appears between the theme sign (-uln first person object) and the inner suffix indexes third person (-g). This shows that it patterns with the other mixed forms with a singular SAP argument, in that third person is indexed by the inner suffix.

(i) Mu   ges-al-uln-u-**g**
    NEG   love-AN-1OBJ-NEG-**3**
    '**S/he** doesn't love you'

5. Note that in (3b) third person plural is indexed by the outer suffix (-ig), but not the inner suffix.

6. Note that fourth person refers to obviative third person forms, which are relatively less topical than proximate third person forms.

7. Although a reviewer points out that many analyses of LDA involve the structurally highest argument, regardless of whether the pattern is restrictive or not, there is an interesting difference in what typical analyses of nonrestrictive and restrictive patterns of LDA refer to when they use the term "structurally highest." Analyses of less-restrictive LDA patterns, e.g., Bruening 2001 and Branigan and MacKenzie 2002, often posit the structurally highest argument to be in a derived position in the left-periphery of the embedded clause. However, in analyses of more-restrictive LDA patterns, e.g., Dahlstrom 1991 and Hamilton 2015, the structurally highest argument typically refers to the one highest in the argument structure (or verbal domain) with the potential exception of inverse forms in some languages, e.g., (9b) in Mi'gmaq.

8. Note that the LDA forms presented here were checked with multiple speakers over multiple sessions. Acceptability judgments remain constant when presented in isolation or within a context.

9. Although this derives the specific pattern in Mi'gmaq, this can be reversed for languages in which second person is preferred over first person via a different feature, e.g., [ADDRESSEE].

10. The motivation for object shift here is twofold. It allows the object (i) to be local enough to be probed by Infl^0, and (ii) to escape the edge of the verbal domain, under the assumption that if it remained in situ, it would be opaque to higher probes outside of the verbal domain, i.e., trapped in a phase (Chomsky 2000).

11. One possibility that Oxford (2014) suggests is the Activity Condition (Chomsky 2000), which would make the object unable to undergo further instances of agreement after already being the target of a previous instance of agreement.

12. In both revisions of Oxford's (2014) account discussed below, an EPP feature attracts one of the arguments independent of which argument is indexed by the inner suffix. As such, the post-syntactic account would fit these revisions better, since under a purely syntactic account, we would have to assume that a probe could agree with one argument, but raise another.

REFERENCES

Béjar, Susana, and Milan Rezac. 2009. Cyclic agree. *Linguistic Inquiry* 40(1):35–73.

Bloomfield, Leonard. 1946. Algonquian. *Linguistic structures of Native America*, ed. by Harry Hoijer, pp. 85–129. Viking Fund Publications in Anthropology, vol. 6. New York: Wenner-Gren Foundation.

Bobaljik, Jonathan David. 2008. Where's phi? Agreement as a post-syntactic operation. *Phi-theory: Phi features across interfaces and modules*, ed. by David Adger, Daniel Harbour, and Susana Béjar, pp. 295–328. New York: Oxford University Press.

Branigan, Phil, and Marguerite MacKenzie. 2002. Altruism, A'-movement, and object agreement in Innu-aimûn. *Linguistic Inquiry* 33(3):385–407.

Bruening, Benjamin. 2001. Syntax at the edge: Cross-clausal phenomena and the syntax of Passamaquoddy. PhD thesis, MIT.

———. 2009. Algonquian languages have A-movement and A-agreement. *Linguistic Inquiry* 40(3):427–445.

Chomsky, Noam. 2000. Minimalist inquiries: The framework. *Step by step: Essays on minimalist syntax in honor of Howard Lasnik*, ed. by Roger Martin, David Michaels, and Juan Uriagereka, pp. 89–156. Cambridge, MA: MIT Press.

Coon, Jessica and Alan Bale. 2014. The interaction of person and number in Mi'gmaq. *NordLyd* 41(1):85–101.

Dahlstrom, A. 1991. *Plains Cree morphosyntax*. New York: Garland.

Despić, Miloje, Michael David Hamilton, and Sarah E. Murray. 2016. Multiple and Cyclic Agree: Person/number marking in Cheyenne. *34th West Coast Conference on Formal Linguistics,* ed. by Aaron Kaplan, Abby Kaplan, and Edward J. Rubin, pp. 167–176. Somerville, MA: Cascadilla Press.

Halle, Morris. 1997. Distributed morphology: Impoverishment and fission. *PF: Papers at the interface*, ed. by Benjamin Bruenung, Yoonjung Kang, and Marth McGinnis, pp. 425–449. MIT Working Papers in Linguistics, vol. 30. Cambridge, MA: MIT Working Papers in Linguistics.

Hamilton, Michael David. 2015. Phrase structure in Mi'gmaq: A configurational account of a 'non-configurational' language. *Lingua* 167:19–40.

Lochbihler, Bethany, and Eric Mathieu. 2016. Clause typing and feature inheritance of discourse features. *Syntax* 19(4):354–391.

Macaulay, Monica. 2009. On prominence hierarchies: Evidence from Algonquian. *Linguistic Typology* 13(3):357–389.

MacKenzie, Marguerite Ellen. 1980. Towards a dialectology of Cree-Montagnais-Naskapi. PhD thesis, University of Toronto.

Nevins, Andrew. 2011. Multiple agree with clitics: Person complementarity vs. omnivorous number. *Natural Language & Linguistic Theory* 29(4):939–971.

Oxford, William Robert. 2014. Microparameters of agreement: A diachronic perspective on Algonquian verb inflection. PhD thesis, University of Toronto.

Polinsky, Maria, and Eric Potsdam. 2001. Long-distance agreement and topic in Tsez. *Natural Language & Linguistic Theory* 19(3):583–646.

Rhodes, Richard. 1994. Agency, inversion, and thematic alignment in Ojibwe. *Proceedings of BLS* 20, ed. by Susanna Gahl et al., pp. 431–446. Berkeley, CA: Berkeley Linguistics Society.

Toward a Detailed Plains Cree VAI Paradigm

Atticus G. Harrigan, Antti Arppe, and Arok Wolvengrey

lgonquian languages, and North American indigenous languages in general, have lacked substantial development of technological applications such as intelligent electronic dictionaries (I-DICTs), which are able to recognize and generate any inflected word forms, and intelligent computer-aided language learning (ICALL) applications, which allow for the extension of exercise templates to cover any inflected word form types using a computational model. Such applications could be useful in supporting revitalization efforts. However, Plains Cree, unlike some other Algonquian languages, does have a substantial number of printed dictionaries, grammars, and teaching materials. The language already also has an online dictionary that allows users to search from Cree-to-English as well as from English-to-Cree. This dictionary, the Online Cree Dictionary,[1] conglomerates multiple dictionaries (LeClaire et al. 1998; Wolvengrey 2001; *Maskwacîs Cree Dictionary* n.d.) into a single resource.

Although useful, this online resource is limited in its simplicity. Since no morphological analysis is implemented, searches only return results that match the search input string. Thus, search strings need to be in the form of the item lemma (or lexical entry—not necessarily exactly the same as lemma). Verbal lemmata are mostly in the third person singular, independent, present form, so looking up other inflected forms requires sufficient knowledge about the morphological composition of words that one may come up with the appropriate lemma corresponding to the inflected form. As a result, a user coming across the imperative form *nâs* ('fetch someone!') must actually have sufficient linguistic knowledge to know to search for *nâtêw* ('s/he fetches someone') in order to retrieve the relevant definition, and even then the definition given will only be for the lexical entry *nâtêw*. This can prove difficult for a language learner, especially at the beginner level, and is further complicated by the need to exclude all preverbal morphology.

In order to help address this problem, we are developing an I-DICT based in terms of its lexical content on Wolvengrey's (2001) Cree dictionary (Arppe et al. 2015; Arppe et al. 2016). The dictionary, *itwêwina*,[2] incorporates a computational morphological model of Plains Cree (Snoek et al. 2014; Harrigan et al. 2016), which allows for the morphological analysis of any Cree word, e.g., to (1) enable users to search with the imperative form *nâs* and receive a definition matching the lemma of this inflected form, alongside information about its morphological features, as well as (2) generate inflected forms as paradigms of various compositions. In order to develop this computational model, we need as extensive as possible descriptions of the (contemporary) morphology of Plains Cree. To be able to deal with morphologically complex forms such as *ni-nôhtê-nitawi-nîmihito-n* ('I want to go and dance'), we require descriptions that cover person circumfixes (*ni- -n*), preverbal morphemes (*nôhtê-* and *nitawi-*), and the stem *nîmihito-*, and ideally the combined use of these different morpheme types, not just individually. While there is no single, unified, comprehensive reference, various resources collectively do contain the necessary information. Focusing on the verb, the aim of this paper is to begin work toward a complete template, as far as is practically possible, of the Plains Cree verb. As a preliminary outcome, we present a detailed paradigm of the Plains Cree animate intransitive verbs (VAIs).

Background

Plains Cree Paradigms

Descriptions of the Plains Cree verb have come in various forms of completeness. One must bear in mind that none of these sources was necessarily attempting to provide full or complete paradigms in any way. Rather, each source provided those forms deemed necessary and comprehensive enough for each audience or research

FIGURE 1. Native studies VAI paradigm sample (2012:31)

INDEPENDENT MODE

PERSON	PERSON INDICATOR	VERB STEM +	SUFFIX
1s	ni		n
2s	ki		n
3s			w or n
1p	ni		nân
21	ki		naw
2p	ki		nâwâw
3p			wak
3'			yiwa

CONJUNCT MODE

PERSON	PERSON INDICATOR	VERB STEM +	SUFFIX
1s	ê		yân
2s	ê		yan
3s	ê		t
1p	ê		yâhk
21	ê		yahk
2p	ê		yêk
3p	ê		cik
3'	ê		yit

question. Resources range from language learning tools (such as Native Studies 2012 and Okimâsis 2004), as well as grammatical descriptions (including Wolfart 1973 and Wolvengrey 2011). Looking at language learning materials we see a basic template for the Plains Cree verb. Teaching materials, such as those from the Cree courses offered at the University of Alberta (Native Studies 2012), provide paradigms composed of independent, conjunct, and imperative forms for first through third persons in both singular and plural, as well as obviative person unspecified for number (3'). Preverbs are considered separate, optional morphemes, and are not included in the paradigms. Similarly, unspecified actor, benefactive, and other such forms are not given as part of main paradigms, but rather as separate forms with verb class allomorphy. In any case, such suffixes are not included in canonical forms of verbal paradigms. Separate paradigms are given for subjunctive/future conditional.[3] Various terms have been used to describe these forms. Some sources use the term "subjunctive" as the form is cited as expressing an irrealis meaning

FIGURE 2. Okimâsis's VAI paradigm sample (2004:152)*

INDEPENDENT MODE

PERSON	PERSON INDICATOR	VERB STEM	SUFFIX
1s	ni		n
2s	ki		n
3s			w or n
3's			yiwa
1p	ni		nân
21	ki		naw
2p	ki		nâwâw
3p			wak
3'p			yiwa

CONJUNCT MODE

PERSON	CONJUNCT PREVERB	VERB STEM	SUFFIX
1s	ê-		yân
2s	ê-		yan
3s	ê-		t
3's	ê-		yit
1p	ê-		yâhk
21	ê-		yahk
2p	ê-		yêk
3p	ê-		cik
3'p	ê-		yit

*For orthographic consistency, all vowel length marks have been regularized to the use of the circumflex (e.g. â, ê, î, ô) even where the source material (e.g. Okimâsis 2004) utilizes macrons.

(translating to *if* or *when* forms of verbs in Native Studies 2012), while Bellegarde (Okimâsis) (1984), Okimâsis and Ratt (1999), and Okimāsis (2004), using similar translations, call this form the "future conditional."

Okimâsis's (2004) description of the Plains Cree verb provides a very similar picture to the instructional materials discussed above. Notably different is how the unspecified actor suffixes are dealt with. While previous materials treated the unspecified actor suffix as a separate, sometimes derivational, morpheme, Okimāsis (2004) includes the unspecified actor forms as a part of her unified paradigms, presented in the summary of the grammar, though only for the Transitive Animate (VTA) paradigm. For VAI paradigms, the unspecified actor form is treated derivationally as above.

FIGURE 3. Wolfart's VAI paradigm sample (1973:43)

	INDEPENDENT INDICATIVE	CONJUNCT SIMPLE AND CHANGED	CONJUNCT SUBJUNCTIVE/ ITERATIVE
Indf*		-hk	-hki
1	ni- -n	-yân	-yâni
2	ki- -n	-yan	-yani
1p	ni- -nân	-yâhk	-yâhki
21	ki- -naw, nânaw	-yahk	-yahko
2p	ki- -nâwâw	-yêk	-yêko
3	-w -ø	-t, -k	-ci, -ki
3p	-wak	-cik, -kik	-twâwi, -kwâwi
3'	-yiwa	-yit	-yici

*As was common at the time, and still may be to some extent, the unspecified actors were referred to as 'indefinite actor' (indf) forms, though the originator of this term later recanted its use (cf. Hockett 1996). For this paper, we will use <X> to mark the Unspecified Actor.

Finally, in dealing with obviative participant marking on verbs, Okimāsis diverges from Native Studies (2012). Most noticeable is her inclusion of both singular and plural forms of obviative participants, which are formally syncretic, but apparently provided to illustrate to students both singular and plural reference.

While clearly divergent, the two sources presented above are similar, particularly in their audiences. Both sources are aimed mainly at second language learners, particularly those with minimal linguistic knowledge. It makes sense then that their presentation and philosophies regarding paradigm makeup would be similar. Shifting to publications less focused on language learning and rather on academic audiences, we find differences in description. Wolfart's (1973) seminal grammar of Plains Cree describes additional modalities not found in Native Studies (2012) and Okimāsis's (2004) materials. Unlike the previous sources, Wolfart (1973) describes as part of main paradigm sets the preterit and dubitative forms. These forms are preserved in some varieties of East Cree and other Algonquian languages such as Ojibwe; however, such forms are all but gone from recently attested forms of Plains Cree. Wolfart's description represents thus, from the current perspective, a historical, though recent, form of Plains Cree.

As in Okimâsis (2004) and Native Studies (2012), the subjunctive (which also, according to Wolfart, shares the same endings as an "iterative" form) is given as a separate paradigm. The changed conjunct and unspecified actor forms are described separately as additional morphemes/processes (Wolfart 1973:42). Further described are the relational forms (created through the addition of a -w suffix), and diminutive

FIGURE 4. EastCree.org's Northern East Cree VAI Paradigm Sample (2016)

				Relational	
	2	**chi**mishikaan		2	**chi**mishikaa**w**aan
	2p	**chi**mishikaan**aawaau**		2p	**chi**mishikaa**w**aan**aawaau**
	21p	**chi**mishikaan**aaniu**		21p	**chi**mishikaa**w**aan**aaniu**
	1	**ni**mishikaan		1	**ni**mishikaa**w**aan
	1p	**ni**mishikaa**naan**		1p	**ni**mishikaa**w**aan**naan**
	3	mishikaa**u**		3	mishikaa**w**aau
	3p	mishikaa**wich**		3p	mishikaa**w**aa**wich**
	4	mishikaa**yiuh**			
unspecified actor	X	mishikaan*iu***u**			
	X'	mishikaan*aaniwi***yiu**			

verb forms (derivationally created through the use of the -*si* suffix), both of which are in continued use in contemporary Plains Cree (cf. Cenerini (2014)), but lack widespread description in contemporary materials such as those described above.

Finally, Wolvengrey's (2011) thesis provides the reader with specific paradigms of verbal inflection used to help argue points unrelated to the documentation of a full verbal paradigm. The paradigms presented cover the basic independent, conjunct, and imperative orders for all classes. Wolvengrey does not include future conditional forms, nor does he include the now defunct dubitative, preterit, or changed conjunct forms, and while he does discuss unspecified actor forms, they are not included in his paradigms.

Verb Paradigms in other Algonquian Languages

While there are similarities in the general structure of verbal paradigms in Algonquian languages, (e.g., the four-way division into conjugation classes according to transitivity and the animacy of the main participant[s]), they also differ from each other in various ways, and there are differences in how the composition of paradigms is represented. Looking toward East Cree/Innu, we see a very different organization of verbal paradigm data. Through the East Cree website,[4] we are presented with a comprehensive set of verbal paradigms for both the Northern and Southern Dialects of East Cree.[5] The paradigm for each verb class is split into 15 potential conjugations (which are not realized for all classes), the first seven of which map to the independent order (for VAI stems, all seven found in the Northern dialect but only four in the Southern), the next six (all for Northern, five for Southern) representing the conjunct order, and the final two conjugations representing the imperative order. Unspecified actor forms are presented within the conjunct and independent conjugations. Furthermore, these conjugations cover the dubitative, habitual, preterit, and changed conjunct forms (cf. Wolfart 1973) (see Figure 4). Where applicable, relational forms are presented alongside regular forms. Similarly for Ojibwe, Valentine's (2001) verbal paradigms contain a variety of features not found in contemporary Plains Cree, including preterit, dubitative, positive and negative, iterative, and participial forms. These forms are presented as a unified, singular, extensive paradigm.

Preliminary Proposed Paradigms

So far we have seen a variety of choices on which parts of the Plains Cree verbal paradigm should be presented. For the purposes of creating a computational model that can analyze and generate the possible, attested verbal forms, none of these sources alone is sufficient. None provides a complete set of paradigms including the independent, conjunct, and imperative orders, the unspecified actors, and the relational forms (in all their possible combinations). Therefore, the paradigms we present will cover all the aforementioned inflected forms, as well as providing for a more comprehensive subdivision of the conjunct not documented for Plains Cree since Wolfart (1973). In addition to the most common (changed) conjunct (as marked by preverbs such as ê- and kâ-), we include the unchanged conjunct (as now usually marked by the preverb ka-/ta-) as a separate form, under a title suggested for it through the work of Cook (2008), the SUBJUNCTIVE.[6] In addition to the (unchanged) future conditional, the (changed) iterative (cf. Wolfart 1973) (or "timeless conditional") must also be included, based on recent fieldwork. In contrast, the dubitative forms cited by Wolfart (1973) no longer seem to be productive in contemporary Plains Cree, essentially superseded in part by the free use of the particle êtokwê. Moreover, the inclusion of preterit forms remains debatable as speakers in some regions at least seem to recognize them; however, there are few (or no) sources of recent data confirming their productive use. As a result, we have opted not to include the preterit forms in our paradigms, but this is clearly an area for future research.

Derivation and Inflection

In creating an inflectional paradigm, we must differentiate between inflection and derivation. In compiling a full paradigm, by convention we would limit ourselves to inflectional morphology. Derivational morphology, unlike inflection, is responsible for lexeme creation (Booij 2007) and changes in word class (Stump 2001). Furthermore, derivation does not rule out further derivation, though inflection often does (e.g., when speaking of the extent to which one can speak another language, one could derive *speaker-ness* from the already derived *speak-er*, while you could not add further inflection or derivation on *speak-s*) (Stump 2001). Moreover, derivation is often seen to produce less regular changes than inflection (Stump 2001; Booij 2006): the third person inflection always indicates that a verbal action is being performed by a third person, while the denominal verbalizing suffix *-ize* has different meanings in *specialize* (to focus on something) than in *prioritize* (to make something a priority) (Stump 2001). Similarly, although inflection is often more productive than derivation, this is not a universal rule (Booij 2006). While the above criteria attempt to demarcate inflection and derivation, it is perhaps better to think of the two processes as opposite ends of a continuum. Stump (2001) argues that context is perhaps the best way to define the type of morphological process, and that a single process may be of an inflectional nature in one case, but a derivational nature in another.

Derivational morphology, in contrast to inflection, is responsible for lexeme creation (Booij 2007). Using this definition, we might reasonably treat benefactives, which create VTA constructions (e.g., ***atoskêstamawêw*** 'He works for him/her [3']') from VAI stems[7] (e.g., ***atoskêw*** 'He works'), as derivational. However, there is some trepidation in labeling these processes as purely derivational: In the case of Plains Cree, we find the formation of benefactives to be neatly regular. Second, derivation is supposedly less semantically regular, producing forms such as *cooker* (which does not primarily refer to any person who cooks as we might expect from the suffixation of an agentive suffix *-er* onto *cook* [as the term may be used for items like a slow cooker].) (Booij 2006). Conversely, a Plains Cree benefactive derivation will (nearly) always mean that one is doing something for someone (e.g., *nîmihitôstamawêw* 'he dances for someone [3']', from the VAI *nîmihitow* 'He dances'). It therefore seems that Plains Cree does not strictly demarcate inflection as compared to derivation. There exist multiple approaches that attempt to address this, in practice, noncategorical nature of derivation and inflection. For our purposes, we will cover (1) distinguishing between lexical and syntactic derivation, (2) derivation as understood in Functional Discourse Grammar (FDG), and (3) Lexical Functions.

Lexical and syntactic derivation is a proposed differentiation within morphological derivation. According to Kuryłowicz (1936, as cited in Haspelmath et al. 2001), lexical derivation is a process wherein only a lexical change occurs while syntactic derivation is a process wherein syntactic function is altered. Haspelmath et al. (2001) further add that syntactic derivation changes syntactic roles without affecting semantics greatly, while lexical derivation can effect semantic change. Such definitions are particularly apt in differentiating Plains Cree inflection and derivation: a reflexive form retains the verbal meaning of its stem lexeme, but decreases the syntactic valency of the verb (i.e., syntactic derivation of VTA to VAI). The approach taken in FDG is essentially in agreement with this. While derivation proper remains a lexical process (achieved in the lexicon), both inflection proper and "word-class changing inflection" (cf. Haspelmath 2002) are morphosyntactic processes required to be productive and regular (Hengeveld and MacKenzie 2008:229). This middle ground between derivation and inflection is broadly defined as a process by which lexemes are adapted to a formal environment they would not normally be able to occupy. Hengeveld and MacKenzie (2008:229) further state, "For example, if a basically transitive lexeme is inserted into a one-place predication frame, it will in some languages have to be adapted [in its form] so as to show its intransitive use." This explanation describes precisely the creation of reflexives from VTA verbs in Plains Cree. Benefactives, which turn VAIs into "new" stems that follow the VTA paradigm (through the addition of *-stamaw*), adapting the verb to show this alternative usage, are thus also in this in-between world of syntactic derivation. This nevertheless leaves open the best way to account for these changes within our computational model.

Finally, we turn to the concept of lexical functions to help explain the opacity of the derivation/inflection divide. Lexical functions act as a bridge between categorical derivation and inflection. In describing the organization of a Portuguese lexical database, Janssen (2005) describes lexical functions as links between separate lexemes. In our Plains Cree examples, the lexemes *atoskêw* ('s/he works') and the third person benefactive ***atoskêstamawêw*** ('s/he does another's work for him/her [3']') would be treated as separate elements in the lexicon, each with their own inflectional paradigm (the former following the VAI; the latter following the VTA). These lexemes, however, would be linked through a function of benefactivization. This function would allow derived lexemes to stand separate from the stem lexeme, while still encoding a (non-inflectional) path through which one word is derived from another.

Based on the previous discussion, we can synthesize an appropriate definition of inflectional and derivational morphology to best fit paradigm creation: we can consider derivation to be those processes that redirect to another paradigm, but do not fundamentally change how the new paradigm marks actors and goals. The unspecified actor (which creates a VII form that may not always take every form that we expect of a regular VII [e.g., the plural]) seems to restrict the paradigm of the newly created VII, and so we can consider it nonderivational, and thus include it in our VAI paradigm; on the other hand, a VTA derived from a VAI can take ANY form that a regular VTA can, and is thus classified as fully derivational and not included in this paradigm.

Preverbs

Perhaps one of the most striking features of Plains Cree is its extensive usage of preverbal morphemes to encode tense, aspect, and modal characteristics on verbs. Preverbs can express desire, attempts at something, strength in action, and more. Preverbs may also be used to mark tense, through *kî-*, *ka-*, and *wî-* (which encode past tense, future tense, and prospective aspect, respectively; cf. Wolvengrey 2006, 2012). While some preverbs may occur less in some orders, the restrictions of preverbal use and stacking is currently understudied. One could apply the concept of lexical function to link commonly used preverb-verb stem combination (e.g., *pê-mîciso* 'come eat!'). However, as preverb combinations do not affect person inflection, and because the theoretical combinations of these morphemes are far too great to contain in a single paradigm table, the following paradigms will not include preverbs.

Conclusion

The Plains Cree verbal paradigm has been described to various extents, but not comprehensively, in several sources. While most sources cover basic paradigmatic features, such as person, number, and order, additional components such as the future conditional, iterative (or "timeless conditional"), and relational forms are often if not regularly left out. This paper has summarized various philosophies as to paradigmatic construction through an attempt to create a justified paradigm for the VAI class. Various derivational forms, such as the diminutive, reflexive, or benefactive, etc., have been left out for reasons of parsimony and an attempt to restrict these paradigms to what we consider primarily inflectional forms. What follows is the resulting basic inflectional VAI paradigm for Plains Cree.[8]

FIGURE 5. V-final VAI independent order—indicative (e.g., *nipâw* 's/he sleeps')

ABBR	PREFIX	VAI STEM	ENDINGS	EXAMPLE
1s	ni(t)-		-n	ninipân
2s	ki(t)-		-n	kinipân
1p	ni(t)-		-nân	ninipânân
21	ki(t)-		-(nâ)naw	kinipâ(nâ)naw
2p	ki(t)-		-nâwâw	kinipânâwâw
3s			-w	nipâw
3p			-wak	nipâwak
3'			-ýiwa	nipâýiwa
X			-(nâ)niwan	nipâniwan

FIGURE 6. V-final VAI Independent Order—Indicative—Relational
(e.g., *nipâwêw* 'S/he sleeps in relation to him/her')

ABBR	PREFIX	VAI STEM	ENDINGS	EXAMPLE
1s	ni(t)-		-wân	ninipâwân
2s	ki(t)-		-wân	kinipâwân
1p	ni(t)-		-wânân	ninipâwânân
21	ki(t)-		-wâ(nâ)naw	kinipâwâ(nâ)naw
2p	ki(t)-		-wânâwâw	kinipâwânâwâw
3s			-wêw	nipâwêw
3p			-wêwak	nipâwêwak
3'				
X			-wân	nipâwân

FIGURE 7. *V*-final VAI conjunct order—indicative (changed)
(e.g., *ê-nipât* 's/he is sleeping')

ABBR	PREFIX	VAI STEM	ENDINGS	EXAMPLE
1s	ê-		-yân	ê-nipâyân
2s	ê-		-yan	ê-nipâyan
1p	ê-		-yâhk	ê-nipâyâhk
21	ê-		-yahk	ê-nipâyahk
2p	ê-		-yêk	ê-nipâyêk
3s	ê-		-t	ê-nipât
3p	ê-		-cik	ê-nipâcik
3'	ê-		-ýit	ê-nipâýit
X	ê-		-hk*	ê-nipâhk

*In dialects other than Plains Cree, this archaic ending is replaced by -(nâ)nîwahki or a variant.

FIGURE 8. *V*-final VAI conjunct order—indicative (changed)—relational
(e.g., *ê-nipâwât* 's/he is sleeping in relation to him/her')

ABBR	PREFIX	VAI STEM	ENDINGS	EXAMPLE
1s	ê-		-wak	ê-nipâwak
2s	ê-		-wat	ê-nipâwat
1p	ê-		-wâhk	ê-nipâwâhk
21	ê-		-wahk	ê-nipâwahk
2p	ê-		-wêk	ê-nipâwêk
3s	ê-		-wât	ê-nipâwât
3p	ê-		-wâcik	ê-nipâwâcik
3'				
X	ê-		-wiht	ê-nipâwiht

FIGURE 9. *V*-final VAI conjunct order—subjunctive (unchanged)
(e.g., *ta-nipât* '(for him/her) to sleep . . .')

ABBR	PREFIX	VAI STEM	ENDINGS	EXAMPLE
1s	(ta-)		-yân	(ta-)nipâyân
2s	(ta-)		-yan	(ta-)nipâyan
1p	(ta-)		-yâhk	(ta-)nipâyâhk
21	(ta-)		-yahk	(ta-)nipâyahk
2p	(ta-)		-yêk	(ta-)nipâyêk
3s	(ta-)		-t	(ta-)nipât
3p	(ta-)		-cik	(ta-)nipâcik
3'	(ta-)		-ýit	(ta-)nipâýit
X	(ta-)		-hk*	(ta-)nipâhk

*In dialects other than Plains Cree, this archaic ending is replaced by -(nâ)nîwahki or a variant.

FIGURE 10. *V*-final VAI conjunct order—subjunctive (unchanged)—relational
(e.g., *ta-nipâwât* '(for him/her) to sleep in relation to him/her . . . ')

ABBR	PREFIX	VAI STEM	ENDINGS	EXAMPLE
1s	(ta-)		-wak	(ta-)nipâwak
2s	(ta-)		-wat	(ta-)nipâwat
1p	(ta-)		-wâhk	(ta-)nipâwâhk
21	(ta-)		-wahk	(ta-)nipâwahk
2p	(ta-)		-wêk	(ta-)nipâwêk
3s	(ta-)		-wât	(ta-)nipâwât
3p	(ta-)		-wâcik	(ta-)nipâwâcik
3'				
X	(ta-)		-wiht	(ta-)nipâwiht

FIGURE 11. *V*-final VAI conjunct order—future conditional (unchanged)
(e.g., *nipâci* 'if s/he sleeps . . .')

ABBR	VAI STEM	ENDINGS	EXAMPLE
1s		-yâni	nipâyâni
2s		-yani	nipâyani
1p		-yâhki	nipâyâhki
21		-yahko	nipâyahko
2p		-yêko	nipâyêko
3s		-ci	nipâci
3p		-twâwi	nipâtwâwi
3'		-ýici	nipâýici
X		-hki*	nipâhki

*In dialects other than Plains Cree, this archaic ending is replaced by -(nâ)niwahki or a variant.

FIGURE 12. *V*-final VAI conjunct order—future conditional (unchanged)—relational
(e.g., *nipâwâci* 'if s/he sleeps in relation to him/her . . .')

ABBR	VAI STEM	ENDINGS	EXAMPLE
1s		-waki	nipâwaki
2s		-waci	nipâwaci
1p		-wâhki	nipâwâhki
21		-wahko	nipâwahko
2p		-wêko	nipâwêko
3s		-wâci	nipâwâci
3p		-wâtwâwi	nipâwâtwâwi
3'			
X		-wihci	nipâwihci

FIGURE 13. *V*-final VAI conjunct order—timeless conditional (changed)
(e.g., *nêpâci* 'whenever s/he sleeps . . .')

ABBR	IC*	VAI STEM	ENDINGS	EXAMPLE
1s	(i→ê)		-yâni	nêpâyâni
2s	(i→ê)		-yani	nêpâyani
1p	(i→ê)		-yâhki	nêpâyâhki
21	(i→ê)		-yahko	nêpâyahko
2p	(i→ê)		-yêko	nêpâyêko
3s	(i→ê)		-ci	nêpâci
3p	(i→ê)		-twâwi	nêpâtwâwi
3'	(i→ê)		-ýici	nêpâýici
X	(i→ê)		-hki†	nêpâhki

*IC = Initial Change, which is becoming archaic in Plains Cree but retained at least in this paradigm. (a→ê, i→ê, o→wê; î→â/iyî; â→iyâ; ê→iyê; ô→iyô).
†In dialects other than Plains Cree, this archaic ending is replaced by -(nâ)niwahki or a variant.

FIGURE 14. *V*-final vai conjunct order—timeless conditional (changed)—relational
(e.g., *nêpâwâci* 'whenever s/he sleeps in relation to him/her . . .')

ABBR	IC	VAI STEM	ENDINGS	EXAMPLE
1s	(i→ê)		-waki	nêpâwaki
2s	(i→ê)		-waci	nêpâwaci
1p	(i→ê)		-wâhki	nêpâwâhki
21	(i→ê)		-wahko	nêpâwahko
2p	(i→ê)		-wêko	nêpâwêko
3s	(i→ê)		-wâci	nêpâwâci
3p	(i→ê)		-wâtwâwi	nêpâwâtwâwi
3'				
X	(i→ê)		-wihci	nêpâwihci

FIGURE 15. *V*-Final VAI imperative order—immediate and delayed
(e.g., *nipâ* '(you) sleep!')

ABBR	VAI STEM	ENDINGS	EXAMPLE
2s			nipâ
2p		-k	nipâk
21		-tân	nipâtân
2s		-hkan	nipâhkan
2p		-hkêk	nipâhkêk
21		-hkahk	nipâhkahk

FIGURE 16. *V*-Final VAI imperative order—immediate (and delayed)—relational (e.g., *nipâ* '(you) sleep in relation to him/her!')

ABBR	VAI STEM	ENDINGS	EXAMPLE
2s		-wa	nipâwa
2p		-wâ(h)k	nipâwâ(h)k
21		-wâtân	nipâwâtân
2s			
2p			
21			

NOTES

1. Www.creedictionary.com.

2. Http://altlab.ualberta.ca/itwewina.

3. Though "subjunctive" is certainly loaded with Standard Average European baggage, it is primarily problematic as it implies a situation that does not necessarily refer to the future. To the contrary, the term "future conditional" (cf. Okimāsis 2004) seems less loaded, and DOES implies a future setting, which is, in fact, closer to how these Cree "subjunctive" forms (generally derived by adding -*i* to the conjunct ending of the respective verb class) behave. Thus, a construction like *kihc-ôkimâwiyâni* cannot be used to mean 'if I were king' in a past or present hypothetical sense, but can only refer to a future or not yet realized occurrence. For these reasons, we will not use the term "subjunctive" to refer to these forms (cf. also Cook 2008).

4. Http://www.eastcree.org/cree/en/.

5. Http://verbs.eastcree.org/.

6. We recognize that this is not an ideal choice since, as already mentioned (see note 3), this term is loaded with intellectual baggage. However, Cook (2008) argues that the Plains Cree unchanged conjunct seems to function quite similarly to the Romanian subjunctive, both languages completely lacking an infinitival form. "Infinitive" would be another, not necessarily ideal but more readily understood, possible choice.

7. Although benefactives can also derive a VTA from a VTI, this article focuses only on Animate Intransitive verbs.

8. In addition to the vowel-final (V-final) paradigms listed here (which encompass all stems that end in /i, o, â, ê, î, ô/ (i.e., all Plains Cree vowels except /a/), small modifications are required to account for a second major VAI subtype, the /n/-final stems. Additionally,

there are a few exceptional intransitive verbs which inflect identically to VTI class 1 stems (i.e., with the theme sign /-am/ and its variants). These have generally been grouped as VTI stems, but could be classified as a third subtype of VAI (cf. Wolvengrey 2011), depending on whether morphology or syntax are taken to be determinative of class membership.

REFERENCES

Arppe, Antti, Lene Antonsen, Trond Trosterud, Sjur N. Moshagen, Dorothy Thunder, Conor Snoek, Timothy Mills, Juhani Järvikivi, and Jordan Lachler. 2015. Turning language documentation into reader's and writer's software tools. Paper read at the Fourth International Conference on Language Documentation and Conservation (ICDLC 4), Honolulu.

Arppe, Antti, Jordan Lachler, Trond Trosterud, Lene Antonsen, and Sjur N. Moshagen. 2016. Basic language resource kits for endangered languages: A case study of Plains Cree. Paper read at Collaboration and Computing for Under-Resourced Languages (CCURL) 2016—Towards an Alliance for Digital Language Diversity, Portorož, Slovenia.

Bellegarde, Jean L. (Okimâsis). 1984. *Cree: Language of the plains*. 1st ed. Regina, SK: Saskatchewan Indian Federated College.

Booij, Geert E. 2006. Inflection and derivation. *Encyclopedia of language and linguistics*, ed. by Edward Keith Brown, pp. 654–661. Amsterdam: Elsevier.

———. 2007. *The grammar of words*. Oxford: Oxford University Press.

Cenerini, Chantale Anna Marie. 2014. Relational verbs: Paradigm and practice in a Manitoba dialect of Swampy. MA thesis, University of Regina.

Cook, Clare E. 2008. The syntax and semantics of clause-typing in Plains Cree. PhD thesis, University of British Columbia.

Harrigan, Atticus, Lene Antonsen, Antti Arppe, D. Bowers, K. Schmirler, Trond Trosterud, and Arok Wolvengrey. 2016. Learning from the computational modeling of Plains Cree verbs. Paper read at Computational Methods for Descriptive and Theoretical Morphology, Seventeenth International Morphology Meeting, Vienna.

Haspelmath, Martin. 2002. *Understanding morphology*. Understanding Language Series. London: Arnold.

Haspelmath, Martin, Ekkehard König, Wulf Oesterreicher, and Wolfgang Raible (eds.). 2001. *Language typology and language universals: An international handbook*. Vols. 1 and 2. Berlin: Walter de Gruyter.

Hengeveld, Kees, and J. Lachlan Mackenzie. 2008. *Functional discourse grammar*. Oxford: Oxford University Press.

Janssen, M. 2005. Between inflection and derivation: Paradigmatic lexical functions in morphological databases. *East-West encounter: Seconding International Conference on Meaning and Text Theory*, ed. by J. D. Apresjan and L. L. Iomdin, pp. 187–196. Moscow: Slavic Culture Languages Publishing House.

Kuryłowicz, Jerzy. 1936. Dérivation lexicale et dérivation syntaxique: contribution à la théorie des parties du discours. *Bulletin de la société de linguistique de Paris* 37:79–92.

LeClaire, Nancy, George Cardinal, Emily Hunter, and Earle H. Waugh. 1998. *Alberta elders' Cree dictionary: Alperta ohci kehtehayak nehiyaw otwestamâkewasinahikan*. Edmonton: University of Alberta Press.

Maskwacis Cree Dictionary. n.d. Cree-to-English glossary compiled by Cree communities in Maskwacîs, Alberta. Electronic version available as incorporated in the Online Cree Dictionary, http://www.creedictionary.com/.

Native Studies, Faculty of. 2012. *Introductory Cree: Part 1 (NS 152)*. Edmonton: University of Alberta Press

Okimâsis, Jean. L. 2004. *Cree: Language of the plains*. Regina, SK: Canadian Plains Research Center.

Okimâsis, Jean L., and S. Ratt. 1999. *Cree: Language of the plains*. Regina, SK: Canadian Plains Research Center.

Snoek, Conor, Dorothy Thunder, Kaidi Lõo, Antti Arppe, Jordan Lachler, Sjur N. Moshagen, and Trond Trosterud. 2014. Modeling the noun morphology of Plains Cree. *Proceedings of the 2014 Workshop on the Use of Computational Methods in the Study of Endangered Languages*, ed. by Jeff Good, Julia Hirschberg, and Owen Rambow, pp. 34–42. Baltimore: Association for Computational Linguistics.

Stump, Gregory T. 2001. Inflection. *The handbook of morphology*, ed. by Andrew Spencer and Arnold M. Zwicky, pp. 13–43. Oxford: Blackwell.

Valentine, J. Randolph. 2001. *Nishnaabemwin reference grammar*. Toronto: University of Toronto Press.

Wolfart, H. C. 1973. *Plains Cree: A grammatical study*. Transactions of the American Philosophical Society, n.s., vol. 63, part 5. Philadelphia.

Wolvengrey, Arok. 2001. *nēhiyawēwin: itwēwina/Cree: Words*. Vols. 1 and 2. Regina, SK: Canadian Plains Research Center.

———. 2006. ēkosi wī-ispayin. (kwayāciho!): Prospective aspect in the Western dialects of Cree. *International Journal of American Linguistics* 73(3):397–407.

———. 2011. *Semantic and pragmatic functions in Plains Cree syntax*. Utrecht Amsterdam: LOT Universiteit van Amsterdam Host.

———. 2012. The verbal morphosyntax of aspect-tense-modality in dialects of Cree. Paper read at the 2012 International Conference on Functional Discourse Grammar, Ghent, Belgium.

The Role of Final Morphemes in Blackfoot: Marking Aspect or Sentience?

Kyumin Kim

n this paper, I address the role of final morphemes (to be detailed shortly) in Blackfoot.[1] In particular, I aim to find out how verb final (henceforth, final) morphemes in the language interact with lexical aspect (henceforth, aspect) and sentience. I propose that among sentient arguments, only agent arguments can contribute to the organization of aspect in Blackfoot. I show that an event can be telic (i.e., having an endpoint) only when the subject of a verb marked by a final morpheme is sentient and an agent, not a theme. As supporting evidence, I present data showing that transitivity alternations indicated by finals correlate with differences in telicity: events marked by transitive finals correspond to telic events, but those marked by certain intransitive finals correspond to atelic events. Thus, finals that differ in transitivity, in conjunction with sentience, can indicate differences in telicity. The sentient agent-oriented aspect in Blackfoot proposed in this paper is consistent with an atemporal view of IP in the language as in Ritter and Wiltschko (2014) but also raises the important question of how to deal with telicity, which Wiltschko (2012) has suggested is inactive in the language. This issue is briefly discussed in the last section of this paper.

Like other Algonquian languages, final morphemes in Blackfoot indicate the transitivity of verbs as well as the grammatical animacy of a verb's subject or object (Bloomfield 1946). Among four classes of finals, Transitive Animate (TA) and Transitive Inanimate (TI) finals indicate the grammatical (in)animacy of the verb's object and that the verbs are transitive. The other two finals—Animate Intransitive (AI) and Inanimate Intransitive (II)—indicate the (in)animacy of the verb's subject and that the verb is intransitive. Some AI verbs, despite being intransitive, allow an optional object (see (1)). I will not discuss data involving II finals, as grammatically inanimate subjects are not directly relevant to the issues discussed in this paper.

A note on GRAMMATICAL animacy vs. sentience is necessary. In Blackfoot, nouns are categorized into two grammatical classes: animate and inanimate. Nouns in the inanimate class are inanimate objects or things. Nouns in the animate class may be humans or animals, but may also be certain inanimate objects. For instance, nouns such as 'wagon' belong to the animate noun class although they are semantically inanimate (Frantz 2009). On the other hand, sentience refers to real-world animacy, or the ability to sense or perceive (Speas and Tenny 2003). A human or animal can be considered to be sentient, but an object or a thing cannot. The verb finals in Bloomfield's classification indicate grammatical animacy, rather than sentience. Throughout this paper, (in)animate refers to grammatical (in)animacy.

Sentience, Final, and Aspect

Aspectual Classification

In Vendlerian verb classification, verbs are classified into four aspectual types, as shown in Table 1. These four types are classified by two criteria: process and definite. Process denotes whether an event unfolds in time. The presence vs. absence of definiteness correlates with *the* vs. *a/any* in English. Like telicity that indicates having an inherent endpoint, the presence of definiteness captures the fact that achievement is telic like accomplishment. Given the similar effect of telicity to that of definiteness, I use the more commonly used term 'telicity', rather than definiteness, as one of the criteria for aspectual classification.

In the literature, however, another criterion that has been proposed to determine the aspectual classification of verbs is agentivity. For example, Verkuyl (1989) points out that some of Vendler's (1967) aspectual tests identify agentivity, in addition to process. Among Vendler's tests is a progressive test, which is illustrated in (1). A process event such as an accomplishment (1a) is compatible with the progressive,

TABLE 1. Vendler 1967 classification (as represented in Verkuyl 1989)

CLASSIFICATION	PROCESS	DEFINITE
Accomplishment	Yes	Yes
Activity	Yes	No
Achievement	No	Yes
State	No	No

but an event without process such as an achievement (1b) is not. Interestingly, however, the same test is also sensitive to the agentivity of an event (Verkuyl 1989). The verbs in (1a) that are compatible with the progressive are agentive, but the verbs in (1b) that are incompatible with the progressive are nonagentive.

(1)   a.   She is **run**ning a mile, he is **draw**ing a circle, he was **eat**ing a sandwich.

      b.   *She was **recogniz**ing him, he was **reach**ing the top, she was **win**ning
         (As presented in Verkuyl 1989: judgments are Vendler's; emphasis is mine)

Similar observations are made in Dowty (1979) and Pustejovsky (1991). In Dowty (1979), a semantic operator DO, which invokes agentivity, was proposed as a criterion that corresponds to process. Moreover, Pustejovsky (1991) argues that the only difference between accomplishment and achievement predicates is the presence of an agentive subject in the former but not in the latter. In a recent study of aspect, Travis (2010) proposes a related idea: process corresponds to a head that introduces an external argument, which is arguably an agent.

    Pursuing the same direction as these scholars, I assume that in some languages the agentivity of a subject is one of the criteria for aspectual classification. For aspectual classification in Blackfoot, however, I exclude process, which is a temporal property, in keeping with a recent proposal that IP in Blackfoot is atemporal (Ritter and Wiltschko 2014).[2] Excluding process, we are left with agentivity and telicity. I show that sentience, when it is an agent, not a theme, is relevant to characterization of aspect in Blackfoot. I also show that a telic event is available only when a sentient agent is present.

Sentience, Final, and Aspect in Blackfoot

In this section, I briefly discuss two recent studies that address the issue of aspect in Blackfoot. One is Ritter and Rosen (2010), and the other is Kim (2015, 2017). Ritter and Rosen (2010) have questioned whether a change in final morphemes indicating transitivity alternations (i.e., alternation between TA/TI and AI+O(bject)) are related to a change in aspectual classification, e.g., from accomplishment to activity. They showed that the transitivity alternations do not indicate a change in aspectual classification. To illustrate, consider the examples of alternating TA-AI+O in (2).[3] In (2a), the verb form is AI and in (2b) it is TA. Both verb forms are compatible with 'finish V-ing', which is known to detect an endpoint and which is present in accomplishment class verbs but not in activity class verbs. The compatibility suggests that both TA/TI and AI+O verbs such as in (2) belong to the same aspectual class, namely accomplishment.

(2) a. Akaa-iksist-ooy-i-wa   (mamii)
         PERF-finish-eat-AI-3S   (fish)
         'S/he's finished eating (fish).'

     b. Akaa-iksist-oow-at-yii-wa   amo   mamii.
         PERF-finish-eat-TA-TH-3S   DEM   fish
         'S/he's finished eating this fish.'   (Ritter and Rosen 2010)

Concluding that finals do not mark different aspectual classes, Ritter and Rosen (2010) argue that finals of alternating TA/TI-AI+O pairs indicate that their subjects are sentient, and they furthermore identify these sentient subjects as agents.[4]

Another study on aspect in Blackfoot is in Kim (2015, 2017). Although this study does not address final morphemes, it questions the relationship between sentience and aspect in the language. Kim (2015) proposed that an endpoint, i.e., telicity, becomes available only in the presence of a sentient argument. Consider the examples of the inherently directed motion verb 'go' in (3). In (3a), the subject 'that boy' is sentient and it is able to co-occur with an endpoint of motion 'that hill' via a direction linker *itap-*. When this subject is switched to an animate but nonsentient subject 'that wagon', an endpoint phrase cannot appear, as shown in (3b).

(3) a. Anna   saahkomaapi   itap-oo-wa   oomi   isspahkoyi.
         DEM   boy   GOAL-go.AI-3S   DEM   hill
         'The boy went to that hill.'

     b. *Anna   ainaka'si   itap-oo-wa   oomi   isspahkoyi.
         DEM   wagon   GOAL-go.AI-3S   DEM   hill
         'The wagon went to that hill.'   (Kim 2015)

Note that it is not the case that an animate but nonsentient subject is not allowed with the motion verb 'go'. As shown in (4), 'that wagon' is grammatical as a subject when an endpoint is absent. Taking these data as core evidence, it is argued that a sentient subject conditions a telic event in Blackfoot: a telic event is available only when sentient subjects are present (Kim 2015, 2017). Note that Kim's proposal does not suggest that a telic phrase must be present whenever a sentient subject is present (e.g., (4) or (8)).

(4) Anna   saahkomaapi/ainaka'si   waamis-oo-wa.
     DEM   boy/wagon   up-go.AI-3S
     'The boy/wagon went up/moved upwards.'   (Kim 2017)

To recapitulate, Ritter and Rosen (2010) propose that the TA/TI-AI alternation in finals does not mark aspectual differences, and show that only verbs with sentient agent subjects can enter into the TA/TI-AI alternation itself. Kim (2015, 2017) proposes that a sentient subject plays a role in aspect, being only necessary for making an event telic. Given these two studies, questions arise: what role does sentience—in an agent or theme—play in making an event telic? Is the notion of sentience in Kim 2015 the same as that in Ritter and Rosen 2010, i.e., the sentience of an agent? If so, should alternating finals be related to aspect in some way?[5]

In what follows, I provide evidence that a sentient argument, when it is an agent, and not a theme, can contribute to aspectual properties of an event such as being telic. I also show evidence that different finals (TA/TI vs. AI) indicate differences in aspect in the language. This is not the same result found in Ritter and Rosen 2010, which will be addressed subsequently.

Sentience and Final Morphemes

As discussed earlier, a sentient agent subject is required for TA/TI-AI alternating pairs. If a telic event is possible, only when a sentient argument is present, as shown in Kim 2015, one question that arises is which type of sentient subject—an agent or a theme—is crucial to make it possible to have a telic event? For example, as shown in (3) where an inherently directed motion verb such as 'go' appears, the verb requires a sentient subject in order to have a PP goal, i.e., an endpoint of the event; however, it is unknown whether the sentient subject of the verb is an agent or a theme, both of which are available options for the subject of motion verbs (e.g., Ramchand 2008). If the subject shares the same role as the sentient subject of TA/TI-AI alternating verbs whose role is established as an agent (Frantz 2009; Ritter and Rosen 2010; Kim 2017), it may be concluded that only sentient arguments that are agents can contribute to the organization of aspect in the language. In this section, I provide evidence that demonstrates that this hypothesis is correct.

I make use of independently known contrasts between two affixes that appear on the Blackfoot verb: an accompaniment final suffix and an associative linker prefix. The two affixes can be shown to impose distinct role requirements on subjects (Frantz 2009). In particular, the accompaniment final suffix requires an agent, and the associative linker prefix requires a theme (Meadows 2010).[6] Illustrative examples are provided in (5). Accompaniment final -m in (5a) has to appear with a prefix *iihpok-*, and in (5a) it appears with the verb 'work', introducing an accompaniment 'my son' to the event of working. In (5b), an associative linker *iihp-* appears with a verb 'fall' and introduces an associate 'my daughter' to the event of falling.

(5)   a.   Accompaniment final

       Nitana   iihpok-a'po'taki-m-yii-wa   nohkoyi.

       my   ACCOMP-work.AI-ACCOMP-TH-3s   my son

       'My daughter worked with my son.' (Frantz 2009)

    b.   Associative linker

       Anna   saahkomaapi   iihp-innisi-wa   nitana.

       DEM   boy   ASSOCI-fall.AI-3s   my daughter

       'That boy fell with my daughter.'

Importantly, as shown in (6a), an accompaniment final cannot occur with the verb 'fall', which is compatible with an associative linker. In (6b), on the other hand, the associative linker is incompatible with the verb 'work', which occurs with the accompaniment final. The contrast between the examples in (5) and (6) shows that the verb 'work' is more like an unergative verb whose subject is an agent, while the verb 'fall' is more like an unaccusative verb whose subject is a theme.

(6) a. *Nitana   iihpok-innisi-m-yii-wa   nohkoyi.
       my   ACCOMP-fall.AI-ACCOMP-TH-3s   my son
       Intended meaning: 'My daughter fell with my son.'

    b. *Anna   saahkomaapi   iihp-a'po'taki-wa   nitana.
       DEM   boy   ASSOCI-work.AI-3s   my daughter
       Intended meaning: 'That boy worked with my daughter.'

In order to find out which thematic role of the subject (i.e., an agent or a theme) is relevant to telicity, I tested a range of motion verbs, as illustrated in the left side of Table 2 (Kim 2015, 2017), with respect to whether the verbs could appear with the accompaniment final or the associative linker. The right side of the same table shows restrictions on the available interpretations of the subjects of these verbs as diagnosed by their compatibility with either the accompaniment final or the associative linker.

Relevant data are presented in (7)–(9), and the discussion of the results follows subsequently.[7]

TABLE 2. Interpretation of sentient subject of motion verbs

	FINDINGS IN KIM 2015	FINDINGS IN THIS PAPER	
	GOAL PP CONDITIONED BY SENTIENT SUBJECT	INTERPRETATION OF SENTIENT SUBJECT	
		AGENT (ACCOMPANIMENT FINAL)	THEME (ASSOCIATIVE LINKER)
oo 'go.AI'	Yes	Yes	No
okska'si 'run.AI'	No	Yes	No
inaka'si 'roll.AI'	No	No	Yes

(7) a. Anna   saahkomaapi   itap-oo-wa   anni   isspahkoyi.
      DEM   boy   GOAL-go.AI-3S   DEM   hill
      'That boy went to the hill.'

   b. **Accompaniment final (Agent) ✓**

      Anna   saahkomaapi   **iihpok**-itap-oo-**m**-yii-wa   anni   isspahkoyi
      DEM   boy   ACCOMP-GOAL-go.AI-ACCOMP-TH-3S   DEM   hill

      oksisstyi.
      his mom

   c. Associative linker (theme) ✗

      *Anna   saahkomaapi   **iihp**-itap-oo-wa   anni   isspahkoyi   oksisstyi.
      DEM   boy   ASSOCI-GOAL-go.AI-3S   DEM   hill   his mom
      Intended meaning for (7b) and (7c): 'That boy went to the hill with his mom.'

(8) a. Anna   saahkomaapi   (itap)-okska'si-wa   (anni   isspahkoyi).
      DEM   boy   (GOAL)-run.AI-3S   (DEM   hill)
      'That boy ran (to that hill).'

   b. **Accompaniment (Agent) ✓**

      Anna   saahkomaapi   **iihpok**-(itap-)okska'si-**m**-yii-wa   (anni
      DEM   boy   ACCOMP-GOAL-run.AI-ACCOMP-TH-3S   DEM

      isspahkoyi)   oksisstyi.
      hill   his mom

   c. Associative (theme) ✗

      *Anna   saahkomaapi   **iihp**-okska'si-wa   (anni   isspahkoyi)oksisstyi.
      DEM   boy   (ASSOCI)-run.AI-3S   (DEM   hill)   his mom
      Intended meaning for (8b) and (8c): 'That boy ran with his mom (to the hill).'

(9) a. Anna   saahkomaapi /   anna   oohkotok   (itap)-inn-inaka'si-wa   (anni

    DEM   boy /   DEM   stone   (GOAL)-down-roll.AI-3S   (DEM

    niitahtaayi).

    river)

    'That boy/that stone rolled down (to the river).'

   b. Accompaniment final (Agent) ✗

     *Anna   saahkomaapi   **iihpok**-(itap)-inn-inaka'si-**m-yii**-wa

     DEM   boy   ACCOMP-GOAL-down-roll.AI-ACCOMP-TH-3S

     anni   niitahtaayi   oksisstyi.

     (DEM   river)   his mom

   c. **Associate linker (Theme) ✓**

     Anna   saahkomaapi   iihp-(itap-)inn-inaka'si-wa   (anni   niitahtaayi)

     DEM   boy   ASSOCI-GOAL-down-roll.AI-3S   DEM   hill

     oksisssтyi.

     his mom

     Intended meaning for (9b) and (9c): 'That boy rolled down with his mom (to the river).'

Discussion

The results of the tests show that all motion verbs except *inaka'si* 'roll.AI' (9) require a sentient agent, as the compatibility with an accompaniment final and the incompatibility with an associate linker indicate. The subject of the verb 'roll' turns out to be a theme, regardless of it being sentient ('boy') or not ('stone'): 'roll' is grammatical only with an associative linker, not with an accompaniment final. This is interesting, as the status of the subject being sentient does not determine the role of the subject as an agent or a theme, unlike in English (see, e.g., Levin and Rappaport Hovav 1995).

The data in this section show that a sentient subject that allows a PP endpoint (e.g., a subject of the verb 'go') is always an agent, which is the same thematic role of the sentient subjects of alternating TA/TI verbs. This provides support for the proposal made in this paper that sentient agents are relevant to the determination of the aspectual properties of an event, such as telicity. Turning to the next section, I provide evidence that telicity can be semantically expressed in Blackfoot in a way that is consistent with Kim 2015 (although telicity is not active syntactically, e.g., not represented in aspectual structure in the language; see relevant discussion in the last section), and more importantly I show that different finals indicate differences in aspect.

Final Morphemes and Telicity

In order to identify whether different forms of finals in Blackfoot indicate differences in telicity, I employ two diagnostics used to identify telicity in Bar-el's 2005 study on aspect in Squamish. The two tests are: (i) culmination (i.e., endpoint) cancellation, and (ii) event continuation. The tests are illustrated in (10a) and (10b), respectively.

(10)   a. Culmination cancellation
         # The president was assassinated . . . but he isn't dead.

      b. Event continuation
         He/She X-ed, and (maybe) he/she is still X-ing. (Bar-el 2005)

A culminated event has an inherent endpoint, which means that it is telic. For example, in (10a), the first conjunct expresses a culminated event, assassination of the president. If the culminated portion of the event is cancelled, as expressed in the second conjunct in (10a), it results in contradiction (indicated by #). In this way, a culmination cancellation can be used to determine whether the event in question has an inherent endpoint. The event continuation test in (10b) indicates whether the event in question is ongoing or not. An ongoing event can be continued with a progressive phrase, while a culminated event is incompatible with such a continuation, suggesting that it has an inherent endpoint and is therefore telic. For these diagnostics to work, the event in question (in the first conjunct, as in (10)) should be expressed as a perfective (Bar-el 2005). According to Bar-el, this is because perfectivity can indicate that the event has reached its endpoint, if it has one, which is the element that these diagnostics are testing. Bare forms or forms that indicate past in Blackfoot have perfective interpretations, so the verbs used to set up the tests (i.e., the verbs in the first conjuncts) are expressed in one of those forms.[8]

TA/TI vs. Their Alternating AI+O Verbs

When applied to TA/TI and their alternating AI+O verbs in Blackfoot, the tests in (10) show that TA/TI verbs are telic, but AI verbs are atelic.[9] The verbs that are tested are 'eat' and 'catch'. The results of the tests are illustrated in (11–14) after which the discussion follows.

(11) *oowatoo* 'eat.TI'

    a. Anna   saahkomaapi   ii-oowatoo-m-wa   anni   koopis.

        DEM   boy   PAST-eat.TI-TH-3s   DEM   soup

        'That boy ate the soup.'

    b. # ki   saaki-ohksisstaa-wa-ayi.

        and   still-have.leftover.AI-3s-PRO

        'but it (the soup) is still left.'

    c. # ki   annohk   saaki-a-oowatoo-m-wa.

        and   now   still-IMP-eat.TI-TH-3s

        'but he is stilling eating it.'

(12) *ooyi* 'eat.AI'

    a. Anna   saahkomaapi   ii-ooyi-wa   koopis.

        DEM   boy   PAST-eat.AI-3s   soup

        'That boy ate soup.'

    b. ki   saaki-ohksisstaa-wa-ayi.

        and   still-have.leftover.AI-3s-PRO

        'but it (the soup) is still left.'

    c. ki   annohk   saaki-a-oowatoo-m-wa.

        and   now   still-IMP-eat.TI-TH-3s

        'but he is stilling eating it.'

Discussion

The TI verb in (11) cannot be followed by a sentence that cancels its inherent endpoint, as shown in (11b); the same verb cannot be understood to be ongoing, as shown by the contradiction of the sentence that indicates event continuation in (11c). The corresponding AI+O verb in (12) shows the opposite pattern: it is compatible with culmination cancellation (12b) or event continuation (12c). This result suggests that TA/TI verbs have an inherent endpoint, i.e., are telic, while AI+O verbs do not have such an endpoint, i.e., are atelic. The result also suggests that telicity is clearly present in Blackfoot, and is indicated by different alternating finals (i.e., TA/TI-AI+O pairs).[10]

 This result seems to be in contradiction with the results in Ritter and Rosen 2010 discussed earlier. In the next section, I clarify this conflict with new data.

Are AI+O Finals Aspectually the Same as TA/TI Finals?

Recall the findings of Ritter and Rosen (2010) discussed previously. They show that transitivity alternations indicated via different finals do not correlate with aspectual distinctions; thus, AI+O verbs are not different from their corresponding TA/TIs in their aspectual classification. Their findings appear to conflict with the findings of the current paper, where AIs are shown to be different from TA/TI verbs in their aspectual properties. In order to probe this conflict, I replicated one of Ritter and Rosen's tests with different speakers and in a slightly different manner (see discussion below (13)). I tested the 'finished V-ing' diagnostic (2), using the same consumption verb *ooyi* 'eat.AI' and a new consumption verb *simi* 'drink.AI'. These are illustrated in (13).

(13) a. Anna saahkomaapi ii-ooyi-wa (koopis).
    DEM boy   PAST-eat.AI-3S soup
    'That boy ate (soup).'

   b. Anna saahkomaapi ii-simi-wa (aohkii).
    DEM boy   PAST-drink.AI-3S water
    'That boy drank (water).'

Rather than directly asking whether the verbs in (13) can be used with 'finish V-ing' in Blackfoot, I used the sentences in (13) as contexts and asked the consultants whether the sentences in (14) can serve as continuations. This is because the objects of AIs used in Ritter and Rosen (2010) are optional, and thus it may be hypothesized that they may not be crucial to the interpretation of 'finish V-*ing*'. Interestingly, the result shown in (14) seems to confirm this hypothesis. The sentences in (14) are acceptable as continuations of the sentences in (13) but only with the meanings indicated in (14). For example, the phrase 'finished drinking' in (14) indicates the event of drinking is finished, but it does not necessarily mean that the object 'water' has been all consumed. Regardless of whether water has been completely consumed, (14) indicates only that the action of drinking has been completed.

(14) Akaa-iksist-ooyi/simi-wa.
      PERF-finish-eat.AI/drink.AI-3s
      'He has finished EATing (soup).'/'He has finished DRINKing (water).'

Although more of the aspectual tests used by Ritter and Rosen need to be verified, the result in (14) seems compatible with the proposal made in this paper: an event represented by alternating AI+O verbs is not the same as an event indicated by TA/TI verbs. Moreover, alternating AI+O verbs do not seem to specify an inherent endpoint, i.e., they are unspecified with respect to telicity, which is supported by the data in (15). In (15), the alternating AI+O verbs in (15) can also be continued with sentences of event continuation.

(15) Ki   annohk   saaki-a-ooyi/simi-wa.
      And   now   still-IMP-eat.AI/drink.AI-3s
      'He is still eating/drinking (it).'

The compatibility of AI verbs with 'finish V-ing' does not necessarily mean that the object of the event in question introduces an inherent endpoint for the event; for example, it does not indicate that the object in question is fully consumed.[11]

Concluding Remarks

Summarizing the results of this study, this paper argues that a sentient agent, not a theme, argument contributes to the organization of aspect in Blackfoot. I have also shown that different finals in transitivity may indicate aspectual differences in the Blackfoot VP, in contrast to the findings in Ritter and Rosen (2010).

The consequence of this paper—i.e., that aspect in Blackfoot is sentient agent–oriented—is consistent with a recent atemporal view on IP in the language (Ritter and Wiltschko 2014). However, it also raises an important question of how telicity conditioned by a sentient agent argument should be incorporated into the aspectual structure (e.g., Asp(ect)P) of the language, considering a suggestion that telicity is not syntactically salient in the language (Wiltschko 2012). Following Jackendoff (1991), Wiltschko (2012) assumes that the [bounded] feature distinguishes telic and atelic events. It was proposed that the [±bounded] feature in an English-type language corresponds to [±animate] in Blackfoot. Under this view, TA and TI verbs are expected to pattern differently in telicity: events denoted by TA verbs should pattern with telic events, as their objects are [+animate], while events denoted by TI verbs should pattern with atelic events as their objects are [-animate]. The data provided in this study is consistent with Wiltschko (2012), except that the relevant split between telicity and atelicity does not correspond to the [±animate] specification of the object but rather whether the verb shows morphological agreement with the [±animate] specification of the object—i.e., whether a TA/TI final is present. Importantly, this consequence suggests that Asp in the language is not simply specified for [±animate] as a corresponding feature to [±telic]. A remaining question is then what feature constitutes the syntax of aspect in the language that can be consistent with the result in this paper and the proposed atemporal IP in the language. I leave these issues for another paper. To conclude, the consequences of this paper provide a basis toward an atemporal characterization of event structure in Blackfoot.

NOTES

1. I wish to thank Sandra Manyfeathers (formerly Sandra Crazybull) and Brent Prairie Chicken for sharing their language with me. I also thank Betsy Ritter for helpful discussion on various stages of this project. All errors are my own. Unless otherwise noted, all data presented in this paper are from my own fieldwork.
2. Assuming that atemporal IP must be compatible with other functional categories (such as aspect) in the language, it is expected that aspect should also be atemporal. The atemporal IP does not mean that the language is lacking temporal elements or concepts such as perfectivity or past. What Ritter and Wiltschko's (2014) proposal suggests is that

those temporal elements, despite being available, are not the heads of clausal functional projections.

3. The following abbreviations are used: 1/3 = 1st/3rd person; ACCOMP = accompaniment suffix; ASSOCI = associate linker; AI = intransitive animate; AN = animate; DEM = demonstrative; DUR = durative; IMP = imperfective; II = intransitive inanimate; INA = inanimate; PER = perfective; PRO = pronoun; S = singular; TA = transitive animate; TH = theme; TI = transitive inanimate.

4. Sentient subjects of nonalternating AIs can be nonagents (Ritter and Rosen 2010; Kim 2017).

5. This paper does not address issues of detailed aspectual structure represented by each of an individual verb, e.g., consumption (2) vs. motion verb (3–4). For both types of verbs, this paper suggests that a sentient agent is an important criterion for the aspectual characterization of these verbs.

6. These morphemes do not impose a particular restriction on verb morphology (e.g., stem or final). As long as the role of the subject of a verbal complex of stem and final suits, either morpheme can be compatible with the complex, as shown in (5).

7. With sentences like (9b) and (9c), the same result is found when the subject is a nonsentient noun such as 'that stone' in (9a).

8. Perfectivity is thus required to set up the tests in (10); however, I neither assume nor argue that perfectivity induces telicity in Blackfoot (see note 2 for relevant discussion).

9. For reasons of space, I cannot present data showing how these diagnostics interact with the motion verbs discussed in the third section. What I found is that, in contrast to the verbs *okska'si* 'run' or *inaka'si* 'roll', which do not require an endpoint PP, the verb *oo* 'go', which does require an endpoint PP, can neither be followed by a sentence that cancels its inherent endpoint (test (i)) nor continued with a sentence that indicates event continuation (test (ii)). Thus, the telicity associated with an inherently directed motion verb is consistent with the telicity associated with the TA/TI verbs discussed here.

10. In passing, note that imperfective prefixes (as in the (c) examples in (11–12)) are required to cancel the culmination, consistent with the findings in Dunham (2007).

11. This may suggest that AI objects are not structurally the same as TA/TI objects, supporting previous studies on this issue (e.g., Glougie 2000; Bliss 2013), which I do not question further.

REFERENCES

Bar-el, L. 2005. Aspectual distinction in Sḵwx̱wú7mesh. PhD thesis, University of British Columbia.

Bliss, Heather. 2013. The Blackfoot configurationality conspiracy: Parallels and differences in clausal and nominal structures. PhD thesis, University of British Columbia.

Bloomfield, Leonard. 1946. Algonquian. *Linguistic structures of Native America,* ed. by Harry Hoijer, pp. 85–129. Viking Fund Publications in Anthropology, vol. 6. New York: Wenner-Gren Foundation.

Dowty, David. 1979. *Word meaning and Montague grammar.* Dordrecht: Reidel.

Dunham, Joel. 2007. The "durative" in Blackfoot: Understanding imperfectivity. *Proceedings of SULA 4: Semantics of under-represented languages in the Americas,* ed. by Amy Rose Deal, pp. 49–46. University of Massachusetts Occasional Papers in Linguistics 35. Charleston, SC: BookSurge Publishing.

Frantz, Donald. G. 2009. *Blackfoot grammar.* Toronto: University of Toronto Press.

Glougie, Jennifer. 2000. Topics in the syntax and semantics of Blackfoot quantifiers and nominals. MA thesis, University of British Columbia.

Jackendoff, Ray. 1991. Parts and boundaries. *Cognition* 41:9–45.

Kim, Kyumin. 2015. Spatial PPs and the structure of motion verbs in Blackfoot. *Proceedings of WSCLA 19*, ed. by Natalie Weber and Sihwei Chen, pp. 129–135. UBC Working Papers in Linguistics.

———. 2017. Animacy and transitivity alternation in Blackfoot. *Papers of the Forty-Sixth Algonquian Conference*, ed. by Monica Macaulay and Margaret Noodin. East Lansing: Michigan State University Press.

Levin, Beth, and Malka Rappaport Hovav. 1995. *Unaccusativity: At the syntax-lexical semantics interface.* Cambridge, MA: MIT Press.

Meadows, Kim. 2010. On the role of sentience in Blackfoot: Evidence from the accompaniment and associative constructions. MA thesis, University of Calgary.

Pustejovsky, James. 1991. The syntax of event structure. *Cognition* 41:47–81.

Ramchand, Gillian. 2008. *Verb meaning and the lexicon: A first phase syntax.* New York: Cambridge University Press.

Ritter, Elizabeth, and Sara T. Rosen. 2010. Animacy in Blackfoot: Implications for event structure and clause structure. *Lexical semantics, syntax, and event structure,* ed. by Malka Rappaport-Hovav, Edit Doron, and Ivy Sichel, pp. 124–152. Oxford: Oxford University Press.

Ritter, Elizabeth, and Martina Wiltschko. 2014. The composition of INFL: An exploration of tense, tenseless languages, and tenseless constructions. *Natural Language and Linguistic*

Theory 32:1331–1386.

Speas, Margaret, and Carol Tenny. 2003. Configurational properties of point of view roles. *Asymmetry in grammar*, ed. by Anna Maria di Scuillo, pp. 315–344. Amsterdam: Benjamins.

Travis, Lisa. 2010. *Inner aspect*. Dordrecht: Springer.

Vendler, Zeno. 1967. *Linguistics in philosophy*. Ithaca, NY: Cornell University Press.

Verkyul, Henk. 1989. Aspectual classes and aspectual composition. *Linguistics and Philosophy* 12:39–94.

Wiltschko, Martina. 2012. Decomposing the count-mass distinction: Evidence from languages that lack it. *Count and mass across languages*, ed. by Diane Massam, pp. 146–171. Oxford: Oxford University Press.

Subjects, Animacy, and Agreement in Mi'gmaq Transitive Verbs

Carol-Rose Little

T his paper's two main goals are to investigate the status of animate and inanimate subjects in the Eastern Algonquian language Mi'gmaq and the consequences for agreement morphology when the subject is animate or inanimate. Inanimate nouns can be in subject position of transitive verbs. When there are two third person arguments, the verb only indexes the animacy of one. However, number (singular or plural) of each third person argument is always indexed on the verb.

Nouns are classified into two grammatical categories in Algonquian languages: animate and inanimate.[1] For the most part, nouns that are living are classified as animate, but nonliving nouns can be grammatically animate or inanimate (Dahlstrom 1995; Quinn 2001). There is a semantic basis for this noun grouping: generally, people and animals are animate, but beyond this semantic basis, grammatical animacy does not seem to be predictable. Animacy has consequences for verbal morphology. In intransitive verbs the verbal morphology agrees with the subject's animacy. In transitive verbs, the topic of this paper, the object's animacy is marked on the verb. A verb is classified as transitive animate if the object is animate and transitive inanimate if the object is inanimate (Bloomfield 1946). It has been reported that the Algonquian language Blackfoot completely disallows semantically inanimate nouns in subject position of a transitive verb (Frantz 1991). Focusing on Mi'gmaq (Eastern Algonquian), I investigate agreement patterns with the transitive verb when the animacy of the subject is varied. To do this, first I explore if inanimate subjects are even possible with transitive verbs, and if they are possible, what the consequences are for verbal morphology.

These new data from Mi'gmaq are important for documenting the variation of animate and inanimate subjects across Algonquian languages. As mentioned above, in Blackfoot, only semantically animate nouns are allowed to function as subjects (Frantz 1991; Ritter and Rosen 2010). Ojibwe allows semantically inanimate subjects but only if the object is semantically animate (Valentine 2001). I provide evidence that Mi'gmaq allows all combinations of animate and inanimate subjects and objects with transitive verbs. Furthermore, I provide evidence that transitive verbs do not index the subject's animacy. In other words, with two third person arguments, the transitive verb only indexes the animacy of one of the arguments. In the cases that follow, the verb only reflects the object's animacy.

The paper is organized as follows: First, I give background on animacy in Algonquian languages. Then, I describe my methodology, results, and observations from elicitation sessions on the status of inanimate subjects in Mi'gmaq and consequences for the morphology of transitive verbs. The final section concludes the paper with notes on how we can capture differences across Algonquian languages with respect to animacy.

Background

In this section, I give background on the animate and inanimate noun classes in Mi'gmaq, then discuss relevant transitive verb morphology.

Animate and Inanimate Noun Classes

In Algonquian languages, nouns are classified into two grammatical genders: animate and inanimate. Most semantically animate nouns (i.e., living things) are grammatically animate whereas semantically inanimate nouns can be either grammatically animate or inanimate. In other words, the animate class of nouns has a semantic basis (i.e., living things), but there are exceptions like *pu'tai* 'bottle' or *tlawo'q* 'knife', which are also grammatically animate. This is summarized in Table 1.

TABLE 1. Noun classification in Mi'gmaq

		GRAMMATICAL	
		ANIMATE	*INANIMATE*
SEMANTIC	*ANIMATE*	ji'nm 'man' jagej 'lobster'	—
	INANIMATE	tlawo'q 'knife' pu'tai 'bottle'	tma'gittaqan 'saw' tepaqan 'car'

Table 1 provides examples of the three categories of nouns found in Mi'gmaq: semantically and grammatically animate, semantically inanimate and grammatically animate, and semantically inanimate and grammatically inanimate.[2]

For the most part, in Mi'gmaq, it is not possible to discern grammatical animacy from a noun's phonological shape alone. Instead, agreement morphology reflects the noun class. Below we see that grammatical animacy is important for agreement morphology (third person markers and plural markers), rather than semantic animacy.[3] The plural marker is *-ig* for the animate nouns in (1) and (2) but *-l* for the inanimate noun in (3). The third person maker is *-j* for the animate nouns but *-g* for the inanimate nouns.

(1) Semantically and grammatically animate

Ji'nm-u-**g**   apje'j-i-**j**-**ig**.[4]

man-LV-PL.AN   small-AI-3.AN-PL.AN

'The men are small.'

(2) Semantically inanimate, grammatically animate

a. Tlawoq-**q**   apje'j-i-**j**-**ig**.

    knife-PL.AN   small-AI-3.AN -PL.AN

    'The knives are small.'

b. Pu'tai-**g**   apje'j-i-**j**-**ig**.

    bottle-PL.AN   small-AI-3AN -PL.an

    'The bottles are small.'

TABLE 2. Plural and singular morphemes and their allomorphs in Mi'gmaq

NOUN CLASS	PLURAL MORPHEME	ALLOMORPH	ALTERNATION RULE
Animate	-g	-q	g → q /q_
Inanimate	-l	-n	l → n / n_

(3)   Semantically inanimate, grammatically inanimate

    a. Tma'gittaqan-**n**   apje'j-**g**-**l**.

        saw-PL.AN   small.II-3.IN-PL.IN

        'The saws are small.'

    b. Wasueg-**l**   apje'j-**g**-**l**.

        flower-PL.IN   small.II-3-PL.IN

        'The flowers are small.'

Allomorphs of animate and inanimate plural morphology are given in Table 2. I give the morphemes using the orthographic system. There is no voicing contrast in Mi'gmaq so -*g* is a velar stop, -*l* is a lateral approximate, -*q* is a uvular obstruent (subject to phonological variation; see Quinn 2012 for discussion), and -*n* is an alveolar nasal.

Transitive Verbs in Mi'gmaq

In Mi'gmaq, as with other Algonquian languages, the animacy of the object is marked in the transitive verb's agreement morphology. Transitive verbs in Algonquian languages are traditionally classified based on the animacy of the object (Bloomfield 1946). Morphemes that mark whether the transitive verb takes an animate or inanimate object are called finals. When the object of a transitive verb is grammatically animate, the verb has a transitive animate (TA) final on it. When the object is grammatically inanimate, the verb has a transitive inanimate (TI) final. Sometimes this final is overt (in which case I separate the stem and final); in other cases the final is null. I detail null finals below in examples (6–7). The following examples in Mi'gmaq demonstrate these two types of verbs for the verb *wissugwa-* 'to cook'. In (4a), the TA final -*al* indexes the animate object *tap'tang* 'potatoes', and the TI final -*atm* in (5a) indexes the inanimate object *wa'wl* 'eggs'. The examples in (4b) and (5b) show that any mismatch of transitive animate or transitive inanimate final marker is ungrammatical. If the object is plural then a plural marker is suffixed to the end of the verb. I follow Oxford (2014) by calling this the outer suffix. This plural suffix is also sensitive to animacy with -*ig* for animate objects and -*l* for inanimate objects, as discussed for nouns above. Verb finals and plural suffixes are in bold in (4) and (5).

(4) Animate object

    a. Wissugw-**al**-oq-**ig**   tap'tan-g.

       cook-**TA**-2.PL-**PL.AN**   potato.AN-PL.AN

       'You all cook the potatoes.'

    b. *Wissugw-**atm**-oq-l   tap'tan-g.

       cook-**TI**-2.PL-**PL.IN**   potato.AN-PL.AN

       Intended: 'You all cook the potatoes.'

(5) Inanimate object

    a. Wissugw-**atm**-oq-**l**   wa'w-l.

       cook-**TI**-2.PL-**PL.IN**   egg.IN-PL.IN

       'You all cook the eggs.'

    b. *Wissugw-**al**-oq-**ig**   wa'w-l.

       cook-**TA**-2.PL-**PL.AN**   egg.IN-PL.IN

       Intended: 'You all cook the eggs.'

Examples of finals that mark animate objects on the verb are: *al, a'l, a, i,* and Ø.[5] Finals when the object is inanimate are *atm, a'tu, (i)tu,* and Ø (Fidelholtz 1968; Hamilton 2015; McCulloch 2013). The verb root's selection of these finals seems to be lexically determined; hence verb roots are listed with their finals. Even when the TA or TI final is not visible, it is still possible to determine if the verb is TA or TI from other suffixes, such as the theme sign. A theme sign is sensitive to the features of the subject and the object and can change depending on the person hierarchy second person > first person > third person proximate > third person obviative. A direct theme sign signifies that something higher on the person hierarchy is acting on something lower on the person hierarchy. The inverse theme sign signifies the opposite: something lower on the person hierarchy acting on something higher. In this paper, I focus solely on data with the direct theme sign. For TA or TI finals that are not visible, I use the notation of 'verb root.TI/TA'. Example (6) shows a TA verb where the TA final is not visible but the direct (DIR) theme sign signifies that the verb is TA. Note that theme signs do not appear on TI verbs.

(6) TA with nonvisible final, but direct theme sign

Tems-**a**-t-l.

cut.TA-**DIR**-3-OBV

'He cuts it (animate).'

Example (7) shows a TI final where the TI is not visible with a third person subject:

(7) TI with nonvisible final

Tems'-g.

cut.TI-3

'He cuts it (inanimate).'

However, with other persons, like the first person exclusive, the TI marker is visible. This is given in (8).

(8) TI final resurfaces with first person exclusive

Tems-**m**-eg.

cut-**TI**-1.EXCL

'We cut it (inanimate).'

The next relevant morpheme is the inner suffix, which comes after the TA or TI marker and the theme sign in TA verbs.[6] The inner suffix indexes person features of the subject or object (whether it indexes the subject or object features is dependent on person hierarchies). For third person singular arguments with TA verbs the third person marker is -*t*, as in examples (9a) and (10a). For TI verbs the third person marker is -*g* (in (9b) or -*q*[7] in (10b)). The selection of -*g* or -*q* is dependent on the TI final.

(9) Inner suffix with *ges*- 'to love'

a. Ges-al-a-t-l.

love-TA-DIR-**3**-OBV

'He loves him/her/it (animate).'

b. Ges-at-**g**.

love-TI-**3**

'He loves it (inanimate).'

(10) Inner suffix with *nem-* 'to see'

a. Nem-i-a-t-l.

see-TA-DIR-**3**-OBV

'He sees it (animate).'

b. Nem-ito-**q**.

see-TI-**3**

'He sees it (inanimate).'

Tables 3 and 4 summarize the relevant parts of a TA verb, where the object is animate (Table 3), and a TI verb, where the object is inanimate (Table 4). The TI/ TA markers (finals) and inner suffix markers are bold.

Animacy, Subjects, and Transitive Verbs in Other Algonquian Languages

Both Ojibwe and Blackfoot are examples of Algonquian languages where animacy restricts subjects and objects of transitive verbs. Valentine (2001:426) comments that in Ojibwe "[b]oth actors and goals may be animate, or either the actor or the

TABLE 3. TA verb morphology

wissugw	-al	-a	-t	-l
cook	**TA**	DIR	**3**	OBV
verb root	**final**	theme sign	**inner suffix**	outer suffix
'He/she cooks it (animate).'				

TABLE 4. TI verb morphology

wissugw	-at	-g	-l
cook	**TI**	**3**	IN.PL
verb root	**final**	**inner suffix**	outer suffix
'He/she cooks them (inanimate).'			

goal may be inanimate, but both cannot be inanimate—a transitive predication in Nishnaabemwin must have at least one animate argument." In other words, if there is an inanimate subject, the object must be animate.[8]

Even more restrictive is Blackfoot, a Plains Algonquian language, which only allows semantically animate nouns to be subjects of transitive verbs (Frantz 1991; Ritter and Rosen 2010). Consider the following examples.

(11) Blackfoot (Ritter and Rosen 2010)

 a. *Oma isttoána ikahksínima annstsi ikkstsíksiistsi

om-wa	isttoán-wa	ikahksíni-m-wa	ann-istsi
DEM-3.PROX.AN	knife-3PROX.AN	cut.TI-TH-3SG	DEM-IN.PL

ikkstsiksi-istsi

BRANCH-IN.PL

Intended: 'That knife cut those branches.'

 b. oma isttoána iihtsikahksínii'pi annistsi ikkstsíksiistsi.

om-wa	isttoán-wa	iiht-ikahksíni-'p-yi	ann-istsi
DEM-3PROX.AN	knife-3PROX.AN	INST-cut.TI-TH-PL.INAN	DEM-IN.PL

ikkstsiksi-istsi

branch-IN.PL

'By means of the knife (animate), the branches were cut off.'

(11a) shows that with an active transitive verb with the direct theme sign (-*m*), the subject 'knife' is ungrammatical because it is not semantically animate or capable of performing the action as an agent, even though 'knife' is grammatically animate. The grammatical way to express the event where a knife cuts branches is given in (11b). There is an instrumental prefix on the verb 'cut' signifying that the instrument of the action is the saw. The verb's theme sign is -*p*, the impersonal marker.

Thus, animacy plays more than simply a morphological role. Ojibwe does not allow a sentence with an inanimate subject and inanimate object. Blackfoot restricts all semantically inanimate nouns from functioning as subjects of transitive verbs. Given these empirical facts about Blackfoot and Ojibwe, I next investigate the status of inanimate subjects in Mi'gmaq.

The Status of Inanimate Subjects of Transitive Verbs

In the following subsections I discuss elicitation methodology, results, and generalizations about the results.

Methodology

In order to test environments involving different combinations of animate and inanimate arguments I used 29 short (<four seconds) videos depicting various events
with two participants. These videos were originally used in a study on animacy,
topicality, and agentivity in Yucatec Maya (Butler et al. 2012, n.d.). Speakers were
asked to provide one-sentence descriptions of these videos. Three Mi'gmaq speakers
(also bilingual in English), two men and one woman aged 50–70, participated in
describing the videos. After showing these videos, I asked follow-up questions
where I varied the plurality of the subjects and objects. So, instead of 'the carriage
bumps into the pot' (one of the events depicted by the videos), I asked speakers to
translate 'The carriages bump into the pot/pots'.

I also showed participants drawings, asking them to describe events with
one-sentence answers.[9] Examples are given in Figures 1 and 2.

FIGURE 1. Drawing of a saw
cutting a branch, by Shoshana Isaac

FIGURE 2. Drawing of a man
cutting a branch , by Shoshana Isaac

Results

The data speakers provided gives evidence that inanimate subjects of transitive verbs are possible.[10] For instance, after seeing the video where a carriage rolls and hits a pot, speakers gave the following description.

(12) Mijua'ji'j-ewei   tepaqan   migutesgu-a-t-l   wow-u-l
      child-POSS   car.IN   bump.TA-DIR-3-OBV   pot.AN-LV-OBV
      'The carriage bumps into the pot.'

Below I discuss some new generalizations about the order of arguments when both arguments are inanimate singular or animate plural. Then I present more data that demonstrate that not only are inanimate subjects possible, but also that the transitive verb does not reflect animacy of the subject with third person objects.

WORD ORDER

Usually in Mi'gmaq, the ordering of arguments in a sentence is flexible: in a sentence with a subject, verb, and object all six orders are possible (Hamilton 2015:22). Order of arguments, however, is important for determining which noun is the subject and the object in a context with two inanimate arguments or two animate plural arguments. The first noun is always interpreted as the subject.

(13) a. Tepaqan   migutesg'-g-'p   altesgasimgewei.
          car.IN   bump.TI-3-PST   bike.IN
          'The car hit the bike.'
          NOT: 'The bike hit the car.'

      b. Tepaqan altesgasimgewei migutesg'-g-'p.
          'The car hit the bike.'

(14) a. Altesgasimgewei   migutesg'-g-'p   tepaqan.
          bike.IN   bump.TI-3-PST   car.IN
          'The bike hit the car.'
          NOT: 'The car hit the bike.'

b. Altesgasimgewei tepaqan migutesg'-g-'p.
'The bike hit the car.'

These data also reflect a similar pattern observed for two animate plural arguments. Examples (15–16) show that the first noun is always interpreted as the subject whereas the second is the object when the arguments of the verb are 'women' and 'babies'. Note that there is no special morphology on animate plural nouns that distinguish animate plural proximate nouns from animate plural obviative nouns.

(15)   a.   E'pij-ig   ges-al-a-'tij-ig   mijua'jij-g
             woman.AN-PL.AN   love-TA-DIR-3.PL-PL.AN   baby.AN-PL.AN
             'The women love the babies.'
             NOT: 'The babies love the women.'

       b.   E'pij-ig mijua'jij-g ges-al-a-'tij-ig
             'The women love the babies.'

(16)   a.   Mijua'jij-g   ges-al-a-'tij-ig   e'pij-ig.
             baby.AN-PL.AN   love-TA-DIR-3.PL-PL.AN   woman.AN-PL.AN
             'The babies love the women.'
             NOT: 'The women love the babies.'

       b.   Mijua'jij-g e'pij-ig ges-al-a-'tij-ig.
             'The babies love the women.'

ANIMACY AND AGREEMENT

Here I detail the effects of animacy on verbal morphology. When there are two third person arguments, the verb only indexes the animacy of one. In the cases below, the verb only indexes the object's animacy. Although the verbal morphology does not index the animacy of the subject noun, it does index the plurality of the subject. For singular subjects of TI verbs, the inner suffix is -*g*, and for plural subjects -*i'tij* (or -*i'tit* before an inanimate plural marker). These inner suffixes are in bold throughout the section.

The first set of data are the TI verbs with possible combinations of singular semantically and grammatically animate and inanimate subjects. The sentence given is "x cuts the branch(es)." The possible subjects are: *ji'nm* 'man' (grammatically and semantically animate), *tlawo'q* 'knife' (grammatically animate), and *tma'gittaqan* 'saw' (grammatically inanimate). In order to firmly establish the context where a knife or saw cuts a branch, I used the picture in Figure 2 as well as the following context where the knife or saw is so sharp, it can cut through anything:

(17) Ula   tlawo'q/tma'gittaqan   tems'-**g**   ta'n   pas   goqwei.
     DEM   knife.AN/saw.IN   cut.TI-3   COMP   PART   what
        'This knife/saw cuts through anything.'

After this context was established, the following sentences were elicited with the three possible subjects 'man', 'knife', and 'saw'. In the (a) examples the object is singular, in the (b) examples the object is plural.

(18) Grammatically animate and semantically animate subject
    a. Ji'nm   tems'-**g**   psetgun.
       man.AN   cut.TI-3   branch.IN
       'The man cuts the branch.'

    b. Ji'nm   tems'-**g**-l   psetgun-n.
       man.AN   cut.TI-3-PL.IN   branch.IN-PL.IN
       'The man cuts the branches.'

(19) Grammatically animate, semantically inanimate subject
    a. Tlawo'q   tems'-**g**   psetgun.
       knife.AN   cut.TI-3   branch.IN
       'The knife cuts the branch.'

    b. Tlawo'q   tems'-**g**-l   psetgun-n.
       knife.AN   cut.TI-3-PL.IN   branch.IN-PL.IN
       'The knife cuts the branches.'

(20) Grammatically inanimate and semantically inanimate subject
    a. Tma'gittaqan   tems'-**g** psetgun.
       saw.IN   cut.TI-3 branch.IN
       'The saw cuts the branch.'

b. Tma'gittaqan   tems'-**g**-l   psetgun-n.
   saw.IN   cut.TI-**3**-PL.IN   branch.IN-PL.IN
   'The saw cuts the branches.'

Regardless of the animacy of the subject, the inner suffixes across all three examples are marked with the third person singular marker (*-g*). When the object is plural, the inanimate plural marker (*-l*) appears after the inner suffix.

The examples below show that the marker for plural subjects 'men', 'knives', and 'saws' is *-i'tij* (or *-i'tit* before the inanimate plural marker *-l*).

(21)   Grammatically animate and semantically animate subject

      a. Ji'nm-u-g   tems'-m-**i'tij**   psetgun.
          man.AN-LV-PL.AN   cut-TI-**3PL.SUBJ**   branch.IN
          'The men cut the branch.'

      b. Ji'nm-u-g   tems'-m-**i'tit**-l   psetgun-n.
          man.AN-LV-PL.AN   cut-TI-**3PL.SUBJ**-PL.IN   branch.IN-PL.IN
          'The men cut the branches.'

(22)   Grammatically animate, semantically inanimate subject

      a. Tlawo'q-q   tems'-m-**i'tij**   psetgun
          knife.AN-PL.AN   cut-TI-**3PL.SUBJ**   branch.IN
          'The knives cut the branch.'

      b. Tlawo'q-q   tems'-m-**i'tit**-l   psetgun-n.
          knife.AN-PL.AN   cut-TI-**3PL.SUBJ**-PL.IN   branch.IN-PL.IN
          'The knives cut the branches.'

(23)   Grammatically inanimate and semantically inanimate subject

      a. Tma'gittaqan-n   tems'-m-**i'tij**   psetgun.
          saw.IN-PL.IN   cut-TI-**3PL.SUBJ**   branch.IN
          'The saws cut the branch.'

      b. Tma'gittaqan-n   tems'-m-**i'tit**-l   psetgun-n.
          saw.IN-IN.PL   cut-TI-**3PL.SUBJ**-PL.IN   branch.IN-PL.IN
          'The saws cut the branches.'

Note again that the plural marker stays the same regardless of the animacy of the subject.

In the next two data sets, I show examples with a TA verb, *migutesgua-* 'to bump into', with the animate object *wow* 'pot'. The subjects tested are *ji'nm* 'man', *tu'aqan* 'ball' (grammatically animate), and *mijua'ji'jewei tepaqan* 'baby carriage' (grammatically inanimate). In all these examples, the inner suffix (*-t*) indexes the third person subject. This marker does not vary according to the animacy of the subject. The *-t* palatalizes to *-j* (the alveopalatal affricate) before the animate plural object marking *-ig* in the (b) series.

(24) Grammatically animate and semantically animate subject

a. Ji'nm   migutesgu-a-**t**-l   wow-u-l.
    man.AN   bump.TA-DIR-**3**-OBV   pot.AN-LV-OBV
    'The man bumps into the pot.'

b. Ji'nm   migutesgu-a-**j**-ig   wow-g.
    man.AN   bump.TA-DIR-**3**-PL.AN   pot.AN-PL.AN
    'The man bumps into the pots.'

(25) Grammatically animate and semantically inanimate subject

a. Tu'aqan   migutesgu-a-**t**-l   wow-u-l.
    ball.AN   bump.TA-DIR-**3**-OBV   pot.AN-LV-OBV
    'The ball bumps into the pot.'

b. Tu'aqan   migutesgu-a-**j**-ig   wow-g.
    ball.AN   bump.TA-DIR-**3**-PL.AN   pot.AN-PL.AN
    'The ball bumps into the pots.'

(26) Grammatical inanimate and semantically inanimate subject

a. Mijua'ji'j-ewei   tepaqan   migutesgu-a-**t**-l   wow-u-l.
    child-POSS   car.IN   bump.TA-DIR-**3**-OBV   pot.AN-LV-OBV
    'The carriage bumps into the pot.'

b. Mijua'ji'j-ewei   tepaqan   migutesgu-a-**j**-ig   wow-g.
    child-POSS   car.IN   bump.TA-DIR-**3**-PL.AN   pot.AN-PL.AN
    'The carriage bumps into the pots.'

Examples (27–29) show that with plural animate and inanimate subjects the inner suffix is -'tit before the obviative marker -l and palatalizes to -'tij before the animate plural -ig. As with the previous data sets, the animacy of the subject does not affect the verb form.

(27) Grammatically animate and semantically inanimate

    a. Ji'nm-u-g   migutesgu-a-'tit-l   wow-u-l.
        man.AN-LV-PL.AN   bump.TA-DIR-3PL.SUBJ-OBV   pot.AN-LV-OBV
        'The men bump into the pot.'

    b. Ji'nm-u-g   migutesgu-a-'tij-ig   wow-g.
        man.AN-LV-PL.AN   bump.TA-DIR-3PL.SUBJ-PL.AN   pot.AN-PL.AN
        'The men bump into the pot.'

(28) Grammatically animate and semantically inanimate subject

    a. Tu'aqan-g   migutesgu-a-'tit-l   wow-u-l.
        ball.AN-PL.AN   bump.TA-DIR-3PL.SUBJ-OBV   pot.AN-LV-OBV
        'The balls bump into the pot.'

    b. Tu'aqan-g   migutesgu-a-'tij-ig   wow-g.
        ball.AN-PL.AN   bump.TA-DIR-3PL.SUBJ-PL.AN   pot.AN-PL.AN
        'The balls bump into the pots.'

(29) Grammatically inanimate and semantically inanimate subject

    a. Mijua'ji'j-ewei tepaqan-n   migutesgu-a-'tit-l   wow-u-l.
        child-POSS   car.IN-PL.IN   bump.TA-DIR-3PL.SUBJ-OBV   pot.AN-LV-OBV
        'The carriages bump into the pot.'

    b. Mijua'ji'j-ewei tepaqan-n   migutesgu-a-'tij-ig   wow-g.
        child-POSS   car.IN-PL.IN   bump.TA-DIR-3PL.SUBJ-PL.AN   pot.AN-PL.AN
        'The carriages bump into the pots.'

These data provide evidence that: (i) inanimate nouns can be in subject position in Mi'gmaq, and (ii) that the verb is only sensitive to the animacy features of the object. In third person environments the verb final consistently indexes the animacy of the object, and the outer suffix does as well when the object is plural.[11] The inner suffix, however, is only sensitive to person and number features of the subject (i.e., third person, singular/plural) but not animacy. In sum, there is an asymmetry between animacy agreement in transitive verbs: transitive verbs in third person environments in Mi'gmaq do not agree with the subject for animacy, but do with the objects' animacy. In other words, with two third person arguments, the verb only indexes the animacy of one of the arguments. In the cases listed above, the verb only indexes the object's animacy.

Conclusions

Mi'gmaq allows inanimate subjects, as evidenced by the data presented above. Furthermore, the animacy of the subject in third person contexts is not indexed by agreement morphology—only the animacy of the object is important for agreement morphology. So, when a transitive verb has two third person arguments, only one argument's animacy is indexed on the verb. On the other hand, number (singular or plural) of the third person arguments is always clearly indexed on the verb. I have also illustrated that the order of arguments is important in contexts with two singular inanimate nouns and two plural animate nouns for determining which is the subject and which is the object.

The importance of this study lies in the fact that though all Algonquian languages share GRAMMATICAL features like animacy, there is variation across languages in terms of SEMANTIC animacy. For instance, in Blackfoot and Mi'gmaq grammatical animacy governs the agreement forms. Blackfoot, however, has a semantic animacy restriction where only semantically animate nouns can be subjects of transitive verbs. Ritter and Rosen (2010) posit that the verb final imposes a strict semantic restriction on the external argument. Mi'gmaq, on the other hand, is not so restrictive on what can function as a subject of a transitive verb. Extending Ritter and Rosen's analysis, in Mi'gmaq, the final would not impose such a strict semantic restriction on the external argument of the transitive verb. To this end in the transitive verb domain at least, we can see a spectrum of the restrictions that the final places on the subjects of transitive verbs within the Algonquian language family: strict (Blackfoot), lax (Mi'gmaq), or somewhere in between (Ojibwe).

Finally, during fieldwork, participants had varying intuitions about certain semantically inanimate subjects. This brings up the question: semantically, what types of inanimate subjects are then possible in Mi'gmaq? Instrument subjects like *tma'gittaqan* 'saw' or *tu'aqan* 'ball' are possible in Mi'gmaq, as exemplified above. However, the acceptability of causer subjects like *mtugunoqt* 'storm' or *ugju'sn* 'wind' varies across speakers:

(30) ?Mtugunoqt/ugju'sn   sewiste'-g-'p   tuop'ti.
      storm.IN/wind.IN   break.TI-3-PST   window.IN
      'The storm/wind broke the window.'

Perhaps there is a continuum of acceptable inanimate subjects: instruments are possible but causers are less acceptable. I leave an investigation of this for further research.

NOTES

1. First and foremost, I would like to gratefully acknowledge Mi'gmaq speakers and experts Mary Ann Metallic, Roger Metallic, Katherine Sorbey, Janice Vicaire, Lillian Moffat Vicaire, and Joe Wilmot. Without them, this paper would not have been possible. I would also like to thank Miloje Despić, Michael Hamilton, Sarah Murray, Conor Quinn, John Whitman, the members of the Cornell Syntax Circle, and the audiences of the Forty-Seventh Algonquian Conference and the 2016 Meeting of the Society for the Study of the Indigenous Languages of the Americas for comments during various stages of this paper. Unless otherwise cited, the data from this paper comes from the author's fieldwork in the Mi'gmaq First Nations community of Listuguj, Quebec. All Mi'gmaq text has been adapted to the Listuguj orthography by the author. Glosses are also the author's. An apostrophe (') is used to mark vowel length (e.g., *su'n* [suːn] 'cranberry') and represent a schwa (ə), e.g., *almag'tg* [almagətk] 'it is soggy', 'g' is used to represent the velar stop, in place of the 'k' seen in other orthographies (e.g., Smith-Francis).

2. Goddard (2002:213) reports that animacy can play a derivational role in deriving collectives. For instance, in Massachusetts the collective noun *nuppometuonk* 'my descendants' and in Fox the collective noun *owiye×he×hi* 'animals, small game' are both inanimate. Mathieu (2012) also argues that animacy in Algonquian (namely, Ojibwe) is used syntactically to create individuals. In other words, he asserts that gender shift from animate to inanimate is used to mark singulativization.

3. Abbreviations: 1 = first person; 2 = second person; 3 = third person; AI = animate intransitive verb; AN = animate; COMP = complementizer; DEM = demonstrative; DIR = direct; II = inanimate intransitive verb; IN = inanimate; INST = instrumental; LV = linking

vowel; POSS = possession suffix; PART = particle; PL = plural; PST = past; TA = transitive animate verb; TI = transitive inanimate verb; TH = theme sign.

4. I follow Quinn's (2006:31) analysis of Penobscot verb finals in glossing -*i* as what marks that the verb is animate intransitive (AI). Also note that some AI and II verbs are identical in the singular form as shown below in (i). See Little (to appear) for more discussion.

    i.   Megwe'-g.
       red.AI/II-3.AN/3.IN
       'It (animate or inanimate) is red. (Mi'gmaq Online Dictionary entry 2227)

5. It is possible that the final -*a* is a causative morpheme, but more research is needed to confirm this.

6. I follow Oxford (2014) and Hamilton (2015) by calling this morpheme slot the inner suffix. This slot corresponds to what Bloomfield (1962) calls slot 5.

7. It is probable that the -*o* in the TI final -*ito* is actually underlying -*itu* and phonological interactions with the uvular obstruent lowered the vowel *u* to *o*. Compare (10b) *nemitoq* 'he or she sees it' to *nemituoq* 'you (pl) see it'. In the second person plural form, -*itu* is the TI final with the second person plural subject indexed by -*oq*. Further investigation is needed to confirm that -*ito* is -*itu* underlyingly in (10b).

8. It is unclear if Valentine means that the Ojibwe constraint is sensitive to grammatical or semantic animacy. It may be safe to assume a SEMANTIC animacy constraint based on the fact that he further says that "[m]ost commonly actors, as initiators and controllers of actions, are animate" (2001:426), assuming initiators or controllers must have will or volition and, for the most part, are animate.

9. To download these drawings visit http://conf.ling.cornell.edu/carolroselittle/.

10. Indeed, Hewson and Francis (1990) mention that inanimate nouns are possible as subjects of transitive verbs in Mi'gmaq.

11. Note that with first person subjects of TA verbs, the inner suffix does index animacy. This is exemplified with the TA verb *gesnugu-* where -*g* indexes the inanimate noun *nunji* 'my head' in (ii) and -*t* indexes the animate noun *njigun* 'my knee' in (iii):

    ii. N-unji   gesnugu-i-**g**.
        1-head.IN   ache.TA-1.OBJ-**3.IN**
        'My head aches.'

iii. N-jigun   gesnugu-i-**t.**

    1-knee.AN   ache.TA-1.OBJ-**3.AN**

    'My knee aches.'

REFERENCES

Bloomfield, Leonard. 1946. Algonquian. *Linguistic structures of Native America,* ed. by Cornelius Osgood and Harry Hoijer, pp. 85–129. Viking Fund Publications in Anthropology, vol. 6. New York: Wenner-Gren Foundation.

———. 1962. *The Menomini language.* New Haven, CT: Yale University Press.

Butler, Lindsay K., T. Florian Jaeger, and J. Bohnemeyer. 2012. Animacy is mediated by topicality in the production of word order in Yucatec Maya and Spanish. Paper read at the International Workshop on Language Production (IWOLP), New York University.

———. n.d. Animacy effects on sentence production: Ease of retrieval or topicality? Unpublished manuscript.

Dahlstrom, Amy. 1995. Motivation vs. predictability in Algonquian gender. *Papers of the Twenty-Sixth Algonquian Conference*, ed. by D. H. Pentland, pp. 52–66. Winnipeg: University of Manitoba.

Fidelholtz, James L. 1968. Micmac morphophonemics. PhD thesis, Massachusetts Institute of Technology.

Frantz, D. G. 1991. *Blackfoot grammar.* Toronto: University of Toronto Press.

Goddard, Ives. 2002. Grammatical gender in Algonquian. *Papers of the Thirty-Third Algonquian Conference*, ed. by H. Wolfart, pp. 195–231. Winnipeg: University of Manitoba.

Hamilton, Michael. 2015. The syntax of Mi'gmaq: A configurational account. PhD thesis, McGill University.

Little, Carol-Rose. To appear. Inanimate nouns as subjects in Mi'gmaq: Consequences for agreement morphology. *Proceedings of the Twenty-First Workshop on the Structure and Constituency of Languages of the Americas*, ed. by Megan Keough. University of British Columbia Working Papers in Linguistics.

Mathieu, Éric. 2012. Flavors of division. *Linguistic Inquiry* 43(4):650–679.

McCulloch, Gretchen. 2013. Verb stem composition. MA thesis, McGill University.

Mi'gmaq online dictionary. 2015. http://mikmaqonline.org/.

Oxford, William Robert. 2014. Microparameters of agreement: A diachronic perspective on Algonquian verb inflection. PhD thesis, University of Toronto.

Quinn, Conor. 2001. A preliminary survey of animacy categories in Penobscot. In *Papers of the*

Thirty-Second Algonquian Conference, ed. by John D. Nichols, pp. 395–426. Winnipeg: University of Manitoba.

———. 2006. Referential-access dependency in Penobscot. PhD thesis, Harvard University.

———. 2012. Listuguj Mi'gmaq: Variation and distinctive dialectal features. Paper read at the Forty-Fourth Algonquian Conference, University of Chicago.

Ritter, Elizabeth, and Sara T. Rosen. 2010. Animacy in Blackfoot: Implications for event structure and clause structure. *Syntax, lexical semantics and event structure*, ed. by Malka Rappaport-Hovav, Edith Doron, and Ivy Siche, pp. 124–152. Oxford: Oxford University Press.

Valentine, J. Randolph. 2001. *Nishnaabemwin reference grammar*. Toronto: University of Toronto Press.

Nominal TAM and the Preterit in Potawatomi

Hunter Thompson Lockwood

T ense, aspect, and mood (TAM) are generally considered solely properties of verbs, but Nordlinger and Sadler (2004, 2008; hereafter N&S) argue that many American Indian languages show systems of nominal tense (NT) or nominal TAM.[1] Citing two examples, they include Potawatomi among them (N&S 2004:781). Using new data from fieldwork, I discuss whether or not NT applies to the preterit in Potawatomi; ultimately, I argue that the preterit is not tense and demonstrate that nominal preterits are lexically restricted.

This paper proceeds as follows: in the next section, I provide a brief overview of NT. Then, I revisit Hockett's remarks on the preterit and NT. Finally, I highlight issues brought up by new data before concluding.

Brief Overview of Nominal TAM

Based on data from languages around the world, N&S (2004:778) offer two broad categories of NT: propositional and independent. Propositional NT is when TAM marked on the noun applies to the entire proposition, either with or without an inflected verb (N&S 2004:790–796). N&S provide an example from Sirionó, a Tupí-Guaraní language:[2]

(1) Ési-ke   óso ñá   ií-ra

    woman-PST go near water-LOC

    'The woman went near the water.' (Firestone 1965, cited in N&S 2004:795)

In this example, a past tense marker *ke* is suffixed to the noun ési, 'woman', and there is no tense information given on the verb.

The focus of this paper is Independent NT, where TAM marked on the noun is independent of the proposition. A comparable English example is *former friend* (N&S 2004:779), where *former* modifies only the local noun *friend* and does not supply TAM information for the clause. N&S offer another example from a Tupí-Guaraní language, this time Guaraní:

(2) h-emiapò-rǎ

    his-work-FUT

    'his future work' (Gregores and Suárez 1967:127, cited in N&S 2004:780)

This possessed noun does not supply TAM information for an entire clause, but rather "locate[s] the time at which the property denoted by the nominal holds of the referent (N&S 2004:779).

Overall, N&S consider both types of NT to have the following core features in common (summarized from N&S 2004:778):

(3) a. Nouns show a distinction in tense, aspect, and/or mood as defined for verbs

     b. This distinction is productive and widespread, not restricted . . .

     c. . . . applicable to adjuncts, and not just arguments

     d. . . . morphological, and not a syntactic clitic.

N&S do not offer a comprehensive definition of TAM or tense in their work; Tonhauser offers the following general definitions of tense, aspect, and modality (summarized from Tonhauser 2006:15, 20, 22):

(4) a. *Tense*: a relation between times, one of which is the perspective time

b. *Aspect*: an operation on eventuality descriptions

c. *Modality*: the relation between the actual world and the worlds of evaluation

Tonhauser discusses tense in much more detail (2006:23 and onward, 2007:858–863) than aspect and modality, arguing for core features of tense that include a lack of semantic restrictions (cf. N&S's criteria (3b) above), no co-occurring tense markers, and no encoding a state change. In the sections that follow, I argue that the preterit in Potawatomi does not display the core features of tense, and as such, Potawatomi cannot be considered an NT language.

Revisiting Hockett

N&S base their argument that Potawatomi is an NT language on remarks from Hockett's landmark description of Potawatomi, so we must first briefly revisit his comments on both the verbal and nominal preterit.

When marked on verbs, Hockett says that the preterit "relegat[es] the reference of the verb to a time prior to the time of speech" (1939a:40). He describes many allomorphs of the preterit suffix, which I will refer to as *-ben* while noting that there is much variation (Hockett 1939a:92–94, 96, 98–104). Before moving to the nominal preterit, I must make a note on translating the verbal preterit: in his dissertation (1939a) and IJAL (1948a) articles, preterit is translated with the English present perfect, as in example (5), which would seem to straightforwardly be interpreted as a sort of past tense:[3]

(5) nissébeninek
     nissé-ben-inek
     fall-PRET-INFL
     'They have fallen down.' (Hockett 1948c:145)

In later work, Hockett changes the way he translates these forms, avoiding the present perfect and instead using words like "formerly" and parentheticals to indicate a contrast from previous states to the current state. This can be seen in (6).[4]

(6)   ngezhadzeben

       ne-gezhadeze-ben

       1-warm.personality-PRET

       'I was formerly happy (but not now).' (Hockett 1958:238)

In the sections that follow, I argue that this later translation is more accurate.

Hockett found the same suffix *-ben* on possessed nouns, both animate and inanimate, where he says it indicates that "the possessive relation no longer exists at the time of speaking" (1948a:8–9); see examples (7) and (8) below.

(7)   nosben

       n-os-ben

       1-father-PRET

       'my (late) father' (Hockett 1948b:73)

(8)   njimanmeben

       ne-jiman-em-eben

       1-canoe-POSS-PRET

       'The canoe I had (but no longer have—stolen or destroyed or lost).'

       (Hockett 1939a:83, 1948a:8–9, 1948b:73)

Examples (7) and (8) are ordinary possessed nouns, animate and inanimate respectively, suffixed with the preterit marker *-ben* previously seen on verbs. N&S take this as evidence that an apparent tense marker can straightforwardly attach to both nouns and verbs. In the next section, I argue against both the claim that *-ben* on verbs is a tense marker and that it can freely attach to nouns.

Rethinking the Preterit in Potawatomi

In this section, I argue against N&S's classification of Potawatomi as an independent NT language. First, I demonstrate that the preterit is not a simple tense marker in Potawatomi, despite repeated claims from the non-Algonquianist literature. Second, I show the results of new fieldwork that show that the nominal preterit is severely lexically restricted, going against N&S's core features of NT described in section 2.

Finally, I argue that the nominal preterit has a lexical meaning (hinted at above) rather than a grammatical function (as argued by N&S).

Preterit Is Not Verbal Tense

First, I must address the notion in the literature that the default past tense marker in Potawatomi is the preterit (Crystal 1987:92; Halle and Marantz 1993:139–141 and numerous papers citing it; N&S 2004:780, 789). Just as in Ojibwe, past tense in Potawatomi is represented with a preverb, written by Hockett as *ki-* (Hockett 1939a:85–86,149, 1939b:238, 245, 1948a:9, 1948c:139, 140) and Buszard and modern Potawatomi speakers as *gi-* (Buszard 2003:25–26). Going further, a tense suffix in Potawatomi would be highly unusual; all tense morphemes in Potawatomi are preverbs and can never appear on nouns.[5]

Consider the following minimal pair in (9) and (10), where (9) is marked with the preterit and (10) has the past tense preverb.

(9) Zhode ma tében

    zhode   ma   té-ben
    here   but   be.located-PRET
    'It was here (but isn't anymore).'

(10) Zhode ma gi-té

    zhode   ma   gi-té
    here   but   PST-be.located
    'It was here.' (OK: and it still is)

Speakers report that (9) crucially involves a change of state; the object described by the sentence must have been present at a point in the past and must now be absent. In (10), on the other hand, speakers report that the sentence with the past tense preverb can be true if the object is absent or if the object is still present.

Importantly, preterit marking can also combine with tense morphemes. For example, the preterit suffix combined with the volitional future preverb *wi-* results in a hypothetical meaning, something like "Subject was supposed to have VERBed, but failed" (cf. Valentine 2001:800; James 1991:291 for similar cases in Ojibwe and Cree).

(11) Nwi-**zigwébtewaben** nesh je ngi-nondéwabmek.

      ne-wi=zigwébtewa-ben . . .

      1-FUT-splash.with.water-PRET

      'I was going to splash him but he saw me before I could do it.'

(12) Gin gé na gwi-**zhyanaben**.

      Gin   gé   na   ge-wi=zhya-naben

      2   EMPH   EMPH   2-FUT-go-PRET

      'You were the one that was supposed to go.'

In (11), the water-splashing event was unfulfilled, and the reason is given in the clause that follows; compare the version of the verb without the preterit, *nwi-zig-wébtewa* "I will splash water on him." In (12), no reason for the unfulfilled event of going is offered, but the preterit is sufficient to make clear that the action of the verb is hypothetical.

    Preterit marking combined with past *gi-* can also be hypothetical, as in (13), or have a slightly different reading, as in (14).

(13) Ngi-**kwtegwi'naben** wi na.

      ne-gi=kwtegwi'-naben   wi   na

      1-PST-refuse-PRET   EMPH   EMPH

      'I was going to back out (but they found me).'

(14) Nmech je ga-**zhewébzeben**.

      nmech   je   ga-zhewébeze-ben

      do.not.know   and   IC.PST-happen-PRET

      'I don't know what happened to him.'

In short: on verbs, the preterit is not tense, but rather is probably better analyzed as mood, since it conveys the notion of possible worlds or perhaps aspect. More research is needed here to present a more complete picture of the function of the verbal preterit in Potawatomi, but the point stands that preterit is not tense in Potawatomi.

Nominal Preterit Is Lexically Restricted

The data provided above is not sufficient to argue against N&S's claim that the nominal preterit in Potawatomi is nominal TAM, since the nominal preterit could be argued to be a sort of mood marker rather than tense. However, one of N&S's core features of NT is the lack of lexical restrictions, and the nominal preterit is only applicable to a small subset of nouns in Potawatomi.

First, as discussed above, the nominal preterit is only found on possessed nouns. Going further, the 'canoe' example from Hockett is the only attested inanimate noun preterit in any of the Potawatomi materials I have seen; modern speakers reject attempts to add the preterit to 'canoe' as well as all forms where the preterit is attached to alienably possessed inanimates like 'book'. Speakers also reject inalienably possessed inanimates like 'foot' (*n-zed-ben* intended meaning: 'the foot I lost [due to diabetes e.g.]' is rejected by all the speakers I interviewed). More specifically, speakers seem to show a strong preference for attaching the preterit suffix only to once-living animate referents—like *nosben* 'my late father', the other (obligatorily possessed) kinship words, and personal names. This fact is much more damaging to the N&S hypothesis; if preterit is a nominal mood, why is it restricted to such a small subset of the lexicon? In the next section, I suggest an answer.

Nominal Preterit Has Lexical Meaning

My position is that, on nouns, the preterit suffix simply means that the referent is deceased. Modern speakers, when asked the meaning of the preterit, explain that it is a way to use a person's name or title respectfully, without calling their spirit to you. In addition to 'father' we can add preterit marking to the possessed form of 'dog' as in (15) and to personal names like Dan in (16), but not the free form *nemosh*, shown in (17)—another example of lexical restriction.

(15) gdeyben
       g-dey-ben
       2-dog-PRET
       'your late dog'

(16) nDanben
      Dan-PRET
      'the late Dan'

(17) *nemoshben
      nemosh-ben
      dog-PRET
      Intended: 'the late dog'

This is identical to the nominal preterit usage in Cree described by James (1991:282), which N&S cite but importantly do not claim is NT.

Conclusion

In this paper, I argue that Potawatomi data cited by N&S does not support their model of NT and is insufficient to analyze Potawatomi as a case of NT. I have shown that the preterit is not a simple past tense, as it has been inaccurately described in the past by non-Algonquianists; rather, there is a set of true tense morphemes that never attach to nouns. I have also shown that the nominal preterit is generally restricted to once-living, now deceased animate referents (generally kinship terms but also personal names) where it does not and cannot serve the same function as the verbal preterit.

Finally, I call for more research on Algonquian TAM both synchronically and historically; the picture of the Potawatomi preterit that I have presented here is largely consistent with what has been found in previous work on other Algonquian languages. In the appendix below, I show examples of preterit marking in Cree, Ojibwe, Menominee, and Miami-Illinois, which all show strong similarities.[6]

Appendix

Cree

As noted above, James (1991:282) finds that the preterit marker on nouns "serves primarily to denote that while the individual in question was formerly alive or present, s/he is no longer so." In the example below, the preterit attaches to the dependent noun 'grandfather' to give a meaning of 'deceased'—importantly, all such examples offered by James are dependent nouns.

(i) nimoso:mi**pan**
    'my late grandfather'

James also finds similar combinations of tense prefixes and preterit marking as the ones described above for Potawatomi; below, preterit marking together with the future preverb *ta-* indicates a hypothetical circumstance.

(ii) kiša:spin   iskwe:wit   *ta*-miloma:kosi:-**pan**
     if   he.be.woman   he.will-be.good.looking-PRET
     'If he were a woman, he would be good-looking.' (James 1991:286)

As in Potawatomi, James provides evidence that *ki:-* is the "more unmarked past tense marking device" (1991:285) while preterit marks "imperfective aspect in the past" (1991:282) and modality (1991:285).[7]

Ojibwe

Nichols's dissertation notes a similar combinations of tense marking plus preterit marking (1980:122–124) resulting in hypothetical or counterfactual meanings in Minnesota Ojibwe.

(iii) nin*kii*-kikkenimaa   *kii*-aakkosi**ppan**
      I knew him   that he had been sick
      'I knew that he had been sick (but then wasn't).' (Nichols 1980:122)

He also shows examples of the negative preterit, which "contrasts prior non-oc-currence with subsequent actual or possible occurrence" (Nichols 1980:122) and gives examples of preterit marking and tense marking combinations; the examples below show first past, then future marking on the verbs.

(iv) kaawiin   nin*kii*-aakkosissii**naapan**
     not   I had not been sick
     'I had not been sick (but may be now).' (Nichols 1980:122)

(v) ni*wii*-wiiciiwaa**pan**ek

'I had wanted to go with them (but didn't).' (Nichols 1980:122)

Nichols also offers an interesting minimal pair, where, in main clauses, warnings are given in independent mode unless the outcome is considered unlikely, in which case the preterit conjunct is used. Note that the preterit example also shows a combination of future tense and preterit.

(vi) kiišpin   minikkweyan   ki*ka*-aakkos

if   that you drink   you will get sick

'If you drink, you'll get sick.' (definite outcome) (Nichols 1980:123)

(vii) kiišpin   minikkweyan   mii   *ci*-aakkosiyam**pan**

if   that you drink   thus   that you will have been sick

'If you drink, you could get sick.' (unlikely outcome) (Nichols 1980:123)

Valentine (2001:862–864) describes similar counterfactual uses of the preterit with or without dubitative marking in the dialects of Ojibwe that he discusses.

(viii) Giishpin   bwaa-ndamtayaam**ba**   ndaa-gii-zhaa

if   I were not busy   I would go there

'If I were not busy I would go there.' (Valentine 2001:864)

Valentine (2001:862) also provides examples of future tense and preterit combinations, which I omit for reasons of space.

Menominee

Macaulay (2003:236–237) argues that preterit marking conveys mirativity in Menominee.

(ix) kemēwano**pah**!

kemewan-w-epa-h

rain.II-3-PRET-MOD

'But it was raining!' (Macaulay 2003:236)

Macaulay also gives an example reminiscent of the hypotheticals and counterfactuals arising from combinations of preterit marking and future tense.

(x) **enepaq**   k̲a̲ēta-mam̲ā̲ēk!
     enepaq   katāēw-mam-E-k
     that.INAN.PRET   going.to-take.TI-TH-3.CONJ
     'But (I thought) it was that one that he was going to take!' (Macaulay 2003:236)

More research is needed to determine the extent to which analyses that appear to hold for Potawatomi, Cree, and Ojibwe also hold for Menominee.

Miami-Illinois

Finally, Costa (2003:353–361) provides examples of the preterit suffix in Miami-Illinois, which differs from the above-described languages in that it is "the only true tense/aspect suffix found in Miami-Illinois" (Costa 2003:353). This is rather unlike the languages cited above, and yet despite this, there are still contexts where the preterit in Miami/Illinois denotes a proposition that is hypothetical, unreal, or counterfactual.

(xi) Neehi-'hsa ceeki eempahwilici. Sakiinaa**hpa**-hka, naahpa-'hsa eempahwalikoci.
      'And (the birds) all flew up. (Wissakatchakwa) meant to catch them, but instead they carried him up.'

The verb *sakiinaahpa-hka* 'He meant to catch them (but didn't)' also shows the dubitative clitic *-hka* and lacks initial change; in Miami/Illinois, all three of these are indications of the nonreality of a proposition.

NOTES

1. Examples without citations come from the author's fieldwork. Examples from other languages are given in the authors' orthographies. Abbreviations used in this paper are as follows: CONJ = conjunct, EMPH = emphatic, FUT = future (tense), IC = initial change, II = inanimate intransitive verb, INAN = inanimate, INFL = inflection, LOC = locative, MOD = modal, POSS = possessive, PRET = preterit, PST = past, TH = theme sign, TI = transitive inanimate verb.

2. However, see Tonhauser 2007, 2008 for critique of N&S's analysis of NT in Tupí-Guaraní.
3. Hockett gives this with a single fortis /s/ but modern records show it with /ss/, reflecting the deletion of the connective vowel due to syncope /ni:s+ə+sɛ:.../.
4. Modern speakers of Potawatomi define this word as "friendly, having a warm personality"; I have kept Hockett's wording here to illustrate his mode of translation.
5. Tense preverb–noun combinations are both completely unattested in all Potawatomi materials I have access to from the nineteenth through the twenty-first centuries and rejected by modern speakers in elicitation.
6. As some authors omit morphological analysis, preterit marking is bolded and tense preverbs are underlined in this section where relevant.
7. James (1991:289, fn.13) specifically cites Potawatomi as a similar language in this regard.

REFERENCES

Buszard, Laura Ann. 2003. Constructional polysemy and mental spaces in Potawatomi discourse. PhD thesis, University of California, Berkeley.

Costa, David J. 2003. *The Miami-Illinois language.* University of Nebraska Press.

Crystal, David. 1987. *The Cambridge encyclopedia of language.* Cambridge University Press.

Halle, Morris, and Alec Marantz. 1993. Distributed morphology and the pieces of inflection. *The view from building 20: Essays in linguistics in honor of Sylvain Bromberger*, ed. by Kenneth Hale and S. Jay Keyser, pp. 111–176. Current Studies in Linguistics, vol. 24. MIT Press.

Hockett, Charles F. 1939a. The Potawatomi language. PhD thesis, Yale University.

———. 1939b. Potawatomi syntax. *Language* 15:235–248.

———. 1948a. Potawatomi I: Phonemics, morphophonemics, and morphological survey. *International Journal of American Linguistics* 14:1–10.

———. 1948b. Potawatomi II: Derivation, personal prefixes, and nouns. *International Journal of American Linguistics* 14:63–73.

———. 1948c. Potawatomi III: The verb complex. *International Journal of American Linguistics* 14:139–149.

———. 1958. *A course in modern linguistics.* Macmillian.

James, Deborah. 1991. Preterit forms in Moose Cree as markers of tense, aspect, and modality. *International Journal of American Linguistics* 57:281–297.

Macaulay, Monica. 2003. Negation, dubitatives, and mirativity in Menominee. *Papers of the Thirty-Fourth Algonquian Conference*, ed. by H. C. Wolfart, pp. 217–240. Winnipeg: University of Manitoba Press.

Nichols, John David. 1980. Ojibwe morphology. PhD thesis, Harvard University.

Nordlinger, Rachel, and Louisa Sadler. 2004. Nominal tense in crosslinguistic perspective. *Language* 80:776–806.

———. 2008. When is a temporal marker not a tense? Reply to Tonhauser 2007. *Language* 84:325–331.

Tonhauser, Judith. 2006. The temporal semantics of noun phrases: Evidence from Guaraní. PhD thesis, Stanford University.

———. 2007. Nominal tense? The meaning of Guaraní nominal temporal markers. *Language* 83:831–869.

———. 2008. Defining crosslinguistic categories: The case of nominal tense (Reply to Nordlinger and Sadler). *Language* 84:332–342.

Valentine, J. Randolph. 2001. *Nishnaabemwin reference grammar*. Toronto: University of Toronto Press.

Noun Categorization in Ojibwe: Animacy Is Gender and Gender Is Separate from the Count/Mass Distinction

Cherry Meyer

n this paper, I put forth a novel analysis of noun categorization in Ojibwe.[1] The noun categorization devices under discussion include the gender system and nominal aspect in the sense of Rijkhoff (1991, 2010). Gender is defined by morphosyntactic agreement in associated material outside of the noun (Corbett 1991:4, 105). Nominal aspect refers to the linguistic representation of a property in space, similar to how verbal aspect refers to the representation of a property or relation in time (Rijkhoff 1991:291). Consider the example below, in which a pair of nouns have identical surface forms, different gender values, and related meanings; the pattern shown is that an inanimate noun refers to a substance (mass), while the corresponding animate noun refers to an individual portion of that substance (count).

(1) a. Inanimate Mass Noun   b. Animate Count Noun
         zhooniyaawaabik   zhooniyaawaabik
         'silver'   'coin'

Wiltschko (2009, 2012) accounts for the pattern shown in (1) by claiming that grammatical animacy in Blackfoot, and Algonquian more generally, is not gender at all, but the functional equivalent of the count/mass distinction.[2] In a more

199

moderate proposal, Mathieu (2012a, 2012b) maintains grammatical animacy as gender and accounts for the above pattern by positing a singulative system. A singulative system is one in which a mass noun undergoes recategorization of gender to create an individual (count noun), called the singulative form. He shows that Ojibwe has both gender and the count/mass distinction, and thus the two cannot be functionally equivalent.

Further, Mathieu claims that the singulative system accounts for why certain mass nouns can be pluralized in Ojibwe, since one of the main diagnostics to identify mass nouns is resistance to pluralization. An example is given in (2).

(2) a. Singular Noun   b. Plural Noun
         wanagek   wanagek-ag
         'bark'   'pieces of bark'

My proposal is twofold: first, I maintain that grammatical animacy is a gender distinction and the pattern in (1) is explainable solely on the basis of semantic assignment in the gender system. I argue, contra Wiltschko (2009, 2012), that animacy is not equivalent to the count/mass distinction, and contra Mathieu (2012a, 2012b), that the language does not embed a singulative system. A consequence of semantic factors motivating gender assignment is that gender may participate in derivational processes, such that a change in gender may be used to differentiate a new lexical item, which I term LEXICAL RECATEGORIZATION. This accounts for the pattern shown in (1), as well as others detailed below. I show how the framework of Construction Morphology (Booij 2010) is capable of capturing lexical recategorization.

Second, the ability to pluralize certain nouns referring to substances in Ojibwe is due to the presence of a third type of nominal aspect, in addition to count and mass nouns, called GENERAL nouns. It is a flexible noun type, meaning spatial specifications can alternate between those of count and mass nouns. Contra Mathieu (2012a, 2012b), the fact that certain substance-denoting nouns may pluralize is not due to a singulative system that links nominal aspect and gender. Nominal aspect and gender are separate devices of nominal classification, evidenced by the three types of nominal aspect cutting across both gender values.

In the following sections, I give a brief introduction to gender in Ojibwe before moving on to a more detailed discussion of semantic assignment and several examples of semantic factors in Ojibwe. I define lexical recategorization and show that this is not a problem for animacy as gender, as has been claimed. The formalization of semantic assignment and lexical recategorization within Construction Morphology is then demonstrated. Finally, I introduce the apparent connection between gender and the mass/count distinction by considering Wiltschko's (2009, 2012) and Mathieu's (2012a, 2012b) analyses, before presenting my own analysis and evidence of disjunction between gender and nominal aspect.

Dialects and Data Collection

The research presented here is focused on the dialects of Southwestern Ojibwe, Eastern Ojibwe, and Odawa. The Southwestern dialect is spoken around the Great Lakes region in Michigan, Minnesota, Wisconsin, and west to the Dakotas and Montana. The Eastern dialect is spoken in Ontario, and Odawa is spoken on the shores of Lake Huron in Ontario and Michigan (Valentine 2001:15–16). Data were collected through dictionaries and grammars. For the Odawa and Eastern dialects, data are drawn from Valentine's (2001) *Nishnaabemwin Reference Grammar*. For the Southwestern dialect, data are from Nichols and Nyholm's (1995) *A Concise Dictionary of Minnesota Ojibwe*, as well as the invaluable *Ojibwe People's Dictionary*, which is accessible online.

Animacy as Gender

Ojibwe has a rather straightforward bipartite gender system based on animacy; all nouns are allocated to either the animate or inanimate value (Valentine 2001:114). Gender is reflected in the choice of the verb class and, if present, the demonstrative pronoun (Valentine 2001:115–116, 132–134, 546). Other pronouns such as indefinites, dubitatives, etc. also agree in gender. Singular nouns have covert gender (Corbett 1991:62), but gender is visible on the noun in the plural number marking.[3] Animate plural suffixes end in /-g/, while those of inanimates end in /-n/ (Valentine 2001:115).

Semantic Assignment: One Motivating Factor or Many

Assignment specifies how the gender value of a noun in a particular language is determined (Corbett 1991:3). Assignment may be of two main types: semantic or formal. With semantic assignment, the meaning of a noun alone is sufficient to predict its gender value, whereas with formal assignment, reference to the phonological or morphological form of the noun is necessary. All gender systems have at least a core of nouns that are semantically assigned, which is most commonly based on biological sex, but this may be heavily supplemented by formal assignment (Corbett 2014:114). The animacy of nouns in Ojibwe is semantically determined, with animate nouns including humans, animals, spirits, and many plants (Valentine 2001:115). There are a number of apparent exceptions to clear semantic assignment, however. Some nouns are grammatically animate but notionally inanimate. A few examples of these exceptions in Odawa are *sab* 'net', *kik* 'kettle', and *aagam* 'snowshoe' (Valentine 2001:114).

There has been much debate over the proper way to characterize these apparent exceptions across Algonquian languages. Greenberg's (1954:15–16) view was that any exceptions to semantic assignment should render the description of the entire system as arbitrary. Hallowell (1955:109, 1960, 1976:361–363) countered that what appear to be exceptions to outsiders are not exceptions for speakers, once the cultural significance of the exceptions are taken into account. The latter position was adopted by Darnell and Vanek (1976) for Cree, Black (1969) and Black-Rogers (1982) for Ojibwe, and Straus and Brightman (1982) for Cheyenne. The single, unifying feature of animate nouns that they propose is POWER. This analysis has since been abandoned, since not all culturally significant items are grammatically animate and such items are, in fact, a source of language and dialect variation (Goddard 2002).

These opposing positions are actually two sides of the same coin, as Dahlstrom (1995:52–53) points out, since both assume predictability constitutes semantic assignment, "where predictable means that there is a single semantic feature which all members of the category have in common, and which does not occur with any nonmembers of the category." Her work on Meskwaki was the first of several applications of a modern approach to semantic assignment in Algonquian, including Quinn (2001) for Penobscot, and Goddard (2002) for Algonquian languages generally. These three studies outline not one, but multiple semantic factors that motivate gender assignment.

Multiple factors are only unpredictable in the sense that they are less obvious than a single factor.[4] They must be conventionalized within a community of speakers. This approach results in a more nuanced form of semantic assignment. Goddard (2002:224) says, "the application of the semantic opposition between the genders to many specific cases involves a cultural component that can vary and that leads to different gender-class membership in different speech communities."[5] In the next section, I give a brief sketch of a few semantic factors that appear to be shared between Odawa, Eastern Ojibwe, and Southwestern Ojibwe.

Factors of Semantic Assignment

While it is true that a certain amount of variability in assignment exists between dialects, the following semantic factors were chosen due to considerable commonality across the three dialects.[6] The following factors are not meant to be exhaustive or to account for the gender assignment of all nouns, as that would require a much larger study. The semantic factors illustrated here include proper names of animate beings (Valentine 2001:120), the part/whole relation,[7] anthropomorphism (see also Dahlstrom 1995:57), and grain/grain products (Valentine 2001:116). Examples are provided in Tables 1–4, taken from the Southwestern dialect unless otherwise noted.

TABLE 1. Animate gender as proper names of animate beings

FORM	INANIMATE NOUN GLOSS	ANIMATE NOUN GLOSS
gichi-mookomaan	big knife	American, white person
wezhgonid*	fishtail	Fishtail (name)

* This example is from Eastern Ojibwe/Odawa (Valentine 2001:120).

TABLE 2. Inanimate as part and animate as whole

FORM	INANIMATE NOUN GLOSS	ANIMATE NOUN GLOSS
mitig	stick, wood	tree
wiigwaas	birch bark	birch tree

TABLE 3. Animate as anthropomorphic

FORM	INANIMATE NOUN GLOSS	ANIMATE NOUN GLOSS
odaminowaagan	toy	doll

TABLE 4. Animate as grain or grain product

FORM	INANIMATE NOUN GLOSS	ANIMATE NOUN GLOSS
abwaajigan	roasted meat or fish	bread roasted over fire
biisiboojigan	grinder or mill	corn meal

TABLE 5. Nishnaabemwin nouns of analogical extension

FORM	INANIMATE NOUN GLOSS	ANIMATE NOUN GLOSS
mkizin*	shoe	tire
baashkzigan†	gun, rifle	penis

* This example is from Eastern Ojibwe/Odawa (Valentine 2001:115).
† This example is dialectal slang from Eastern Ojibwe spoken at Curve Lake (Rhodes 1985). The unsyncopated form is baashkizigan, which exists as an inanimate noun in other dialects, though I'm unaware of its status as an animate noun.

For *abwaajigan,* there is nothing in the word form to contribute the meaning bread or meat, only that something is roasted over a fire. The specific meaning of the animate noun becomes clear as a result of the semantic factor motivating grain/grain products as animate. Likewise, the meaning of the inanimate noun is tied to the fact that *wiiyaas* 'meat' and related words are inanimate. Further research into the semantic opposition of animate and inanimate gender will reveal more factors of semantic assignment. Table 5 shows examples that may be motivated solely on the basis of analogy.

The use of *mkizin* as animate 'tire' is by analogy to the similar function of inanimate 'shoe'. A slang word for 'penis' may be animate in opposition to the word it is an analogical extension of, but a more formal term *wiinag* 'his penis' is inanimate.[8] At times, recategorization of gender makes sense only in light of creating new lexical items. The next section discusses this derivational use of gender in Ojibwe and why this does not cause a problem for the characterization of animacy as gender.

Lexical Recategorization

A change in gender may be used to derive new words in Ojibwe (cf. Mufwene 1980 for Bantu). As shown above, there are plenty of nouns that share a form and have related meanings but differ in gender. The ability of gender to enter into derivational processes is tied to multiple semantic factors of assignment; the gender value itself may distinguish meaning in the derived word, as is the case with *abwaajigan*.

This derivational use of gender may be termed LEXICAL RECATEGORIZATION, as opposed to gender shift in stories (aka nonce recategorization), which does not correlate with a change in meaning and is more a matter of speaker stylistics (Goddard 2002:202–210).[9] It should be noted that the direction of derivation most often proceeds from inanimate to animate, but this is not always the case. The animate noun *ishkodekaan* 'fire-steel' denotes the earlier fire starter, and the inanimate noun denotes the later, more modern device, the lighter (Goddard 2002:211); Nichols and Nyholm 1995:69).[10]

Lexical recategorization has led to some doubt about the appropriateness of labeling animacy as a gender distinction. This is one of the main pieces of evidence that Wiltschko (2009, 2012) uses to support her claim that animacy is not gender. She writes, "There are no German nouns that are associated with two distinct genders and still related in meaning. If a given form has two possible genders associated with it, it is for one of the following two reasons. We are either dealing with accidental homophony or else gender is in free variation and does not correlate with a meaning difference" (2009:7–8, 2012:166). However, though certainly not a productive strategy of derivation, nouns with identical forms, different genders, and related meanings do exist in German. Some examples are given below, with differing gender values visible through agreement on the determiners.[11] Cross-linguistically, it is not uncommon for nouns that differ only in gender to have related meanings.[12] Further examples are given from Spanish and Lak (Friedman 1996:195).[13]

(3) German

a. der see   b. die see
'the.M lake.M'   'the.F sea.F'

c. der erbe   d. das erbe
'the.M heir.M'   'the.N inheritance.N'

e. der ekel   f. das ekel
'the.M revulsion.M'   'the.N obnoxious.person.N'

(4) Spanish

a. cerez-o   b. cerez-a
'cherry.tree-M'   'cherry.fruit-F'

c. manzan-o   d. manzan-a
'apple.tree-M'   'apple.fruit-F'

(5) Lak kurču

    a. Class 1
       MALE
       'widower'

    b. Class 2
       FEMALE
       'widow'

    c. Class 3
       OTHER ANIMATE
       'barren cow'

    d. Class 4
       RESIDUE
       'fallow land'

In short, it is not necessary to conclude that identical forms that differ in animacy and have related meanings are the same noun, and thus that animacy is not gender. This is the result of covert gender on singular nouns (Corbett 1991:62) in Ojibwe and semantic assignment. The derivational use of gender across languages varies in productivity, so it is a gradient and not categorical distinction. In the next section, I show how Construction Morphology may be used to capture multiple semantic factors of assignment and their consequent derivational utility.

Construction Morphology

Booij (2010) applies the constructionist approach to morphology. Construction Morphology takes paradigms of related words as the basis for morphological analysis, hence deriving new words depends on abstractions over sets of existing words. A CONSTRUCTION is a pairing of form and meaning, shown through SCHEMAS, which are data structures representing these abstractions. Morphological schemas express predictable properties of existing complex words and indicate how new words can be derived. An example schema, representing the English agentive -*er*, which is added to a verb to derive a noun, is shown in (6). The left side is a morphosyntactic description, and, on the right side, SEM stands for a meaning component. The symbol ↔ represents a relation of correspondence between these different kinds of information (Booij 2010:14). The 'X' in square brackets serves as the variable word form. Subscript capital 'V' and 'N' represent the part of speech as a verb and noun, respectively, and subscript lowercase letters co-index the properties on the left with those on the right.

(6) Agentive English -*er*

$[[X]_{V_i} er]_{N_j} \leftrightarrow [\text{SEM of one who } V_i s]_j$

This is compatible with semantic assignment and lexical recategorization of gender; speakers generalize multiple semantic factors over a gender value based on sets of nouns that bear that value, represented as schemas, and use those schemas to coin new words.

The lexicon may be manifested as a hierarchy of types; at the top are very broad distinctions, such as syntactic categories, and at the bottom are more specific distinctions, such as individual nouns. The notion of DEFAULT INHERITANCE states that a particular property of a word is inherited from the dominating node unless otherwise specified in its lexical entry, allowing for the expression of an exceptional property. I co-opt this term to describe inanimate as the 'elsewhere' gender value (Corbett 1991:206; Dahlstrom 1995:64; Quinn 2001:1; Goddard 2002:221–224); thus only semantic factors of the animate value need to be specified with a schema.

The schema in (7) captures the semantic core of the animate category, that of beings who possess animateness, while schema (8) captures the fact that animate nouns derived from inanimate ones may also express the semantics of a proper name of an animate being.

(7) Animateness

$[X]_{N[+animate]i} \leftrightarrow [\text{SEM include animateness}]_i$

(8) Proper name of animate being

$[[X]_{N[-animate]i}]_{N[+animate]j} \leftrightarrow [\text{SEM}_i \text{ and SEM of proper name}]_j$

One advantage of this approach is that it allows for the creation of new lexical items through analogical extension between individual words, as well as schemas.[14] An example of this is shown with the animate noun *mkizin* in (9). The line connecting the animate and inanimate nouns represents the transfer of information. The semantic relatedness of the two nouns is shown through semantics from the inanimate noun forming part of the semantics of the animate noun, in addition to new semantic material as a result of the recategorization of gender ($\uparrow\downarrow_{gender}$).

(9) Analogical extension of animate *mkizin* 'tire'

$[mkizin]_{N[-animate]k} \leftrightarrow [shoe]_k$

$[mkizin]_{N[+animate]j} \leftrightarrow [\text{SEM}_{[\uparrow\downarrow gender]k} \text{ and new SEM}]_j$

Morphological constructions may carry specific, noncompositional meaning (Booij 2010:10). In the animate noun *abwaajigan,* although there is no morpheme express-ing the meaning of bread, this semantic content can be derived from the gender value. Since new words may be coined based on schemas or analogical extension, the meaning of *abwaajigan* could be demonstrated by referring to a schema that specified grain/grain products as animate, or by analogical extension with the model word *bakwezhigan*. The latter is illustrated in (10).[15] The information on the right says that the semantics of the verb *abwaad*$(_i)$ combine with the semantics and gender value of the lexical item *bakwezhigan*$(_k)$ to provide both the gender and semantics of the derived noun $(_j)$.

(10)   Analogical extension of animate *abwaajigan* 'bread cooked over a fire'

   $[\text{bakwezhigan}]_{N[+animate]k} \leftrightarrow [\text{bread}]_k$

   $|$

   $[[\text{abwaad}]_{Vi}\text{igan}]_{N[+animate]j} \leftrightarrow [\text{SEM}_i \text{ with SEM}_{[gender]k]j}$

In the next sections, I discuss how semantic assignment and lexical recategorization have been interpreted by researchers as a link between animacy and the count/ mass distinction.

Gender and the Count/Mass Distinction

In Wiltschko's comparison of English, German, and Blackfoot, it appears that no language has both grammatical animacy and the count/mass distinction (2009, see also 2012). This leads her to claim that animacy is structurally identical to the count/mass distinction. Thus, the example in (1) seems to support her claim that animacy acts like the count/mass distinction in German (2009:9, 2012:168). While this analysis may work for Blackfoot, it fails for Ojibwe because the language has a count/mass distinction, evidenced by a lack of pluralization on certain nouns (Valentine 2001:182; Mathieu 2012a, 2012b), as well as animacy. Table 6 offers some examples that lack a plural form in dictionaries. They are found in both genders, though the majority are inanimate.

   In another proposal aimed at formalizing a connection between grammatical animacy and the count/mass distinction, Mathieu (2012a, 2012b) maintains the gender label for animacy and instead posits a singulative system. In a singulative

TABLE 6. Southwestern Ojibwe mass nouns

ANIMACY	SINGULAR NOUN	GLOSS	*PLURAL
inanimate	agajiwin	shame	*agajiwin-an
inanimate	bimide	oil	*bimide-n
inanimate	doodooshaaboo	milk	*doodooshaaboo-n
inanimate	miskwi	blood	*miskwi-n
animate	waabigan	clay	*waabigan-ag
animate	giizhig	sky	*giizhig-ag
animate	goon	snow	*goon-ag

system, mass nouns undergo recategorization of gender to create portions of that mass, called the singulative form. This singulative form, as a count noun, can then be pluralized. Mathieu says singulative systems are attested in Breton, Welsh, Arabic, and Dagaare (2012a:195). He proposes that Ojibwe and other Algonquian languages have a singulative system whereby inanimate mass nouns recategorize to animate to become count, as in (1).

In data from the Southwestern, Eastern, and Odawa dialects, (1) from the Southwestern dialect is the only example I found of the inanimate/mass > animate/count pattern. The other Ojibwe example provided by Mathieu, inanimate *mitig* 'wood, forest' and animate *mitig* 'tree', is not listed as such in my sources.[16] The inanimate form can mean 'wood' or 'stick' but not 'forest'.

The inanimate nouns meaning 'wood' and 'silver' and their counterpart animate nouns meaning 'tree' and 'coin' easily fit the semantic assignment factor of 'inanimate as part and animate as whole' shown in Table 2. Wood is part of a whole tree; there are also leaves, bark, etc. Likewise, silver is part of a coin, but not every hunk of silver is a coin; there is also the circular shape and stamping. It is more efficient to account for noun pairs such as (1), as well as those that do not fit the count/mass pattern, with a gender system and semantic assignment than by structural identity of animacy and the count/mass distinction or a singulative system.

While it was shown above that mass nouns in Ojibwe do resist pluralization, there are what appear to be mass nouns that have a pluralized form. Such nouns are presented as further evidence of a singulative system by Mathieu and are discussed next.

TABLE 7. Southwest Ojibwe nouns with ambiguous singular meanings

ANIMACY	NOUN	SINGULAR MEANING	PLURAL MEANING
animate	wanagek(-wag)	bark, piece of bark	pieces of bark
animate	mandaamin(-ag)	corn, kernel of corn	kernels of corn
animate	mikwam(-iig)	ice, chunk of ice	chunks of ice
inanimate	mishi (mis-an)	firewood, log of firewood	logs of firewood
inanimate	aasaakamig(-oon)	moss, piece of moss	pieces of moss

The Puzzle of Pluralized Mass Nouns

Wiltschko (2012) concludes from her work on Halkomelem Salish that number is not inflectional in that language, which she says explains why there is systematic pluralization of all nouns, including substance-denoting nouns, and no formal count/mass distinction. Mathieu shows that number is inflectional in Ojibwe (2012b:174–183), but says this leaves a puzzle as to why certain mass nouns can be pluralized, as in (2) (2012b:175). Table 7 provides more examples of the sort of nouns Mathieu references.[17]

The nouns in Table 7 are actually ambiguous between a mass and count reading in the singular and are disambiguated in the plural; only the count reading is available. They are both animate and inanimate and show no recategorization of gender from the singular to plural. In fact, the majority of the data provided by Mathieu (2012a:666, 2012b:184) in favor of a singulative system do not show recategorization. He comments that this may be due to the loss of the singulative, but in light of this, it may be helpful to ask whether another explanation exists for this set of nouns. I propose that this set of nouns are not mass nouns at all, but display a separate type of nominal aspect.

Nominal Aspect and Disjunction with Gender

Rijkhoff's (1991, 2010) work on nominal aspect is broader than the count/mass distinction. Count and mass nouns are just two of six types of nominal aspect found across the world's languages. There are four rigid types (sort, mass, singular object (count), and collective) and two flexible types (general and set). The singular object

FIGURE 1. Rijkhoff's flexible and rigid types of nominal aspect

	– HOMOGENEITY	+ HOMOGENEITY
– SHAPE	*General*	
	Sort	Mass
+ SHAPE	*Set*	
	Singular Object	Collective

is the equivalent of a count noun. The different types arise from specifications of the features of shape and homogeneity, as shown in Figure 1.

The third type of nominal aspect identified here for Ojibwe is one of the flexible types, i.e., a general noun, characterized as not having a definite outline. Rijkhoff (2010:735) says that "a general noun can be used to refer to, for example, a single concrete object or to a mass entity." This type of nominal aspect is found in languages with classifiers, such as Ojibwe, further supporting this analysis. Examples of general nouns in Yucatec Maya are given below (Lucy 2000:329). In each, the noun may be interpreted as a single concrete object or a mass, e.g., (11a) could be a single banana fruit or the substance of banana fruit.

(11)   *Há'as* 'banana' with multiple classifiers

   a. 'un-tz'íit   há'as   'one 1-dimensional banana (i.e., the fruit)'

   b. 'un-wáal   há'as   'one 2-dimensional banana (i.e., the leaf)'

   c. 'un-kúul   há'as   'one planted banana (i.e., the plant/tree)'

To summarize, nouns of both animate and inanimate gender values in Ojibwe may be categorized with respect to nominal aspect in three ways: as singular object (count), mass, or general. Tables 8 and 9 show that these three types of nominal aspect cut across both gender values.

Conclusion

In conclusion, animacy in Ojibwe is a gender system with semantic assignment, whereby nouns are assigned gender values based on multiple factors. This assignment

TABLE 8. Three types of nominal aspect with animate gender

NUMBER	SINGULAR OBJECT	MASS	GENERAL
Singular	zhooniyaawaabik 'coin'	giizhig 'sky'	wanagek 'bark, piece of bark'
Plural	zhooniyaawaabik-oog 'coins'	*	wanagek-ag 'pieces of bark'
Singular	bineshiinh 'bird'	goon 'snow'	mandaamin 'corn, kernel of corn'
Plural	bineshiin-yag 'birds'	*	mandaamin-ag 'kernels of corn'

TABLE 9. Three types of nominal aspect with inanimate gender

NUMBER	SINGULAR OBJECT	MASS	GENERAL
Singular	mookomaan 'knife'	miswki 'blood'	mishi 'log of firewood, firewood'
Plural	mookomaan-an 'knives'	*	mis-an 'logs of firewood'
Singular	makak 'box'	azhashki 'mud'	aasaakamig 'moss, piece of moss'
Plural	makak-oon 'boxes'	*	aasaakamig-oon 'pieces of moss'

mechanism enables lexical recategorization, which Construction Morphology is well-suited to describe. Rather than explain the rare pattern of inanimates as mass nouns and animates as count nouns by formalizing it in relation to gender, it is more accurate to characterize this pattern using semantic assignment. Nouns that may alternate between count and mass in the singular but are only count in the plural represent a third type of nominal aspect that is flexible, GENERAL nouns. Gender and nominal aspect are separate noun categorization devices, evidenced by the three types of nominal aspect found in both gender values.

NOTES

1. I would like to thank Amy Dahlstrom, Salikoko Mufwene, and John Goldsmith, as well as attendees of the Forty-Seventh Algonquian Conference and reviewers, for their very helpful comments and suggestions on this project in progress. All remaining errors are

my own.

2. The count/mass distinction refers to the presence or absence of both count and mass nouns in a language. For example, English has both count and mass nouns and therefore has the count/mass distinction, while Mandarin Chinese has neither count nor mass nouns and therefore lacks the count/mass distinction. Nominal aspect includes the concepts of count and mass nouns, but it is not synonymous with the count/mass distinction. Nominal aspect allows for more variety in spatial representation across and within languages, outside of simply having count/mass nouns or having unspecified nouns.

3. Covert gender on singular nouns is due to a sound change resulting in the loss of the final vowels -*a* for animates and -*i* for inanimates. Final vowels are retained in Meskwaki (Dahlstrom 1995) and Miami (Costa 2003:205–211). In Ojibwe, final vowels remain on bisyllabic words, such as *makw-a* 'bear' and *mish-i* 'firewood' (Piggott 2007:15; see also Mathieu 2012a:194, 2012b:664).

4. The labels ANIMATE and INANIMATE aid in identifying the semantic core of each gender value, but may also impede our understanding of the gender system with respect to identifying additional semantic motivations. Corbett (1991:9–10) comments, "While names for genders are helpful, there is much to be said for the numbering system, since it prompts us to spell out exactly which types of nouns are included." This is in reference to the tradition followed by linguists working on North-East Caucasian languages, who use Roman numerals to label gender values.

5. See Corbett (1991:7–8, 92–104) for further support of the validity of an assignment mechanism involving multiple semantic factors, as opposed to arbitrariness.

6. Valentine (2001:116) notes that while grain is animate across most communities, *bkwezhgan* 'bread' is inanimate at Walpole and on Manitoulin Island.

7. A reviewer commented that the 'animate as whole and inanimate as part' semantic factor predicts that all body parts should be inanimate. However, when multiple assignment criteria exist, there is likely to be a hierarchy or ranking (see also Plaster et al. 2013). The applicability of an assignment factor does not preclude another from superseding it. There may be other factors governing the assignment of body parts, e.g., reproductive power.

8. Rhodes (1985:166–167) identifies this example as part of a larger metaphor in Eastern Ojibwe, SEX IS HUNTING. Another example is inanimate *wiiyaas* 'meat', which means 'sexual object' when animate.

9. Goddard (2002:211) briefly discusses lexical recategorization when addressing lesser known shifts from inanimate to animate. He states that certain examples of

recategorization are 'lexicalized', in contrast to other nonce shifted examples, but he does not create a formal term for this type of recategorization. The term 'lexical recategorization' is inspired by his discussion.

10. See Goddard (2002:211) for another example of derivation proceeding from animate to inanimate.

11. The Collins German dictionary was used to verify these forms. See references for full citation.

12. In these examples, M = masculine gender; F = feminine gender; N = neuter gender.

13. Since gender is defined by agreement, this includes languages such as Lak, which are often spoken of as having noun classes (Corbett 1991:5).

14. Booij (2010:89) writes, "The implication of assuming a hierarchical lexicon with different levels of abstraction is that . . . there is both analogical word formation, based on an individual model word, and word formation based on abstract schemas."

15. "Schemas are based on lexical knowledge, and this type of knowledge varies from speaker to speaker. Hence, speakers may also differ in the number and types of schemas that they deduce from their lexical knowledge" (Booij 2010:89).

16. Other Algonquian examples provided by Mathieu are from Meskwaki.

17. While this phenomenon seems common to all dialects of Ojibwe, dialectal variation exists so that the nouns referenced by Mathieu are slightly different than those given in Table 7. For example, *waabigan* 'clay' and *asemaa* 'tobacco' do not appear in the dictionaries I referenced with plural forms.

REFERENCES

Black, Mary. 1969. A note on gender in eliciting Ojibwa semantic structures. *Anthropological Linguistics* 177–186.

Black-Rogers, Mary. 1982. Algonquian gender revisited: Animate nouns and Ojibwa 'power'— an impasse? *Research on Language and Social Interaction* 15(1): 9–76.

Booij, Geert. 2010. *Construction morphology*. Oxford University Press.

Collins German Dictionary 2016. http://www.collinsdictionary.com/dictionary/english-german.

Corbett, Greville. 1991. *Gender*. Cambridge: Cambridge University Press.

———, ed. 2014. *The expression of gender*. The Expression of Cognitive Categories (ECC), vol. 6. Berlin: Walter de Gruyter.

Costa, David. 2003. *The Miami-Illinois language*. University of Nebraska Press.

Dahlstrom, Amy. 1995. Motivation vs. predictability in Algonquian gender. *Proceedings of the*

Twenty-Sixth Algonquian Conference, ed. by David H. Pentland pp. 52–66. Winnipeg: University of Manitoba.

Darnell, Regna, and Anthony L. Vanek. 1976. The semantic basis of the animate/inanimate distinction in Cree. *Research on Language and Social Interaction* 9(3–4):159–180.

Friedman, Victor A. 1996. Gender, class and age in the Daghestanian Highlands: Towards a unified account of the morphology of agreement in Lak. *NSL.8: Linguistic studies in the non-Slavic languages of the Commonwealth of Independent States and the Baltic Republics,* ed. by Howard I Aronson, pp. 187–199. Chicago: Chicago Linguistic Society.

Goddard, Ives. 2002. Grammatical gender in Algonquian. *Papers of the Thirty-Third Algonquian Conference*, ed. by H.C. Wolfart, pp. 195–231. Winnipeg: University of Manitoba.

Greenberg, Joseph H. 1954. Concerning inferences from linguistic to nonlinguistic data. *Language in culture: Conference on the interrelations of language and other aspects of culture*, pp. 3–10. Chicago: University of Chicago Press.

Hallowell, Alfred I. 1955. *Culture and experience*. Philadelphia: University of Pennsylvania Press.

———. 1960. Ojibwa ontology, behavior and world view. *Culture in history: Essays in honor of Paul Radin*, ed. by S. Diamond, pp. 19–52. New York: Columbia University Press.

———. 1976. *Contributions to anthropology: Selected papers of A. Irving Hallowell*. Chicago: University of Chicago Press.

Lucy, John A. 2000. Systems of nominal classification: A concluding discussion. *Systems of nominal classification*, ed. by Gunter Senft, pp. 326–341. Cambridge: Cambridge University Press.

Mathieu, Éric. 2012a. On the mass/count distinction in Ojibwe. *Count and mass across languages*, ed. by Diane Massam, pp. 172–198. Oxford: Oxford University Press.

———. 2012b. Flavors of division. *Linguistic Inquiry* 43(4):650–679.

Mufwene, Salikoko. 1980. Noun class prefixes: Inflectional or derivational? *Papers of the Sixteenth Regional Meeting of the Chicago Linguistics Society*, pp. 246–258.

Nichols, John D., and Earl Nyholm. 1995. *A concise dictionary of Minnesota Ojibwe*. University of Minnesota Press.

Ojibwe People's Dictionary. Department of American Indian Studies, University of Minnesota. http://ojibwe.lib.umn.edu.

Piggott, Glyne. 2007. Deriving word minimality by phase. MA thesis, McGill University.

Plaster, Keith, Maria Polinsky, and Boris Harizanov. 2013. Noun classes grow on trees: Noun classification in the North-East Caucasus. *Language typology and historical contingency: In honor of Johanna Nichols*, ed. by Balthasal Bickel, Lenore A. Grenoble, David A. Peterson, and Alan Timberlake, pp. 153–170. Amsterdam: John Benjamins.

Quinn, Conor. 2001. A preliminary survey of animacy categories in Penobscot. *Papers of the Thirty-Second Algonquian Conference*, pp. 395–426.

Rhodes, Rich. 1985. Metaphor and extension in Ojibwa. *Papers of the Sixteenth Algonquian Conference*, pp. 161–169.

Rijkhoff, Jan. 1991. Nominal aspect. *Journal of Semantics* 8(4): 291–309.

———. 2010. On flexible and rigid nouns. *Parts of speech: Empirical and theoretical advances*, pp. 227–252. Benjamin Current Topics, vol. 25. Amsterdam: John Benjamins.

Straus, Anne Terry, and Robert Brightman. 1982. The implacable raspberry. *Papers in Linguistics* 15:97–137.

Valentine, J. Randolph. 2001. *Nishnaabemwin reference grammar*. University of Toronto Press.

Wiltschko, Martina. 2009. How do languages classify their nouns? Cross-linguistic variation in the manifestation of the mass count distinction. *Proceedings of WSCLA 14*, ed. by Heather Bliss and Raphael Girard, pp. 223–236.

———. 2012. Decomposing the mass/count distinction: Evidence from languages that lack it. *Count and mass across languages*, ed. by Diane Massam, pp. 146–171. Oxford: Oxford University Press.

Vowel-Consonant Coalescence in Blackfoot

Mizuki Miyashita

lackfoot has three variants of a back fricative: palatal [ç], velar [x], and labial-velar [xʷ].[1] In this paper, they are referred to as DORSAL FRICATIVES. According to the historical account suggested by Proulx (1989), these dorsal fricatives developed from various consonants before another consonant (i.e., *hp → xp, *tp → xp, *Hm → xp, *nt → xt, *ʔt → xt, *hk → xk, *tk → xk, *łk → xk, *ŝk → xk). In terms of synchronic study, Frantz (2009) and Elfner (2006b) claim that [ç], [x], and [xʷ] are surface forms of the same phoneme, /x/, preceded by /i/, /a/, and /o/, respectively. However, to my knowledge, a formal account of these sounds has not been made. The goal of this paper is to provide a formal analysis that depicts the distributions of the dorsal fricative variants with acoustic descriptions of sample recordings and also makes and supports the claim that dorsal fricatives in Blackfoot are examples of typologically rare vowel-consonant coalescence.

Data shown in this paper are from the Blackfoot dictionary (Frantz and Russell 1995) and grammar (Frantz 2009) unless otherwise indicated. The forms in these resources are represented in the orthography; this paper uses orthographic representation except the symbol <x>—which is <h> in the orthography—in order to avoid confusion. Examples that are given in IPA transcription have been

TABLE 1. Blackfoot consonant chart

	LABIAL	DENTAL	PALATAL	DORSAL	GLOTTAL
Plosive	p	t		k	ʔ
Nasal	m	n			
Fricative		s		x	
Affricate		t͡s		k͡s	
Glide	w		j		

confirmed by native speaker consultants, and the transcriptions represent their pronunciation.[2]

The organization of this paper is as follows: In the next section, the Blackfoot sound inventory is given briefly as background. The section after that describes the distribution of the dorsal fricatives in Blackfoot. In the following section, I claim that the dorsal fricatives are the result of vowel-consonant coalescence and provide support for this claim. In the last section, I discuss the significance of this study and the broader implications of the vowel-consonant analysis.

Sound Inventory in Blackfoot

Blackfoot has three vowel phonemes: /i/, /a/, and /o/. All of them have long counterparts: /ii/, /aa/, and /oo/. There are also three diphthongs: /ai/, /ao/, and /oi/ (Frantz 2009), which are realized as various surface forms, including monophthongized segments. The Blackfoot consonants are shown in Table 1. They occur in long and short forms except the glides, back fricative, and glottal stop, which are always short.[3]

Note that the phoneme in question, /x/, although orthographically written as <h>, is not a glottal fricative. This is clear from a number of descriptive sources such as Uhlenbeck (1938), Taylor (1969), and Frantz (2009).

Surface Distribution of /x/

Previously, Frantz (2009) and Elfner (2006b) described [ç], [x], and [xʷ] as surface forms of the same phoneme, /x/, preceded by /i/, /a/, and /o/, respectively. These surface forms occur regardless of morphology as long as the appropriate phonolog-ical environment is given. For example, they may be observed within a morpheme, as shown in (1a–c), or across morphemes, as in (1d–f).[4]

(1)   a.   [piçksso]
           piixksso
           'nine'

      b.   [paxtóm²xksikimi]
           paaxt-omaxk-ikimi
           inside-big-water
           'Waterton Lake'

      c.   [poxʷsapoot]
           pooxsap-oo-t
           toward.speaker-go-IMP
           'Come here!'

      d.   [niʦiomaniçpinnaan]
           nit-ii-omaanii-xpinnaan
           1-PST-be.right(AI)-1PL
           'We (excl.) were right.'

      e.   [niʦiomiçkaxpinnaan]
           nit-ii-omiixkaa-xpinnaan
           1-PST-catch.fish(AI)-1PL
           'We (excl.) caught fish.'

      f.   [niʦitapoxʷpinnaan]
           nit-itapoo-xpinnaan
           1-go.there(AI)-1PL
           'We (excl.) went there.'

Thus, a morpheme beginning with /x/ (1d–f) surfaces as three allomorphs based on the final vowel of the preceding morpheme.

Phonologically, dorsal fricatives are observed in two major environments. One is the postvocalic environment, where they are preceded by a short vowel and followed by a consonant. The examples in (1d–f) show postvocalic /x/ in inflected forms of three animate intransitive (AI) verb stems: *omanii* 'to be right', *omiixkaa* 'catch fish', and *itapoo* 'go there'.[5] In this environment, only the three combinations in the examples are observed: [iç], [ax], and [oxʷ]. There is no occurrence of other combinations of vowel and dorsal fricative: *[aç], *[oç], *[ix], *[ox], *[axʷ], *[ixʷ], except when the preceding vowel is underlyingly a diphthong. Each variant of the back fricative has its "favorite" vowel, and, notably, they share articulatory features with those vowels: [i] and [ç] are palatal; [a] and [x] are velar; and [o] and [xʷ] are labial-velar.

The other environment in which dorsal fricatives appear is interconsonantal, where the three variants of the dorsal fricative can occur in the same environments. The examples in (2) show forms including interconsonantal /x/ in various environments such as between [n] and [k], [m] and [k], two [k]s, and [ts] and [k]. Note that these environments are not exhaustive.

(2)   a.   [inˀçkíw]
          in**ix**ki-wa
          sing-3SG
          'He sang.'

       b.   [issímˀçkaa]
          issím**ix**kaawa
          sniff-3SG
          'He sniffed.'

       c.   [pa**x**tómˀx͡ksikimi]
          paaxt-om**ax**k-ikimi
          inside-big-water
          'Waterton Lake'

       d.   [ik**x**tsíw]
          ika**x**tsi-wa
          gamble-3SG
          'He gambled.'

e. [sikxʷkiaajo]
   sik-**ox**kiaayo
   black-bear
   'black bear'

f. [annˀxʷką̃]
   anno-**x**ka
   this-INVS
   'now'

Thus, the interconsonantal environments for the three variants overlap, and the overlapping environments may make the dorsal fricatives appear contrastive. If this were true, the statement made by previous authors that [ç], [x], and [xʷ] are phonetic variations of the same phoneme /x/ becomes questionable. However, I do not believe these are separate phonemes, and I instead support the previous studies' claim.

In order to maintain the view that these dorsal fricatives are phonetic variants of the same phoneme /x/, it must be the case that there are three noncontrasting underlying environments. Specifically, in the interconsonantal cases, the three variants [ç], [x], and [xʷ] must be underlyingly preceded by [i], [a], and [o], respectively. Such environments are supported by the complementary distribution of postvocalic /x/: If the interconsonantal dorsal fricatives [ç], [x], and [xʷ] are independently occurring, it is difficult to explain why these variants have favorite vowel pairs in their postvocalic counterparts.

Vowel-Consonant Coalescence

Both postvocalic and interconsonantal dorsal fricatives can be observed at morpheme boundaries. The final vowel of a morpheme plus a following /x/ that is the initial consonant of the subsequent morpheme create the environment for coalescence. The examples in (3) show coalescence across a morpheme boundary between a short vowel and a dorsal fricative. At the surface, the short vowels are no longer realized as full vowels. Instead, we see a merging of the underlying vowels and the following /x/.

(3) a. [sikxʷkiaajo]
   sik-**ox**kiaayo
   black-bear
   'black bear'

   b. [annˀxʷką]
   ann**o**-**x**ka
   this-INVS
   'now'

The next examples, in (4), show the merging of sounds between a long vowel and a dorsal fricative across a morpheme boundary. Long vowels surface as short vowels followed by the variants of the phoneme /x/.

(4) a. [nifsiomaniçpinnaan]
   nit-ii-omaan**ii**-**x**pinnaan
   1-PST-be.right(AI)-1PL
   'We (excl.) were right.'

   b. [nifsitapoxʷpinnaan]
   nit-itap**oo**-**x**pinnaan
   1-go.there(AI)-1PL
   'We (excl.) went there.'

The examples in (5) have no coalescence because the consonants following the vowels are not dorsal fricatives. The vowels remain short, in (5a–c), and long, in (5d–f).

(5) a. [ajimmɨw]
   á-yimmi-wa
   DUR-laugh(AI)-3.SG
   'He/She is laughing.'

   b. [ponokáw]
   ponoká-wa
   elk-3.ANIM
   'It is an elk.'

c. [natájow]
   natáyo-wa
   lynx-3.ANIM
   'It is a lynx.'

d. [iimaniiw]
   ii-omanii-wa
   PST-be.right(AI)-3SG
   'He was right.'

e. [ejpottaaw]
   á-ipottaa-wa
   DUR-fly(AI)-3SG
   'He is flying.'

f. [áakitapoow]
   áak-itapoo-wa
   FUT-go.there(AI)-3SG
   'He is going there.'

The examples above show that vowel change is observed only when /x/ is involved. This peculiarity, thus, is a phonological, not morphological requirement.

Based on the observation above, I propose the analysis that the phoneme /x/ always underlyingly follows a vowel and that the fricative sound surfaces with shared features from the preceding vowel. During the process of feature-sharing, vowel-consonant coalescence must occur. The term COALESCENCE refers to a phonological phenomenon in which two successive segments merge into a single segment, usually maintaining some characteristics of the original segments (Trask 1996). Under this analysis, the back fricative merges with a vowel or part of a vowel. When an underlying long vowel is followed by the phoneme /x/, the consonant and part of the long vowel merge into one, forming a diphthong-like unit, as illustrated in (6a). Similarly, a back fricative between consonants is developed by the merging of an entire short vowel and a back fricative, as illustrated in (6b).

(6) a.   /ii/   /x/   [i ç]

b.   /i/   /x/   [ç]

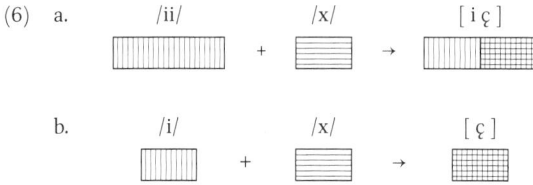

This analysis is supported perceptually by the fact that the coalesced segments [ç], [x], and [xʷ] are phonetically more complex than the symbols reflect (Donald Frantz, personal communication, 2015). I agree with this view because the vowel qualities of [i], [a], and [o] are quite audible in the fricatives [ç], [x], and [xʷ] in spite of their voicelessness, as the frication in the vocal tract is radically loud. Below, I describe other supporting factors for the coalescence analysis.

Length of the Preceding Vowel

Vowels preceding dorsal fricatives are always short. That is, sequences such as *[iiç], *[aax], and *[ooxʷ] do not occur.[6] One could argue that it is natural for the preceding vowel to be shortened, assuming that the sound /x/ is a syllable coda, as vowel shortening always occurs before a coda consonant. This is described as a phonological phenomenon by Elfner (2006a, 2006b), referring to the general process that vowels followed by a consonant cluster are shorter than those in other contexts. However, as shown in (7), not all long vowels are shortened in this context. They remain long before consonant clusters and geminates.[7]

(7) a. iikkamí'niwa   'he fainted'
     b. nitsiinnohkatsimmoka   'she found me burdensome'
     c. iippotsi'kiniisiwa   'he became winded on impact'
     d. nitsimmsowaakka   'she muddied waters for me'
     e. ksikksinaattsiwa   'it is white'
     f. nitaapsstsitsikini   'I took off my shoes'
     g. ikookssiwa   'he regretted'
     h. otahkoottsiiksi   'prickly pear cacti'
     i. koonsskoyi   'snow covered area'

On the other hand, long vowels never retain their length before /x/. Thus, the shortening of long vowels before /x/ needs its own explanation and cannot be categorized with the shortening phenomena previously analyzed. This peculiarity of /x/—that its preceding vowel is never long—is explained when coalescence is assumed.

Diphthongs

The case of the postvocalic environment when the vowel is a diphthong also provides strong support for the vowel-consonant coalescence analysis. I mentioned above that there is no occurrence of a vowel and a dorsal fricative with mixed articulatory features: *[aç], *[oç], *[ix], *[ox], *[axʷ], and *[ixʷ] do not occur. However, the sequence [eç] is attested when the vowel preceding /x/ is underlyingly the diphthong /ai/.

Frantz (1978, 2009) states that the diphthong /ai/ is often realized as a front, nonhigh vowel: [ɛ], [ej], and [æ:].[8] The diphthong /oi/ is pronounced [oj] or [y], and /ao/ is [ɔ] or [aw]. Thus, some are realized as monophthongs. The cases that usually surface as diphthongs present important evidence for coalescence, because when the diphthongs are followed by the dorsal fricative /x/, the off-glide element [j] is not realized, and the sound [ç]—a variant of /x/—surfaces instead. For example, as shown below, /aix/ surfaces as [eç] (8a) and /oix/ as [oç] (8b).

(8) a. [niteçpiyi]
        nit-a-ixpiyi
        1-DUR-dance
        'I am dancing.'

     b. [ɛsoçtaa]
        Ø-a-isoixtaa
        3-DUR-place.one's.own.food.on.a.dish
        'He is placing his own food on a dish.'

This can be analyzed as the second element of the diphthong, /i/, merging with the following /x/. Note that while the first example could be analyzed as the spreading of a [front] feature from the preceding vowel, the latter example does not support this analysis. This, in turn, supports the idea that the last half of a long vowel merges with a following dorsal fricative /x/, assuming that diphthongs and long vowels are alike in terms of quantity (i.e., vowel length).

Duration of Coalesced Segments

As a result of vowel-consonant coalescence, an interconsonantal dorsal fricative has the duration of a short vowel and a postvocalic dorsal fricative plus its preceding vowel has the duration of a long vowel. This observation is shown below using phonetic measurements.

The sound samples in (9) and (10) are taken from the recording supplement for the *Basic Beginning Blackfoot* teaching material. This is a 12-page, unpublished document consisting of vocabulary and conversations developed in 2008 by an instructor at the Cuts Wood School (a Blackfoot immersion school) in the Piegan Institute. The sample utterances were produced by the developer of the materials, who is a native speaker from the Kainai reserve in Alberta and regularly uses the language. She was in her mid-50s at the time of recording.

The image in (9) is a spectrogram of the word /omaxkinaa/ [om²xkinaa] 'old man' along with the values of the segments' durations. As shown in Table 2, the duration of the interconsonantal coalesced segment, a velar fricative [x], is 149ms. This is close to the duration of the word's short vowels: 138ms for [o] and 110ms for [i]. On the other hand, the duration of the long vowel [aa] is 304ms, twice as long as [x]'s. This durational fact is explained by the coalescence analysis.

(9)   Spectrogram of /omaxkinaa/ [om²xkinaa] 'old man'

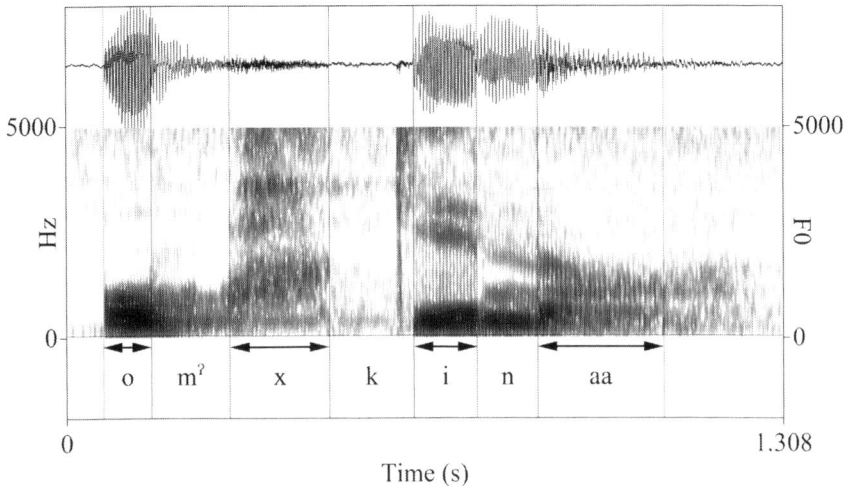

TABLE 2. Vowel durations

vowels	[o̞]	[x]	[i]	[aa]
ms	138	149	110	304

Turning to a postvocalic coalesced segment, the duration of a coalesced segment with its preceding vowel, V[x], is similar to that of a long vowel. The image in (10) shows a spectrogram of the word /saaxkomaapiiwa/ [saxkʊmaapiiwa̰] 'boy'. As shown in Table 3, the total duration of the coalesced segment with its preceding vowel is 221ms, which is close to the 248ms duration of the long vowel [aa] in the same word. (The duration of the postvocalic [x] is only 143ms.) Again, this durational correspondence is explained by the coalescence analysis that /x/ is fused with the last half of a long vowel, even though the coalesced portion is longer than exactly half of the vowel-plus-coalesced-segment combination.

(10) Spectrogram of /saaxkomaapiiwa/ [saxkʊmaapiiwa̰] 'boy'

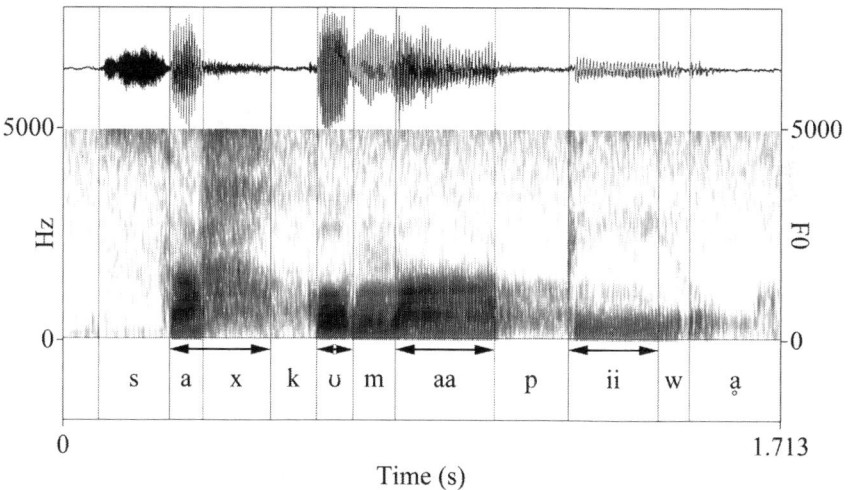

TABLE 3. Vowel durations

vowels	[ax]	[ʊ]	[aa]
ms	221	75	248

Thus, coalescence across morpheme boundaries, the length of preceding vowels, diphthongs, and the duration of coalesced segments all support the idea of a "merger," with /x/ having coalesced with a vowel.

Implications of the Coalescence Analysis

Coalescence Typology

This study is typologically significant. In the phonological literature, the majority of the coalescence examples reported occur between two vowels or two consonants. For example, monophthongization of [ɔ] from /a/ and /o/ in Blackfoot is an occurrence of vowel-vowel coalescence (Frantz 2009). The Kpokolo vowel system also shows a case in which a vowel feature matrix is a result of fusing two separate vowel matrices (Kaye et al. 1985). Odden (1994) shows an example of two vowels that fuse into one syllable in Kikuyu. Bámisilè (1994) reports vowel coalescence in Yoruba. As for consonantal coalescence, Avery and Rice (1989) present fusion as an example of coronal underspecification. Additionally, Indonesian's nasal substitution is shown as an example of coalescence (Pater 1999; Kager 1999).

Examples of coalescence between a vowel and consonant are not uncommon, but they generally involve a consonant that is either nasal or [−consonantal]. The predominant case of vowel-consonant fusion is perhaps the vowel-nasal coalescence observed in French (e.g., Morin 2002) as well as in Choctaw (Lombardi and McCarthy 1991). Examples where the merging segment is [−consonantal] are seen in two other Algonquian languages: Wolfart (1996), for example, describes a contraction in Cree in which interconsonantal [w] followed by [i] or [e] is realized as [o]. Similarly, in Ojibwe [w] and [a] coalesce to [o] (Malone 1997) and [y] and [e] to [ii] (Valentine 2002). In these cases, the merging consonants are glides, which are [−consonantal], and they surface as a vowel with features of the glides. Another example is Capanahua (Elías-Ulloa 2009), in which a vowel and a glottal stop (which is also [−consonantal]) coalesce to form a glottalized vowel. Thus, the vowel-consonant coalescence shown in all these examples is the fusion of two [−consonantal] segments or a vowel and a nasal consonant. Since two nonnasal segments with opposite values of the feature [consonantal] merge in Blackfoot, as described in this paper, the present study adds a rare example to the typology of coalescence.

Mora Analysis

The coalescence analysis can be made with reference to moras (Hayes 1989), giving support to this theoretical unit. In the analysis of postvocalic coalescence, the second mora of a long vowel merges with the following /x/. In the case of interconsonantal coalescence, the entire monomoraic short vowel merges with the following /x/. This moraic analysis is shown in (11).

(11) a. $/V_{\mu 0} V_{\mu 1} x_2 / \;\rightarrow\; [V_{\mu 0} x_{\mu 1,2}]\;(V_0 = V_1)$

    b. $/V_{\mu 1} x_2 / \;\rightarrow\; [x_{\mu 1,2}]$

Thus, in a mora-based analysis, the dorsal fricative /x/ merges with its immediately preceding mora. This analysis unifies the two environments.

Elfner (2006b) notes that if /x/ is assumed to be moraic, then the shortening of the long vowel before /x/ can be analyzed as an avoidance of a super-heavy syllable. With respect to a short vowel merging with /x/, however, she states that "it is less clear how this process can be accounted for under a moraic analysis" (Elfner 2006b:49) and also discusses the difficulty of analyzing it as underlyingly moraic or as the result of weight-by-position. The coalescence analysis in this paper implies that /x/ does not have an inherent or underlying mora but receives one from the preceding vowel.

Place Feature of /x/

The dorsal fricative consonant underlyingly must occur following a vowel. The surface form of /x/ is always a coalesced segment, and it is either [ç], [x], or [xʷ], underlyingly preceded by [i], [a], or [o], respectively. In other words, the place feature of the phonetic forms of /x/ entirely depends on the preceding underlying vowel. This leads to the possibility that /x/ may be placeless. In fact, Goad and Shimada (2014) propose that this consonant is inherently placeless for three theoretical reasons: it does not pattern with other place-bearing lingual consonants (e.g., it does not occur as an onset); it is always a coda, which cannot license its own place features; and it has the same distribution as /ʔ/, which is generally accepted as placeless. The present study provides additional description that supports the idea of the phoneme being /X/, without a place specification.[9]

Syllabic Consonant or Voiceless Vowel?

The interconsonantal coalesced segments are represented as syllabic consonants in Elfner (2006b): [ç̩], [x̩], and [x̩w]. However, it is worth examining whether interconsonantal coalescence results in a syllabic consonant or a voiceless vowel, as this paper's analysis suggests that segments that are heterogenous with respect to the feature [consonantal] merge together.

Vowel devoicing in Blackfoot is a well-known phenomenon (Frantz 2009; Bliss and Gick 2009). Devoiced vowels are observed only in phrase-final position, as in the examples in (12).

(12) a. *iniiwa*   [iniiwḁ]   'buffalo'

     b. *apasstaamiinaamma*   [apasstamiinaammḁ]   'apple'

     c. *aakiikoana*   [aakiikoanḁ]   'girl'

The distribution of the devoiced vowels differs from the vowel-consonant coalescence, which occurs phrase-medially, as in (13), and never finally.

(13) a. *omahkokataa*   [omx̩kokataa]   'gopher'

     b. *nitaakahkayii*   [nitaakx̩kayii]   'I will go home'

     c. *nitssokimmohsi* [nitssokimmx̩ʷsi̥]   'I feel good'

In addition to the fact that the distributions of devoiced vowels and coalesced segments do not pattern together, the noise of the coalesced segments is perceptually and acoustically louder than that of voiceless vowels.[10] Acoustic evidence for this is shown in the spectrograms in (14) and (15). The sound samples are taken from the same source as (9) and (10). The word portion in (14) contains a voiceless vowel at the end, and the noise is hardly detected. On the other hand, (15) contains an interconsonantal coalescence word-medially, and the noise is quite visible as dark scattered prints.

(14) Spectrogram of a voiceless vowel: [iikoaną] < *aakiikoana* [aakiikoaną] 'girl'

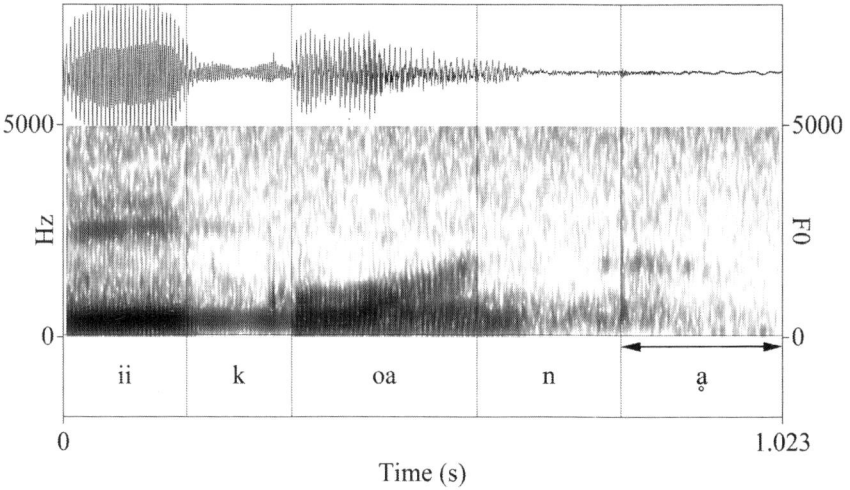

(15) Spectrogram of an interconsonantal coalescence: [ɔtxko] < *aotahkoinamm* 'yellow'

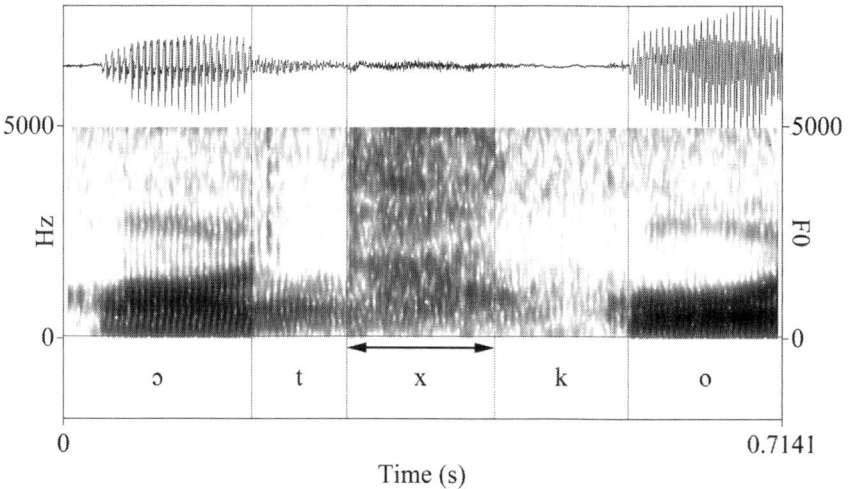

Thus, the coalesced segment shows characteristics that are distinct from voiceless vowels in the language, supporting the idea that the coalesced segment is better analyzed as a consonant.

Further Topics for Research

This study suggests several topics for further research. For example, since the three variants of /x/ are distinct in the case of interconsonantal coalescence, there must be vowel features retained from the underlying vowel. The retaining vowel features in coalescence may be [+high] for [ç], [+back] for [x̞], and [+back] and [+round] for [x̞ʷ]. Also, according to the universal sonority scale, fricatives are lower than nasals in sonority, and this is true in Blackfoot (Elfner 2005). If the dorsal fricatives can be syllabic, this presents a typologically interesting instance because nasals in Blackfoot do not occur as syllabic. Thus, implicational universals regarding syllabic sononants and fricatives would need to be revisited. Additionally, this may suggest that sonority may not be the only measure for syllabification (cf. Clements 1992).

Conclusion

The three variations of the dorsal fricative in Blackfoot occur interconsonantally and postvocalically. They never surface after a long vowel, as other consonants do. The variants are examples of V-C coalescence, which is typologically rare. This coalescence analysis offers an explanation for the peculiarity of the dorsal fricatives. It also leads to other interesting phonological questions regarding, for example, moras, segment status, and syllabicity. Further research is needed.

NOTES

1. I would like to acknowledge my appreciation of the late Darrell R. Kipp for having supported the ongoing Blackfoot research; Rosella Many Bears and Bernadine Tallman for serving as native speaker language consultants; Donald G. Frantz and Joyce McDonough for their mentorship; Diana Archangeli, Ryan Denzer-King, Amy Fountain, Kate Hohenstein, Robert Kennedy, and Michael Kenstowicz for their comments on the earlier version of this paper; and Cavan Wagner and Scott Schupbach for their assistance. I also thank the editors, Monica Macaulay and Margaret Noodin, as well as the anonymous reviewers. All errors are mine. This study is partially supported by NSF DEL grant [BCS 1251684].

2. The symbol <a> is used instead of <ɑ> for the low vowel to be consistent with the orthography, as this is not a main concern of the analysis.

3. The sound in question, /x/, is represented as h in the orthography. The same symbol represents a glottal fricative. The glottal fricative /h/ is excluded here because it only occurs in discourse markers such as *hannia* 'really?', *hoaa* 'wow!', etc., and seems to occur as a word-initial onset filler for these exclamation words. Also, the initial sounds of these words are often very close to onsetless (Donald Frantz, personal communication 2015). For this reason, I hesitate to include /h/ in the set of legitimate phonemes.

4. Abbreviations: DUR = durative, PL = plural, SG = singular, INVS = invisible post-inflectional suffix, ANIM = animate, INAN = inanimate, PST = past, FUT = future, NONAFF = nonaffirmative, REFL = reflexive, IMP = imperative.

5. Note that the forms given in the dictionary (Frantz and Russell 1995) for (1d–e) are slightly different from the forms produced by the consultant, of which expected forms based on the dictionary are [nitsíímaniçpinnaan] and [nitsíímiçkaxpinnaan], respectively.

6. Note that *naaáhs* 'my grandparent' is not an example of VV+/x/. Instead, this is an example of vowel hiatus. This is evident from the location of accent: the first vowel is long, immediately followed by an accented vowel, [na:.áxs]. I do not discuss Vx when the vowel is short but accented.

7. General vowel shortening may be a phonetic phenomenon rather than phonological. Further investigation is necessary regarding this topic.

8. [aj] is also documented as a dialectal variation found in North Piegan. It is [ej] in other Blackfoot-speaking bands.

9. Goad and Shimada (2014) represents the sound as /h/, without specifying a gestural feature, which may imply that it is a glottal sound. The traditional and impressionistic view, however, is that its phoneme is a velar fricative /x/ (Frantz 2009; Elfner 2006b). My analysis still holds the traditional view that this sound is a dorsal fricative, with the difference that there is no underlying place feature.

10. There is also a phonetic difference. Bliss and Gick (2009) report their finding that Blackfoot devoiced vowels are articulatorily present but acoustically null and posit an interaction between an articulatory speech sound and morphosyntactic distinction strategy. In my own experience working with several native speakers of Blackfoot, I observed similar articulatorily positive but soundless vowel production as well as vowels that were fully voiced, aspirated, and completely deleted (with and without the gestures). However, it is unknown whether these phonetic variations are conditioned.

REFERENCES

Avery, Peter, and Keren Rice. 1989. Segmental structure and coronal underspecification. *Phonology* 6:179–200.

Bámisilè, Rémí. 1994. Justification for the survival of vowel coalescence as a phonological process in Yorubá. *African Languages and Cultures* 7(2):133–142.

Bliss, Heather, and Bryan Gick. 2009. Articulation without acoustics: 'Soundless' vowels in Blackfoot. *Proceedings of the 2009 Annual Conference of the Canadian Linguistic Association*, ed. by Frédéric Mailhot, pp. 1–15. Albany: SUNY Press.

Clements, George N. 1992. The sonority cycle and syllable organization. *Phonologica 1988: Proceedings of the Sixth International Phonology Meeting*, ed. by Wolfgang Dressler, pp. 63–76. Cambridge: Cambridge University Press.

Elfner, Emily. 2005. The role of sonority in Blackfoot phonotactics. *Calgary Papers in Linguistics* 26:27–91.

———. 2006a. Contrastive syllabification in Blackfoot. *Proceedings of WCCFL 25,* ed. by Donald Baumer, David Montero, and Michael Scanlon, pp. 141–149. Somerville, MA: Cascadilla Press.

———. 2006b. The mora in Blackfoot. MA thesis, University of Calgary.

Elías-Ulloa, José. 2009. The distribution of laryngeal segments in Capanahua. *International Journal of American Linguistics* 75(2):159–206.

Frantz, Donald G. 1978. Abstractness of phonology and Blackfoot orthography design. *Approaches to language: Anthropological issues*, ed. by William C. McCormack and Stephen A. Wurm, pp. 307–325. The Hague: Mouton de Gruyter.

———. 2009 [1991]. *Blackfoot grammar.* Toronto: University of Toronto Press.

Frantz, Donald G., and Norma Jean Russell. 1995. *Blackfoot dictionary of stems, roots, and affixes.* Toronto: University of Toronto Press.

Goad, Heather, and Akiko Shimada. 2014. In some languages, /s/ is a vowel. *Proceedings of the Annual Meetings on Phonology 2013*, ed. by John Kingston, Claire Moore-Cantwell, Joe Pater and Robert Staubs, pp. 1–12. Washington, DC: Linguistic Society of America.

Hayes, Bruce. 1989. Compensatory lengthening in moraic phonology. *Linguistic Inquiry* 20:253–306.

Kager, René. 1999. *Optimality theory*. Cambridge: Cambridge University Press.

Kaye, Jonathan, Jean Lowenstamm, and Jean-Roger Vergnaud. 1985. The internal structure of phonological elements: A theory of charm and government. *Phonology Yearbook* 1:305–328.

Lombardi, Linda, and John McCarthy. 1991. Prosodic circumscription in Choctaw morphology. *Phonology* 8(1):37–72.

Malone, Joseph L. 1997. On reduplication in Ojibwa. *Anthropological Linguistics* 39(3):437–458.

Morin, Yves C. 2002. The phonological status of nasal vowels in sixteenth-century French. *Interpreting the history of French: A festschrift for Peter Rickard on the occasion of his eightieth birthday,* ed. by Rodney Sampson and Wendy Ayres-Bennet, pp. 95–129. Amsterdam–New York: Rodopi.

Odden, David. 1994. Adjacency parameters in phonology. *Language* 70(2):289–330.

Pater, Joe. 1999. Austronesian nasal substitution and other NC effects. *The prosody-morphology interface.* Cambridge Studies in Linguistics, vol. 79, ed. by René Kager, Harry van der Hulst and Wim Zonneveld, pp. 310–343. Cambridge: Cambridge University Press.

Proulx, Paul. 1989. A sketch of Blackfoot historical phonology. *International Journal of American Linguistics* 55(1):43–82.

Taylor, Allan R. 1969. A grammar of Blackfoot. PhD thesis, University of California, Berkeley.

Trask, R. L. 1996. *A dictionary of phonetics and phonology.* New York: Routledge.

Uhlenbeck, C. C. 1938. *A concise Blackfoot grammar, based on material from the Southern Peigans.* Verhandelingen der Koninklijke Nederlandsche Akademie van Wetenschappen te Amsterdam, Afdeeling Letterkunde, n.s., part 41.

Valentine, J. Randolph. 2002. Variation in body-part verbs in Ojibwe dialects. *International Journal of American Linguistics* 68(1):81–119.

Wolfart, H. C. 1996. Sketch of Cree, an Algonquian language. *Handbook of North American Indians,* Vol. 17, *Languages,* ed. by Ives Goddard, pp. 390–439. Washington, DC: Smithsonian Institution.

Blackfoot Sibling Terms: Representing Culturally Specific Meanings in a Blackfoot-English Bilingual Dictionary

Madoka Mizumoto and Inge Genee

ecent discussion of dictionaries of Native American languages has often tended to focus on grammatical matters such as verb forms at the expense of the investigation of lexical semantics (e.g., Pulte and Feeling 2002; Munro 2002; Montgomery-Anderson 2008).[1] The representation of culturally specific lexical meanings and concepts in such dictionaries is less discussed. However, if one of the goals of language documentation and description is to provide resources that can contribute to language and culture revitalization efforts (Himmelmann 1998; King 2001; Austin 2012; Mizumoto 2016), then it is equally important to pay attention to the representation of culturally specific meanings. It is important to document such cultural knowledge very precisely because "[w]hen a language disappears so do a culture and a speech community's unique way of seeing and ordering the world" (Ogilvie 2011:392). This is especially crucial in the case of largely orally transmitted endangered languages like Blackfoot and other Indigenous languages.

An example will illustrate the point. Blackfoot has a Transitive Animate verb stem (VTA)[2] *waahko'sskat*, which is translated in the dictionary as 'give gifts of livestock [or] (dry) goods to parents-in-laws (of males only)' (Frantz and Russell 1995:237). A full understanding of the meaning of this verb would require an explanation of customs around marriage and the appropriate treatment of a man's wife's family in traditional Blackfoot society. A simple translation such as that given in the dictionary may suffice for people still intimately familiar with the set of customs it refers to, especially if they are fluent speakers, but others may need more information to fully grasp the meaning of this verb in its cultural context. Providing additional context, details, and relevant examples is important not only in order to document the underlying cultural practices but also to assist the learner in understanding and using the word correctly (see Whaley 2011 for a critique of preserving old meanings at all costs). By providing sufficient context for the interpretation of culturally specific lexical items, a dictionary can assist community members learning their ancestral language as a second language in learning not just the lexical item and its meaning but also the cultural concepts and practices encompassed in them.

In this paper we explore two related questions:

1. In general terms, how can we improve the representation of culturally specific meanings in bilingual dictionaries of endangered Indigenous languages?
2. More specifically, what is the best way to translate kinship terms and to represent their cultural meanings in a Blackfoot-English bilingual dictionary?

These questions are raised in the context of the Blackfoot Digital Dictionary project, under development at the University of Lethbridge (see blackfoot. atlas-ling.ca). The main goal of this project is to produce a lexical resource that is user-friendly for speakers, learners, and teachers. This is important because most younger Blackfoot now no longer acquire the Blackfoot language as a mother tongue in the home, instead usually learning it as a second language, often in a school environment. User-friendly elements to be added to the digital dictionary include audio files, images, and stories, as well as "richer" translations of important lexical items. Such additions were indicated as desirable by Blackfoot speakers who were consulted in the planning of the project. Speakers often mention the need for sufficient detail and context in the translations of culturally specific items as a high priority in a useable dictionary. Providing better translations and contextual and cultural information is therefore one of the main objectives of the project. For example, we have begun to add information about various plants used for food and medicine to the dictionary.

In this paper, we focus on kinship terms, in particular sibling terms. Representing and interpreting kinship terms and their meaning and use is a common subject of discussion in communities involved in reclaiming their language in the context of reclaiming traditional family bonds (Noori 2013). Thomason (2015) suggests that kinship systems provide an important window on the relationship between language and culture and that, when an endangered language's complex kinship terminology is replaced by simple English kinship terms, this may correlate with the breakdown of traditional kin categories and family relationships in that community.

The Blackfoot language is spoken in Southern Alberta, Canada, and Montana, US, in four different communities, each with its own dialect; Siksiká / Blackfoot, Kainaa / Blood, Aapátohsiipikani / (North) Peigan (Canada), and Aamskáápipikani / (South) Piegan, Blackfeet (US). According to the latest census, in Canada, 3,250 people speak Blackfoot as their mother tongue, and 97.5% of these speakers reside in Southern Alberta (Statistics Canada 2011). In Montana, 1,075 people speak Blackfeet (US Census Bureau 2015). There are very few monolingual speakers left in any community, and home transmission is severely limited (Frantz 2009:viii).

The paper is organized as follows: First, we give some general background on the documentation of lexical semantics and in particular of culturally specific lexical items in endangered languages. Second, we provide an outline of the handling of Blackfoot kinship terminology as represented in Frantz and Russell (1995) in particular in relation to the representation of sibling terms. Third, we discuss some possible alternative ways to represent the meaning of these terms. Last, we give some concluding comments and suggestions for further work in this area.

Background

Documentation has long benefited the scholarly linguistic community and/or the teachers and missionaries who were working in Indigenous communities. More recently, linguists have begun to discuss the ways in which our work can and should be of benefit to the community of speakers (e.g., Rice and Saxon 2002; Corris et al. 2004; Mosel 2004; Rice 2006; Thieberger and Musgrave 2007; Czaykowska-Higgins 2009; Austin 2012; Wilhelm 2013; Junker 2014). Some of this literature considers more user-friendly presentation of grammatical matters such as verb forms (e.g., Pulte and Feeling 2002; Munro 2002; Montgomery-Anderson 2008) or the development of online language learning materials such as mobile apps (e.g., Begay 2013) and online games (e.g., Junker and Torkornoo 2012).

One way to create more user-friendly dictionaries is to organize lexical information by culture-specific semantic fields rather than by alphabetical order, such as the thematic dictionaries by Visitor et al. (2013) for Eastern James Bay Cree and Kari (2007) for Dena'ina. Relevant themes will vary depending on how the language categorizes concepts. For instance, in our dictionary the theme "traditional values" was added at the request of Blackfoot contributors.

Another way to increase user-friendliness, especially for younger learners, is to include illustrations with the entries for things such as body parts, animals, and plants. A good example of a dictionary that includes pictures for culturally specific items is the Iñupiaq dictionary by MacLean (2014). While this is not a thematic dictionary (its main sections are organized alphabetically), it includes line drawings of some culturally specific items as part of some lemmas, as well as a set of appendixes with pictures representing vocabulary relating to culturally specific concepts such as locational terms, names of ocean currents, names of winds, kayaks, sleds, parts of whales, and traditional sod houses. Some other examples of lexicographic work that is sensitive to culturally specific semantic distinctions include work by Cablitz (2011) on plants in Marquesan, Rau et al. (2009) on fish in Yami, and Stephens and Boyce (2011) on traditional customary legal terminology in Māori.

Anisomorphism is of course the main challenge in the compilation of any bilingual dictionary. Anisomorphism is taken here to mean the lack of one-to-one correspondences between two languages in the widest sense of the word, including their lexicon, semantics, grammar, and culture (Hartmann and James 1998). Two languages rarely have exactly matching equivalent lexical items (Ilson 2013), and as a result many lexical items end up with an "approximate translation" (Cablitz 2011:450) in bilingual dictionaries. That approximate translation may then result in the loss of the original flavor of many items in the lexicon (Chan 2004). Important cultural concepts are often felt to be untranslatable. It is especially crucial to take this into account when working on the lexicography of endangered minority languages and to work very hard on translations that are as specific and detailed as possible, since the full flavor and meaning of the lexical items may disappear with the lexical items themselves if the language ceases to be spoken. Alternatively, as discussed by Whaley (2011:234), a word may remain in use but its original meaning may be lost if cultural practices around that item or concept are abandoned (other examples include the loss of mother-in-law language in Dyirbal, described in Lyovin 1997; see also Fishman 2000 on the difficulties involved in reversing language shift in culturally unstable environments). Possibilities for making more precise translations are obviously much more restricted when working with small languages with a limited number of fully competent speakers.

The Representation of Blackfoot Kinship Terms

The most up-to-date print dictionary for the Blackfoot language is the *Blackfoot Dictionary of Stems, Roots, and Affixes* (Frantz and Russell 1995). This is a Blackfoot-English dictionary with an English-Blackfoot index: items in the index refer back to headwords in the Blackfoot-English part. As the title indicates, lexical entries in this dictionary are not complete Blackfoot words but building blocks of words, i.e., stems, roots, and affixes. This presentation format means that using the dictionary requires an understanding of some linguistic terminology and, more important, of the grammatical structure of the Blackfoot language. For instance, a user of the dictionary needs to know that an expression like *Aahkstamai'tsi'poyo'p* 'Let's (just) speak Blackfoot!' contains a stem *iitsi'poyi* 'speak Blackfoot', lit. 'speak (the) genuine (language)', and that the verb would therefore be found in the dictionary alphabetized under *i*. Fortunately, many of these issues resolve themselves quite naturally in a digital representation (Corris et al. 2004; Montgomery-Anderson 2008).

Most lexical items in the dictionary are provided with a brief idiomatic translation (gloss) into English, sometimes followed by a literal translation. This is followed by inflected "diagnostic forms," which are intended to help the user work out how the stem or root behaves morphologically and phonologically (in particular what its allomorphs are). These often represent forms that are unlikely to occur in natural conversations.

Translations are often fairly cryptic glosses, as in the example *waahko'sskat* given in section 1 above. Similar comments can be made with regard to the translation of Blackfoot kinship terms. We illustrate this in more detail with the lemmas relating to Blackfoot sibling terms (including spouse's siblings). (Note only terms of reference are included here; terms of address [vocatives] are not included.)

- **aaáhs** *nar;* elder relation (grandparent, parent-in-law, paternal aunt/uncle, husband's older brother, etc.)
- **áákiim** *nar;* sister/female cousin of a male (includes **insst** and female **isskan**)
- **iihsiss** *nar;* younger sibling of female
- **ínsst** *nar;* older sister
- **isahkínaim** *nar;* same generation older male relative of a male, e.g., an older brother, cousin, etc.
- **iss** *nar;* son-in-law/husband's younger brother
- **isskán** *nar;* younger sibling of a male
- **isstamo** *nar;* brother-in-law of a male, i.e., his sister's husband
- **isstamoohko** *nar;* brother-in-law of a male, i.e., his wife's brother
- **i's** *nar;* older brother
- **niitsistowahsin** *nar;* brother/relative
- **ootoohkiimaan** *nar;* sister-in-law of male; lit. 'distant wife'
- **ootoyoom** *nar;* brother-in-law of female; lit. 'distant husband'
- **oyínnaa** *nar;* male relative of a female (e.g., brother, uncle, cousin), may refer to **i's** and male **iihsiss**

As the above sample demonstrates, the Blackfoot kinship terms are quite different from the English kinship terms: there are no one-to-one matches. Some of the Blackfoot terms make distinctions not present in the English terms, such as age and gender of the possessor,[3] and some of the English terms make distinctions not present in the Blackfoot terms, such as gender of the possessum (Mizumoto 2016: 60–71). In-laws (spouse's siblings) are conceptualized not as a kind of sibling but as a kind of spouse. The point here is not to provide an anthropological analysis of the entire Blackfoot kinship system, which has been done elsewhere (Wissler 1912; Hanks and Richardson 1945), but to consider how we can represent the complex meanings of these terms in ways that are meaningful to speakers, learners, and teachers who may not be familiar with the traditional Blackfoot kinship and family relations. The terms as given might be difficult to comprehend on the basis of the close translation alone without additional elaboration and context.

We focus here on the representation of age and gender in sibling terms. One way to show how the Blackfoot and English sibling terms are different in these respects is to represent them in table form. In English, sibling terms distinguish only the gender of the possessum, and both the siblings of one's spouse and the

TABLE 1. Age and gender in English sibling terms

ENGLISH	POSSESSOR				POSSESSUM			
	AGE		GENDER		AGE		GENDER	
	O	Y	M	F	O	Y	M	F
sister	✔	✔	✔	✔	✔	✔		✔
brother	✔	✔	✔	✔	✔	✔	✔	
sister-in-law (both spouse's sister and brother's wife)	✔	✔	✔	✔	✔	✔		✔
brother-in-law (both spouse's brother and sister's husband)	✔	✔	✔	✔	✔	✔	✔	

TABLE 2. Age and gender in selected Blackfoot kinship terms

BLACKFOOT	ENGLISH TRANSLATIONS	POSSESSOR				POSSESSUM			
		AGE		GENDER		AGE		GENDER	
		O	Y	M	F	O	Y	M	F
ínsst	older sister (of male or of female)		✔	✔	✔	✔			✔
i's	older brother (of male or of female)		✔	✔	✔	✔		✔	
iihsiss	younger sibling (brother or sister) of female	✔			✔		✔	✔	✔
isskán	younger sibling (brother or sister) of male	✔		✔			✔	✔	✔
ootoyoom	brother-in-law of female, husband's brother, lit. 'distant husband'	✔	✔		✔	✔	✔	✔	
isstamo	brother-in-law of male, man's sister's husband	✔	✔	✔		✔	✔	✔	
isstamoohko	brother-in-law of male, wife's brother, lit. 'brother-in-law son'	✔	✔	✔		✔	✔	✔	
(no term?)	sister-in-law of female	✔	✔		✔	✔	✔		✔
ootoohkiimaan	sister-in-law of male, wife's sister, lit. 'distant wife'	✔	✔	✔		✔	✔		✔

spouses of one's siblings are treated as a type of sibling ("in-laws"). Relative age is not distinguished in these terms at all, as shown in Table 1.

In Blackfoot, sibling terms distinguish gender and relative age of both possessor and possessum, as shown in Table 2. Spouse's siblings and siblings' spouses are distinct: in particular, the same-gender siblings of ego's spouse are treated as a type of spouse (lit. 'distant wife/husband'; this distinction is not represented in the tables).

A comparison of the tables makes it clear that there is significant semantic anisomorphism between the English and Blackfoot terms, representing two world-views. Even when we only consider age and gender, the Blackfoot terms are difficult to fully comprehend for speakers with English as their first language, because they do not give enough contextual information and do not tell us anything about the role of these individuals in the family group. The question arises, what is the best way to handle these items in the context of a dictionary? How do we convey the worldview encompassed in the Blackfoot terms to nonnative speakers?

Some Possible Solutions

Learners' dictionaries often include pictures and illustrations, especially for beginners' levels of vocabulary development. Examples include the *Oxford Picture Dictionary* series, published both in monolingual and 13 bilingual editions (e.g., the Canadian edition of Shapiro and Adelson-Goldstein [1999]) and *The Heinle Picture Dictionary* (monolingual). This is helpful for users from a variety of cultural and linguistic backgrounds. Pictures are usually interpretable to all levels of language learners, make it easier to visualize or conceptualize meanings, especially of concrete items, and help avoid misinterpretation and misunderstanding.

The anthropological literature often represents kinship relations visually in the form of a kinship chart, as in the two-generation charts in Figure 1.

This kind of presentation has obvious advantages. The family relations are indicated clearly by a combination of symbols (circles for females, triangles for males, lines for relations by blood, equal signs for relations by marriage) and colors (not fully visible in grayscale; individuals with the same color are considered identical and may be referred to with the same kinship term). Levels in the chart indicate generations. In terms of sibling relations, for instance, the full color version of this chart (available on the Wikipedia page from which it was taken) visualizes clearly

FIGURE 1. An example of a kinship chart

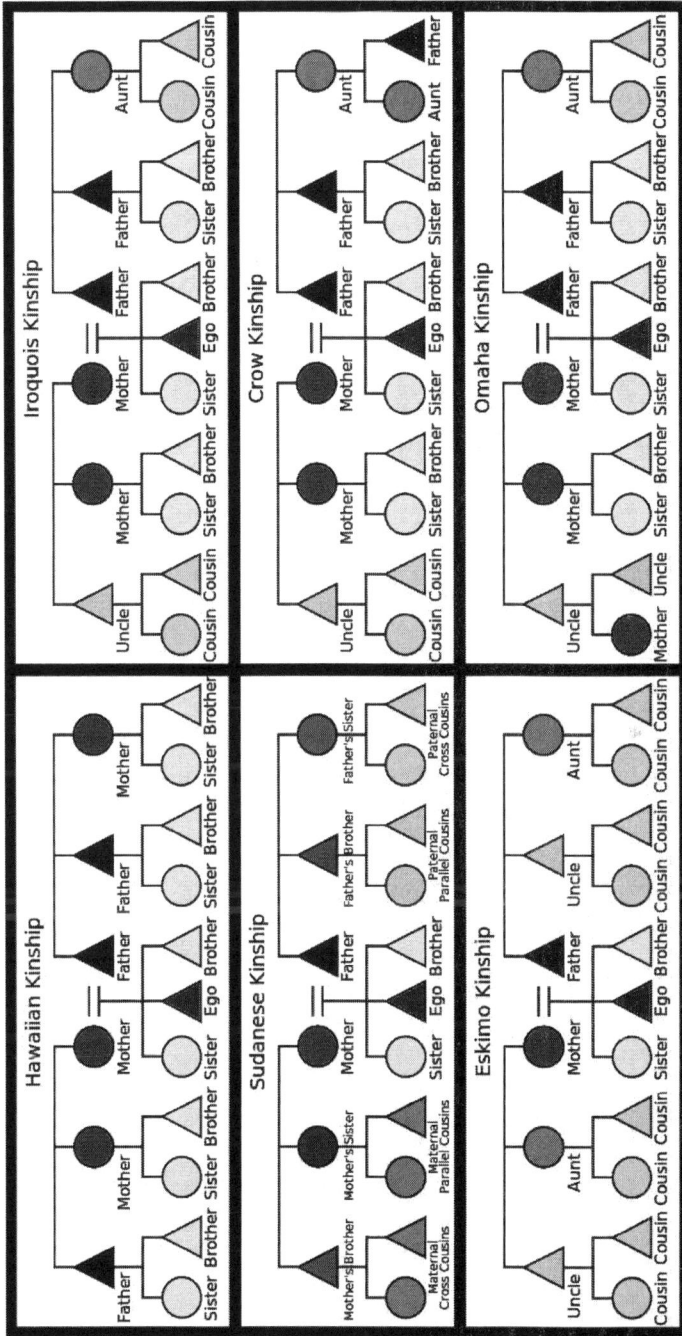

that the Hawai'ian system treats cousins and siblings as identical while the Eskimo system separates them, as English does.

This type of chart does not represent every potentially important kinship distinction, such as age differences within one generation (older and younger siblings) and gender of ego, parameters that are important for the Blackfoot kinship system, although it could certainly be refined to include these. A weakness from a learner's point of view lies in the prior knowledge of the symbols required to interpret the terms and relations correctly. For elderly and very young learners and learners with limited formal education and/or literacy, this kind of chart is still likely to be confusing.

A common way to represent family relations for learners, especially children, is in the form of a family tree with face illustrations and/or names (e.g., Parnwell and Yellowhair 1989; Shapiro and Adelson-Goldstein 1999; *Heinle Picture Dictionary* 2014 [2005]). Face illustrations eliminate the need for abstract symbols to represent gender, and names can help learners connect the terms with specific people in their own family.

A partial family tree with face illustrations for Blackfoot, focusing on sibling terms, could look as in Figures 2 and 3. Notice that two separate trees are needed as Blackfoot sibling terms differ depending on whether ego (*niistówa* 'I/me') is male or female. Equal signs represent relations by marriage. Age differences within the same generation are represented by placing siblings older than ego to the left and slightly higher in the tree, while siblings younger than ego are represented to the right and slightly lower in the tree.

All terms are given in the form of a full word with appropriate affixes. Because kinship terms are dependent (relational) nouns in Blackfoot, they must have a possessor. For instance, the dependent noun stem *i's* is represented as *ni'sa* (n-*i's*-wa 1SG-older_brother-AN.SG) 'my older brother'.

For a comparison with the English sibling terms, see Figure 4.

These charts clearly visualize two crucial differences between English and Blackfoot sibling relations. Triangles represent males, circles represent females, and boxes represent terms not distinguished for gender. A comparison between the charts shows clearly that in Blackfoot it matters whether ego's sibling is older or younger than ego, and for siblings that are younger than ego, it matters whether ego (not the sibling) is a boy or a girl. In English, the only thing that matters is whether ego's sibling is a boy or a girl. In a classroom setting a comparison of these charts could be used as a prompt for a discussion of traditional Blackfoot sibling

FIGURE 2. Blackfoot sibling terms from woman's point of view

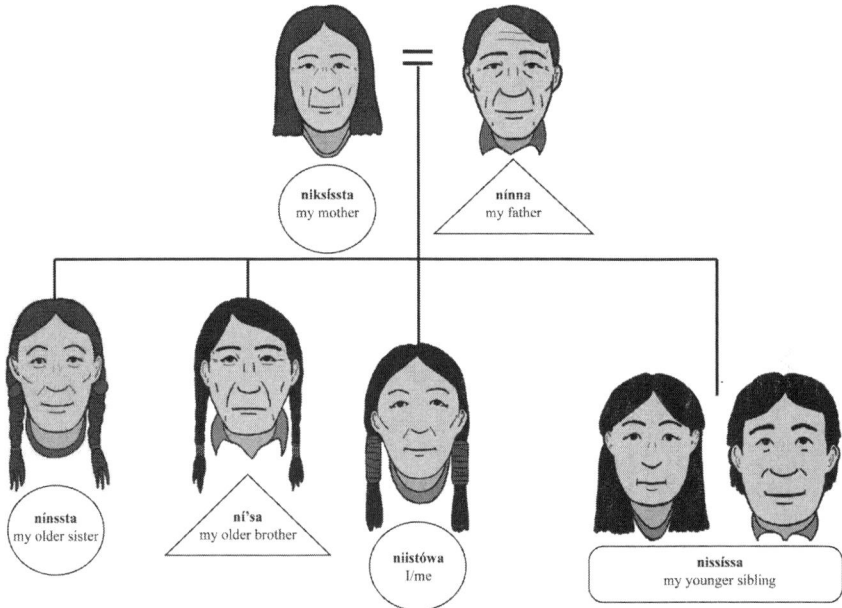

niksíssta
my mother

nínna
my father

nínssta
my older sister

ní'sa
my older brother

niistówa
I/me

nissíssa
my younger sibling

FIGURE 3. Blackfoot sibling terms from man's point of view

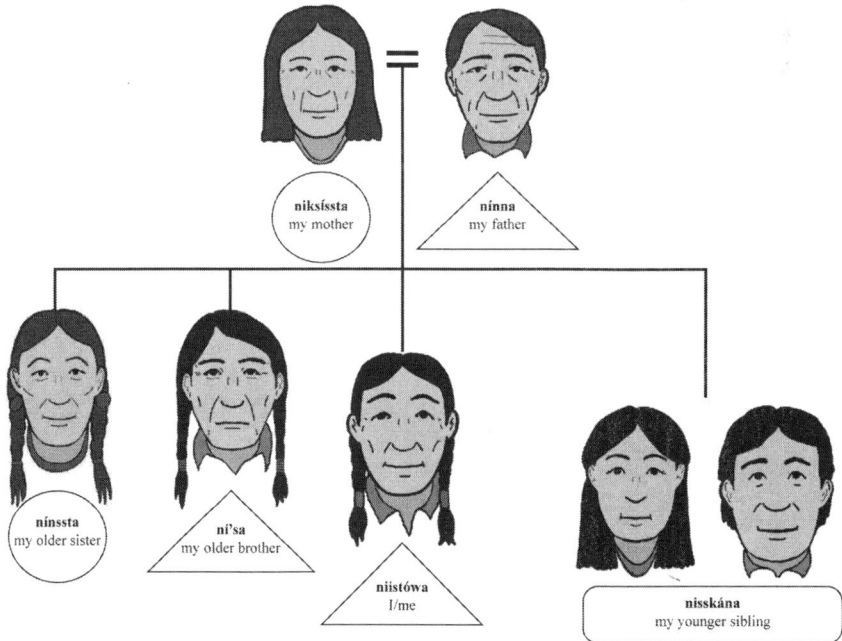

niksíssta
my mother

nínna
my father

nínssta
my older sister

ní'sa
my older brother

niistówa
I/me

nisskána
my younger sibling

FIGURE 4. English sibling terms from man and woman's point of view

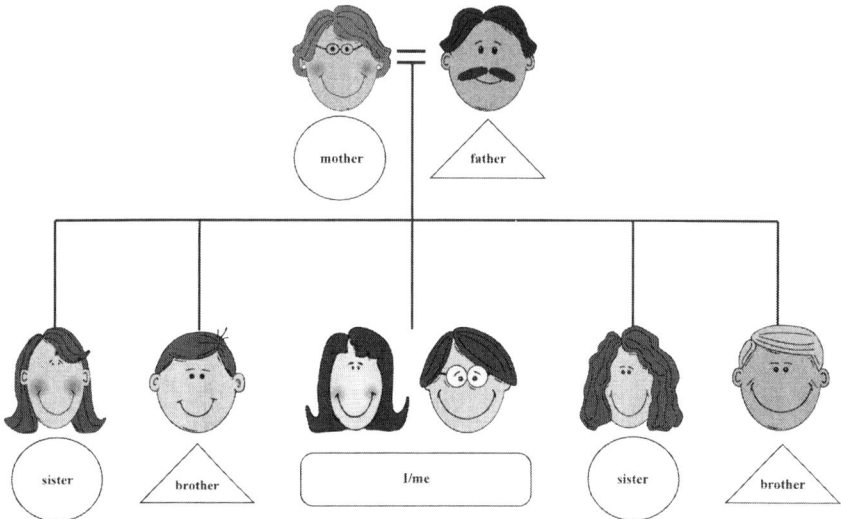

relations and the roles and responsibilities attached to these terms. (See Mizumoto 2016 for further discussion.)

Discussion and Conclusion

This paper has explored some possible ways to represent culturally specific lexical items such as sibling terms in a Blackfoot-English bilingual dictionary. We suggest that a slightly adapted form of a traditional family tree could capture some of the Blackfoot-specific distinctions in a culturally appropriate way that represents their semantics in visual form. This obviously needs additional investigation since we have only considered a very partial family tree based on the direct relations of a person with parents and siblings. Other family members such as children and grandchildren, grandparents, parents' siblings ("aunts and uncles"), and parents' siblings' children ("cousins") are not included, nor are relations by marriage. Neither did we include culture-specific terms such as *miníí'pokaa* 'favorite child', *kipitáípokaa* 'child raised by elderly persons, usually grandparents (and so more familiar with traditional ways and language)', or general nouns such as *pookáá* 'child' (Frantz and Russell 1995 s.v.). We also ignored terms of address (vocatives).

Despite all these limitations, even a comparison between the English and Blackfoot sibling terms represented in this way already illustrates quite well some of the significant differences between the Blackfoot and English kinship systems. We feel that this type of representation will not only be a good addition to a bilingual learner's dictionary but can also fairly straightforwardly be turned into a classroom exercise resource—for instance, by making a blank version of the sibling trees in Figures 2 and 3, omitting the English translations, letting students put the names of their own family members in the correct slot, and then using the completed charts as a prompt for an exploration of the roles and responsibilities of siblings within a family.

NOTES

1. We would like to thank Francis First Charger, Annabelle Chatsis, Rhonda Crow, Lena Russell, and Rod Scout from the Blackfoot community for sharing their language with us; Donald G. Frantz for sharing his kinship chart; and Hendrika H. Beaulieu for sharing her knowledge of kinship with us. The face illustrations in Figures 2 and 3 were made by William Singer III/Api'soomaahka. We are grateful to the audience at the Forty-Seventh Algonquian Conference, and to Mizuki Miyashita and an additional anonymous reviewer for PAC, for some very helpful comments and feedback. This research is supported by SSHRC grant 435-2015-1082 (awarded to Inge Genee) and a grant from the Jacobs Research Funds 2015 (awarded to Madoka Mizumoto).
2. List of abbreviations: 1SG = first person singular, AN.SG = animate singular, NAR = relational (dependent) animate noun, VTA = transitive animate verb. In Tables 1 and 2: O = older, Y = younger, M = male, F = female.
3. In kinship expressions like *my sister* the possessor is *my* and the possessum is *sister* (Payne 1997).

REFERENCES

Austin, Peter. 2012. Language documentation. *Oxford bibliographies in Linguistics*, ed. by Mark Aronoff. www.oxfordbibliographies.com.

Begay, Winoka Rose. 2013. Mobile apps and Indigenous language learning: New developments in the field of Indigenous language revitalization. MA thesis, University of Arizona.

Cablitz, Gabriele H. 2011. Documenting cultural knowledge in dictionaries of endangered languages. *International Journal of Lexicography* 24:446–462.

Chan, Sin Wai. 2004. Dictionaries and translators. *Translation and bilingual dictionaries*, ed. by Sin Wai Chan, pp. 1–3. Tübingen: Max Niemeyer Verlag.

Corris, Miriam, Christopher Manning, Susan Poetsch, and Jane Simpson. 2004. How useful and usable are dictionaries for speakers of Australian Indigenous languages? *International Journal of Lexicography* 17:33–68.

Czaykowska-Higgins, Eva. 2009. Research models, community engagement, and linguistic fieldwork: Reflection on working within Canadian Indigenous communities. *Language Documentation & Conversation* 3:15–50.

Fishman, Joshua A. 2000. *Can threatened language be saved?* Clevedon, UK: Multilingual Matters.

Frantz, Donald. G. 2009. *Blackfoot grammar*. Toronto: University of Toronto Press.

Frantz, Donald. G., and Norma Jean Russell. 1995. *Blackfoot dictionary of stems, roots, and affixes*. Toronto: University of Toronto Press.

Hanks, Lucien M., and Jane Richardson. 1945. *Observations on northern Blackfoot kinship*. Monographs of the American Ethnological Society, vol. 9, ed. by Irving Hallowell, pp. 1–39. Seattle: University of Washington Press.

Hartmann, R.R.K., and Gregory James. 1998. *Dictionary of lexicography*. London: Routledge.

The Heinle picture dictionary. 2014 [2005]. Independence, KY: National Geographic Learning.

Himmelmann, Nikolaus P. 1998. Documentary and descriptive linguistics. *Linguistics* 36:161–195.

Ilson, Robert. 2013. The explanatory technique of translation. *International Journal of Lexicography* 26:386–393.

Junker, Marie-Odile. 2014. Developing thematic dictionaries of Eastern James Bay Cree. http://www.canadacouncil.ca/council/blog/2014/08/creedictionary.

Junker, Marie-Odile, and Delasie Torkornoo. 2012. *Online language games for endangered languages: Jeux.tshakapesh.ca, www.eastcree.org/lessons*. Paper presented at the EDULEARN 12: International Conference on Education and New Learning Technologies, Barcelona.

Kari, James. 2007. *Dena'ina topical dictionary*. Fairbanks: Alaska Native Language Center.

King, Kendall A. 2001. *Language revitalization: Processes and prospects*. Clevedon, UK: Multilingual Matters.

Lyovin, Anatole V. 1997. *An introduction to the languages of the World*. Oxford: Oxford University Press.

MacLean, Edna Ahgeak. 2014. *Iñupiatun Uqaluit Taniktun Sivuninit: Iñupiaq to English dictionary*. Fairbanks: University of Alaska Press.

Mizumoto, Madoka. 2016. Translating Blackfoot kinship terms in a Blackfoot-English bilingual dictionary. MA thesis, University of Lethbridge. http://hdl.handle.net/10133/4769.

Montgomery-Anderson, Brad. 2008. Citing verbs in polysynthetic languages: The case of the Cherokee-English dictionary. *Southwest Journal of Linguistics* 27(1):53–75.

Mosel, Ulrike. 2004. Dictionary making in endangered speech communities. *Language Documentation and Description* 2:39–54.

Munro, Pamela. 2002. Entries for verbs in American Indian language dictionaries. *Making dictionaries: Preserving Indigenous languages of the Americas*, ed. by William Frawley, Kenneth C. Hill, and Pamela Munro, pp. 86–107. Berkeley: University of California Press.

Noori, Margaret. 2013. Anishinaabemowin: Language, family, and community. *Bringing our language home: Language revitalization for families*, ed. by Leanne Hinton, pp. 118–140. Berkeley, CA: Heyday.

Ogilvie, Sarah. 2011. Linguistics, lexicography, and the revitalization of endangered languages. *International Journal of Lexicography* 24:389–404.

Parnwell, E. C., and Marvin Yellowhair. 1989. *The new Oxford picture dictionary: English/Navajo edition*. Oxford: Oxford University Press.

Payne, Thomas Edward. 1997. *Describing morphosyntax: A guide for field linguistics*. Cambridge: Cambridge University Press.

Pulte, William, and Durbin Feeling. 2002. Morphology in Cherokee lexicography: The Cherokee-English dictionary. *Making dictionaries: Preserving Indigenous languages of the Americas*, ed. by William Frawley, Kenneth C. Hill, and Pamela Munro, pp. 60–69. Berkeley: University of California Press.

Rau, D. Victoria, Meng-Chien Yang, Hui-Huan Ann Chang, and Maa-Neu Dong. 2009. Online dictionary and ontology building for Austronesian languages in Taiwan. *Language Documentation & Conservation* 3:192–212.

Rice, Keren. 2006. Ethical issues in linguistic fieldwork: An overview. *Journal of Academic Ethics* 4:123–155.

Rice, Keren, and Leslie Saxon. 2002. Issues of standardization and community in Aboriginal language lexicography. *Making dictionaries: Preserving Indigenous languages of the Americas*, ed. by William Frawley, Keneth C. Hill, and Pamela Munro, pp. 125–154. Berkeley: University of California Press.

Shapiro, Norma, and Jayme Adelson-Goldstein. 1999. *The Oxford picture dictionary: Canadian edition*. Oxford: Oxford University Press.

Statistics Canada. 2013. 2011 Census in brief, Aboriginal language in Canada. Catalog no.98-314-X2011003. Ottawa.

Stephens, Mamari, and Mary Boyce. 2011. Finding a balance: Customary legal terms in a modern Maori legal dictionary. *International Journal of Lexicography* 24:432–445.

Thieberger, Nicholas, and Simon Musgrave. 2007. Documentary linguistics and ethical issues. *Language Documentation and Description* 4:26–36.

Thomason, Sarah G. 2015. *Endangered languages: An introduction.* Cambridge: Cambridge University Press.

U.S. Census Bureau. 2015. *Detailed languages spoken at home and ability to speak English for the population 5 years and over for states: 2009–2013.* https://www.census.gov/data/tables/2013/demo/2009-2013-lang-tables.html.

Visitor, Linda, Marie-Odile Junker, and Mimie Neacappo. 2013. *Eastern James Bay Cree thematic dictionary (Northern dialect).* Chisasibi, QB: Cree School Board.

Whaley, Lenore A. 2011. Some ways to endanger an endangered language project. *Language and Education* 25:339–348.

Wissler, Clark. 1912. *Social organization and ritualistic ceremonies of the Blackfoot Indians.* Anthropological Papers of the American Museum of Natural History, vol. 7. New York: The Trustees.

Lexicographical Dilemmas from the Perspective of *Bezhik ENshinaabemat*

Mary Ann Naokwegijig-Corbiere

S ince first getting involved in teaching Nishnaabemwin in 1989, I have become acquainted with a growing number of *Nishnaabek* with a profound desire to "get their language back."[1] Some have taken the courses I teach at the University of Sudbury. Others have contacted me to inquire about learning resources. Some after hearing through word of mouth about the correspondence courses on the language that were developed by the Indigenous Studies department have asked me about purchasing them. Still others I have met at the conference that Anishinaabemowin Teg holds near the end of March every year in Sault Ste. Marie.[2] These learners, to whom I will refer as *aapji waa-Nishnaabemjik*,[3] are widely dispersed, with most away from a Nishnaabemwin speech community. Nonetheless, they continue their pursuit of fluency by whatever means they can. The efforts of one group are especially notable.

In 2015, several *aapji waa-Nishnaabemjik* in Ontario, mainly in the areas east and north of Lake Huron, came together to establish an initiative called the Language House.[4] This is not a specific facility and it is not a formal organization. Rather, it is the name under which the group comes together periodically throughout the year for three or four days at a time to learn through immersion. The participants have obtained such resources as the correspondence course manuals from the University of Sudbury and similar materials from Algoma University and Trent University, as well as materials by community organizations such as the Wikwemikong Heritage Organization and by individuals like Shirley Williams, Isadore Toulouse, and Helen Roy. They also make use of the *Eastern Ojibwe-Chippewa-Ottawa Dictionary* (Rhodes 1985) and/or *A Concise Dictionary of Minnesota Ojibwe* (Nichols and Nyholm 1995). These dictionaries understandably were constrained in the amount of Nishnaabemwin vocabulary and examples they could include. Students with particular words in mind that they want to say in Nishnaabemwin often are unable to find them in the existing works, hence the genesis of the current project that will provide a more comprehensive Nishnaabemwin dictionary,[5] a need that grows ever more urgent as the population of *eNshinaabemjik* ages.

The needs of such a dedicated group have shaped my paramount objective from the outset: to produce a resource that will enable *aapji waa-Nishnaabemjik* to speak with the eloquence and the humor of their forebears and thereby fully reconnect with their roots. In this paper, I discuss the implications the learners' situation has for certain aspects of dictionary design. To do so, I first outline the type of background knowledge *aapji waa-Nishnaabek* typically bring to their learning endeavor. Then I touch on the considerations that bear on the production of a Nishnaabemwin dictionary tailored to help this category of users. These considerations include ethical ones associated with my dual position as a member of both the Nishnaabe community and academia. I close by providing some examples to illustrate some of the more difficult dilemmas the objective of serving learners of Nishnaabemwin as a second language poses to the lexicographical task.

Aapji waa-Nishnaabemjik: Their Background Knowledge and Motivational Factors

Aapji waa-Nishnaabemjik are quite a diverse group in terms of their interests and aptitudes. Some are artistic-minded and bring a creative impulse to their studies; others are motivated primarily by a desire to be able to converse with family members in the language and to join in the joking *eNshinaabemjik* do. Especially salient to all of them is the spirituality embodied in Native culture. With regard to background knowledge of a technical nature, a fair proportion of *aapji waa-Nishnaabemjik*—like a good proportion of the general undergraduate population—struggles with grammatical concepts. It would likely be too facile on my part to attribute the lack in this area to a deficient elementary and secondary education. Yong and Peng, in writing of foreign language learners, remind us that their "native language and culture are deeply rooted in their minds ... and [they] tend to use their own norms to pass judgments and distort what is foreign to conform to their own customs and habit" (2007:48). For Nishnaabe students who have not grown up in their ancestral language, English is their native language. Sentence patterns of the sort used to say "I come from a family of six" and "That's a great idea" are standard to them, and they expect that such commonplace nouns as *family* and *idea* must have equivalent terms in Nishnaabemwin. Teaching the language entails frequent explanations that Nishnaabemwin uses different "sentence templates" to convey the same sorts of information. Learning to indicate family size in the way *eNshinaabemjik* generally do—through phrasing that literally means "We number six [siblings]," for example, and that uses a verb formed from the number term (*ngodwaachi* from *ngodwaaswi* in this example)—is a major change to their ways of expressing such concepts.

It is apparent that very few have ever taken a linguistics course. The reason for this may be that this discipline seems irrelevant to learning Nishnaabemwin or it may simply be a matter of opportunity. The oral nature of Nishnaabemwin leads some to regard theoretical concepts as irrelevant to learning this language. Some *aapji waa-Nishnaabemjik* do find linguistics concepts helpful and express an interest in learning those that would serve their goal. Unfortunately, linguistics courses are generally either not available or are not readily accessible. If offered at an institution where Nishnaabemwin is also taught, they may be intended primarily for linguistics majors.[6] That focus, coupled with the prevailing ethos of Indigenous studies departments (where Nishnaabemwin courses are typically housed), also inhibits Nishnaabemwin instructors from drawing more fully on linguistics discursive resources.[7] Linguistics is regarded by some as another of the prongs in the historical incursion of the social sciences into the Indigenous sociocultural domain. A related view is that linguistic analysis is a dissection of the language, a practice antithetical to Nishnaabe epistemology. The various situational factors related to education systems and ideas concerning what is epistemologically and pedagogically appropriate make *aapji waa-Nishnaabemjik* a heterogeneous group. The specific words they will look for in the dictionary and how they will go about using the information they find we can only try to anticipate. Our aim is to create entries that are as clear a set of lexical signposts as possible and will thus aid *aapji waa-Nishnaabemjik* to express themselves in ways that sound authentic in terms of phraseology.

Ethical Considerations in Creating a Resource
for *Aapji waa-Nishnaabemjik*

My membership in both an Aboriginal community and the academic community presents me with an ethical dilemma. Whose needs do I accord primacy—my own to produce work that meets the scholarly standards of linguistics, or those of *aapji waa-Nishnaabek* for whom needing to learn relevant linguistics concepts may be an added impediment? Also a consideration is the obligation I feel I have as a faculty member in a particular type of program, one that was founded to accord a place for Indigenous epistemology within the academy, a thrust now articulated as decolonization. Within the Indigenous studies context, the latter term has a connotation beyond that of "(a state) withdraw[ing] from (a colony), leaving it independent" (Barber 1998:364).

A leading Aboriginal scholar alludes to the sense it has in the educational context when she writes,

> Indigenous knowledge, embraced in Aboriginal languages, is . . . being supplanted in First Nations schools with Eurocentric knowledge. . . . Instead of draw[ing] from . . . [Indigenous people's] social and cultural frames of reference, embodying their philosophical foundations of spiritual interconnected realities, and building on the enriched experiences and gifts of their people . . . , education has been framed as a secular experience with fragmented knowledge imported from other societies and cultures. This fragmented accumulation of knowledge builds on Eurocentric strategies that maintain their knowledge is universal, that it derives from standards of good that are universally appropriate, that the ideas and ideals . . . need not be questioned, and that all questions can be posed and resolved from within it. (Battiste 1998:21)

Another scholar recalling an evening noncredit Nishnaabemwin course he took in Toronto attributes the declining attendance by other Native students in the course to resistance against colonization. Some Aboriginal people, he remarks, perhaps "feel that language is the last frontier for the colonizer" (Corbiere 1997:104). Neeley and Palmer (2012:273) note that some Kiowa speakers express a desire that Native languages not be exploited any further. The situation that often prevails has been characterized as that of two solitudes.

A view ... sometimes found in the literature on language revitalization and the role
of linguists in this endeavor is that linguists and language activists represent two
solitudes, each with their own ideas, perhaps even their own legends, about what
a language is and what language revitalization is all about. (Rice 2009:1)

Anishinaabemowin Teg's vision statement as it appears in the 2016 conference
program, "We will provide a stable foundation and the place that allow Anishinaabe
[*sic*] ... to come together to maintain culture and language for ourselves and future
generations," expresses the desire for autonomy that Rice also notes. She notes as
well the distrust language activists have regarding linguists and touches on other
factors behind the resistance to their involvement. "One hears many comments
made to academics about their goals. ... Indigenous people sometimes remark that
everything else has been taken from them, and now the linguists are trying to steal
their language as well" (Rice 2009:45). The question of who can rightly engage in
scholarship on Indigenous languages and develop courses if not voiced remains
part of the subtext of most discussions on this issue.

Straddling the Aboriginal and the academic communities imposes on me two
sets of expectations (and makes me potentially subject to questions concerning
whether I have been seduced by Eurocentric thought). Theories posited from
the Indigenous realm do not always accord with those found within linguistics
scholarship. This situation puts me in a position somewhat akin to that of the
mzhinwe, although this comparison might not be entirely apt. This term that has
been rendered archaic I have heard in only two instances. Once was in an anecdote
my late mother related about a wedding reception she had attended as a young
woman; she remarked of a person, "Mii wa gaa-mzhinwewit." I gathered from
the context that this person ensured each guest found a seat. The meaning this
suggests, 'be an usher', seems not entirely appropriate since wedding receptions
in our community at the time were not very formal affairs. The second instance
was when Alan Corbiere mentioned having come across the term in a historical
document. It referred to one of the positions that were filled in a band election
in 1889. Upon researching the term further, he found it was interpreted in several
ways including: "the person who would gather food and supplies for people that
were less fortunate or had recently experienced a tragedy" (Corbiere 2010:2);
maitre d'; steward; property administrator; one whose role is rather like that of an
aide-de-camp (2); and one who conveys state messages, a role regarded as a key

one in diplomacy (3). Nishnaabemwin is regarded as a resource to be treasured, safeguarded, and whose integrity must be maintained. In writing a dictionary, I am a go-between striving to integrate the vital contributions that the two solitudes each bring to the work at hand.

I have often explained to dictionary workshop participants the linguistics- or lexicographical-based rationale for asking about particular inflections or range of usage for certain words. And in writing a guide to using the dictionary, it will be important to explain pertinent linguistics and lexicographic principles clearly to *aapji waa-Nishnaabemjik* and in a manner that achieves "a balance between the analytical study of the language and the responsibilities to the community" (Rice 2009:47). The project, we hope, promotes mutual respect for each other's perspective on the part of the two "solitudes" by utilizing effectively and honoring appropriately the respective contributions of each.

An aspect of the dictionary's function of which I am also conscious is to aid translators. Organizations that deal with First Nations often commission translations of assorted documents ranging from the brief (greeting cards and flyers) to lengthier texts in brochures and factsheets. Individuals who teach or have taught Nishnaabemwin are often approached to do such work. In the future, that task (should it still be desired then) will fall to those for whom Nishnaabemwin is a second language. While some who will have learned "their language" in this way will no doubt be cognizant that their mastery is not at a mother-tongue level, they may feel obliged to provide translations when requested. For them, the dictionary will be an especially vital resource.

Translation of course entails skills and knowledge beyond simply being bilingual. Otherwise there would be no programs and resources for training translators and interpreters. Experiences such as one recounted by a bilingual *eNshinaabemat* demonstrate the crucial role such training can play—training that is not available for Nishnaabemwin. In recounting the time she was asked to interpret for a Nishnaabe man in court, it was apparent she had overlooked that a key term has a second sense. She recalled being totally flustered when she heard "Do you swear to tell the whole truth … ?" and thinking in Nishnaabemwin, "I can't ask him to swear!?"

Accuracy entails not only using correct grammar in rendering ideas in the target language (TL); they need to be expressed in characteristic TL phraseology that reflects the ways its mother-tongue speakers conceptualize phenomena. The concept of dynamic equivalence is one name given to this aspect of the translation task. "The message has to be tailored to the receptor's linguistic needs and cultural expectation and '[aim] at complete naturalness of expression'" (Munday 2008:42). To illustrate the type of challenge culture-specific concepts present, Baker gives the example of *privacy*, "an abstract English concept which is notoriously difficult to translate into other languages" (2011:18). Recognizing that a sense of what sounds natural in a given language comes with mastery of that language, my hope is that the dictionary will enable English-Nishnaabemwin translators of the future to produce text that approaches that tone.

At the same time, I am mindful of the caution Yong and Peng offer as to how ambitious the lexicographer ought to be:

> A general-purpose bilingual dictionary . . . attempts to cover as wide a range as possible of the general vocabulary of the source language. The general vocabulary should not be interpreted as the whole lexicon . . . which is impossible for any bilingual dictionary to cover and describe. (2007:71)

Nonetheless, my goal is to compile as comprehensive a lexicon as possible. My reasons are twofold. The situation of Nishnaabemwin differs from that of other languages that seem to be the primary concern of Yong and Peng. Other languages have a wealth of written materials—novels, history books, biographies, and books on the sciences and business—that demonstrate the full range of uses of the language. That breadth of literature facilitates production of a range of dictionary types: diachronic; synchronic (Yong and Peng 2007:21); "college" dictionaries; and national language and regional dialect dictionaries (74), for instance. Literature in Nishnaabemwin by contrast is sparse. Another reason is the declining number of mother-tongue speakers of Nishnaabemwin who can fill full-time faculty positions that facilitate long-term projects of this sort. Undeniably, the opportunity I was afforded to compile from a mother-tongue speaker position as comprehensive a listing of terms as possible for future reference by *aapji waa-Nishnaabemjik* is likely never to occur again.

Helping *Aapji waa-Nishnaabemjik* to Sound like *Pane Bi-Nishnaabemjik*

The features that make Nishnaabemwin and English so different from each other create many dilemmas as we strive to design a dictionary that will foster authentic

Nishnaabemwin expression on the part of learners. Some of the questions I struggled with when I was envisaging just a print dictionary are not pressing at the moment now that the immediate goal is an online dictionary.[8] However, some questions are germane to both versions. These will be the focus for the remainder of this discussion.

In order to foster characteristic Nishnaabemwin expression on the part of adult learners of the language, we need to try and anticipate how they are apt to phrase thoughts in their first language and their unconscious assumptions regarding the meanings of the words they use. Fluent speakers rarely give thought to the precise meanings of their utterances and just as rarely realize a given word can have a different sense in another context. As an example, when *until* first comes up in my course, it is rendered as *biinish*, as in *Biinish ko 5:00 nakii* 'She usually works until 5:00'. It was only in giving another example later, 'He won't get here until around 6:00', that I realized there's a second Nishnaabemwin term for 'until', *baamaa,* and that this dictates affirmative phrasing, *Baamaa ngoji 6:00 da-bi-dgoshin.* The negative pattern in which I have schooled my students does not make sense when the idea is 'not . . . until'. Scholarship on lexicography and on translation and interpretation elucidates this aspect thoroughly emphasizing the need to be mindful of this behavior.

Baker (2011:11) identifies "four main types of meanings in words and utterances: propositional . . . , expressive . . . , presupposed . . . , and evoked meaning." Yong and Peng utilize a typology proposed by Leech which "distinguished seven types of meaning: conceptual . . . , connotative . . . , social . . . , affective . . . , reflected . . . , collocative . . . , and thematic" (2007:47). Conceptual meaning is what Baker calls propositional meaning: "the meaning of a word or utterance [that] arises from the relation that arises between it and what it refers to or describes in a real or imaginary world as conceived of by the speakers of a particular language" (2011:11). Yong and Peng (2007:47), like Baker, note that this type of meaning is the most readily grasped. They add that the other six types of meaning (which they subsume under the heading "non-conceptual meaning") create the greatest challenge for the bilingual lexicographer and warrant equal, if not greater, attention (49).

As my students consult the handbook they use in the course of composing Nishnaabemwin remarks, I am regularly reminded that non-conceptual meanings are a natural part of their unconscious understanding of words. This experience has alerted me to the kinds of questions to bear in mind as I flesh out dictionary articles. What sorts of situations, sentiments, and attitudes prompt particular word choices and remarks? How does the vocabulary range of users influence their choices in terms of register or pithiness of expression? Like any fluent speaker using his or her language informally, learners also are not conscious of the tacit or contextual knowledge that determines their choice of words. How can we convey most clearly and succinctly the meanings of those words whose usage varies greatly? The already difficult task of "finding exact equivalents in two different languages . . . [is] even greater when the source and target languages are not closely related etymologically" (Yong and Peng 2007:129). Munday, having noted how *cheese* and *syr*, a Russian term, are not fully equivalent, explains that "for the message to be 'equivalent' in [the source text and target text], the code-units will be different since they belong to different sign systems (languages) which partition reality differently (the *cheese/ syr* example)" (2008:37). How do we facilitate ready recognition of idioms and metaphors and enable *aapji waa-Nishnaabemjik* to use such devices to the same effect in characteristic Nishnaabemwin ways? Yong and Peng (2007:176) explain that "from the semantic point of view, idioms must be interpreted in connection with the historical and cultural contexts from which they emerged." They go on to state: "When establishing equivalence between idioms in the language pair, bilingual lexicographers will have to pay equal attention to linguistics aspects of idioms and their cultural aspects" (186).

ENshinaabemjik, like any other group, deploy words and use the language's fabled morphological precision not only for denotative purposes. *Skanaabiigzi*, for example, is rarely used in the literal sense of one of its possible glosses, 'be scrawny', using the adjective one dictionary defines as "very thin and bony" (Collins English Dictionary, 2016). It's often used to achieve the same effect as "He's rail-thin." To quote again from Yong and Peng (2007:128), "it is [the lexicographers'] responsibility to . . . create lexical associations and images that are as close as possible to those existing in the mind of the native speakers." The section that follows that concludes this paper gives some examples of Nishnaabemwin words that leave me keenly aware that I will not have fulfilled that responsibility satisfactorily.

Leading *Aapji waa-Nishnaabemjik* to Apt Phraseology

While an online dictionary has a vastly greater capacity and a web-based interface allows greater design flexibility than the printed page, some significant challenges remain regarding how to guide learners to Nishnaabemwin phrasing that would sound natural and resonate in the way they intend. Granted, particular words evoke the images and feelings they do because of the era and milieu in which they are used. Phraseology that would evoke an inane image in the minds of those who acquired Nishnaabemwin as children fifty or more years ago would not necessarily have the same effect on those for whom Nishnaabemwin is the second language. Suppose, for example, a learner moving into a new place has been lugging boxes up and down the stairs and wants to text a friend, "My arms are so tired." *Ekzi*, a verb describing a state typically associated with people and meaning 'He's tired' might come readily to mind.[9] If the learner is aware that such verbs can be applied to an inanimate subject (which *nnik* 'my arm' would be) by adding the morpheme /*mgad*/, his English-patterned thoughts might lead him to write *Gwetaani-ekziimgadoon nnikan* denoting what's tired: *nnikan* 'my arms', using the discrete noun. That would likely make perfect sense to most learners; to a mother-tongue speaker that phrasing would be quite odd. At this point, I have not settled on the extent to which the dictionary ought to try and address this sort of contingency. Undoubtedly, certain aspects of usage can be learned more effectively from teachers whether in a formal context or through immersion.

Aptness of phraseology extends beyond conveying propositional meanings fittingly. It takes in characteristic figures of speech by which experiences are cast in a particular light. Therefore, I feel it important that the dictionary also show common figurative usages of particular words and also if some words are typically used just in that way. Continuing with the example of tired arms, there are a couple of equally viable options for describing this state: *Ngwetaani-eknike* and *Ngwetaani-ekwaabiignike*. Both mean 'My arms are so tired'. To convey how the verbs *eknike* and *ekwaabiignike* differ in meaning they could be glossed as, respectively, 'one's arms be tired' and 'one's arms be tired [speaking of arms as if they're "stringlike"]'.[10] Explanation concerning usage is in keeping with the advice of Yong and Peng (2007:189): "In cases where both literal and free translation cannot get the meaning across to the user, explanation (often in the form of glosses in brackets) becomes a useful supplementary technique to make the meaning intelligible." Noting that arms are being characterized AS IF they are stringlike will I hope make it clear that *ekwaabiignike* should be taken as a metaphor rather than a literal description. Nishnaabemwin is rich in such figurative speech. Some figures of speech are equivalent to English ones, for instance, *boozgwaashkni* (hop on [in boarding a vehicle]), and *boozoode* (crawl on [in boarding a vehicle]), and some such as *ekwaagmi-shkiinzhgwe* (one's eyes be tired [making salient the "wateriness" of eyes]) are particular to Nishnaabemwin.

Another aspect of glossing terms appropriately are levels of hyperbole. This is related to the concept of "cultural substitution," one of the translation strategies available to translators. As Baker (2011:29) explains, "this strategy involves replacing a culture-specific item or expression with a target language item which does not have the same propositional meaning but is likely to have a similar impact . . . by evoking a similar context in the target culture." The verb *wiisgaate* poses this sort of challenge. One possible gloss for it, 'be blisteringly hot sunshine', strikes me as being too hyperbolic. *Wiisgaate* would be said when the sunshine seems in a way painful on the skin, but it neither generally suggests blistering nor does it come across as hyperbole. Should a literal gloss be used? At this point, I have not been able to compose one that is clear and not inordinately wordy. Again, speakers can express the idea more artfully by adding the morpheme /*zhe*/ to make 'skin' the salient feature and remark, "Wiisgizheyaate."

Taking the English-speaker standpoint reveals still other sorts of lexicographical challenges. *Get* and *take* are particularly illustrative in this regard. Each has several propositional meanings as exemplified by such remarks as: *We got in late last night*; *Get on the bus*; *If you take the bus, get off at Third Avenue*; *Get in [the car]*; and *Get out* as uttered to a visitor who has offended his host. As well, there is the range of expressive or other nonpropositional meanings such as: *Get it?* in reference to a joke; *Get out!* to express incredulity or skepticism; *Get lost!* uttered in annoyance with someone; *Get cracking*; and *Get real*. Nichols and Nyholm (1995), who document 19 collocative meanings for *get* and 51 for *take* through appropriate subheadings, make apparent the amount of information learners need to wade through to find the particular term for certain thoughts they may want to express. Some Nishnaabemwin equivalents use code-units (to use Munday's term) that differ markedly from those used in English. *Ngoji maanpii*, for instance, is a verbless expression that is best glossed as 'Get out of here'. *Aanii go naa iidik!* 'Get out' (expressing incredulity) is likewise verbless. Another example uses a verb, *dpine*, whose propositional meaning is 'die at a certain location', to tell someone, 'Get lost': *To go ngoji oo-dpinen*, literally 'Go off and die elsewhere'. Another question is whether to include routinely such wording as *get sick*, *get cold* as alternatives to *be sick*, *turn cold*, and so on. Although an online dictionary can hold a vast amount of data, some users would likely get annoyed if tracking down the closest equivalent Nishnaabemwin term involves scrolling down long lists too often.

What of verbs that are now rarely or no longer used in their original or literal sense? Going about pulling a load (*paamdaabii*) is an activity that few imagine anyone doing today. Should the primary English gloss then be one that expresses the sense it is more likely to have today, 'take a baby out in the stroller', as heard from a speaker at Walpole Island? Conversely, what about the practice *eNshinaabemjik* do more and more: fashioning Nishnaabemwin verbs, for example, *late-wi,* from English words. This can be done with virtually any English verb. This practice I prefer to show just when I teach. Some such terms appear in example sentences included in the dictionary database.

Example sentences are another important aspect of lexicography. As Yong and Peng (2007:157) explain: "The role of examples in dictionaries varies . . . with users. . . . Non-native speakers will expect examples to help them to understand not only the meaning of the lexical item but also its use." They point out the five functions they serve: semantic, grammatical, collocational, stylistic, and pragmatic (157). Thus far, I have not done exemplification systemically in terms of those functions. My main concern has been to document any remarks that seem particularly illustrative promptly upon hearing them. The code-unit issue also arises when translating some sentences into English as the wording of a particular concept in an example sentence may differ markedly from that in the gloss, creating another challenge for learners. Suppose a learner wants to say, 'I'll be right back'. The Nish-naabemwin expression that has the same force and sounds most natural is *Mii eta ge-piiskaayaanh.* Two possible glosses for *piiskaa,* 'take a certain amount of time in getting somewhere' and 'take a certain amount of time to return from somewhere', give no clue that this verb can be used to say 'I'll be right back'. How do we lead the learner directly to the verb *piiskaa*? Perhaps by including the English sentence in the entry for 'be back' and using as a subheading 'be right back'.

A code-unit problem also arises with *ntam,* usually glossed as 'first, turn'. Taking an English speaker standpoint again, "You wash the dishes this time" might be a common enough remark. A search for 'this time' would lead the learner to *nongo.* However, "Giin nongo gziinaagnen" has a rather different sense. It does not convey the tacit annoyance the last dishwasher feels and that prompts him to tell another to do the dishes THIS time. That feeling seems more evident in the phrasing, "Giin ntam gziinaagnen." Thus, it seems that 'this time' should be added as another gloss for *ntam.* I have yet to determine in which contexts it would have this sense so I can delimit its usage accordingly. It definitely is not fully synonymous with *nongo* as it cannot replace the latter in *Wiiba wii nongo nga-zhiitaa* 'This time I'll get ready early'. Perhaps such fine points of usage are more than a dictionary can reasonably be expected to convey.

Finally, I would like to touch on a couple of other aspects briefly. One is the matter of sample inflections. It is general practice to show initial change as part of the entry for verbs. However, this practice seems to be diminishing noticeably. Rather than changing *bskaabii* to *beskaabiit* when asking when someone is returning, for instance, it seems quite common now to say "Aaniish pii e-bskaabiit?" where the prefix *e-* indicates present tense. Many speakers have also dropped the first consonant in a consonant pair from their speech when a word begins with that sound. I have at times tried to ascertain whether they retain unconsciously a sense of the full word by inquiring upon hearing "skaabii" instead of *bskaabii*, for example, how they would ask "When is he coming back?" Not infrequently, they say, "Aaniish pii e-skaabiit?" But a good number of speakers do restore elided consonants when they form such sentences. The use of the prefix *e-* to mark present tense if the verb is in conjunct form (*doo-* if it is in independent form with first or second person actor) tends to occur more with rarely used verbs that likewise have consonant clusters at the beginning of the word. This is likely due to their infrequent use having made us less familiar with the full range of their various possible inflections. If I wanted to say that I am particularly moved by an unexpected gesture such as being presented with a gift, I would say "Ndoo-gshkwendam." I have not heard this verb in the first person tense often enough to have a sense of how it should be said with initial change. When I feel this kind of uncertainty, I feel safer giving *doo-* and *e-* forms rather than guessing how the words would likely sound with initial change. While such choices may be regarded as problematic from a linguistics perspective, they reflect what is occurring in the speech community. Although Nishnaabemwin speakers of the future will also inevitably alter the language, the spirit of their forebears will come through.

Conclusion

This paper has discussed the implications the learners' situation has for the design of the Nishnaabemwin dictionary that I, with the invaluable assistance of Rand Valentine, undertook to produce. The aspect of the learners' situation that was discussed is the background knowledge *aapji waa-Nishnaabek* typically bring to their learning endeavors. The paper then discussed some considerations that bear on the production of a dictionary tailored to help this category of users. The ethical dilemmas of my dual membership in my community of birth and in the academy was another aspect discussed. A number of examples were then presented to illustrate a few different types of challenges posed by the objective of serving primarily second-language learners of Nishnaabemwin.

NOTES

1. This spelling variation of Anishinaabemowin is used in the courses I have developed during my tenure in the Department of Native Studies (since renamed Indigenous Studies). Similarly, *Nishnaabek* is used in reference to the people.
2. This organization was established in 1994; its mission is the preservation of the language.
3. For the reader not versed in Nishnaabemwin, this phrase means "those who really want to speak [this language]". "Those who speak [this language]" is *eNshinaabemjik*.
4. My knowledge of the group comes through my acquaintance with one who is a former student of mine and my participation, at their request, in one of their immersion weekends.
5. I commenced the project in 1997 with the naive expectation that it would be completed in five years at most. It is only now that my coeditor, Rand Valentine, and I feel that it is approaching completion, though it is hard to estimate how long final editing will take. I suspended work on it from 2000 to 2007 when I enrolled in a doctoral program on theory and policy studies in education. One more series of workshops with the communities being consulted remains to be completed.
6. Most of Laurentian University's linguistics courses, for instance, serve the program Etudes Français. Modern Italian linguistics is also offered. Trent University has what it calls an "Emphasis in linguistics," which "enables students to add . . . a series of courses designed . . . to complement their studies in a language or languages" by selecting courses from various departments such as modern languages, ancient history, and classics after taking introductory linguistics. The description does not reference Indigenous studies. Algoma University, which offers a B.A. in Anishinaabemowin, has no linguistics program.
7. The foundational premise of Indigenous studies programs—the need to bring the Native perspective to Aboriginal topics of study—is manifested in the approach to delivering Nishnaabemwin courses. The expertise *eNshinaabemjik* possess by virtue of their fluency, it is felt, best facilitates the teaching of the language and obviates the need for grounding in linguistics.
8. The online dictionary will be among the suite of resources comprising the Algonquian Linguistic Atlas being developed through a five-year project coordinated by Marie-Odile

Junker. A print dictionary remains a major goal. Elders and undoubtedly a number of others want something to pick up and leaf through. Questions concerning print layout design and the microstructure of dictionary articles will become pressing when we turn to that goal.

9. This spelling reflects its pronunciation in Wikwemikong; one would hear *yekzi* in other dialects, for example, Walpole Island.

10. The way I glossed *eknike*, 'have one's arms get tired, have tired arms', looks in retrospect much too odd.

REFERENCES

Algoma University. n.d. *Academic calendar 2015–2016*. https://www.algomau.ca/media/style_assets/pdf/academic_calendar/Academic_Calendar_2015–2016.pdf.

———. 2015. *Anishinaabemowin courses*. https://www.algomau.ca/anishinaabemowin/courses/.

Baker, Mona. 2011. *In other words: A coursebook on translation*. 2nd ed. New York: Routledge.

Barber, Katherine. 1998. *The Canadian Oxford dictionary*. Toronto: Oxford University Press.

Battiste, Marie. 1998. Enabling the autumn seed: Toward a decolonized approach to aboriginal knowledge, language and education. *Canadian Journal of Native Education* 22(1):16–27.

Collins English Dictionary. 2016. http://www.collinsdictionary.com/dictionary/english/scrawny.

Corbiere, Alan. 1997. One learner's journey. *Beyond rhetoric: Exploring linkages between language, literacy and First Nations social security programming*, pp. 101–116. Unpublished manuscript, Assembly of First Nations, Ottawa.

———. 2010. Mizhiniwe: A defunct Anishinaabe title to be re-considered. *Ojibwe Cultural Foundation Newsletter* 5(1):1–3.

Munday, Jeremy. 2008. *Introducing translation studies: Theories and applications*. 2nd ed. New York: Routledge.

Neeley, Amber, and Gus Palmer Jr. 2012. Which way is the Kiowa way? Orthography choices, ideologies, and language renewal. *Native American language ideologies: Beliefs, practices and struggles in Indian country*, ed. by Paul Kroskrity and Margaret Field, pp. 271–297. Tucson: University of Arizona Press.

Nichols, John, and Earl Nyholm. 1995. *A concise dictionary of Minnesota Ojibwe*. Minneapolis: University Minnesota Press.

Rice, Keren. 2009. *Must there be two solitudes? Language activists and linguists working together*, pp. 1–24. http://jan.ucc.nau.edu/~jar/ILR/ILR-4.pdf.

Rhodes, Richard. 1985. *Eastern Ojibwa-Chippewa-Ottawa dictionary.* New York: Mouton Publishers.

Trent University. *Emphasis in linguistics.* http://www.trentu.ca/modernlanguages/emphasis.php.

Yong, Heming, and Jin Peng. 2007. *Bilingual lexicography from a communicative perspective.* Philadelphia: John Benjamins.

Baraga's *Jesus o Bimadisiwin*

Richard A. Rhodes

There is an impressive collection of missionary materials published in varieties of Ojibwe throughout the nineteenth century.[1] Among the most prolific sources of nineteenth-century Ojibwe materials were the Catholic missionary efforts in the territory that was to become the state of Michigan, and within that the most prolific individual was the Rev. (later Rt. Rev.) Frederic Irenej Baraga. In the twentieth century Algonquianists, following Bloomfield's lead, reflexively rejected missionary sources as inferior and untrustworthy. But Ojibwe studies have come a long way. Most of the lexical items in the nineteenth-century corpus have been either intentionally reelicited or independently elicited. Our knowledge of Ojibwe dialectology is extensive. As I have argued elsewhere (Rhodes 2011), the value of nineteenth-century Ojibwe sources is enormous. A case in point is the topic of this paper.

Here we will take a preliminary look at one of the earliest extensive exemplars, Baraga's *Jesus o Bimadisiwin* (*Life of Jesus*). The work itself is impressive. The text is just over 19,000 words long in the original orthography. It is provably Ottawa, as I shall show below. It was published in Paris in 1837, but the composition of the work itself must have preceded that date by some years. All the work done must have been done between 1831 and 1835, the period Baraga lived in Arbre Croche, Michigan,

Ottawa-speaking territory. In 1835 he moved to La Pointe (now Wisconsin) where Southwestern Ojibwe is spoken, the variety he documented in his grammar (1850) and dictionary (1853).

Jesus o Bimadisiwin is a text that weaves together the material of the Gospels into a single coherent narrative. Although the attempt to meld the four Gospel accounts into a single narrative dates back as far as the second century CE, with Tatian's *Diatessaron* (see, e.g., Shedinger 2002), the nineteenth century saw hundreds of attempts to write a Life of Jesus, driven by theological thinking that by assembling the material of the Gospels into a single coherent historical narrative one could reveal the "historical" Jesus (Powell 1998:13). At the same time, missionaries wrote single narratives, too, although for different reasons. Catholic missionaries needed Scripture readings for the mass, and so their products owe more to the demands of the lectionary than to any theological movement.[2] That Baraga's *Jesus o Bimadisiwin* was created to serve as a lectionary is evident from the indices at the end. See Figure 1, the first page of the lectionary index (page 209).

The particular kind of lectionary that *Jesus o Bimadisiwin* represents is an evangeliary (or evangeliarium), which contains only the year's Gospel readings for the Mass. The title in Figure I asserts that. It reads as in Figure 1:

INDEX EVANGELIORUM
quae diebus Dominicis, et iis festis, quae in diocesibus Statuum
unitorum Americae de praecepto sunt servanda, leguntur

IN USUM MISSIONARIORUM
apud Ottawas, Otchipweos, Potewatamos, Manominos, et Algonkinos:
mutatis paucis mutandis

Index of the Gospels which are read on Sundays and Holy Days of Obligation in the United States of America in use by missionaries among the Ottawas, Otchipwes, Potawatamis, Menominees, and Algonkins: with a few changes

Jesus o Bimadisiwin contains things that are not referenced in the Index Evangeliorum, but very little of *Jesus o Bimadisiwin* is extrabiblical, unlike the theological work of the time. Thus the source of *Jesus o Bimadisiwin*, that is the original from which it was translated, is effectively the Bible.

So the question becomes: which Bible? The two most likely candidates are

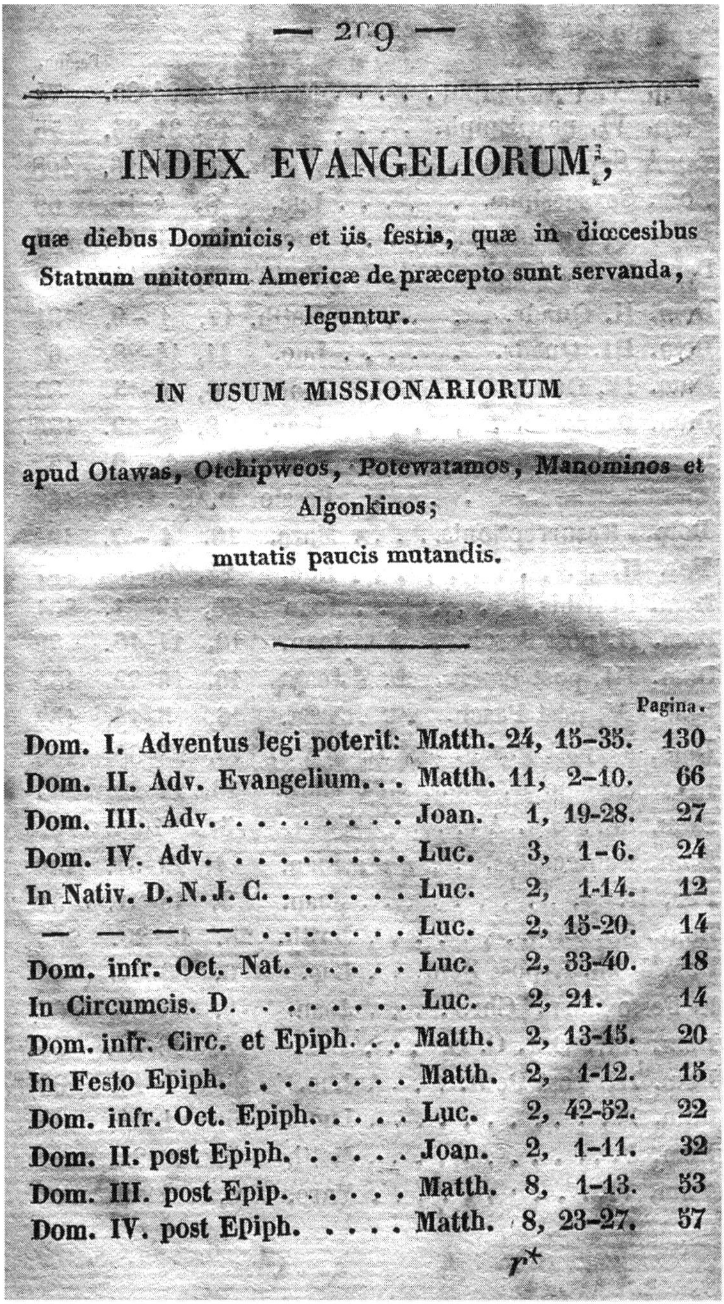

— 2r9 —

INDEX EVANGELIORUM,

quæ diebus Dominicis, et iis festis, quæ in diœcesibus Statuum unitorum Americæ de præcepto sunt servanda, leguntur.

IN USUM MISSIONARIORUM

apud Otawas, Otchipweos, Potewatamos, Manominos et Algonkinos;

mutatis paucis mutandis.

			Pagina.
Dom. I. Adventus legi poterit.	Matth.	24, 15-35.	130
Dom. II. Adv. Evangelium...	Matth.	11, 2-10.	66
Dom. III. Adv.	Joan.	1, 19-28.	27
Dom. IV. Adv.	Luc.	3, 1-6.	24
In Nativ. D. N. J. C.	Luc.	2, 1-14.	12
— — — —	Luc.	2, 15-20.	14
Dom. infr. Oct. Nat.	Luc.	2, 33-40.	18
In Circumcis. D.	Luc.	2, 21.	14
Dom. infr. Circ. et Epiph. . .	Matth.	2, 13-15.	20
In Festo Epiph.	Matth.	2, 1-12.	15
Dom. infr. Oct. Epiph.	Luc.	2, 42-52.	22
Dom. II. post Epiph.	Joan.	2, 1-11.	32
Dom. III. post Epip.	Matth.	8, 1-13.	53
Dom. IV. post Epiph.	Matth.	8, 23-27.	57

r*

FIGURE 1. First page of the lectionary index in Baraga's *Jesus o Bimadisiwin*

the Vulgate and the 1744 French Bible translation, the Bible Martin, which was in wide use in the French-speaking world early in the relevant time period. The most obvious evidence that the European language in question was French rather than German (which was the working language of the Diocese of Cincinnati at the time; see Rhodes 2010) or English is that Baraga used consistent French spelling conventions in his transcription of Ojibwe, at least for the consonants, as in (1).

(1) Baraga   value
       s   [z]
       ss   [s·]
       j   [ʒ]
       ch   [ʃ·]
       dj   [dʒ]
       tch   [t·ʃ]

In later work on Southwestern Ojibwe he changes slightly and spells [ʃ] with *sh* rather than *ch*. His later work includes his 1858 *Gagikwe-Mazinaigan*, which, in spite of its title—*Preaching Book*—is a synopsis of the whole Bible in Southwestern Ojibwe and contains a Life of Jesus section (which we will use later in this paper).

The most obvious evidence that the source document was a French Bible is in the names. As shown in (2), where proper names have different spellings in the Vulgate and in the Bible Martin, *Jesus o Bimadisiwin* follows the French overwhelmingly, even to the point of spelling the acute accent. The sole exception is *Capharnaum,* shown in (2c).

(2)	*JoB*	*Bible Martin*	*Vulgate*
a.	Jean	Jean	Johannes
	Pierre	Pierre	Petrus
	Jerusalem	Jérusalem	Hierusalem
	Israel	Israel	Israhel
b.	Marie	Marie	Maria
	Galilée/Galilee	Galilée	Galilaea
	Zachée	Zachée	Zaccheus
	Zacharie	Zacharie	Zaccharia
c.	Capharnaum	Capernaüm	Capharnaum

TABLE 1. Comparison of wordings in the Bible Martin and the Vulgate

	BIBLE MARTIN	GLOSS	VULGATE	GLOSS
Matthew 27:29	Et ayant <u>fait</u> une couronne d'épines entrelacées, ils la mirent sur sa tête,	and having <u>made</u> a crown of woven thorns, they placed it on his head.	et <u>plectentes</u> coronam de spinis posuerunt super caput eius	and <u>weaving</u> a crown of thorns they placed it on his head
Mark 15:17	et ayant <u>fait</u> une couronne d'épines entrelacées l'une dans l'autre, ils la lui mirent sur la tête;	and having <u>made</u> a crown of thorns woven one on the other, they placed it on his head.	et inponunt ei <u>plectentes</u> spineam coronam	and <u>weaving</u> a thorny crown, they place it upon him
John 19:2	Et les soldats <u>firent</u> une couronne d'épines qu'ils mirent sur sa tête,	and the soldiers <u>made</u> a crown of thorns which they put on his head	et milites <u>plectentes</u> coronam de spinis inposuerunt capiti eius	and the soldiers, <u>weaving</u> a crown of thorns placed it on his head.

The forms in (2b) lose their final e when they are inflected—either with the obviative (*an*) or with the locative (*ing*).

(3)   *uninflected*   *inflected*

Marie   Mariian

Galilée/Galilee   Galileing

Zacharie   Zacharian

Note the convention that the obviative of Marie is always spelled with an extra *i*. There is no evidence whether this was a spelling convention or whether the spelling reflects a distinct pronunciation.

Teasing out whether the translation is from the Vulgate or from the Bible Martin is a bit tricky. The provenance of the 1744 version of the Bible Martin is a second-generation revision of Calvin's translation that was based on the Textus Receptus of Erasmus, who depended on the Vulgate for many of his editorial decisions (Metzger and Ehrman 2005). However, there are a few places, very few, where slight differences in wording between the Bible Martin and the Vulgate allow us to discern that the Ottawa text has a closer affiliation with the Bible Martin. One example is the passage in which the soldiers mock Jesus before his crucifixion. It is found in Matthew 27:27–31, Mark 15:16–20, and John 19:2–3. The crucial verses refer to the crown of thorns. In Latin the expression in all three places uses the verb *plectere* 'braid'. In French the expression in all three places uses the verb *faire* 'make'. This is shown in Table 1.

The corresponding passage in *Jesus o Bimadisiwin* is given in (4), where the verb is *odoozhitoonaawaa* 'they make it'.[3]

(4) Wiokwan gaie **odojitonawa**, minessagawajin aj-awawad, obassikwebinawan.

wiiwikwaan	gaye	**od-oozhit-oo-naawaa**
hat	and	3SBJ-make.INAN-INAN.OBJ-3PL
miinesaagawanzh-iin		azh=aw-aa-waa-d
hawthorn-OBV		COMP=use-3OBJ-3PL-3.CONJ
o-basikwebin-aa-waa-n		
3SBJ-round.on.head.tie.AN-3OBJ-3PL-OBV		

'And **they made** a hat, using (haw)thorns. They placed it on his head.'

This suggests that the translator of *Jesus o Bimadisiwin* is following the French *faire* rather than the Latin *plectere*. The argument is all the more cogent because Baraga's dictionary explicitly attests a way to say 'braid/pla[i]t thorns':

(5) okadenag minessagawanjig, (nind).

nind-ookaaden-aa-g	miinesagaawanzh-iig
1SBJ-braid.AN-3OBJ-3PL	hawthorn-PL

'I pla[i]t thorns together.'

The final argument that the source text for *Jesus o Bimadisiwin* was a French Bible is that, to the extent Baraga was using native speakers, the second language in the area was French, as reflected in the French place names for older settlements in Michigan, starting with Arbre Croche (now abandoned), but most notably Detroit and Sault Ste. Marie.

Let me turn now to the question of the quality of the translation. The example in (3) gives one a very good idea of how the translation is both literal and by sense. It translates to how one would convey the concept in Ottawa, but it is literal at the second level. It also has a very wooden Ottawa style. In particular it fails to use narrative conjuncts, uses *dach* as de facto sentence marker, and gives the climax of the story in a cleft sentence, using the *mi dash eji-* construction.

The literalness of sense makes it quite easy to identify which Gospel is being translated as well as making it clear that Baraga did not use a merged narrative of the sort the theologians of the time were creating.

A comparison of the three versions of this calming of the storm passage shows that it is the Matthew account that is the basis for this passage in *Jesus o Bimadisiwin*. The different Evangelists highlight and background different parts of the story, and, in this case, the Ottawa wording follows Matthew's version, as can be seen from Table 2.

Now let us turn to more directly linguistic questions starting with the matter of dialect. All the externals point to the dialect being Ottawa. Some of the key markers presently used to distinguish Ottawa from other dialects are present, including the loss of final *n* from certain inflections, as in (5), the nasalization of the first person singular conjunct, as in (6), and words with first syllable *a* for *i*, as in (7).

(5) a. Zacharie ijinikasogo**ba**

        Zacharie   izhinikaazo-go-**ba**(**n**)

        Zechariah   be.so.named-3.IRR-PRET

        'His name was Zechariah.' (Lk. 1:5)

    b. **Ninawi** dach kakina gego nin ginagada**mi** tchi nopinanigoian

        niinawi(**n**)   dash   gakina gegoo   nin-gii=nagad-aa-**mi**(**n**)

        1PL.EXCL   EMPH   everything   1SBJ-PST=leave.INAN-INAN.OBJ-1PL

        ji-noopinan-igoo.yan

        FUT-follow.AN-1PL.2SG

        'We left everything to follow you.' (Matt. 19:27)

(6) Debenimiiang, kichpin kin awiian, nandomichin tchi nasikonà ogidibig tchi bimossei**à**

    debenimiyaang   giishpin   giin   aawi-yan   nandom-ishin

    our.Lord   if   2SG   be-2SG   ask.AN-1SG.IMPER

    ji=naazikaw-in-**aanh**   ogid-ibiig   ji=bimose-**yaanh**

    FUT-come.AN-2OBJ-1SBJ   on.top-water   FUT=walk-1SBJ

    'Lord if it is you, tell me to come to you, walking on the water.' (Matt. 14:28)

TABLE 2. Parallel versions of the calming of the storm

JESUS O BIMADISIWIN	BACK TRANSLATION	MATTHEW 8
Iwipi Jesus nabikwanensing bosi enonadjin gaie bosiwag;	At that time Jesus got into a ship, and his disciples embarked too;	23 Et quand il fut entré dans la nacelle, ses Disciples le suivirent.
kitchi mamangachka dach kitchigaming, mojag bosiwag tigowag Jesus dach niba;	There were very big waves on the sea, the waves always came into the boat. Jesus was asleep.	24 Et voici, il s'éleva sur la mer une si grande tempête que la nacelle était couverte de flots ; et Jésus dormait.
enonadjin dach obiodissigon, odamadjiigon, ekitong: Debenimiiang, bimadjiichinang, nin nibomi.	The disciples came to him, they wake him, saying: Lord, save us, we're dying.	25 Et ses Disciples vinrent, et l'éveillèrent, en lui disant : Seigneur, sauve-nous, nous périssons !
Odinan Jesus: Wegone dach wendji segisiieg? Kitchi pangi ki debwetam! Mi dach eji onichkad, gaganondang nodin, kitchigami gaie, pabige dach kitchi dogissin.	Jesus said to them : Why are you afraid? You believe very little of what you hear! Then he got mad, shouting at the wind and the sea and suddenly there was a great calm.	26 Et il leur dit : pourquoi avez-vous peur, gens de petite foi ? Alors s'étant levé il parla fortement aux vents et à la mer, et il se fit un grand calme.
Kitchi mamakadendamog dach anichinabeg, ekitong: Tani ejiwebisid maba? Nodin, kitchigami gaie odebwetagon!	The people were amazed, saying: How does this [person] behave like this? The wind and the sea listen to what he says.	27 Et les gens [qui étaient là] s'en étonnèrent, et dirent : qui est celui-ci que les vents même et la mer lui obéissent ?

(7)	*JoB*	Baraga Dictionary	Nichols and Nyholm	
a.	anini	inini (Ot. anini)	inini	'man'
	akwe	ikwe (Ot. akwe)	ikwe	'woman'
	achkote	ishkote (Ot. ashkote)	ishkode	'fire'
	achkwandem	ishkwandem	ishkwaandem	'door'
	achkwa	ishkwa	ishkwaa-	'finish'
	makam-/makaw-	mikam-/mikaw-	mikam-/mikaw-	'find s.t./s.o.'

MARK 4	LUKE 8
35 Or en ce même jour, comme le soir fut venu, il leur dit : passons delà l'eau. 36 Et laissant les troupes, ils l'emmenèrent [avec eux], lui étant déjà dans la nacelle ; et il y avait aussi d'autres petites nacelles avec lui.	22 Or il arriva qu'un jour il monta dans une nacelle avec ses Disciples, et il leur dit : passons à l'autre côté du lac ; et ils partirent.
37 Et il se leva un si grand tourbillon de vent, que les vagues se jetaient dans la nacelle, de sorte qu'elle s'emplissait déjà.	23 Et comme ils voguaient, il s'endormit, et un vent impétueux s'étant levé sur le lac, [la nacelle] se remplissait d'eau, et ils étaient en grand péril
38 Or il était à la poupe, dormant sur un oreiller ; et ils le réveillèrent, et lui dirent : Maître, ne te soucies-tu point que nous périssions ?	24 Alors ils vinrent à lui, et l'éveillèrent, disant : Maître ! Maître ! nous périssons.
39 Mais lui étant réveillé, tança le vent, et dit à la mer : tais-toi, sois tranquille ; et le vent cessa, et il se fit un grand calme.	Mais lui s'étant levé, parla en Maître au vent et aux flots, et ils s'apaisèrent ; et le calme revint.
41 Et ils furent saisis d'une grande crainte, et ils se disaient l'un à l'autre : mais qui est celui-ci, que le vent même et la mer lui obéissent ?	25 Alors il leur dit : où est votre foi ? et eux saisis de crainte et d'admiration, disaient entre eux : mais qui est celui-ci, qu'il commande même aux vents et à l'eau, et ils lui obéissent ?

b. gagichkam-/-chkaw-	gigishkam-/-shkaw-	gigishkam-/-shkaw-	'have s.t./s.o. on/in one's body'
sakwan-	sikwan-	zikwan-	'spit on s.o.'
c. akinoamaw-	kikinoamaw-	gikinoo'amaw-	'teach s.t.'
wadi	iwidi (Ot. wadi)	iwidi	'there'

Previously noted examples of *a* for *i* are given in (7a). Heretofore unattested examples are given in (7b), and examples with other complications are in (7c). The word 'teach' with first syllable *a* and a missing initial *g* is attested in twentieth-century Ottawa. The word for 'there' has the *a* for *i* in the second syllable—the only known example.

Jesus o Bimadisiwin uses -inin- rather than -ini- in the local inverse, also an Ottawa trait. As shown in (8) the long form is used in the independent but not in the conjunct (where it is arguably a simple object marker), cf. Valentine (2001:287ff), where the opposite distribution is reported for Manitoulin Odawa.

(8) Ki giwindamo**ninim** iwi megwa widjiwi**na**gog;

gi-gii=wiindamaw-**inini**-m   iwi   megwaa   wiidiiw-**in**-agog

2SBJ-PST-tell-**INVER**-2PL   that   while   accompany-**2OBJ**-1SBJ.2PL

'I have told you this while I am with you;' (John 16:4)

Finally, in (9) are given well-known vocabulary items that mark the Ottawa dialect. Function words are in (9a), other probative forms are in (9b). The list is not complete, but it contains the most frequent words in *Jesus o Bimadisiwin*.[4]

(9)		*JoB*	Baraga Dictionary	Nichols and Nyholm	
	a.	weni	awenen (Ot. weni)	awenen	'who'
		tani	anin (Ot. tani)	aaniin	'how'
		ajonda	omâ (Ot. ajonda)	omaa	'here'
		ajiwi	iwidi (Ot. ajiwi)	iwidi	'there'
		maba	mabam, aw, waaw	wa'aw	'this *an. sg.*'
		manda	mandan, ow	ow, o'o(w)	'there'
	b.	ogachiwan	ogin (Ot. ogashiwan)	ogiin	'his/her mother'
		ondib	oshtigwân (Ot. ondib)	oshtigwaan	'his/her head'
		debani-	kitchi- (Ot. debani-)	gichi-	'right (opp. left)'
		mijachk	mashkossiw (Ot. mijashk)	mashkosiw	'grass, hay'
		wakwing	ishpiming (Ot. wakwing)	ishpiming	'heaven'
		kakidoo-	kâdon (Ot. kakis)	gaadoon	'hide'
		gigang	— (Ot. gigang)	—	'virgin'

The forms in (9a) *maba* and *manda* 'this' animate and inanimate, respectively, warrant some discussion. These are distinctively Ottawa forms. There were similar forms in nineteenth-century Ojibwe, *mabam* and *mandan*, respectively. These latter forms did not survive into twentieth-century Ojibwe. It is unclear what the difference in meaning was between *mabam* and *waaw*, and between *mandan* and *ow*, although the *m*-forms were probably emphatic.

As I noted before, Baraga also published a second Life of Jesus as part of a longer Bible synopsis in the Southwestern dialect. The discussion of dialect differences would not be complete without a comparison of at least some passages. We will look at a passage describing the soldiers mocking Jesus. The source text is Matthew 27:27–32. The parallel verses are given in Table 3.

The most notable difference beyond those noted in (5–9) above is the near absence of past tense markers (*gi*) in Ottawa in contrast to the Ojibwe usage where they appear on almost every clause. (For ease of reading I have separated the preverbs with a hyphen, which is not present in the originals.) The parallels are tight enough to believe that the later text was based on *Jesus o Bimadisiwin*, or at the very least *Jesus o Bimadisiwin* was heavily consulted. But the details are different, even ignoring the difference in use of the past tense. The use of *dach/dash* does not line up at all, for example. The very first word is *kitchi ogima* 'king/ big chief' in Ottawa but *ogima* 'chief' in Ojibwe. In the following verse the words are almost all different, although the Ottawa word *makam-* 'to take away by force' is a perfectly fine Ojibwe word. In verse 29 the quote formula is intransitive in Ottawa but transitive in Ojibwe. In verse 30 the soldiers snatch away the reed that was a fake scepter. In verse 31 the Ojibwe has a further obviative, *odagwiwini* 'his *obv.* clothes', but the Ottawa does not *odagwiwinan* 'his *obv.* clothes' even though the syntax is otherwise the same. This is not because Ottawa lacks the further obviative forms; they occur elsewhere in the text (see the examples in (20) below). Both verses 31 and 32 have words in Ojibwe that have no correspondent in the Ottawa, *kitwen* 'reluctantly' and *tibinawe* (*dibinawe*) 'by oneself', here in the meaning 'his *obv.* own'. Furthermore in verse 31 the Ottawa refers to the cross with a noun, but the Ojibwe refers to it only with a medial. Clearly, developing the Ojibwe Life of Jesus was not a simple matter of *mutatis mutandis*, as Baraga suggested on the title page.

There are several more points that need to be addressed. The unchanged preverb *a-* is unique to the Ottawa dialect and is only poorly attested in the twentieth century, limited to a single speaker. However, it is widely attested in this document, as it is in the Sifferath Catechism (Rhodes 2010). In the twentieth-century Ottawa data (approx. 14,000 words) it occurs a mere eight times. All occur in the material collected by Bloomfield in 1939 (Bloomfield 1958); four times in Medler's texts, given

TABLE 3. Comparison of Ottawa and Southwestern Ojibwe versions of Matthew 27:27–32

VS.	OTTAWA	OJIBWE
27	Kitchi ogima ojimaganichiman dach ododapinawan Jesusan, opindiganawan dach gigitowigamigong, kakina dach omawandjiawan jimaganichan.	Ogima o jimaganishiman dash o gi-odapinawan Jesusan, gi-pindiganawad gigitowigamigong, kakina dash ogi-mawandjiawan jimaganishan.
28	Omakamawan dach obisikawagani, miskobisikawagan odagwanawan.	Ogi-gisikwanaiebinawan, miskwegino-babisikawaganish dash o gi-bisikonawan.
29	Wiokwan gaie odojitonawa, minessagawajin aj-awawad, obassikwebinawan; apakwechkwai dach ominawan odebaninindjing; odotchitchingwanitawan dach, a-bapinodawawad ekitong: Kit anamikon, Judawininiwag wegimakandawadwa!	Wiwakwan gaie o gi-ojitonawa, minessagawanjin gi-awawad, o gi-bassikwebinawan dash; obiwaiashkinan dash o gi-minawan o kitchinindjing; o gi-otchitchingwanitawawan dash, gi-bapinodawawad, gi-inawad: Kid anamikon, Judawininiwag wegimakandawadwa !
30	Osakwanawan dach gaie, omakamawan apakwechkwai, mi dach eji-wepotawawad ondibaning.	O gi-sikwanawan gaie, o gi-odapinawan obiwaiashkinan, gi-papakitewawad oshtigwanining.
31	Ga-achkwa- bapinodawawad dach, omakamawan misko-bisikawagan. Win odagwiwinan dach obisikonawan, mi dach eji- madjinawad tchi-badakakwoond tchibaiatigong.	Ga-ishkwa-bapinodawawad o gi-gisikonawan miskwegino-babisikawaganish, tibinawe dash od agwiwini o gi-bisikonawan, mi dash gi-madjinawad awi-sassagakwawawadigong
	Odanibiminiganan dach Jesus otchibaiatigoman;	O gi-ani-biminiganan Jesus o tchibaiatigoman
32	saiagaamowad dach (odenawing Jerusaleming), omakawawan aniniwan, Cyrenening ga-ondjibad, Simon ijinikasogoba, ogandomawan dach tchi anitakonad Jesus otchibaiatigoman	ba-sagaamowad dash odenang Jerusaleming, o gi- mikawawan ininiwan, Simon ga-ijinikasonidjin, kitwen dash o gi-anonawan tchi ani-takonanid Jesusan o tchibaiatigomini

in (10); and four times in the elicited sentences, given in (11).[5] Two of the instances in the texts (10a) and (10b) are in two versions of the same story.

(10) a. Pii dash debshkooseg ngii-zhaami **widi a̲-bmi-noogbizod** aw mshkode-daabaan.

widi	a̲=bmi=noogibizo-d
there	COMP=along=stop.moving-3.CONJ

'When the time came around, we went to **where** the train **stops**.' (8:7)

BACK TRANSLATION OF THE OJIBWE	BIBLE MARTIN
The king's soldiers take Jesus. They take him into the council hall. They gather all the soldiers.	27 Et les soldats du Gouverneur amenèrent Jésus au Prétoire, et assemblèrent devant lui toute la cohorte.
Then they take away [Jesus] clothes, and wrap him in a red cloak.	28 Et après l'avoir dépouillé, ils mirent sur lui un manteau d'écarlate.
and they make a hat using hawthorn branches. They bind it around his head. They give him a reed in his right hand. They kneel to him, ridiculing him, saying: I greet you, who rule the Jews!	29 Et ayant fait une couronne d'épines entrelacées, ils la mirent sur sa tête, avec un roseau dans sa main droite ; puis s'agenouillant devant lui, ils se moquaient de lui, en disant : nous te saluons, Roi des Juifs!
And they spit on him. They snatch the reed, and they hit him on the head (with it).	30 Et après avoir craché contre lui, ils prirent le roseau, et ils en frappaient sa tête.
When they finished ridiculing him, they take away the red-coat. Then they clothe him with his coat, and they take him away to be nailed to a cross.	31 Et après s'être moqués de lui, ils lui ôtèrent le manteau, et le vêtirent de ses vêtements,
Then Jesus carries his cross away on his shoulder.	et l'amenèrent pour le crucifier.
Going out (of the city of Jerusalem), they meet a man, who came from Cyrene. His name was Simon. They made him carry Jesus cross.	32 Et comme ils sortaient, ils rencontrèrent un Cyrénéen, nommé Simon, lequel ils contraignirent de porter la croix de Jésus.

b. Mii dash maaba nini gii-wzhibiihang iw ndanoozwin maa mzinhigning, gye go mii gii-dbaajmod pii miinwaa ge-bi-dgoshing **maa a-bmi-noogsed** aw shkode-daabaan.

> maa   a=bimi=noogise-d
> there   COMP=along=stop-3.CONJ

'Then the man wrote my name in a book, and explained when he would be returning to **where** the train **stops**.' (9:6)

c. Gye go mii **a̲-ngwahang**.

        a̲=ningwah-an-g

        <u>COMP</u>=bury.INAN-INAN.OBJ-3.CONJ

'And **she buried it** there.' (25:7)

d. Ngoding kiwenziinh ngii-noondwaaba **a̲-dbaajmod** shkniikwen gii-ndodmaagod
iw wiikwebjigan.

        a̲=dibaajimo-d

        <u>COMP</u>=tell-3.CONJ

'Once I heard an old man **tell about** a young woman seeking love medicine.' (28:1)

Two instances in the elicited sentences (11b) and (11c) are adjacent and bear parallel
meanings:

(11)   a. Gii-shkwaa-biindaakweyaan mii-sh dash **a̲-nbaayaan**.

        a̲=nimbaa-yaan

        <u>COMP</u>=sleep-1SG.CONJ

'After I have smoked then I shall **go to bed**.' (483)

b. Wnjiiyenh ngii-nmadab **a̲-nmadbid**.

        a̲=namadabi-d

        <u>COMP</u>=sit-3.CONJ

'I sat next to him **where he sat**.' (534)

c. Gzhaatemgad maanpii **a̲-nmadbiyaan**.

        a̲= namadabi-yaan

        <u>COMP</u>=sit-1SG.CONJ

'The sun shines hot here **where I am sitting**.' (535)

d. Ngashi gii-bi-zhaa maa **a̲-nbaayaan** gii-bi-waabmid nembaawaanen.

        maa   a̲=nimbaa-yaan

        there   <u>COMP</u>=sleep-1SG.CONJ

'My mother came to **where I was sleeping** to see whether I was asleep.' (668)

There are enough instances of the preverb *a-* in *Jesus o Bimadisiwin* that we can be sure that the variant *azh-* is, in fact, the allomorph that appears before verb stems starting with *a*, as the examples in (12) show.

(12)   *azh-* before *a*-initial stems

a. ijan dach kikaniss **aj'**aiad

   izhaa-n   dash   g-iikaanis   **azh**-ayaa-d

   go.to-IMPER.SG   EMPH   2POSS-(man's).brother   COMP=be.there-3.CONJ

   'Go to your brother.' (Matt. 5:24) (lit. 'where your brother is')

b. Binaan kit ajawechk **aj'**ategiba

   biina'-a-n   gid-azhaweshk   **azh**-ate-g-iba(n)

   put.in-INAN-IMPER.SG   2POSS-sword   COMP=be.there-3.CONJ-PRET

   'Put your sword where it belongs.' (Matt. 26:52) (lit. 'where it was')

c. Mi dach eji otchitchingwanitawad, **aj'**anamietawad.

   mii   dash   ezhi=ojijiingwanitaw-aa-d   **azh**-anami'etaw-aa-d

   CLEFT   EMPH   REL.thus=kneel.to-3OBJ-3.CONJ   COMP=pray.to.AN-3OBJ-3.CONJ

   'Then he knelt before him and worshiped him.' (John 9:38) (lit. 'to worship him')

The unchanged *a-* occurs in *Jesus o Bimadisiwin* in the same classes of environments that I reported for the Sifferath Catechism (Rhodes 2010), exemplified in (13).

(13)   a. *a-* marked complement in simple *mii* clefts

   Mi dach **a**gisagaamowad odenawing, **a**nasikawawad.

   mii   dash   **a**-gii-zaaga'am-owaad

   CLEFT   EMPH   COMP=PAST=go.out-3PL.CONJ

   oodenaw-ing   **a**-naazikaw-aa-waad

   town-LOC   COMP=go.to.AN-3OBJ-3PL

   'Then they came out of the town and came to him.' (John 4:30)

b. *a-* in simple temporal clauses

Nongo **a**gijigak jawendjigewin gidagwichinomagad manda wigiwaming

noongo	**a**-giizhiga-k	zhawenjigewin
today	COMP= be.day-3.CONJ	blessing

gii=dagwishinoo-magad-Ø	maanda	wiigiwaam-ing
PST=arrive.INAN-3SBJ	this.INAN	house-LOC

'Today blessing has come to this house.' (Luke 19:9)

c. *a-* marked complement of *megwaa* (probably just a special case of (12b))

megwa abimadisid, giikito: Ginissogwanagak nin gaabitchiiba.

megwaa	**a**-bimaadizi-d	gii=ikido-Ø	gii=nisogwanagad-g
while	COMP=be.alive-3.CONJ	PST=say-3SBJ	PST=be.three.days-3.CONJ

nin-ga=aabijiibaa
1SBJ-FUT=resurrect

'While he was alive he said: after three days I will rise from the dead.' (Matt. 27:23)

d. *a-* in locative clauses

   i. ijan dach kikaniss **aj**'aiad

izhaa-n	dash	g-iikaanis	**azh**-ayaa-d
go.to-IMPER.SG	EMPH	2POSS-(man's).brother	COMP=be.there-3.CONJ

'Go to your brother.' (Matt. 5:24) (lit. 'go to where your brother is')

   ii. Marie dash pasigwigoba iwipi, **a**babikwadinanig dash kakejdine ijagoba odenawing Juda

Marie	dash	bazigwii-go-ba	iwipii
Mary	EMPH	stand.up-3SBJ-PRET	at.that.time

a=baa=bikwadinaa-ni-g	gakezhidine	izhaa-go-ba
COMP=around=be.hills-OBV-3.CONJ	immediately	go.to-3SBJ-PRET

'Mary got up and immediately went to the hill country to a town Judah.' (Luke 1:39)

e. *a-* in purpose clauses

Jesus dach ija Pharisien endad, namadabi dach awiwissinid.

Jesus	dash	izhaa-Ø	Pharisie-n	en-daa-d
Jesus	EMPH	go.to-3SBJ	Pharisee-OBV	COMP=dwell.at-3.CONJ

namadabi-Ø	dash	a=wii=wiisini-d
sit.down-3SBJ	EMPH	COMP=FUT=eat-3.CONJ

'Jesus went to where a Pharisee lived, and sat down to eat.' (Luke 7:37)

There remain a number of smaller issues that should at least be mentioned. There are three spelling issues. First, the first person subject/possessor marking is always spelled *nin* even if it should be written *nim* to reflect the obligatory assimilation, as shown in (14).

(14) a. osam ni**n b**ataijiwebis.

ozaam   nim-baataa=izhiwebiz

too.much   1SBJ-antisocial=behave

'I behaved very badly.'

b. ni**n b**imadisiwin

nim-bimaadizi-win

1POSS-be.alive-NOM

'my life'

This spelling convention is also followed in Baraga's dictionary (1853).

(15) a. as verb prefix

Bimakwishima, (nin) a. v. *an.* (pr. *ni**n b**imakoshima,*) I put or lay it somewhere, (a piece of wood, *an.*); 3. p. *o bim. .n*; *bem. .mad.*— *Na-bagissag ni**n b**imakwishima wedi,* I lay a board there.

b. as noun prefix

Binakwanininj s. toe; pl. *-in.*— *Ni**n b**inakwanininj,* my finger; *ki binakwanininjin,* thy fingers, etc.

The second spelling issue is that the nasal of the type I TI negative is never written, as exemplified in (16).

(16) a. ka dach omakasin

      gaa   dash   o-mak-**an**-zii-n

      NEG   EMPH   3SBJ-find. INAN-**INAN.OBJ-NEG**-OBJ

      'He did not find it.'

    b. kawi dach ki kikend<u>a</u>sin iwi?

      gaawii dash   gi-gikend-**an**-zii-n   iwi

      NEG   EMPH   2SBJ-know.INAN-**INAN.OBJ-NEG**-OBJ   this.INAN.SG

      'You do not know this?!?'

By the time of the *Gagikwe-Masinaigan*, Baraga was consistently writing this *n*.

The next group of observations are about places in the text where there are inconsistencies. Short *a* before *w* is occasionally spelled *o*, as in (17).

(17) a. odaininamowawan dach ossan;

      od-ay-inin-amaw-aa-waa-n   dash   Ø-oos-an

      3SBJ-REDUP-use.hands-APPL-3OBJ-3PL-OBV   EMPH   3POSS-father-OBV

      'They made signs to his father.'

    b. obidowawan dach aniniwan

      o-biid-aw-aa-waa-n   dash   aniniw-an

      3SBJ-bring-APPL-3OBJ-3PL-OBV   EMPH   man-OBV

      'They brought a man to him.'

Once, but only once in 21 times, the prohibitive is spelled with *k* rather than *g* after *n*.

(18) Kego inendan**k**ego tchi wi ikitoieg: Abraham nossina;

      gego   inendan-**g**ego   ji=wii=ikido-yeg   Abraham   n-oos-inaa

      NEG   think.thus-NEG.IMPER.PL   FUT=FUT-say-2PL   Abraham   1POSS-father-1PL

      'Don't think you can just say, "Abraham is our father."' (Matt. 3:9, Luke 3:8)

Finally, there are a number of inconsistencies in word usage that show either that there was dialect influence from Ojibwe or that there were multiple contributors.

(19) Ot. akinoamaw- (17X) ~ Oj. kikinoamaw- (1X)   'teach'
      akinoo'amaw-   gikinoo'amaw-

      Ot. nibina (61X) ~ Oj. nibiwa (4X)   'much'
      niibina   ~ niibiwa

      Ot. odenawing (27X) ~ Oj. odenang (2X)   'in/to town'
      oodenawing   ~ oodenaang

One point of morphosyntax is worthy of mention. The further obviative, -*(i)ni*, which goes on nouns to mark the fact that the possessor is obviative, fell out of use in the twentieth century, but it is well attested here.

(20) a. Debeniminang osidaning namadabi opisindawan ekitonid.
          debeniminaang   o-zidaa-ni-ng   namadabi-Ø
          our.Lord   3POSS-foot-OBV-LOC   sit-3SBJ

          o-bizindaw-aa-n   CHANGE-ikido-ni-d
          3SBJ-listen.AN-3OBJ-OBV REL-say-OBV-3.CONJ
          'She sat at our Lord's feet and listened to what he said.' (Matt. 3:9, Luke 3:8)

      b. Omakamawan dach obisikawagani,
          o-makam-aa-waa-n   dash   o-biizikawaagan-ni
          3SBJ-take.by.force.AN-3OBJ-3PL-OBV EMPH   3POSS-coat-OBV
          'They ripped off his coat.' (Matt. 27:28)

      c. mi dach ajiwi kakidod debenimigodjin ojoniamini.
          mii   dash   azhiwi   gakid-oo-d
          CLEFT   EMPH   there   hide.INAN-INAN.OBJ-3.CONJ

          CHANGE-dibenim-igo-j-in   o-zhooniyaam-ini
          REL-be.master.of-INVER-3.CONJ-OBV 3POSS-money-OBV
          'That's where he hid his master's money.' (Matt. 25:25)

In conclusion, documents like Baraga's *Jesus o Bimadisiwin* are treasure troves of information about nineteenth-century Ojibwe. Even though there are problems with the fact that they are translated, handled properly they tell us things we would have no other way of knowing.

NOTES

1. This paper has benefited greatly from discussions with various colleagues, John Nichols, Ives Goddard, and Rand Valentine in particular.

2. For those not familiar with the concept, a lectionary is a list of Scriptural readings for particular dates. Lectionaries exist in both Jewish and Christian traditions. The modern Catholic Church has a fixed lectionary that covers the entire Bible in a three-year cycle.

3. The abbreviations used in this paper are: SBJ, subject; OBJ, object; POSS, possessor; AN, animate; INAN, inanimate; SG, singular; PL, plural; EXCL, exclusive; OBV, obviative; FUT, future; PST, past; PRET, preterite; DUB, dubitative; IRR, irrealis; CONJ, conjunct; IMPER, imperative; INVER, inverse; PST, past; CHANGE, initial change; COMP, complementizer; REDUP, reduplication; APPL, applicative; EMPH, emphatic; REL, relative; NOM, nominalizer; LOC, locative.

4. Baraga's dictionary (1853) cites only the middle form of *kakis* for Ottawa, nin kakiz, i.e., *gakizo-* AI 'hide (oneself)'. The corresponding transitive forms are: *gakin-* TA 'hide him', *gakidoo-* TI 'hide it'.

5. Medler spoke a mixed dialect (see text 4, Bloomfield 1958). So he regularly dropped the final *n* from endings like Ottawa speakers, but unlike Ottawa speakers he did not nasalize *-yaanh* '1SG.CONJ' or *-enh* 'dub'.

REFERENCES

Baraga, Frederic. 1850. *A theoretical and practical grammar of the Otchipwe language.* Detroit: Jabez Fox.

———. 1853. *Dictionary of the Otchipwe language, explained in English.* 1st ed. Cincinnati: Jos. A. Hemann.

Bloomfield, Leonard. 1958. *Eastern Ojibwa: Grammar, texts, and word list*, ed. by C. Hockett. Ann Arbor: University of Michigan Press.

Metzger, Bruce M., and Bart D. Ehrman. 2005. *The text of the New Testament: Its transmission, corruption and restoration.* Oxford: Oxford University Press.

Powell, Mark Allan. 1998. *Jesus as a figure in history: How modern historians view the man from*

Galilee. Louisville, KY: Westminster John Knox Press.

Rhodes, Richard A. 2010. The language of Sifferath's Ottawa Catechism Paper read at the Forty-Second Algonquian Conference, St. John's, Newfoundland, 23 October.

———. 2011. The value of 19th Century Ojibwe sources. Presidential address read to the Society for the Study of the Indigenous Languages of the Americas, Pittsburgh, 6 January.

Shedinger, Robert F. 2002. *Tatian and the Jewish scriptures*. Leuven: Peeters.

Valentine, J. Randolph. 2001. *Nishnaabemwin reference grammar*. Toronto: University of Toronto Press.

Expressing Comparison in Cheyenne

Todd Snider and Sarah E. Murray

n this paper, we examine the expression of comparison in Cheyenne, based on existing language materials (Leman 2011, 1980a, 1987; Fisher et al. 2006) and follow-up fieldwork.[1] We identify and analyze the ways Cheyenne encodes comparison, looking in particular at comparatives but also discussing related constructions, including superlatives and equatives. First we consider the types of comparative structures found across languages and then turn to the strategies employed in Cheyenne.

Comparison Across Languages

Comparative structures are those that express a comparison in degree, quantity, or quality between two things. For example, English (1–3) all compare Annie and Dale, but in different ways.

(1) Annie is taller than Dale.   DEGREE
(2) Annie has more berries than Dale.   QUANTITY
(3) Annie is better at painting than Dale.   QUALITY

Regardless of the type of comparison, or the particular things being compared, comparative structures make use of the same three components: a SUBJECT being described (e.g., in (1), Annie),[2] a SCALE along which the subject is measured (in (1), the scale of height, introduced by the predicate *tall*), and a STANDARD OF COMPARISON marking the point against which the subject is compared (in (1), Dale). Each comparative in (1–3) expresses a particular kind of comparison, with the subject exceeding the standard. These components are also used to form other kinds of comparisons, such as equatives, as in (4); superlatives, as in (5); and excessives, as in (6).

(4) Laura is as tall as Maddy.

(5) Denise is the tallest person in her family.

(6) Shelly is too tall to wear that jacket.

Equatives compare a subject with a standard and assert that they are equal on the relevant scale. Superlatives compare a subject with a standard—usually a set of individuals, rather than a single individual—and assert that the subject ranks highest on the relevant scale. Excessives compare a subject with a standard, where the standard is a threshold associated with some action, and assert that the subject exceeds that threshold.[3] Taken broadly, the class of comparative structures include equatives, superlatives, and excessives, as they all involve some form of comparison. In its more narrow usage, however, comparatives describe specifically expressions of simple inequality, those that English marks with *more* or with *-er* *than*, as in (1–3).

Even taking comparatives at their narrow definition, there has been significant interest among scholars to identify the different ways that different languages encode comparison. Stassen 1984 identifies six types of comparative constructions, which Bobaljik 2012 simplifies into three types.[4] We follow the typology in Bobaljik 2012, so we briefly introduce it below.

A Comparative Typology

Bobaljik 2012 divides the ways languages build comparatives into three types—conjoined comparatives, exceed comparatives, and standard comparatives—which we introduce and exemplify in turn. It is not uncommon for a single language to make use of more than one of these strategies. It is usually assumed, however, that languages have a default or unmarked strategy, and so languages can be classified by which strategy they treat as grammatically primary (Stassen 1984; Bobaljik 2012).

CONJOINED COMPARATIVES express comparison by means of two contrasting simple statements, with the contrast flagged grammatically by negation or intensification. For example, in English we can say:

(7)　Annie is tall, Dale is **not**.

One could take (7) to mean that Annie is taller than Dale, even though that is not strictly what the sentence says.[5] Or, for a language that uses this strategy as its primary mode of forming comparatives, consider this example from Mian (Ok-Awyu, Papua New Guinea; Fedden 2007):

(8)　Mosbi ó-le　　sum　eka　Banimo　ó-**ta**　　　gwaab-ó-be.
　　　Mosbi NEUT-TOP　big　and　Banimo　NEUT-**EMPH**　small-PRED-DECL
　　　'Port Moresby is big and Vanimo is small.'　　　　(Mian; Fedden 2007 (3–36))

In (8), the subject is Mosbi, the scale on which it is being measured is size, introduced by *sum* 'big', and the standard of comparison is Banimo. The somewhat literal translation above shows that (8) is composed of two simple predications, connected by conjunction, but this is taken as a whole to mean that Port Moresby is bigger than Vanimo. Note the emphatic marker (in boldface) in the second conjunct, which helps to mark the contrast in size between the two places.

Conjoined comparatives are used as the primary means of building comparatives in languages like Mian and Itelmen (Chukotko-Kamchatkan, Eastern Russia; Bobaljik 2000), approximately one in four/five languages (Bobaljik 2012). Bobaljik 2012 notes that this strategy may be endangered across the languages of the world. This may be due to an inherent instability in the linguistic structure itself, or it may be a coincidence due to extralinguistic factors.

EXCEED COMPARATIVES make use of a verb that means 'exceed' or 'surpass', taking the standard as a direct object and introducing the scale along which the comparison is made in a separate clause. For example, in English, we can say:

(9)　Annie **exceeds** Dale in height.

Note that in (9) the verb is *exceed*, the standard (Dale) is the direct object, and the scale (height) is introduced in an adverbial adjunct. In a language that uses exceed comparatives as its default strategy, consider this example from Tamashek (Berber, Mali; Heath 2005):

(10) Ø-ojǽr   abbà-nnet   t-əššəjrət-t.
      3.MASC.SG-**surpass**.RESULT   father-3.SG.POSS   FEM-length-FEM.SG
      'He is taller than his father.'   (Tamashek; Heath 2005 (222c))

In (10), the subject of comparison is 'he' (the third-person masculine grammatical subject); the scale is height, introduced by *əššəjrət* 'length'; and the standard of comparison is his father('s height). To see that this is an exceed comparative, note that the verb (in boldface) means 'surpass', and has nothing to do with height or tallness; the scale is introduced separately from the verb. The standard, meanwhile, is the direct object.

Exceed comparatives are the primary means of comparison in Tamashek, Amele (Madang, Papua New Guinea; Roberts 1987), and Mandarin, and are about as common worldwide as the conjoined comparative (Stassen 2008; Bobaljik 2012).

STANDARD COMPARATIVES are so called not because of their prevalence, but because they involve marking on the standard of comparison with a case-marker or a particle; they also may optionally mark the scale-introducing predicate in some way. For example, English uses standard comparatives as the primary means of forming comparatives, as in (11).

(11) Annie is taller **than** Dale.

The comparative standard, Dale, is introduced with a special particle, *than* (in boldface), and the adjective *tall*, which introduces the scale of height, is marked with -*er*, or alternately *more*. Another language that uses standard comparatives is Hebrew, as in (12), constructed by the first author.

(12) bə-manitoba   joteɣ   kaɣ   mə-jisɣael.
      in-Manitoba   more   cold   **from**-Israel
      'Manitoba is colder than Israel.'   (Hebrew, constructed)

In (12), the subject is Manitoba; the scale is coldness, introduced by *kaɣ* 'cold';

and the standard of comparison is Israel. The standard, Israel, is marked with a preposition/case marker.

Even though marking on the standard of comparison is the characteristic feature of standard comparatives, the standard can be implicit, as in (13).

(11) Annie is taller.

English (13) is still considered a standard comparative, even though there is no overt standard, and thus no overt marking on the standard. In such cases, the standard is provided by context, including previous linguistic material, e.g., *Dale is tall, but Annie is taller.*

Standard comparatives are used as the primary means of forming comparatives in languages such as English, Hebrew, and Japanese. Languages like these make up the remainder of languages spoken in the world—more than half—and perhaps because of that, standard comparatives have been the primary focus of cross-linguistic analyses of comparatives.

To sum up, conjoined comparatives involve contrasting two statements, exceed comparatives have a predicate that means 'exceed', and standard comparatives involve marking on the standard of comparison. With this typology in hand, we now have the tools to look for what sort of comparative strategy (or strategies) a language uses. Before we turn to Cheyenne, however, we look at which of these strategies are represented in other Algonquian languages.

Comparatives in Algonquian

Both conjoined comparatives and standard comparatives are argued to be present in Algonquian languages. Menominee has been said to use a conjoined comparative, as in (14), originally from Bloomfield 1962.

(14) Apaeqsek   tatāhkesew,   nenah   taeh   **kan.**
      more   he.is.strong   I   and   **not**
      'He is stronger than me.' (Menominee, Dahlstrom 2015)

In (14), the subject is 'he'; the scale is strength, introduced by *tatāhkesew* 'he is strong'; and the standard of comparison is the speaker. We can see that it is a conjoined comparative by the presence of two simple clauses connected by conjunction, with the contrast between the two marked with negation (in boldface). There is no marking on the standard (the speaker) and no predicate that means 'exceed', so it is neither a standard nor an exceed comparative. Meskwaki has also been argued to use a conjoined comparative (see Dahlstrom 2015 and the conclusion below).

Standard comparatives are also attested in Algonquian, as in (15) from Nishnaabemwin, originally from Valentine 2001.

(15) Washme   ndoo-gnooz   **pii**   **dash**   mBill.
     more   I.am.tall   **than** **then**   Bill
     'I am taller than Bill.' (Nishnaabemwin, Dahlstrom 2015)

In (15), the subject is the speaker; the scale is height, introduced by *ndoo-gnooz* 'I am tall'; and the standard of comparison is Bill. We can see that it is a standard comparative because the standard (Bill) is marked—here, with two particles (in boldface). There is only one clause, and the main verb is the scale-introducing predicate, so it is neither a conjoined nor an exceed comparative. In a footnote, Dahlstrom 2015 notes that through personal communication, Richard Rhodes suggested (15) may be "a calque on English, due to language contact."

To our knowledge, there are no other explicit discussions of the kinds of comparative structures found in Algonquian languages. Notably, we are unaware of any Algonquian languages that are claimed to use an exceed comparative.

A Typological Prediction

Before we turn to the Cheyenne data, it is worth considering what existing theories predict; doing so not only allows us to leverage data to support or challenge the theory itself, but can also inform the investigation of the data.

Stassen 1984 argues that the behavior of a language's comparative structures is determined by other properties of that language, in particular the syntax of conjunction—whether conjoined clauses are both independent, or if one is dependent on the other—and the availability of deletion under identity. The particular combination of these features, Stassen 1984 argues, shapes the way a language builds comparatives.

Cheyenne can conjoin independent clauses without subordination—there need not be "deranking" of one clause (see Leman 2011; Murray 2017). Under the analysis in Stassen 1984, this limits Cheyenne to either a conjoined or standard comparative.[6] As far as Stassen's second property, identity deletion, the facts for Cheyenne have not been fully investigated. If any deletion under identity is allowed in Cheyenne, Stassen 1984 predicts that Cheyenne should use a standard comparative. If there is no deletion under identity in Cheyenne, then comparative structures should make use of two full clauses: a conjoined comparative. This leaves us with a partial prediction that Cheyenne should have either a conjoined comparative or a standard comparative. We turn next to the actual Cheyenne data to see if this prediction is borne out.

Comparatives Expressing Inequality

In this section, we look at the 'strict' comparatives in Cheyenne, those structures of comparison that express inequality between two things, where the subject exceeds the standard of comparison. In the next section, we widen our scope and look at other comparative structures, such as equatives.

Background and Methodology

Cheyenne is an Algonquian language spoken in Montana and Oklahoma. Ethnologue (Lewis et al. 2016) lists Cheyenne as having 2,100 native speakers, though a recent Montana survey places the number closer to 500, with most speakers over the age of 50.

In order to investigate how Cheyenne expresses comparison, we looked at a number of existing written texts (e.g., from Leman 2011, 1980a, 1987; Cheyenne Bible Translation Committee 2007) and the online dictionary (Fisher et al. 2006), supplemented with primary elicitation. We looked through the Fisher et al. 2006 dictionary for common English comparatives (like *taller, bigger, better*) to see how they were translated into Cheyenne, and we also looked through every translation with the English words *than* and *more*, which frequently mark comparison, to see which Cheyenne forms they were used to translate. For the texts, we looked for the various forms we had identified through dictionary searching, and we also looked at sections where the corresponding English translations used comparisons.

hehpe-

The most common form used for expressing comparison in Cheyenne is the preverb *hehpe-*. Compare a form without this preverb in (16) and the *hehpe-* form in (17), respectively.[7]

(16)   É-háa'ëstahe.
       3-be.tall
       'He is tall.' (Fisher et al. 2006, *-háa'ëstahe*)

(17)   É-hehpė-háa'ëstahe.
       3-*hehpe*-be.tall
       'He's taller.'

Looking at (17), the subject is the third person, and the scale is height, introduced by *-háa'ëstahe* 'be tall'. The standard of comparison, though, is not given explicitly. Without any context, it is hard to be sure that this is really a comparative (as opposed to, say, an excessive), and even if it is, the lack of an explicit standard prevents us from reaching a conclusion about what kind of comparative structure it is.

Fortunately, however, we also find *hehpe-* in sentences that do have explicit standards of comparison. For example, (18) takes an explicit standard as a direct object (with an initial variant of *hehpe-* and a reduplicated form of the final for 'be tall').

(18)   Ná-hehp-ó'ëstàhe-m-a.
       1-*hehpe*-REDUP:be.tall-FTA-INV(3:1)
       'He's taller than me.' (Fisher et al. 2006, *-hehpó'ëstàhem*)

In (18), the subject is again the third person, and the scale is again height, introduced by *-'ëstahe* 'be tall'. But here the standard of comparison is explicitly given: the speaker is the direct object, marked by the inverse 3:1 voice suffix, indicating the speaker as the comparative standard. An additional example of this transitive construction is given in (19), with two names.

(19) Will   é-hehp-ó'èstáhe-m-ó-ho   Wayne-va-ho.
      Will   3-*hehpe*-REDUP:be.tall-FTA-DIR-OBV   Wayne-OBV-OBV
      'Will is taller than Wayne (obviative).'

Examples (18) and (19) allow us to rule out *hehpe-* as an excessive marker: when there is an explicit standard, the interpretation is 'taller than', not 'too tall for'.

As far as the type of comparative construction exemplified in (18) and (19), it is plainly not a conjoined comparative, as the standard of comparison is introduced as a direct object of the main predication in that same clause, not in its own predication, in its own clause. Whether we consider, e.g., (19) to be an example of an exceed comparative or a standard comparative is somewhat up to our interpretation of the sentence. If we understand *-o'èstahe* 'be tall' as the main predicate of the sentence, then (19) is most similar to a standard comparative: it is one clause, with the main predication introducing the scale, though there is no overt marking on the standard. On the other hand, if we interpret *hehpe-* as forming a complex predicate with 'be tall', then (19) might be analyzed as an exceed comparative. Fisher et al. 2006 actually translates *hehpe-* as 'more, beyond, farther', which is similar to 'exceed'. But the primary issue is whether *hehpe-* is (part of) the main predication of the sentence. Exceed comparatives, as defined in the previous section, have a predicate meaning 'exceed', take the standard as a direct object, and introduce the scale in a separate clause. For (19) to be an exceed comparative, we would have to interpret *hehpe-* as meaning 'exceed', analyze it as (part of) the main predication, and argue that the predicate 'be tall' is in some sense separate or subordinated within the verbal complex. We do not have a conclusive argument against this for examples like (19), but below give another construction with *hehpe-* that is clearly not an exceed comparative.

In (18) and (19), we saw *hehpe-* in a transitive construction, which is one way to make the standard of comparison explicit (as the direct object). Another way to include an explicit comparative standard is in a conjunct (dependent) clause. Consider (20):

(20) Né-hehpe-'èstahe   Will   tsé-he'èstae-stse.
      2-*hehpe*-be.tall   Will   IND-be.so.tall-CNJ.3SG
      'You are taller than Will.'

Being an intransitive verb, *Néhehpe'éstahe* can only take a subject argument, so in (20) the comparative standard, Will, is introduced in a conjunct clause. This dependent clause involves a second occurrence of the main predicate 'be tall', not unlike the English clausal comparative (*You are taller than Will is* [*tall*]). This should not be taken as a conjoined comparative, though, which would require two independent clauses—(20) is more like 'You are taller than Will's height'. Example (20) is also certainly not an exceed comparative, as exceed comparatives have the comparative standard "invariably constructed as the direct object" (Stassen 1984:157).

The conjunct clause that introduces the standard of comparison has a degree interpretation. In (20), this is derived as part of the predicate 'be tall', which introduces its own scale (namely, height). This degree interpretation can also be flagged explicitly, as in (21) with *he'xóve-*, which Fisher et al. 2006 translate as 'at such time, to the degree of'.

(21) Náhko'éehe   ná-hehpe-méhot-a   tsé-he'xóve-méhót-á'ė-stse   ného'éehe.
      my.mother   1-*hehpe*-love-INV(3:1)   IND-*he'xóve*-love-3:1-CNJ.3SG   my.father
      'My mother loves me more than my father does.' (Fisher et al. 2006, *he'xóve-*)

One could more literally translate (21) as 'My mother loves me more than the degree to which my father loves me'. In (21), the subject is the speaker's mother, the scale is amount of love one holds (for the speaker), and the comparative standard is the speaker's father. As in (20), the comparative standard is introduced in a conjunct clause, which is verbal (akin to 'my father does'), and not just a noun phrase (like 'my father'). Because the predicate 'love' is not associated with a scale in the way that 'be tall' is, this conjunct clause must contain the preverb *he'xóve-* to make 'love' into a degree that can serve as the comparative standard; without *he'xóve-*, (21) would be ungrammatical.

hóno'xe-

Another, less common form that seems to act like a comparative is *hóno'xe-*, as in (22).

(22) Né-hóno'xė-ho'tse-nótse   men-ótse.
      2-*hóno'xe*-have-PL.INAN   berry-PL.INAN
      'You have more berries (than I).' (Fisher et al. 2006, *hóno'xe-*)

The English translation given in Fisher et al. 2006 is a comparative, but given the limited data, it is not clear what the Cheyenne construction is. *Hóno'xe-* could be a comparative morpheme, but it could also be a quantifier akin to *most*, as in 'You have most of the berries'. Having most of the berries, of course, entails having more berries than anyone else, so it would make the English comparative given as a translation true. (22) could also be a superlative construction, as in 'You have the most berries'. There is simply not enough context to (22) to be able to distinguish these possibilities. To illustrate this uncertainty, note that a similar meaning can be conveyed using the comparative *hehpe-*, as in (23).

(23)   É-hehpė-stóhá-nėstse   na-men-ótse.
       3-*hehpe*-be.so.many-PL.INAN   1-berry-PL.INAN
       'I have more berries (than you).' (Fisher et al. 2006, *hehpėstohá-*)

Cheyenne (23) literally means 'my berries are more in number', with an implicit standard. If (22) is indeed a comparative, it, like (23), has an implicit, contextual standard of comparison (hence the parentheses in the English translation), which makes it hard to tell which comparative strategy would be in play. However, there is some evidence in favor of the quantificational interpretation of *hóno'xe-*, from some of the other dictionary entries, given in (24) and below.

(24)   Ná-hóno'xe-mét-o.
       1-*hóno'xe*-give-DIR(1:3)
       'I gave him most of it.' (Fisher et al. 2006, *hóno'xe-*)

(25)   hóno'xė-háahpe'e
       hóno'xe-much
       'the greater portion; most of it' (Fisher et al. 2006, *hóno'xe-*)

The particle in (25) is from a story about how Rev. Petter documented the Cheyenne language. The immediate context is that he worked for forty years and recorded tens of thousands of words, and recorded 'the greater portion' of the old language. Within the context of the story, there is no comparison to anyone else recording the Cheyenne language—the 'greater portion' seems to be in contrast to what was not recorded, which would be a quantificational interpretation. These translations are just suggestive of the semantics of *hóno'xe-*, but point to directions for future research.

Other Comparative Structures

In the previous section, we discussed how Cheyenne deals with expressions of simple inequality. A complete examination of comparison in Cheyenne (or in any language) includes not just expressions of inequality but also of the other comparative structures described in the first section (Schwarzschild 2008). In this section, we discuss comparisons to thresholds associated with an action (excessives), comparisons to sets (superlatives), and comparisons of equality (equatives).

Excessives

In addition to *hehpe-* and *hóno'xe-* there are other preverbs that also seem to deal with degree and comparison, broadly construed. For example, we see the preverb *heóme-* on a scalar predicate in (26):

(26)   [Context: The grasshopper is complaining that the day is too hot to do any work.]
     É-heómė-ho-háaeho'ta.
     3-*heóme*-REDUP-hot
     'It's too hot (to work).' ('The Grasshopper and the Ant', Leman 2011)

The context of the story, a version of one of Aesop's fables, makes it clear that it is not just that it is very hot, but that it is hot beyond some salient threshold—namely, the threshold for working. While this would still be consistent with *heóme-* being an intensifier (like English *very*), there is a different Cheyenne preverb, *osee-*, translated in Fisher et al. 2006 as 'very, really, intensely', which is very commonly used as an intensifier, as in (27).

(27)   É-osee-pėhéva'e.
     3-*osee*-good
     'It's really good.' (Fisher et al. 2006, *osee-*)

We also see a particle variant of *heóme-*, used with the adverbializing *-to*, as in (28).

(28)   Heóme-sto   kásováaheh-o   mó-h-vése-na'h-e-he-vó-he.
     heóme-ADV   young.man-PL   Q-PST-also-kill-PSV-NEG-PL-INF
     'Too many young men had also been killed.'   (Fisher et al. 2006, *heómesto*)

The excessive-denoting *heóme-* is here part of the complex noun phrase *heómesto kásováaheho* 'too many young men' that serves as the subject for the rest of the sentence. It is clear in this context, given the nature of the predicate, that the speaker is describing more young men as having died than whatever the threshold is for such a thing.

Superlatives

Another preverb that deals with comparison looks to be a superlative marker: *náno'se-*, as in (29).

(29)   É-náno'se-pėhéva'e.
      3-*náno'se*-be.good
      'It is the best.' (Fisher et al. 2006, *náno'se-*)

In (29), the subject is inanimate third person, and the scale is goodness, introduced by the predicate *-pėhéva'e*. The superlative preverb describes the subject as exceeding all other contextually salient things on the scale of goodness, making the subject 'the best'. It remains a question for future elicitation just how productive this form is and which predicates it can combine with.

Equatives or Similatives

There are two morphemes that seem to build equatives in Cheyenne: *vé'-* and *séeto'-* (and its variants). As with *hehpe-*, they can combine with an intransitive verb and take a contextual comparative standard, as in (30), or can combine with a transitive verb and take a standard as direct object, as in (31).

(30)   É-vé'-ėhahe.
      3-*vé*-be.old
      'He is of the same age.' (Fisher et al. 2006, *-vé'ėhahe*)

(31)   Ná-vé'-ėhahé-m-o.
      1-*vé*-be.old-FTA-DIR(1:3)
      'I am the same age as him.' (Fisher et al. 2006, *-vézéhahém*)

(32) É-séetó'-éhahe-o'o.
      3-*séese*-be.old-PL
      'They are the same age.' (Fisher et al. 2006, -*séetó'éhahe*)

In (32), *séeto'-* occurs with a plural subject, so the third person plural is taken as both subject and standard.

   Other morphemes that may be semantically related are -*ahé* and -*hehá*. These are nominal suffixes, unlike the verbal forms identified above (Fisher et al. 2006). For example, consider (33) with -*hehá*, which can go with both animate and inanimate nouns:

(33) Hoóhtsetsé-héha   é-he-'ëstahe.
      tree-*hehá*   3-REL-be.tall
      'He's as tall as a tree.' (Fisher et al. 2006, -*hehá*)

The main predication in this sentence—the second word, *éhe'ëstahe*—on its own means simply 'he is that tall'. The work of comparison is done by -*hehá*, which sets the contextual standard against which the main predication is interpreted. Fisher et al. 2006 translate -*hehá* as 'like; similar; same as; as'. It is not entirely clear if this is an equative ('his height is equal to the tree's height') or a similative ('his height is similar to that of a tree') construction. However, the same could also be said for (30–32) above; more work needs to be done to tease apart these interpretations.

   Equatives may also be formed more periphrastically with the degree preverb *he'xóve-* and an anaphor, as in (34).

(34) Náhko'éehe   ná-në-he'xóve-méhot-a
      my.mother   1-AN-*he'xóve*-love-INV(3:1)

      tsé-he'xóve-méhót-á'ë-stse   ného'éehe.
      IND-*he'xóve*-love-3:1-CNJ.3SG   my.father
      'My mother loves me as much as my father does.'

A more literal translation of (34) could be 'My mother loves me to that degree, the degree to which my father loves me'. Unlike in the comparative (21), there are two instances of *he'xóve* in this construction.

TABLE 1. Cheyenne expressions of comparison discussed here

COMPARISON	CHEYENNE	COMPARATIVE STANDARD EXAMPLES
Comparative	*hehpe-*	Context (17), DO (18), conjunct (20)
Quantifier	*hóno'xe-*	Context (22)
Excessive	*heóme-*	Context (26)
Superlative	*náno'se-*	Context (29)
Equative/Similative	*vé'-*	Context (30), DO (31)
	séeto'-	Plural subject (32)
	-heha	Nominal (33)

Discussion

The strategies used in Cheyenne for expressing comparison, as discussed here, are summarized in Table 1.

This is not intended to be an exhaustive list: many of these morphemes likely take forms that we have not yet identified, and there may be other morphemes that express comparison as well.

Based on what we have identified, *hehpe-* is the form most commonly used for building comparatives in Cheyenne. Within the Bobaljik 2012 typology laid out above, Cheyenne seems to primarily use a standard comparative: comparatives do not have two independent clauses, nor do they rely on emphasis or negation, so the Cheyenne examples shown above are not conjoined comparatives. Further, while we might take *hehpe-* to mean 'exceed', the standard is not always introduced as a direct object, so Cheyenne is not making use of an exceed comparative. Cheyenne's primary strategy seems to be the standard comparative, with standards being supplied contextually or introduced in a conjunct clause.

However, Cheyenne's *hehpe-* looks very similar to a Meskwaki comparative preverb that Dahlstrom 2015 argues to be part of a conjoined comparative, as in (35).

(35) a·wasi . . .   [ᵥ ahpi·hči–we·wenesi-wa]
      more . . .   to.such.extent– . . .
      'She is prettier.' (Meskwaki; Dahlstrom 2015 (7b))

While the Meskwaki preverb *ahpi·hči-* and Cheyenne *hehpe-* have obvious similarities, there is at least one important difference: in (35), there is an additional particle, *a·wasi* meaning 'more'. Dahlstrom 2015 argues that this is an oblique argument of the verb, and *ahpi·hči-* 'to.such.extent' is a relative root. Interestingly, in Cheyenne, only the preverb *hehpe-* is needed, and *hehpe-* seems to include the meaning of 'more' or 'beyond' contributed in Meskwaki by *a·wasi*.

NOTES

1. We would like to thank our Cheyenne consultants, and others we have talked with about Cheyenne, for their collaboration and discussions about the language. We would also like to thank Ryan Bochnak, Wayne Leman, Monica Macaulay, Margaret Noodin, William Starr, audiences at the Forty-Seventh Algonquian Conference in Winnipeg, and the PAC 47 reviewers for their helpful comments. Any errors are our own.

2. This is sometimes also called a "target" in the literature.

3. Even if the standard of comparison in an excessive is picked out by an individual, the standard is not the measure of that individual. For example, in *Shelly is too tall for Donna*, Shelly is taller than the threshold identified by Donna for some salient activity. If basketball dunking match-ups are salient in the context, the above sentence is understood like *Shelly is too tall for Donna to dunk on*. While this standard of comparison is fixed by Donna—in these examples, it is the maximum height of a person she can dunk on—it is not the same as the measurement of Donna on this same scale, i.e., Donna's height. Both are perfectly compatible with situations in which Donna is taller than Shelly: Donna exceeds Shelly on the scale of height, but Shelly still exceeds the contextually salient threshold associated with Donna.

4. Bobaljik 2012 collapses the "separative", "allative", "locative", and "particle" classes from the Stassen 1984 typology into a single class, the "standard comparative" (explained in the following subsection). Bobaljik 2012 considers them one type, as they all make use of a particle to mark the standard of comparison, where Stassen 1984 treats them differently depending on the noncomparative meaning of that particle: "separatives" use a *from*-like particle marking a SOURCE, "allatives" use a *to*-like particle marking a GOAL, "locatives" use an *at*-like particle marking a LOCATION, with "particle" comparatives serving as an "other" class, for particles that do not fit those three descriptions.

5. If tallness is interpreted relative to different comparison classes for Annie and Dale in (7), we might well understand Annie to be tall (relative to her comparison class) and for Dale not to be tall (relative to his comparison class), but for Dale still to be taller than Annie.

6. Stassen 1984 does not use the term 'standard comparative'; as mentioned above, that term is from Bobaljik 2012, among others. Here, this would be Stassen's PARTICLE type.

7. Cheyenne orthography: Orthography: V̥ voiceless vowel, V́ high pitch vowel, š = voiceless alveolar fricative (IPA: ʃ), ' = glottal stop (IPA: ʔ). Cheyenne morphological glosses: 1 = first person, 2 = second person, 3 = third person, X:Y = voice suffix indicating X acting on Y, ADV = adverbializer, AN = anaphor, CNJ = conjunct mode suffix, DIR = direct voice, FTA = transitive animate final, INAN = inanimate, IND = indicative, INF = inferential mode suffix, INV = inverse voice, NEG = negation, OBV = obviative, PL = plural, PST = distant past, PSV = passive, Q = interrogative proclitic, REDUP = reduplication, SG = singular.

REFERENCES

Bloomfield, Leonard. 1962. *The Menomini language.* New Haven, CT: Yale University Press.

Bobaljik, Jonathan David. 2000. Implications of Itelmen agreement asymmetries. *Proceedings of the Berkeley Linguistics Society Annual Meeting*, ed. by Josef Ruppenhofer, Steven S. Chang, and Lily Liaw, 25:299–310. Berkeley Linguistics Society.

———. 2012. *Universals in comparative morphology: Suppletion, superlatives, and the structure of words.* Current Studies in Linguistics, vol. 50. Cambridge, MA: MIT Press.

Cheyenne Bible Translation Committee. 2007. *Ma'heonemóxe'éstoo'o: Cheyenne scripture.* Busby, MT: CCEP.

Dahlstrom, Amy. 2015. Meskwaki comparatives: A first look. *Papers of the Forty-Third Algonquian Conference*, ed. by Monica Macaulay and J. Randolph Valentine, pp. 15–27. Albany: State University of New York Press.

Ethnologue. 2015. Cheyenne. http://www.ethnologue.com/language/chy.

Fedden, Olcher Sebastian. 2007. A grammar of Mian, a Papuan language of New Guinea. PhD thesis, University of Melbourne.

Fisher, Louise, Wayne Leman, Leroy Pine Sr., and Marie Sanchez. 2006. *Cheyenne dictionary.* Lame Deer, MT: Chief Dull Knife College. http://www.cdkc.edu/cheyennedictionary/index.html.

Heath, Jeffrey. 2005. *A grammar of Tamashek (Tuareg of Mali).* Mouton Grammar Library, vol. 35. New York: Mouton de Gruyter.

Leman, Wayne (ed.). 1980a. *Cheyenne texts: An introduction to Cheyenne literature.* Occasional Publications in Anthropology, Series No. 6. Greeley: Museum of Anthropology, University of Northern Colorado.

———. 1980b. *A reference grammar of the Cheyenne language.* Occasional Publications in Anthropology, Series No. 5. Greeley: Museum of Anthropology, University of Northern Colorado.

——— (ed.). 1987. *Náéváhóó'óhtséme / We are going back home: Cheyenne history and stories told by James Shoulderblade and others.* Memoir 4. Winnipeg: Algonquian and Iroquoian Linguistics.

———. 2011. *A reference grammar of the Cheyenne language.* Raleigh, NC: Lulu Press. Updated version of Leman 1980b.

Lewis, M. Paul, Gary F. Simons, and Charles D. Fennig (eds.). 2016. *Ethnologue: Languages of the world, nineteenth edition.* Dallas: SIL International.

Murray, Sarah E. 2017. Cheyenne connectives. *Papers of the Forty-Fifth Algonquian Conference,* ed. by Monica Macaulay, Margaret Noodin, and J. Randolph Valentine, pp. 149–162. East Lansing: Michigan State University Press.

Roberts, John R. 1987. *Amele.* London: Croom Helm.

Schwarzschild, Roger. 2008. The semantics of comparatives and other degree constructions. *Language and Linguistics Compass* 2(2):308–331.

Stassen, Leon. 1984. The comparative compared. *Journal of Semantics* 3(1–2):143–182.

———. 2008. Comparative constructions. World atlas of language structures online, ed. by Martin Haspelmath, Matthew S. Dryer, David Gil, and Bernard Comrie, ch. 121. Max Planck Digital Library. http://wals.info/feature/121.

Valentine, J. Randolph. 2001. *Nishnaabemwin reference grammar.* Toronto: University of Toronto Press.

An Overview of Change of State Lexicalization Patterns in Innu

Fanny York

The complexity of the Algonquian verb or, as formulated by Paul Lejeune in 1634 "[*cette*] *infinité de mots qui signifient plusieurs choses en même temps*" (in the *Relations des Jésuites* [1896:26]) has always been a subject of fascination in Algonquian studies. It is now well known that the Algonquian verb is polymorphemic and can bear the meaning of a whole sentence in a language like French or English, similar to other polysynthetic languages. Since Bloomfield (1946), most authors have analyzed the Algonquian verbal stem in terms of a morphological template comprised of three positions. In the latest templatic analysis, Goddard (1990) proposes the three following position classes (in primary derivation): (1) an INITIAL that has be to filled with a root, a nominal stem, or a derived initial; (2) a MEDIAL that can be filled with a derived nominal stem; (3) a FINAL that can be simple (abstract or concrete) or derived from a verbal stem.

This analysis remains rather silent about the semantic content of the morphemes appearing in each position class. The question then arises of the combinatory semantics within the verbal stem. How is the semantic content organized within the verbal stem? What is expressed in each position and with what interaction? Few studies have addressed these questions (see Rhodes 2015 and Rhodes and Valentine 2015 on Ojibwe, and Slavin 2012 on Oji-Cree). Concerning Innu, I have shown in my Master's thesis that Innu verbs of motion follow some very general and regular patterns of lexicalization of motion events (York 2010). In this paper, I explore how change of state events are lexicalized into Innu verbs (or rather, verbal stems).

In order to do this, I use the perspective of cognitive semantics and follow Talmy's (2000) theory of Event Integration. In this framework, change of state is understood as an event with an underlying conceptual structure (a frame) that can be encoded differently into the lexical items of languages, following language-specific lexicalization patterns. Change of state is conceptualized in analogy with Motion. A motion event minimally consists of a Figure (the moving object), a Ground (the reference object), a Path, and Motion (Talmy 1974, 1985). Motion can be dynamic (represented by MOVE) or static (represented by BE). Those semantic elements form a simple event, as in (1).

(1) The cup   is   on   the table
     FIGURE   BE   PATH   GROUND

A motion event is complex when a co-event is added,[1] which typically bears a relation of Manner or Cause as in the examples below:[2]

(2) She   runs   towards   the house
     figure   MOTION+MANNER   PATH   GROUND

(3) The napkin   blew   off   the table
     FIGURE   MOTION+CAUSE   PATH   GROUND

(4) The book   lies   on   the shelf
     FIGURE   BE+MANNER   PATH   GROUND

York (2010) has shown that Innu motion verbs typically lexicalize the Path into the initial, the Ground into the medial, and the element of Motion (MOVE or BE) and Manner or Cause into the final, as in the examples below.[3]

(5) ashukameteu

âšaw-	-(a)kâm-	-e-	-ute-	-w
from.one.point.to.another-	-space-	-PMA-	-by.walking.AI-	-3
path	GROUND		MOTION+MANNER	(FIGURE)

'S/he goes to another place by walking.'

(6) pashtapetshishinu

pašt-	-âpek-	-šin-	-u
over-	-stringlike-	-lie.AI-	-3
PATH	GROUND	BE+MANNER	(FIGURE)

'S/he is lying across something (stringlike).'

Talmy (2000) has generalized this analysis of motion events to other types of events, among which is change of state.[4] The semantic elements implied in a change of state event are similar to those of a motion event, with the exception that Motion is to be understood metaphorically (represented by 'MOTION'). Once again, the element of Motion can be dynamic ('MOVE' in change of state) or static ('BE' in a state). The Figure corresponds to the entity undergoing the change and the Ground to the property acquired through the change. If a co-event is added to make a complex event it most frequently is a Cause. Consider the examples below:

(7)
Marie	got	sick	from	the cold
FIGURE	'MOVE'	GROUND	PATH	CAUSE

(8)
The lake	froze	to	ice
FIGURE	'BE'+CAUSE	PATH	GROUND

Motion can also be agentive, which is represented by '$_A$MOVE':

(9)
She	burned	him	to	death
AGENT	'$_A$MOVE'+CAUSE	FIGURE	PATH	GROUND

Talmy's (2000) theory of Event Integration proposes that languages systematically lexicalize what he refers to as the CORE SCHEMA of the event into the same constituent. For motion events, the core schema corresponds to the Path where it refers to the Ground (or Path + Ground) for change of state events.[5] Thus, in Innu change of state verbs, the Ground should be encoded into the initial, as it is the case for Path in motion verbs (as in examples (5) and (6)).

In the rest of this paper, I show that in Innu bipartite verbs encoding a change of state, the property acquired (Ground) is, as predicted, systematically encoded into the initial whereas the change (metaphorical Motion) and the Cause are lexicalized into the final. If the verb is tripartite, the medial typically encodes the entity undergoing the change (Figure). I begin by presenting Innu verbs encoding a simple change of state event (i.e., without a Cause) and continue with verbs encoding a complex change of state event (i.e., with a Cause). Both types of verbs can be intransitive (the subject is the Figure, i.e., the entity undergoing the change) or transitive (the object is the Figure). The data used for this study are drawn from a lexical database (Drapeau 2015), which is an updated version of the *Dictionnaire Montagnais-Français* (Drapeau 1991). It contains approximately 17,000 verbal entries. Only the most frequent lexicalization patterns are presented here.

Verbs Encoding a Simple Change of State

Intransitive Verbs Encoding a Simple Change of State

An overwhelming number of intransitive verbs expressing a simple change of state (without a specified cause) are built with the final *-pal*. This final lexicalizes Motion and a continuous Manner of motion in motion verbs such as *atimipanu* in (10), whereas in change of state verbs it encodes the element of metaphorical Motion (i.e., the change itself, 'MOVE') such as *pimipanu* in example (11).

(10) atimipanu

atim	-i-	-pal-	-i-	-w
inverse.direction	-EP-	-in.a.continuous.manner.of.motion	-AI/II	-3/0
PATH		MOTION+MANNER		(FIGURE)

'S/he, it goes away by flying, swimming, or motorboat.'

(11) pimipanu

pîm-i-pal-i-w

twist-EP-'MOVE'-AI/II-3/0

'S/he, it becomes twisted.'

In change of state verbs, the final *-pal* is combined with initials that lexicalize a property (GROUND) but not necessarily the element of metaphorical Motion, i.e., the process that activates the change ('MOVE' in an inchoative verb) or a state ('BE' in a static verb). Hence, a great number of initials allow for an inchoative/static alternation depending on the final they are associated with. For example, the initials *cîtû-* 'stiff' and *pîm-* 'twist, twisted' build a change of state verb when combined with the final *pal* as in *pimipanu* in (11) and *katshitupanu* in (12).[6]

(12) katshitupanu
      kacîtaw-pal-i-w
      RED.stiff-'MOVE'-AI/II-3/0
      'S/he, it stiffens, becomes stiff.'

By contrast, the same roots combined with a static final such as the abstract final *-â* (Denny 1977, 1984) build up a static verb as in *pimau* and *tshituau*:

(13) *pimau*
      pîm-â-w
      twist-'BE'.II-0
      'It is twisted.'

(14) *tshituau*
      cîtaw-â-w
      stiff-'BE'.II-0
      'It is stiff.'

These examples show that metaphorical Motion ('MOVE') is not encoded into the initial root but only into the concrete final *-pal* (and 'BE' into the abstract final *-â*). Hence, using a final automatically disambiguates the aspect (inchoative/static) of the initial. The pattern of lexicalization for this type of change of state verb is schematized in (15). Recall that Ground corresponds to the property acquired through the change.

(15) [GROUND]$_{initial}$ + ['MOVE']$_{final}$

However, not all initials have an inchoative/static alternation (with a dynamic final such as *-pal* or a static final such as *-â*). Indeed, according to our corpus, a small number of initials can only be combined with a dynamic final like *-pal* as in *apupanu* and *apapanu*. As such, this type of initial seems to lexicalize not only a property (GROUND) but also the change of state itself (i.e., 'MOVE' + GROUND according to our theoretical framework).

(16)   apupanu
       âpaw-pal-i-w
       warm-'MOVE'-AI/II-3/0
       'S/he, it warms up.'

(17)   apapanu
       âpâ-pal-i-w
       thaw-'MOVE'-AI/II-3/0
       'S/he, it thaws.'

This suggests that the final *-pal* has grammaticalized into an inchoative marker. In simple change of state verbs, the final *-pal* seems to be obligatorily used, even with initials that already lexicalize a change of state (and not just a property).[7] The Manner of continuous motion that *pal* encodes when combined with an initial of Path in motion verbs (as illustrated in example (10)) seems to be bleached in the case of change of state verbs. Indeed, the final *-pal* can refer to a continuous, progressive change of state, but also to a sudden change of state, as in *mikukuepanu*.[8]

(18)   mikukuepanu
       miku-kw-e-pal-i-w
       red-face-PMA-'MOVE'-AI/II-3/0
       'S/he, it is blushing.'

The lexicalization pattern for this type of verb is represented in (19).

(19)   ['MOVE'+GROUND]$_{initial}$ + ['MOVE']$_{final}$

To sum up, there are two major morphological constructions for Innu verbs encoding a simple non-agentive change of state:[9]

1. One that is built with an initial encoding a property and with the final -*pal* that activates the change of state;
2. One that is built with an initial encoding a change of state (a property and metaphorical Motion), and with the final -*pal* that redundantly encodes the change.

When a medial is added to any one of these types, it typically lexicalizes a property of the figural entity undergoing the change, such as -*assûk*- 'viscous' in the example below.

(20) ashinassutshipanu
ašin-assûc-i-pal-i-w
rock-viscous-EP-'MOVE'-AI/II-3/0
'S/he, it (viscous) stiffens.'

The pattern of lexicalization with a medial is represented in (21).

(21) [GROUND]$_{initial}$ + [FIGURE]$_{medial}$ + ['MOVE']$_{final}$

Transitive Verbs Encoding a Simple Change of State

Transitive verbs encoding a simple agentive change of state are constructed with the causative final -*y*, as in the examples below.

(22) tshituieu
cîtaw-y-ew
stiff-CAUSATIVE.TA-3:3'
'S/he makes him/her, it (animate) stiff.'

(23) akuieu
âku-y-ew
sick-CAUSATIVE.TA-3:3'
'S/he hurts, makes him/her suffer, makes him/her sick.'

This type of verb is somewhat uncommon in the Innu lexicon, as the majority of transitive change of state verbs encode a specified cause, as we shall see below. The lexicalization pattern for simple agentive change of state events is represented in (24).[10]

(24) $[\text{GROUND}]_{\text{initial}} + [\text{'}_\text{A}\text{MOVE'}]_{\text{final}}$

Verbs Encoding a Complex Change of State

In this section, I present the intransitive and transitive verbs encoding a complex change of state, i.e., a main event that expresses a change of state and a co-event of Cause.

Intransitive Verbs Encoding a Complex Change of State

There are more than a dozen intransitive finals in Innu that refer to a natural force (Drapeau 2014:420–421). A few examples are given below:

- -âši (AI) /-âštan (II) 'by the wind'
- -(a)ci (AI) /-(a)tin (II) 'by the cold'
- -âkatušu (AI) / -âkatute (II) 'by drying'
- -âpuku (AI) / -âpute (II) 'by the current'

These intransitive finals can build complex change of state verbs when combined with a root lexicalizing a property (GROUND), such as the roots previously mentioned.

(25) pimakatushu
      pîm-âkatušu-w
      twist-by.drying.AI-3
      'It becomes twisted as it dries.'

(26) pimashkatshu
      pîm-âškaci-w
      twist-by.freezing.AI-3
      'It becomes twisted as it freezes.'

Notice that in these examples the subject of the verb is the Figure undergoing the change. It is possible to add a medial, in which case it refers to a property of the Figure, as in (27):

(27) pashtaneiakatushu
      pâšt-ân-e-y-âkatušu-w
      crack-skin-PMA-LNK-by.drying.AI-3
      'It (skin) cracks as it dries.'

The lexicalization pattern is the following:

(28) [GROUND]$_{\text{initial}}$ (+ [FIGURE]$_{\text{medial}}$)+ ['MOVE'+CAUSE]$_{\text{final}}$

Transitive Verbs Encoding a Complex Change of State

In nearly all verbs encoding an agentive change of state, the transitive final encodes a Cause. Some finals, such as in the verb in example (29), are the transitive counterparts of the natural force finals presented above while others are "regular" instrumental finals as in examples (30) to (32).

(29) tshituakatusham^{u}
      cîtaw-âkatuš-am-w
      stiff-by.drying-THTI-3:0
      'S/he dries it up stiff.'

(30) tshituapikateu
      cîtaw-âpikât-ew
      stiff-by.tying.TA-3:3'
      'S/he tied him/her up stiff.'

(31) shitaim^{u}
      šît-ay-am-w
      tight-with.an.instrument-THTI-3:0
      'S/he tightens it with an instrument.'

TABLE 1. Finals encoding Cause versus Manner in motion and change of state verbs

	MOTION VERB	CHANGE OF STATE VERB
Natural force final Ex. *-ašu* 'by the wind'	*ashaiashu* 's/he moves backward because of the wind' (Cause)	*nanikashu* 'it is torn by the wind' (Cause)
Other concrete final Ex. *-ay* 'with an instrument, by canoe, by swimming, by flying, by walking'	*atimaim^u* 's/he catches up by canoe, by swimming, etc.' (Manner)	*atshuekaim^u* 's/he makes it (sheetlike) smaller by using an instrument' (Cause)

(32) shitineu

 šît-in-ew

 tight-with.hands.TA-3:3'

 'S/he tightens him/her, it with their hands.'

Rhodes (2015) has noted that the expression of instrumentality is obligatory in Ojibwe agentive change of state verbs. Transitive finals referring to an instrument (such as *-ah* 'use an instrument') or to what he calls a "kind of action" (such as *-bi* 'by pulling') are obligatory when used with initials encoding a resultant state (Rhodes 2015:203–204). Innu is similar, as the use of the causative *-y* is very limited in change of state verbs and since concrete finals encoding a Cause build up the overwhelming majority of agentive change of state verbs. However, my analysis does not distinguish between instrumental and "kind of action" finals considering that they both encode the same co-event of Cause.

More precisely, natural force finals (both transitive and intransitive) always lexicalize the Cause of the event, whether it is a motion or change of state event. On the other hand, other instrumental and "kind of action" finals tend overwhelmingly to encode either a Manner in a motion verb (with an initial encoding a Path) or a Cause in a change of state verb (with an initial encoding a property). The examples in Table 1 compare the use of the same finals in both types of verbs.

Agentive complex change of state verbs can be tripartite, in which case the medial refers to the entity undergoing the change (i.e., the Figure) as in (33) and (34). The medial classifies the syntactic object.

(33) shiteiecipiteu

šît-eyek-i-pit-ew

tight-sheetlike-EP-by.pulling.TI-3:0

'S/he stretches it (sheetlike) tight by pulling it quickly.'

(34) tshinuapetshinam^u

cinw-âpek-in-am-w

long-stringlike-with.hands-THTI-3:0

'S/he lengthens something (stringlike) with their hands.'

This lexicalization pattern is represented in (35).

(35) $[\text{GROUND}]_{\text{initial}}$ (+ $[\text{FIGURE}]_{\text{medial}}$)+ $[\text{'}_{\text{A}}\text{MOVE'+CAUSE}]_{\text{final}}$

To conclude this paper, the various patterns of lexicalization that I have presented for each subtype of change of state verbs can be generalized into one main lexicalization pattern for change of state in Innu, schematized in (36).

(36) $[\text{GROUND}\ (\text{+'MOVE'})]_{\text{initial}}$ (+$[\text{FIGURE}]_{\text{medial}}$)+ $[\text{'}_{(\text{A})}\text{MOVE'}\ (\text{+CAUSE})]_{\text{final}}$

Recall that Talmy's (2000) model predicted that the core schema of change of state events, the Ground property, is encoded into the same constituent as the core schema of motion events, namely the Path (as seen for Innu in example (5)). This core schema corresponds to the initial in Innu. Moreover, both the Cause of the change of state and Manner of a motion event are constantly lexicalized as the final. Furthermore, in tripartite verbs, the medial typically encodes the entity undergoing the change (i.e., the Figure).

Two important points must be noted. First, in Talmy's model, the element of Metaphorical Motion is expected to be always encoded into the verbal root. Yet in Innu change of state verbs, the change (or metaphorical Motion) is not necessarily encoded into the initial but is always lexicalized into the final. Second, the Cause of a change of state is extremely salient in Innu, especially when the change is agentive. Accordingly, a contrastive set of finals is readily available in Innu in order to specify the Cause of an event.

In the literature on motion verbs, a sizable part of the discussion has focused on MANNER SALIENCE.[11] Slobin (2004, 2006) has demonstrated that some languages have a strong tendency to express the Manner of motion (by walking, by running, by flying, etc.) and display an accessible slot to encode Manner, whereas in other languages Manner is optionally expressed and is syntactically subordinated to the Path. I conclude that in Innu, both Manner and Cause are salient categories: the Manner of motion or localization is nearly always specified in motion and locative verbs (York 2010, 2013) while the Cause is almost obligatorily encoded into agentive change of state verbs (and is frequently encoded into nonagentive change of state verbs and motion verbs as well).[12]

Coming back to the tripartite template of the Algonquian verbal stem, the analysis that I propose in this paper shows that the positions are not just arbitrary derivational position classes but that they are cognitively motivated. Finals are used to background salient information such as the Manner of motion or localization or the Cause of the change of state, whereas initials typically encode the core schema of the event. From a diachronic point of view, it means that finals can only be derived (or rather, grammaticalized) from initial stems that lexicalize a Manner or a Cause.[13] Behind the apparent morphological complexity of verbs, the articulation of the semantic content can be brought down to very general and simple conceptual schemas that map into lexicalization patterns. This analysis sheds new light on speaker competence in the use and creation of polysynthetic verbs.

NOTES

1. Talmy uses the terms MAIN EVENT for simple events and MACRO-EVENT for complex events in which a main or framing event is associated with a co-event of Manner or Cause. For the sake of clarity and simplification, I use the terms SIMPLE and COMPLEX EVENTS.

2. Note that example (3) in English corresponds to what Goldberg (1995) has analyzed as a caused motion construction.

3. Abbreviations: AI = Animate Intransitive; II = Inanimate Intransitive; LNK = link; PMA = post-medial accretion; TA = Transitive Animate; TI = Transitive Inanimate. 3 = third person subject; 3:0 = third person subject and inanimate object; 3:3' = proximate third person subject and obviative third person object.

    In the examples, the first line follows the Innu standard orthography and the second is the morphemic line spelled with phonological orthography. In the latter, the short vowels /i/ and /a/ are maintained, despite being phonetically realized as schwas. The vowel /u/ can assimilate a short vowel of a preceding syllable (vowel harmony).

4. In this paper, I use the term CHANGE OF STATE, most common in the literature, instead of the Talmian expression of STATE CHANGE.

5. Talmy distinguishes so-called VERB-FRAMED LANGUAGES, in which Path is lexicalized into the verb root and Manner or Cause in a satellite (a closed-class bound affix or free word that is dependent on the verb root) from SATELLITE-FRAMED LANGUAGES, where Path is lexicalized in a satellite, while the verbal root encodes Manner or Cause. For lack of space, I leave aside the discussion of the status of the initial and final with respect to the categories of verbal root and satellite.

6. In this example, the reduplication of the root also plays a role in the aspectual structure of the event denoted by the verb. However, not all the verbs constructed with the final -pal and encoding a change of state have a reduplicated root. As such, reduplication in itself is not obligatory to express a change of state.

7. There are a few exceptions. A small number of initials encoding an inherent change of state, such as *ilnûûw* 's/he is alive, s/he lives, s/he is born' or *nipiw* 's/he dies, s/he is dead' do not need to be combined with -pal to express a change of state. For more information about the stative/inchoative ambiguity, the reader is referred to Rhodes (2016).

8. In this particular example, the initial lexicalizes a property (GROUND) but not the change of state ('MOVE' + GROUND).

9. In this paper, I leave aside forms with preverbs. More research needs to be done on this type of construction encoding a change of state.

10. Notice that the lexicalization pattern does not include a medial position. This is because agentive simple change of state verbs, since they are not a common type of verb, do not usually take a medial.

11. Slobin (2006:6) defines MANNER SALIENCE as "the level of attention paid to manner in describing events." The degree of manner salience in a particular language can be measured by use (the tendency for speakers to provide information about manner when describing an event) and the lexicon (size and diversity of manner expressions available in a language).

12. In my presentation at the Forty-Fifth Algonquian Conference, I demonstrated that a small set of posture verbs have grammaticalized into locative verbs. Those posture verbs encode a Manner of being localized: *takut mîcišwâkanit aštew* 'it is placed (literally, sits) on the table', *tipiškût akutew ûcit* 'it is suspended right above the mountain'.

13. They may also possibly be derived from other semantic elements in verbs that encode an event other than motion or change of state.

REFERENCES

Bloomfield, Leonard. 1946. Algonquian. *Linguistic structures of native America*, ed. by Cornelius Osgood and Harry Hoijer, pp. 85–129. Viking Fund Publications in Anthropology, vol. 6. New York.

Denny, J. Peter. 1977. Semantics of abstract finals in inanimate intransitive verbs. *Papers of the Eighth Algonquian Conference*, ed. by William Cowan, pp. 124–142. Ottawa: Carleton University.

———. 1984. Semantic verb classes conveyed by the abstract finals of the Cree verb. *Papers of the Fifteenth Algonquian Conference*, ed. by William Cowan, pp. 241–271. Ottawa: Carleton University.

Drapeau, Lynn. 1991. *Dictionnaire montagnais-français*. Québec: Presses de l'Université du Québec.

———. 2014. *Grammaire de la langue innue*. Québec: Presses de l'Université du Québec.

———. 2015. Innu lexical database, FileMaker pro.

Goddard, Ives. 1990. Primary and secondary stem derivation in Algonquian. *International Journal of American Linguistics* 56(4):449–483.

Goldberg, Adele. 1995. *Constructions: A construction grammar approach to argument structure*. Chicago: University of Chicago Press.

Lejeune, Paul. 1896 [1634]. Relation de ce qui s'est passé en La Nouvelle France, en l'année 1634, De la langue des sauvages montagnais. *The Jesuit Relations and Allied Documents: Travel and Explorations of the Jesuit Missionaries in New France, 1610–1791; the Original French, Latin, and Italian Texts, with English Translations and Notes* (Reprinted, New York: Pageant, 1959), ed. by Reuben Gold Thwaites, pp. 20–33. Cleveland: Burrows Brothers.

Rhodes, Richard A. 2015. Instrumentality and frames in Ojibwe. *Papers of the Forty-Third Algonquian Conference*, ed. by Monica Macaulay and Randolph Valentine, pp. 195–206. Albany, NY: SUNY Press.

———. 2016. On the semantics of abstract finals: 35 years later. *Papers of the Forty-Fourth Algonquian Conference*, ed. by Monica Macaulay and Randolph Valentine, pp. 289–310. Albany, NY: SUNY Press.

Rhodes, Richard A., and Randolph Valentine. 2015. Transitivity in Ojibwe. *Valency Classes: A comparative handbook*, ed. by Andrej Malchukov, Martin Haspelmath, Iren Hartmann, and Bernard Comrie, pp. 1206–1264. Berlin: de Gruyter.

Slavin, Tanya. 2012. The syntax and semantics of stem composition in Oji-Cree. PhD thesis, University of Toronto.

Slobin, Dan. 2004. The many ways to search for a frog: Linguistic typology and the expression of motion events. *Relating events in narrative*. Vol. 2, *Typological and contextual perspectives*, ed. by Sven Stromqvist and Ludo Th. Verhoeven, pp. 219–257. Mahwah, NJ: Lawrence Erlbaum Associates.

———. 2006. What makes manner of motion salient? *Space in languages: Linguistic systems and cognitive categories*, ed. by Maya Hickmann and Stéphane Robert, pp. 59–82. Amsterdam/Philadelphia: John Benjamins.

Talmy, Leonard. 1974. Semantics and syntax of motion. *Syntax and semantics*, ed. by John P. Kimball, pp. 181–238. New York: Academic Press.

———. 1985. Lexicalization patterns: Semantic structure in lexical forms. *Language typology and syntactic description*, ed. by Timothy Shopen, pp. 3:57–149. Cambridge: Cambridge University Press.

———. 2000. *Toward a cognitive semantics*. Vol. 2, *Typology and process in concept structuring*. Cambridge: Cambridge University Press.

York, Fanny. 2010. La sémantique des verbes de mouvement en innu. MA thesis, Université du Québec à Montréal.

———. 2013. The use of Innu Intransitive posture verbs in static localization. Paper read at the Forty-Fifth Algonquian Conference, University of Ottawa.

CONTRIBUTORS

Antti Arppe received his Ph.D. in general linguistics from the University of Helsinki in 2009 and has been assistant professor of quantitative linguistics at the University of Alberta since 2012 and the founding director of the Alberta Language Technology Laboratory (ALTLab) since 2013. His research interests include lexical semantics, corpus linguistics, statistical methods, as well as exploiting multiple methods and sources of evidence. More recently he has started work in language documentation and developing language technological tools and applications for Indigenous languages to support their revitalization, in particular for Cree but also other Canadian Indigenous languages.

Roland Bohr received his Ph.D. in North American Indigenous history from the University of Manitoba, in Winnipeg, Canada, in 2005. He is the director of the Centre for Rupert's Land Studies at the University of Winnipeg, where he teaches Canadian Indigenous history. Bohr has published several articles and monographs on North American Indigenous archery, including *Gifts from the Thunder Beings— Indigenous Archery and European Firearms on the Northern Plains and the Central Subarctic, 1670–1870* (2014).

Chuck Bourgeois is a doctoral student in the Native Studies Department at the University of Manitoba. His research explores contemporary and critical aspects of Métis identity.

Rose-Marie Déchaine is a faculty member in the Department of Linguistics at the University of British Columbia. Her research areas include Algonquian, Na-Dene, and Niger-Congo languages, with a focus on how syntax interfaces with other parts of the grammar. Her work on Algonquian covers topics such as nominal predication, verbal agreement, morpheme ordering, the morphosemantics of gender, the morphosyntax of pronouns, and the root lexicon.

Inge Genee is associate professor of linguistics at the University of Lethbridge. She has worked on several languages, including Old Irish, Dutch, English, and Blackfoot. Her current SSHRC-funded project, "A digital dictionary for the Blackfoot language" (blackfoot.atlas-ling.ca), aims to create a user-friendly resource for speakers, learners, and teachers.

Ives Goddard is senior linguist, emeritus, in the Department of Anthropology in the National Museum of Natural History, Smithsonian Institution. He has conducted extensive fieldwork on Munsee, Unami, and Meskwaki and has written extensively on Native North American languages, cultures, and ethnohistory, particularly of the speakers of Algonquian languages.

Michael David Hamilton is assistant professor of linguistics in the Department of Languages, Linguistics, and Comparative Literature at Florida Atlantic University. He received his Ph.D. in 2015 from the Department of Linguistics at McGill University and served as a Mellon Postdoctoral Fellow at Cornell University.

Atticus G. Harrigan is a graduate student in the Department of Linguistics at the University of Alberta studying corpus and computational linguistics of North American Indigenous languages. His research focuses on morphosyntax, phonetics, and semantics, as well as endangered language sustainability.

Chris Harvey is a Ph.D. candidate at the University of Toronto. He is working on a detailed corpus, grammar, and lexicon of the historical Mahican language in its recorded dialects and time periods, and is using variationist methodology to analyze the synchronic phonology of the language.

Marie-Odile Junker is a professor in the School of Linguistics and Language Studies at Carleton University. She is active in Indigenous language documentation, maintenance, and revitalization. She uses a participatory-action research framework to work with communities and individuals interested in saving their languages and seeing them thrive in the twenty-first century. Exploring how information and communication technologies can help Indigenous languages, she has developed several websites and online dictionaries for languages of the Algonquian family (Cree, Innu, Atikamekw). She is leading the cocreation of the Algonquian Linguistic Atlas, a large collaborative project that is building a digital infrastructure for Algonquian dictionaries and other resources.

Kyumin Kim is currently assistant professor in the Department of English Language and Literature at Cheongju University, South Korea. Her primary area of research is theoretical syntax, and her recent research topics include aspectual structure and syntax of number in Blackfoot (Algonquian) and East Asian languages.

Carol-Rose Little is pursuing a Ph.D. in linguistics at Cornell University. She has been doing fieldwork on the Eastern Algonquian language Mi'gmaq since 2011. Her research interests include morphology, syntax, semantics, and fieldwork methodologies.

Hunter Thompson Lockwood is a Ph.D. candidate in linguistics at the University of Wisconsin–Madison. His research focuses on Algonquian language documentation. He helped produce the first authoritative dictionary of Potawatomi and is currently writing a descriptive grammar of the language as his dissertation.

Cherry Meyer is currently a doctoral candidate in linguistics at the University of Chicago with a focus on Anishinaabemowin. She has worked on topics such as discontinuous constituents, word order, information structure, and, most recently, gender and classifiers.

Mizuki Miyashita is professor of linguistics at the University of Montana. Her current research focus is Blackfoot prosody. She is also interested in documentary linguistics and has recorded Blackfoot lullabies, narratives, and conversations.

Madoka Mizumoto holds a master's degree from the University of Lethbridge in Alberta, Canada. She is originally from Japan and has been interested in the relationship between grammar and culture from her experiences in English and Japanese. Her master's thesis discusses the translation of culturally specific lexical items in a Blackfoot-English bilingual dictionary.

Sarah E. Murray is associate professor in the Department of Linguistics at Cornell University, as well as a member of the graduate fields of American Indian and Indigenous Studies, Cognitive Science, and Philosophy. She completed her Ph.D. in linguistics with a Certificate in Cognitive Science at Rutgers University in 2010. Since 2006, she has been working with members of the Northern Cheyenne community in Montana on a variety of language projects.

Mary Ann Naokwegijig-Corbiere has taught Nishnaabemwin, her mother tongue from growing up in Wikwemikong, Ontario, in the University of Sudbury's Indigenous Studies Department since 1989. Her research focuses on Nishnaabemwin curriculum and translation issues as well as lexicography as applied to her language.

Richard A. Rhodes's work has centered on topics relating to American Indian languages, particularly those of the Algonquian family. He has worked on the Ottawa dialect of Ojibwe, on Métchif, and on Sayula Popoluca, a Mixe-Zoquean language of southern Mexico. He has written extensively on the descriptive syntax and syntactic typology of Ojibwe, on the historical linguistics of Métchif, and on lexical semantics and lexicography in American Indian languages. His current research focuses on the intersection of language, history, and geography.

Todd Snider is a doctoral candidate in linguistics at Cornell University, focusing on semantics and pragmatics, with a minor in cognitive science. He has worked on tautologies and contradictions, counterfactuals, and continuation semantics for comparatives. His dissertation is on propositional anaphora.

J. Randolph Valentine is an Algonquianist linguist who teaches at the University of Wisconsin–Madison and Lakehead University.

Natalie Weber is a Ph.D. candidate at the University of British Columbia. Her research interests include the Blackfoot language, as well as aspects of the prosody-syntax interface, including how to model that interface in polysynthetic languages.

Arok Wolvengrey is professor of linguistics and head of the Department of Indigenous Languages, Arts and Cultures at First Nations University of Canada (FNUniv). He specializes in Cree language studies, particularly syntax, and Algonquian linguistics in general. He has been active in Cree revitalization efforts in addition to his descriptive and theoretical linguistic research, and he serves as the series editor for the University of Regina Press's First Nations Language Reader series.

Fanny York, M.A. in linguistics (UQAM 2010), is a Ph.D. candidate in linguistics and a lecturer at the University of Quebec in Montreal. Her dissertation proposes a lexical semantic analysis of Innu complex verbs in a cognitive framework. Her research interests are morphology, lexical semantics, polysynthetism, and the history of Algonquian grammar (history of linguistic ideas).